PHOTOGRAPHY

THIRD EDITION

BARBARA LONDON UPTON WITH JOHN UPTON

Adapted from the LIFE LIBRARY OF PHOTOGRAPHY

LITTLE, BROWN AND COMPANY

BOSTON   TORONTO

Library of Congress Cataloging in Publication Data

Upton, Barbara London
  Photography : adapted from the Life Library of Photography.

  Bibliography: p.
  Includes index.
  1. Photography. I. Upton, John,
II. Title.
TR145.U67 1985   770   84-17129
ISBN 0-316-88752-8

Library of Congress Catalog Card No. 84-17129

ISBN 0-316-88752-8

9 8 7 6 5 4 3 2 1

BP

Published simultaneously in Canada
by Little, Brown & Company (Canada) Limited

Printed in the United States of America

The Camera, © 1970 Time-Life Books Inc.
The Camera, Revised Edition, © 1981 Time-Life Books Inc.
Caring for Photographs, © 1972 Time-Life Books Inc.
Caring for Photographs, Revised Edition, © 1983 Time-Life Books Inc.
Color, © 1970 Time-Life Books Inc.
Frontiers of Photography, © 1972 Time-Life Books Inc.
The Great Themes, © 1970 Time-Life Books Inc.
Light and Film, © 1970 Time-Life Books Inc.
Light and Film, Revised Edition, © 1982 Time-Life Books Inc.
Photographer's Handbook, © 1970 Time-Life Books Inc.
Photographer's Handbook, Revised Edition, © 1981 Time-Life Books Inc.
Photographing Nature, © 1971 Time-Life Books Inc.
Photographing Nature, Revised Edition, © 1981 Time-Life Books Inc.
The Print, © 1970 Time-Life Books Inc.
The Print, Revised Edition, © 1982 Time-Life Books Inc.
Special Problems, © 1971 Time-Life Books Inc.
Special Problems, Revised Edition, © 1982 Time-Life Books Inc.

Picture and Text Credits: *Credits from left to right are separated by semicolons; from top to bottom, by dashes.*

Cover photograph of camera:
Copyright © Clint Clemens 1984.

CHAPTER 1 iv: Walker Evans, courtesy Library of Congress. 2: Bruce Davidson / Magnum, courtesy Eli Lilly and Company—Dana Duke. 3: Bruce Davidson / Magnum, courtesy Johnson & Johnson. 4: Jeff Rotman—Urs Mockli. 5: Jeff Rotman. 6: Susan Meiselas—Matthew Naythons / Gamma Liaison. 7: Susan Meiselas. 8: Clint Clemens—Vito Aluia. 9: Clint Clemens. 10: Barbara Kasten—Kurt Kilgus. 11: Barbara Kasten. 12: Bob Peterson—Dick Taylor. 13: Bob Peterson. 12–13: From multi-image show ''Heart Attack'' produced by Watts-Silverstein for Physio-Control Corp. 14: Lisl Dennis. 15: Lisl Dennis. 16: Joyce Wilson—Bill McIntosh. 17: Joyce Wilson. 18: Lois Gervais—Pete Newman. 19: Atlantic Richfield Company,

(Credits continued on page 408)

Photography is essentially a means of visual communication. Just as a typewriter can be used for personal letters, business correspondence, poetry, or a scientific dissertation, so a camera can be used for many types of notation, from objective documentation to fantasy. Whatever *your* interest is in photography, this book is designed to teach the skills that you will need in order to use the medium confidently and effectively.

To learn photography or to get better at it, you need information—for example, from this book—but even more, you need to participate actively. The more pictures you make, the more questions you ask, the more feedback you get, the more photographs you look at, the better your own pictures will be, and probably the more pictures you will want to make.

This book makes the information you will need as accessible and as easy to use as possible. The book is organized so that each two facing pages completes a single idea, skill, or technique. The key topics appear in the text in boldface type, making it easy to pick out the main concepts. Topics are explained using words, drawings, charts —but especially pictures, hundreds of them, the best of many different styles.

Much new material has been added to this edition. Many people have requested more information about various careers in photography. Chapter 1, Photographers at Work, features interviews with eleven photographers who have each developed a successful career. Chapter 5, Exposure, contains extensive new material on automatic exposure: when it works well, and when and how to override it and set the exposure manually. Chapter 11, Lighting, features a completely revised section on electronic flash that includes new material on when automatic flash works

well, and when and how to override it. Chapter 14, Seeing Photographs, expands the material on composition, tonality, sharpness, and other elements that will help you make better pictures and that will help you see other people's photographs with a more sophisticated eye.

Four chapters contain new sections titled What Went Wrong? that describe various problems, their causes and prevention. See, for example, Troubleshooting Camera and Lens Problems, page 83. Six chapters contain new material that illustrates how photographers have put some of the chapter topics to use. For example, see Using Lighting, pages 288–289, which has three examples of lighting techniques such as the use of side lighting to create prominent shadows. In addition to new material, there has been a general technical updating throughout the book.

This third edition of *Photography* has been a collaborative effort. Students, photographers, instructors, editors, manufacturers, curators, gallery people, and other writers participated in its construction. They fielded queries, made suggestions, responded to material, and were unfailingly generous with their time, energy, and creative thinking. Many thanks to all those who made this new edition possible.

Judy Dater, Bruce Davidson, and Beaumont Newhall made the final selection of student photographs on pages 26–31. The history chapter is largely based on the pioneer work of Beaumont Newhall; anyone interested in the history of photography has benefitted from his work.

More than 100 instructors reviewed the previous edition of *Photography* and made suggestions for this one. Ken Kobre, Jack Sal, and Jim Stone contributed suggestions to the book overall.

Many people contributed to specific sections: Fred Bodin, Tom Logan, Helen J. Sisserson, and Julie Trager reviewed Chapter 14, Seeing Photographs; Peter Kloehn reviewed the Cibachrome section; Bill Crawford checked the material on platinum printing; Carson Graves contributed to Chapter 13, Zone System; Paul Mulroney at Eastman Kodak Company clarified many technical points; Henry Wilhelm updated the material on archival processing and toning; Jim Stone updated the Bibliography. Henry Horenstein, Susan Kismaric, Nancy Rosen, Julia Scully, Brent Sikkema, and Karen Skove discussed and suggested pictures and photographers.

Without editorial assistance, a book of this size and complexity would have been impossible to complete. Lista Duren, Kristin Holcomb, Carol Pelletier, and Sue Schultz handled countless details. At Little, Brown, Jane Tufts offered constant encouragement and editorial expertise; Joan Kelly contributed valuable creative efforts; and Elizabeth Schaaf, George McLean, and Linda Bellamarich dealt with the massive amount of production work involved in a complete revision. The credit for originating the idea of a textbook of this type goes to Dennis Curtin, who was at Little, Brown when the first edition was released.

A generation of photographers have used *Photography* since its first edition in 1976. Some of the people who contributed to this edition had used the book themselves when they were studying photography, and still had the dogeared copy that they had used then. As you use the book, suggestions that you might have to improve it will be welcome.

For Michael and for Erica and Sean.

Contents

WALKER EVANS: *Photographer's Window Display, Birmingham, Alabama, 1936*

1

Photographers at Work

This chapter describes the careers that eleven photographers have made in photography. These people like what they do and get enormous satisfaction from their work. When so many people think of their work as something they have to get through before they can relax or play, it is refreshing and encouraging to talk to others who have found work that satisfies them deeply.

You don't have to earn your living in photography to be a good photographer. Even if you don't want to pursue photography as a career and just want to learn how to make better pictures, the people interviewed for this chapter can help you. They spend their days with photography, working at it and thinking about it, and they have a lot to say about it.

The advice they offered about how to improve was surprisingly consistent. ''Photograph more and more.'' ''Take more pictures.'' ''Shoot, shoot, shoot.'' ''Try different ways of doing things.'' ''Try to make the next picture better.'' ''Persevere.'' ''Just keep after it; you can't help but improve if you do.'' If this sounds like obvious advice—no secrets or inside information—it seems to be obvious advice that works. These photographers volunteered such comments often and with feeling. They knew how they had improved their skills, and they knew what you must do to get better, too.

At the end of this chapter are some ideas on how to get started showing your work to others (*pages 24–25*) and some examples from student photographers at work, the finalists in this edition's juried selection of student photographs (*pages 26–31*).

◀ *It is possible to look at photographs on more than one level. For example, this photograph of a display in a photographer's window can be seen as data: a documentary record of the inhabitants of a certain time and place. It can be seen as nostalgia: a bit of Americana, a relic of a simpler time (the past always seems like a simpler time). It can be seen as a pictorial event: the results of the photographer's choices regarding composition, exposure, processing, and display. No matter what you know about how or where a photograph was taken, it is important to stop and look just at the picture itself. What do you actually see when you look at a print? What photographic techniques are apparent? What associations does the print call to mind?*

Throughout this book, background information and possible interpretations are given for some of the pictures, but your own reaction to the print is more important. You may see a photograph in a different way altogether; that is to be expected. You will also find that people may have unpredictable reactions to your own pictures. Responding to photographs is a very personal art.

Corporate Photography: Bruce Davidson

Bruce Davidson is well known for his personal projects of documentary photography, such as *East 100th Street* and The Brooklyn Gang (*see photograph, page 64*). He is also well known in another arena: photography for corporate annual reports. Planning for an annual report starts long before the first day of shooting. One purpose of the report is to convey a specific image of a company, an image that can range from high tech to humanistic. Davidson has to be sure that he, the graphic designer of the report, and the chairman of the company understand one another completely. "I may never see the chairman," Davidson says, "so the designer is a critical link. A good designer creates a graphic point of view that is compatible with the chairman's business notions for that year. Until that's reached and agreed on, you're in dangerous water, because you can come back with pictures that are brilliant but not what the chairman needs or wants."

Davidson's clients include corporations such as Eli Lilly and Company, Occidental Petroleum, H. J. Heinz Company, and Metropolitan Life Insurance Company. He also does editorial illustration for magazines such as *Fortune* and *Vanity Fair*. Davidson's clients hire him because they are familiar with and want his personal style, which does not rely on any tricks, distortion, or other special effects. "I always try for a deeper, more penetrating view, not just a slick graphic solution, whether I am photographing people or products."

Although his commercial style is not unlike his personal work, he thinks about the two differently. "For a client, I'm working more as a craftsman than as an artist. For an annual report, I'm thinking along the lines of the chairman of the board. For an editorial assignment, I'm thinking about what a particular editor or story requires. But when I'm doing my personal work, I'm only trying to come to grips with my own sensibility."

An assistant and 10 cases of equipment accompany Davidson on most assignments, and his control over his craft is formidable, but he says that technique isn't everything. "Diplomacy is very important because I have to get people to do what I want. I alert the contact at a location the night before that we are coming. I bring my other annual reports and I show them that a double-page picture *is* something."

Davidson has worked on movies, and he thinks of his shots as scenes. Like a casting director, he looks for the right type of person for a particular shot, not simply using whoever happens to be at a factory or plant when he arrives. He looks at each location as if it were a set. "You can't just go in and make candid shots when they are going to end up as double-page pictures that will be scrutinized. Shooting is really a small part of the work. Time and energy go into creating the scene, very much like directing a movie. We're building to a shot that will have action, drama, story."

Davidson sees himself and his assistant as a team. His assistants must have some experience before he will hire them. "I don't take apprentices from nothing and train them because there are too many mistakes they can make, but once they work with me, they are learning constantly. They usually stay three or four years and then go off on their own. Good assistants are another pair of eyes. They'll let me know if they see something that isn't quite right."

On location, a work day can be 18 hours long, but "there's nothing greater than when my assistant and I realize that we're getting a really fantastic photograph. If you are not working very hard and not enjoying the work at the same time, there's something wrong."

BRUCE DAVIDSON: *Photograph for Eli Lilly and Company,* 1981

Bruce Davidson often emphasizes the human element in his photographs for corporate reports. Above: one of the products made by Eli Lilly and Company is a fungicide that controls blast, a devastating rice disease. For a Lilly corporate report, Davidson photographed a Japanese farm family who actually uses the fungicide. Opposite: the product itself can be made subtly evident, as here for a Johnson & Johnson corporate report.

DANA DUKE: *Bruce Davidson,* 1981

BRUCE DAVIDSON: *Photograph for Johnson & Johnson*, 1974

3

Freelance Photography: Jeff Rotman

Jeff Rotman begins his day at his apartment in Jerusalem by opening the mail. Rotman is a freelance photographer who shoots various types of assignments but whose specialty is underwater photography. Today his mail contains a check from *Geo* magazine for a story about caves in the Red Sea; a query from a picture researcher working on a biology text asking for pictures of sea turtles; a note from a writer who is coauthoring an article with Rotman, asking about a picture of two Bedouins slaughtering a goat; and a letter from a magazine rejecting an article he proposed on crocodiles. The phone rings with a call from *Life* magazine: they are not interested in his idea for a story on the cocaine trade in Bolivia but want to know what pictures he has of oil spills.

By the end of the day, he will have sent five slides of sea turtles to the picture researcher, given the writer information on the Bedouins and the goat, made a phone call about the crocodile story to another potential publisher, and worked on a new idea for a story on women in the Israeli army.

Rotman feels he has to both photograph and sell. For every hour he spends in the field shooting, he spends at least as much time developing ideas and promoting them to potential clients. He recently mailed a list of his stock photos and some sample reproductions to 3000 picture researchers, art directors, editors, agents, and others who might be interested in his work.

His photographic skills are important, but he says his most valuable skill is persuasiveness in dealing with clients. "I don't want to sell something to someone if they don't want it, but I have to make them see the light. As soon as most editors hear 'fish,' they think it belongs in a wildlife magazine, but many of my pictures can go into *Vogue*; they can go anywhere. You have to believe

in your work and then go out and sell it." Rotman has been very successful persuading people that they need his work. He is one of the few freelancers who make a good living doing mostly underwater shooting.

Lately he has been going after other kinds of assignments. "I don't want to spend eight months a year in the water anymore because I don't want to lose my edge. I want to be hungry when I go in that water. I want to be excited and if I stay dry for two or three months, I can't wait to get in the water." He looks for stories on land that he really wants to do. "If there's nothing else that I like about my work, it's that I'm doing what I like to do. I've lived for years near the Bedouins by the Red Sea, and I was always curious about them, but I never had an excuse to go out and live with them. Doing a magazine story on the nomads of the desert—that was the excuse."

There are drawbacks to Rotman's line of work that most people don't see, such as the paperwork involved in labeling slides and preparing captions for them. "Pictures sell better with good labeling and captions. I have farmed out the paperwork more and more, but I can't eliminate it." Even the shooting, which he loves, has its drawbacks. "Clients have a romantic vision of me at work. They see me coming in with a tan, but they don't see the hours I put in— maybe 8 or 10 hours a day in the water. They don't see me camping out for long periods, eating out of cans and packages, and working in a remote area where I'm 16 hours from a hospital if I have an accident. Underwater equipment is extremely expensive, probably as much as a fashion photographer's full rig, but I don't get the fees that a top fashion photographer gets. So all the more reason why it's important to love the work."

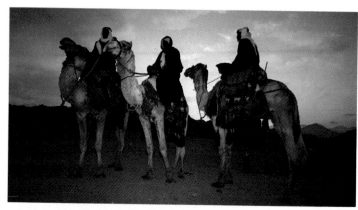

JEFF ROTMAN: *Bedouins, Sinai, 1982*

Rotman often synchronizes an underexposed available-light exposure with a normal flash exposure. He makes a reading of the available light, then sets his camera to underexpose the available light by two stops and sets his automatic flash to expose normally. His 24mm lens takes in a wider angle than is lit by the flash, so the edges of the picture are darker than the center, an effect that Rotman likes because he feels it adds drama.

URS MOCKLI: *Jeff Rotman, Red Sea, 1982*

Jeff Rotman says that before you try to photograph underwater, you should be an excellent diver. "You have to be able to concentrate on the shooting, and to do that you can't worry about your diving." Rotman is using a Nikonos III underwater camera fitted with a 28mm lens and a frame that helps position the camera for close-ups. His right hand is adjusting a light meter. His left hand holds an underwater strobe. Around his neck he has another light meter plus a Nikonos III camera fitted with a 15mm lens.

JEFF ROTMAN: *Shark!* 1979

This 10-ft sand tiger shark lives in the large ocean tank at the New England Aquarium. It would be almost impossible to get a shot like this in open waters—and bring home the film. In the ocean, the shark can be dangerous, but in the tank it has become accustomed to divers. Rotman shot from about 2 ft away. "I am very aggressive underwater. If I am going to take a picture of a shark, then I go in close, head-on with it. I am not going to make it look gentle. I'm going to take its strongest trait and color it up." The photograph epitomizes what most people have in mind when they think of sharks; Rotman has sold it more than twenty times for use in magazines and books.

Documentary Photography/Photojournalism: Susan Meiselas

For Susan Meiselas, there is no typical day in Central America. If the region is quiet, she concentrates on feature pictures, ones that are not linked to a specific news event. But in a country where fighting is taking place, she says, "You get up at 6:30, have breakfast, talk to people, call around, and if nothing is happening you still get on the road. You just go, even if you don't know where you are going and you don't know what you will find. If there is some action, if a town has been taken or an offensive is beginning, obviously that directs the day."

Meiselas went to Central America in 1978 on her own to make some pictures of life in Nicaragua. By chance, she arrived just a few months before the country went into open revolt. When the war heated up, Meiselas was at the center of the action. International attention turned to Nicaragua, and her photographs began appearing in newspapers and magazines all over the world.

Unlike many news photographers, Meiselas did not go to photojournalism school or work on a daily newspaper. She thinks of herself more as a documentary photographer than as a photojournalist, and even though she now gets assignments from *Time* magazine, the *New York Times,* and other periodicals, she avoids working strictly in terms of stories. Her interest is in documenting the ongoing history of the region, so she tries to cover what she perceives as important, not just what she has been assigned to photograph.

Part of what is important in Central America today is conflict. Meiselas has often been in the midst of gunfire, trekked deep into ambush country, and waited out tense periods at barricades. Part of her survival kit is her intuition about when to move forward and when —if she has the choice—to go back. "Obviously, I feel fear. I always watch the people who are alongside the road. You get clues from their faces, or you can feel the anxiety if people won't talk to you." She says it is important to work with people who respond to situations the way you do and with whom you are free to say how you feel. "You have to listen to that inside place. If you are afraid, you are afraid. But you also have to evaluate to what extent those fears are reasonable, or things can become larger than they are so that you paralyze yourself."

She enjoys working with a writer and for a magazine, if they provide an accurate context for her pictures. A photojournalist has very little control over how pictures are used; they may even be used to illustrate the opposite of what actually took place. But ideally, the photographer and writer can form a team in which each complements and extends the meaning of the other's work.

Meiselas does not photograph when she thinks people are posing or performing for her camera. Instead, she tries to wait until she feels people are behaving naturally. She wants people to be comfortable with her presence rather than intruding on them to "take" the pictures she wants. "I know that I affect a situation, but I don't want the picture to be about me or about a relationship the subject has to me." She never asks anyone to re-create something she has seen them do because doing it for the camera would be doing it for a different purpose. "I don't even like to ask people to move someplace else. I try to work myself around them instead."

Her advice to beginning photographers is to become involved with someone, some place, and live close to it. She says she is very fortunate to be part of a living history. "It is an extraordinary experience, a very privileged position."

SUSAN MEISELAS: *Soldiers Searching Bus Passengers, Northern Highway, El Salvador,* 1980

Susan Meiselas's photographs of the political conditions in Central America have been used in many magazines and newspapers. Her work is often more complex than the straightforward news picture that conveys its story without requiring much effort from the viewer. The photograph above is not one a photojournalist would typically make because it does not reveal itself immediately. It is a very powerful image, but, as Meiselas says, "You have to live with it a while before you emotionally connect with it."

MATTHEW NAYTHONS: *Susan Meiselas, Nicaragua,* 1979

SUSAN MEISELAS: *Awaiting Counterattack by the Guard, Matagalpa, Nicaragua, 1978*

During the early days of open fighting in Nicaragua in 1978, Susan Meiselas photographed these men at a barricade awaiting counterattack by government troops. She had to decide whether to stay and continue photographing or to leave to get the pictures on a plane to New York in time to make the deadline for publication that week. "As a documentary photographer, I would have liked to stay, but I had to leave to get the pictures out. It was the first time that I realized what it means to be a photojournalist and deal with a deadline."

Advertising Photography: Clint Clemens

What makes a good advertising photograph? For Clint Clemens, the answer is simplicity, and he thinks that many photographers lose sight of that. "They complicate it too much," he says. "Too often there isn't a simple statement or any purity of thought or elegance." He believes that to get an advertising message across effectively you have to understand the psychology of your audience: how people perceive themselves and what intangibles the product might supply to them. For example, imparting a feeling of sleek luxury to the pen and lighter at right is as important as showing their design.

Lighting can be dramatic in Clemens's pictures, but it always looks natural. "In nature, there is only one source of light—the sun. Lighting in a photograph should have that single-source feeling, whether it is indoors or outdoors." Clemens likes to give light a direction so that it comes from one area and moves across the picture. A viewer's eye tends to go to the lightest part of a picture first, which means that light, especially when it contrasts with a darker background, can direct attention where the photographer wants it to go.

Clemens always visualizes a photograph before he begins to shoot. He has a clear idea in advance of how the product should be presented, how it should relate to the type in the ad, how the picture will be cropped for the layout, and so on. "You have to be able to see the picture beforehand and be able to describe it to others. You would drive everyone crazy if you didn't have a good idea of what you wanted it to look like." He isn't rigidly tied to his ideas and will take advantage of something that happens spontaneously, but often the final picture is exactly what he visualized.

Clemens feels that advertising is a very personalized business. He gets to know his clients and lets them know that their job is the most important one he has. More than that, he makes sure that every job *is* his most important one. "You never, never blow a job. You always have to give it your best, and that requires preplanning and constant attention to detail, especially when you are shooting. But don't get so bottled up and rattled that you can't think. You have to be willing to take chances, too."

Clemens's studio is in Boston. Like his photographs, he knew in advance what he wanted in the studio and had it built to his exact specifications. He says that spending money for the tools you need is a worthwhile investment. Among his lighting tools is an 8 × 8-foot light box hung from a motorized rigging in the ceiling of the huge central shooting area (*right*). The box has total mobility from floor to ceiling at any angle, with output that can be set from a powerful 18,000 watt-seconds down to only 400. His studio staff includes four full-time photographic assistants, an administrator who schedules bookings and makes other arrangements, and two bookkeepers. He keeps two freelance set stylists busy enough not to work for anybody else and provides most of a set builder's business. Clemens also takes on apprentices for six-week stints. The apprentices get no pay, work intensely, and get the kind of experience that is impossible to get in a school or from a book.

Clemens says that if you want to be an advertising photographer, you have to be businesslike: "You have to learn how to deal with people, how to go out and get work, how to present and promote yourself, what to put in a portfolio, and many other things." But the most important attribute is a desire to understand every aspect of photography. "I can teach anybody anything, but you have to want to learn. That is absolute."

CLINT CLEMENS: *Photograph for S. T. Dupont,* 1982

For an ad photograph for a company that manufactures luxury lighters, pens, and watches, Clint Clemens placed two products on highly reflective black window blinds. Then he adjusted the blinds and his light until he got the striped reflection he wanted.

VITO ALUIA: *Clint Clemens in His Studio,* 1984

CLINT CLEMENS: *Photograph for Tech HiFi, 1982*

Camera angle is one way to affect a viewer's attitude. To look down on someone is often condescending. To look up can make someone appear impressive or bigger than life. In a photograph for an audio equipment store's catalog, Clemens placed the camera very low, which created an intimacy with the child because the viewer is joining his world rather than looking down on him from the usual adult point of view. (See also the Clemens photograph on page 256.) "You have to take the viewer's mind," Clemens says, "and put it where you want it."

Artist: Barbara Kasten

Barbara Kasten is an artist who makes photographs of constructions that she builds for the purpose of photographing them. In her studio she arranges objects such as mirrors, solid forms, and flat surfaces into what could be called extremely large still lifes, big enough to walk into (*right, bottom*). She lights the construction, then rearranges and rephotographs it until she arrives at a final image.

Ideas for a new construction come from various sources. Kasten may decide to use a particular object. She looks at paintings, sculpture, set designs, and other work to generate ideas. She sketches possible constructions in a loose way, not making exact layouts but using the sketches themselves as sources of ideas. "Being an artist is hard work," she says. "Ideas come from research. They don't appear like a light bulb going on in your head."

Kasten starts a construction with a simple problem, such as focusing on a mirror reflection and using a three-foot-high pyramid she had built. She puts the first objects in place, then sets up an 8 × 10-inch view camera. She goes back and forth between arranging objects and seeing how they appear in the camera's ground glass. Eventually she makes 8 × 10 color Polaroids to see what the image looks like in a print. At first she works only with objects, concentrating on their composition, then she lights them and adds color from lights covered with colored filters.

When she is satisfied with a setup, she shoots an 8 × 10 color transparency from which she has a custom printer, Michael Wilder, make 30 × 40-inch Cibachrome prints. She and Wilder have the traditional relationship of artist and master craftsman working together to make a final print. "Although an artist should have technical knowledge to discuss a process, I don't feel I need to

make the print myself." Kasten also photographs at a special Polaroid studio that makes 20 × 24 instant prints.

Kasten originally studied painting, then made fiber sculptures. She began making photograms (photosensitive paper exposed under layers of various materials), eventually was adding paint to them, then making photographs of constructions. She feels her work is still evolving and that her main interest has always been in manipulating and using space, whatever medium she uses.

While many artists are unable to earn their living from their art and must take jobs teaching or doing other types of work, Kasten has reached a point where her art is her major source of income. She sells many of her photographs through the John Weber Gallery in New York City which exhibits her photographs, keeps an inventory of her work to show interested collectors, handles the details of placing her work in exhibitions outside the gallery, and, in general, promotes her work. A typical gallery commission is 40 to 50 percent of the sales price. Kasten has also received grants from organizations such as the Guggenheim Foundation and the National Endowment for the Arts and has done commissions for advertising.

A few years ago, Kasten moved from California to New York City. She could make her art anywhere, but in New York she is part of an intensely active art world where she meets other artists, museum curators, critics, and collectors. Kasten's suggestion for anyone interested in developing a career as an artist: perseverance. "Do more and more work. Try new ways of doing what you have done before. Take your work to galleries, as painful as it can be to trudge around, leave a portfolio, and then get a smile and a rejection. Art requires a real commitment. A bit of luck helps, too."

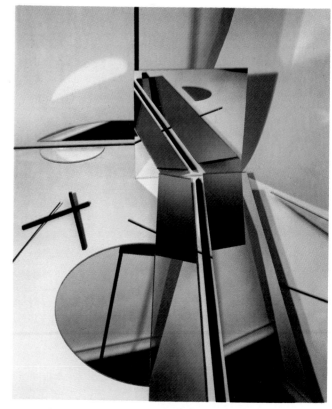

BARBARA KASTEN: *Construct PC/5-B*, 1981. 20 × 24-inch Polaroid print

KURT KILGUS: *Barbara Kasten*, 1984

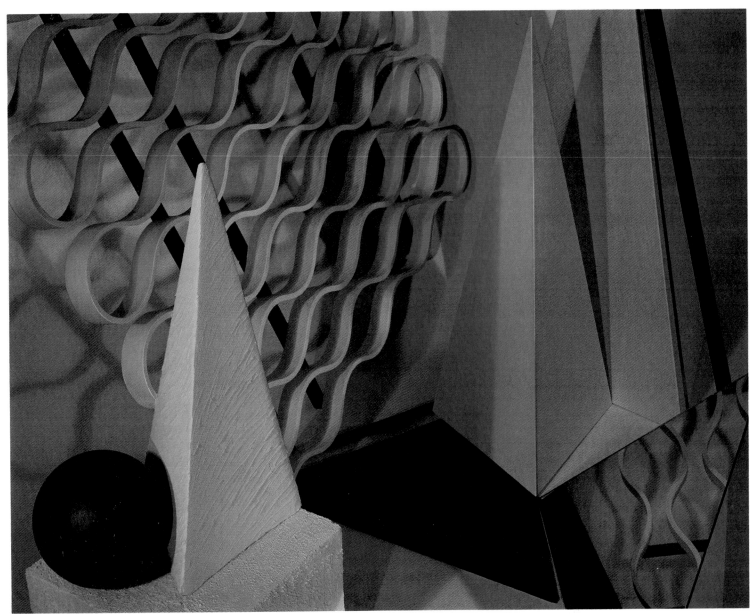

BARBARA KASTEN: *Construct NYC 18*, 1984. 30 × 40-inch Cibachrome print

◄ *Some of the constructions that Barbara Kasten builds and then photographs are as big as 6 ft deep and 9 ft wide (left). "I like the physical nature of being in the setup, being part of the construction as I move the object. I don't want to use little models, but to be part of the set like a dancer."*

Multi-Image Productions: Bob Peterson

If having an audience pay rapt attention to your work and if seeing your images 30 feet wide appeal to you, then you might like to try what Bob Peterson does: multi-image productions. A multi-image show is a fancy cousin of a slide show with sound. It uses 35mm slide projectors, from 2 to 30 or more. Three projectors plug into a dissolver, a device that tells each projector when to change slides and when to turn on and off. Each dissolver is cued by pulses from a tape recording, which also contains a sound track. A typical user for such a show is a corporation that wants an exciting presentation for a sales meeting or conference.

The advantages of a multi-image show are its size (Peterson recently did a nine-projector show onto a 10 × 30-foot screen), its sound (a taped stereo sound track, powerful amplifier, and big speakers produce better portable sound than most movie theaters have permanently installed), and its cost (inexpensive compared with what you would need to get comparable size and sound in a film). The individual slides do not make a movie, of course, but the show creates a compelling display as images on different parts of the screen fade, dissolve, or rapidly change.

Peterson began his career as a newspaper photographer, then shot for several years for magazines such as *Life, Time,* and *Sports Illustrated.* Later he did advertising work. His style has always been strongly journalistic, and that is the type of assignment he has always gotten. "When I went into advertising, people didn't hire me to do a still life of an apple and a pie. They hired me to go out and be with the apple pickers and show what the pickers go through to bring that wonderful apple to you." His journalist's style adapts readily to the storytelling that is part of many multi-image shows.

The size, sound track, and pacing of a multi-image show make it easy to attract and direct an audience's attention and to arouse emotions. If a company's goal is to create an enthusiastic atmosphere at a sales meeting, a multi-image show is far more effective than speeches by corporate officials. The show can give an idea of what some future project will be like—Peterson did one show for a company that was leasing space in an office building that had not been built yet. It is relatively easy to tailor a show to different audiences, such as different ethnic groups, by replacing a few pictures or a sound track.

Peterson says the market is strong for people who do good work. "If you can compose something nicely, if you can tell a story, if you have the intellect to make a medium work for you and communicate something, then you will always be able to get a job." Technical skills are vital, he believes, because not having them will detract from your ability to do what you want to do. He also suggests going to movies—good and bad ones—imagining how various directors would shoot a scene; going to industrial films and other people's slide shows; and looking at art in museums. You may not be able to apply a technique directly, but each will make your eye more sophisticated.

Peterson finds multi-rewards in his work. The financial return is good. He enjoys working in collaboration with other people, as he did in his journalism days. He likes the audience response he gets; once he received a standing ovation at the end of a show. And, especially, he enjoys making things work: "When you get the images into the projector trays, and you have the rough sound track together—the first time you run a show, you do get a little bit of a thrill."

BOB PETERSON: From multi-image show, *Heart Attack,* 1983

The use of multiple projectors in a multi-image show makes special effects possible, such as image build (above). The sequence of partially blocked slides was shown rapidly using several projectors so that the scene seemed to increase in size as the viewer watched. Below, Bob Peterson usually works with projectors in multiples of three because the dissolve unit that controls the projectors coordinates up to three at a time.

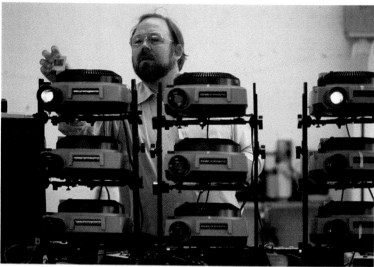

DICK TAYLOR: *Bob Peterson at Work,* 1983

For a company that manufactures defibrillators, devices that can regulate heartbeat, Bob Peterson did a show that dramatized how such a device saved a man's life. Images within a multi-image show have to relate to each other, so shots are made to create a movie-like continuity. Far right, a cutaway, a close-up of an object, a shot used for emphasis or as a transition from one shot to another.

After a stressful day at the office, the man has an equally stressful drive home. Long exposures (center) and zooming during the exposure (far right) streaked the lights of cars, adding to the impression of frenzy as well as creating interesting visuals.

The man has a heart attack. As it progresses, the images change on screen from full color to black and white as a visual indication that his life is slipping away.

Paramedics rush in carrying the device that will save the man's life. Blurred shots used in rapid sequence can give the illusion of speed and movement. As in a movie, Peterson often shoots the same scene several times, in long shots, medium shots, and close-ups or from different points of view.

The sound track of the show consisted of sound effects, music, and realistic dialogue spoken by the actors. The only narration came with the last slide in the show (far right), to give one mention of the product's name: "Physio-Control. When it has to work, it has to work."

BOB PETERSON: From multi-image show, *Heart Attack*, 1983

Travel Photography: Lisl Dennis

Imagine two photographers, a photojournalist and a travel photographer, shooting on Broadway. One seeks out pictures of the tawdry glitz and sleaze; the other tries to convey something of the bright lights and excitement. The photojournalist might shoot either one, but you can bet your passport that the travel photographer will always come back with pictures of the latter. (See Lisl Dennis's picture of Broadway on page 125.)

The purpose of travel photography is not to show the dark side of life but as Lisl Dennis says, "to show whatever is good or beautiful or positive about a place. It is a kind of gratitude for the good time you have had and a desire to share your experiences with others. After all, people don't travel to have a miserable time. That's not the purpose of a vacation."

Lisl Dennis traces her love of travel to her childhood, when she enjoyed wandering through the rural New Jersey countryside near her home. When she began to photograph, she realized that the camera was a kind of passport for her. "It was my introduction and my gateway, my justification for probing and being involved with the world." She has logged more than 18 years of travel-related photography for articles, books, and advertising, often working with her husband, Landt Dennis, a writer. She teaches the annual Travel-Photography Workshop in Santa Fe, New Mexico.

She says that the travel industry tends to publish rather conventional pictures, ones that do not demand much of the viewer. She always supplies clients with the standard shots that she knows will be accepted, but in addition she seeks to expand her personal style and the definition of travel photography in general. "After you have photographed open-air markets in twenty different countries, a pile of oranges in Senegal begins to

look not too different from one in the south of France. The person behind the pile of oranges will have on a different outfit, but he or she isn't going to be doing anything too different." Her solution is to look for unusual ways of approaching a subject (see photograph, opposite).

She believes that the barter system that finances many travel articles contributes to the conventionality of travel writing and illustrations. The fees for travel material tend to be relatively low, so photographers and writers often try to arrange for "hospitality," such as free transportation, lodging, or tour arrangements. They get part of their expenses paid, the publisher gets a less expensive article, and the airline or hotel gets free publicity. The catch is that you must come back with a favorable, publishable article or you won't be offered hospitality again. (Some newspapers, such as the New York Times and the Washington Post, will not publish an article if hospitality was accepted.)

The open-air market of travel publishing is the Society of American Travel Writers. At its regional and national meetings, editors, writers, and photographers meet representatives of national tourist bureaus, airlines, hotels, and other travel-related businesses and discuss ideas and projects. For anyone interested in professional travel photography, membership in SATW is a must. A substantial travel record is needed to qualify for membership.

Much hard work and persistent effort have given Lisl Dennis a successful career, but she suggests that if you enjoy travel photography, have some means of financial support available while you are getting started—and possibly forever. The career is worth millions in memorable experiences, but not always in dollars.

LISL DENNIS: Canal du Midi, France, 1982

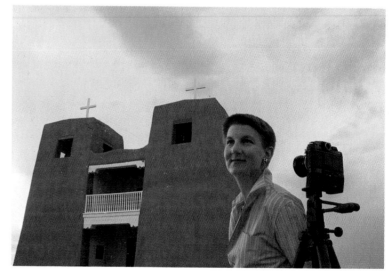

LISL DENNIS: Self-Portrait, New Mexico, 1984

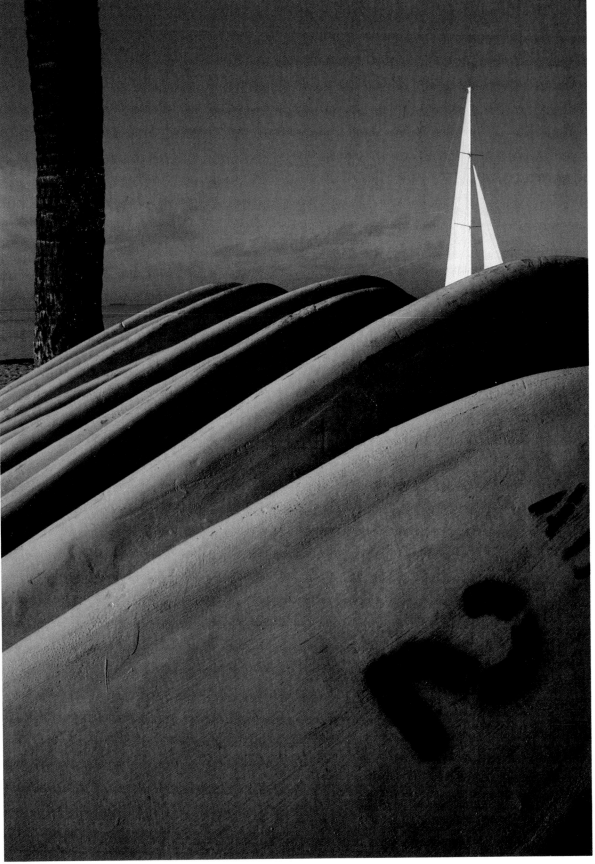

On a trip to the south of France, Lisl Dennis bicycled along the tow paths of an inland waterway, photographing people she encountered along the way. Here, an 85-year-old woman is trying to animate her disgruntled great-granddaughter. Dennis feels she developed a considerable social flexibility during the two years she spent with the Boston Globe as a newspaper photojournalist. At the Globe she photographed everything from drug rehabilitation centers to society teas, and in doing so she learned how to be at ease in any situation. She also learned how to be comfortable working in close with a wide-angle lens; she is about 4 ft from the people shown in this photograph.

Lisl Dennis's travel photographs are often less literal than the standard travel image. Here, only segments of the surfboards, sail, sand, sea, and palm tree are visible. "Compared to conventional travel photography," she says, "my work is more detail oriented. My pictures are apt to be tighter visions of places or things rather than overall views. They are graphic interpretations, but ones that still deal with a sense of place."

LISL DENNIS: *Waikiki, Hawaii,* 1979

Portrait and Wedding Photography: Joyce Wilson

If you have ever had your picture taken while sitting on Santa's lap, you will know something about Joyce Wilson's first job in photography: she was Santa's helper and pushed the button on the camera. After her first year as a helper, she got an offer to do the Santa concession herself and, knowing almost nothing about photography, decided she had better learn more about it. As her skills increased, she began to branch out. At first she photographed only children. In time, she opened a full-scale portrait-wedding studio, became well known in her field, and today teaches photography workshops. With her husband, she operates a studio in Indianapolis, Wilson-Holt Photography.

Wilson loves to take portraits. She describes herself as an extrovert and as someone who likes people and enjoys bringing out the best in them. "I can be depressed and mad at the world, but after about ten minutes into a portrait sitting, I am a totally different human being," Wilson says. "I am having a wonderful time and when it is over, I am on an adrenaline high that just won't quit."

Portraits are the mainstay of Wilson's business. Even though there is a camera in almost every home, many people still go to a professional photographer to have their portrait made. She believes that people respect quality and will pay for it. Many of her clients want a portrait to give to someone else, such as a spouse or other family member. "Grandmothers. If we didn't have grandmothers we'd be out of business. They are always demanding family groups. Snapshots are fine, but they want something to frame and put in the living room or bedroom."

Wilson shoots portraits in the studio and on location in a wooded area behind her studio or at a client's house or office. She discusses the session with clients in advance to fit the style of the portrait to their lifestyle. "You get some people who are very structured, and it wouldn't fit them at all if you tried doing them in casual clothing outdoors." She believes that to get people to look natural, you have to relax and act natural yourself. At the same time, you have to know what you are doing technically so that you don't fumble with the lights or camera. You can't be creative and relate to a client, she says, until you are thoroughly at home with your equipment.

Weddings are also a part of Wilson's business, and she says it is especially important for the photographer to be relaxed and confident at a wedding because other people are likely to be excited. She prices her wedding packages rather high because she prefers portrait photography, but for the price she gives clients 70 prints. One strategy has made portraits and weddings more profitable: instead of giving clients proof prints to take home, she shows them slides of their sitting or wedding in her studio. Clients make their decisions in the studio and no longer have to be hounded to return proofs and place their orders.

Wilson does not market her services as aggressively as some other studios do. She displays prints at various local business establishments and also relies on repeat business from clients and on their recommendation of her to others. She says she enjoys making pictures most of all, so she wants her business to remain small enough for her to spend most of her time photographing rather than managing. "It's important to make money and to run a business efficiently, but that's not my entire purpose. My motivation is my self-gratification and my need to express myself. I feel that because the motive is right, the business is successful."

JOYCE WILSON: *Bride and Groom*, 1982

BILL McINTOSH: *Joyce Wilson in Her Studio*, 1983

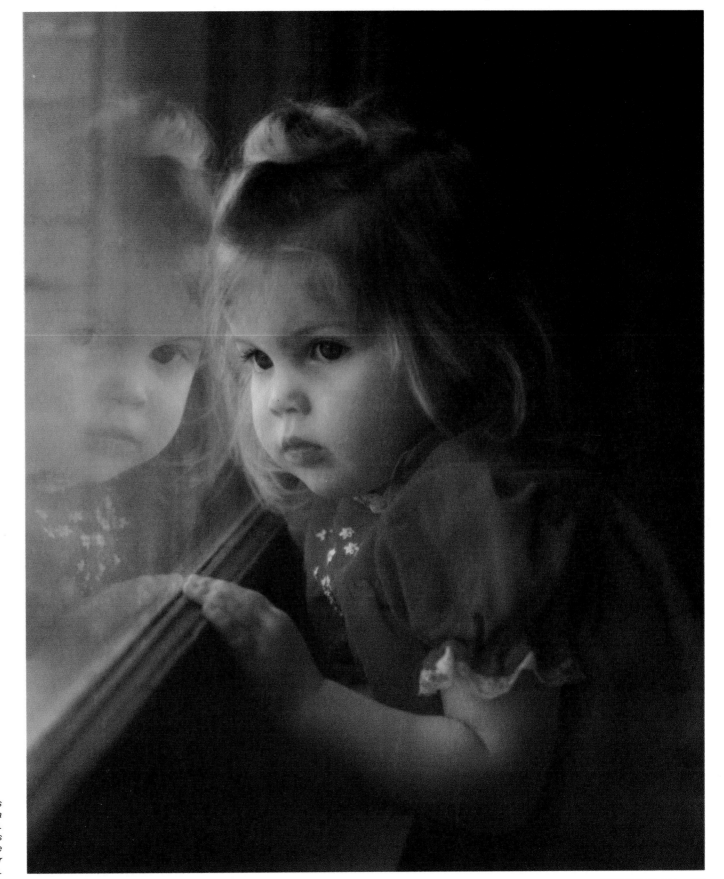

◄ When Joyce Wilson does a wedding, in addition to making the standard candid and posed shots she likes to add a photograph that looks romantic but believable.

The viewer has no clues that this portrait was actually taken in a cramped corner of a small room. Wilson often does portrait sittings in clients' homes and has become adept at finding settings for her subjects.

JOYCE WILSON: *Adrian*, 1981

Photographic Illustration: Lois Gervais

In the seven years that Lois Gervais has worked for Atlantic Richfield Company, she has photographed everything from oil rigs to executive portraits in every location from Alaska to the company's home base in Los Angeles. Her work consists of conceiving and making pictures for annual reports, calendars, brochures, press announcements, and in-house slide shows. Atlantic Richfield provides photographic and design services and other support to community projects, so Gervais's schedule can be as varied as photographing at a refinery in the morning and at a ballet performance in the evening.

Gervais's job is photographic illustration, the creation of photographs that visually interpret or present an idea. "It is *making* a photograph," she says, "not just taking one of whatever happens to be there." She is responsible for the technical execution of the photograph—how it will be made—and often for its conception—what the picture will show. She frequently works as part of a team that includes an art director and a writer. Sometimes they simply ask her to work from a shooting list or layout, they may ask her for advice on how to technically carry out a photograph, or they may ask her for help with the concept itself. People may have different ideas about what will work, but when it comes to executing a photograph, she is the one who knows how to do it and in most cases the art director or writer will take her advice.

Gervais is on the road about half the time. Typically she travels with three 35mm camera bodies, six lenses, two complete electronic flash setups that include stands and umbrellas, Polaroid gear, meter, film, and miscellaneous equipment. Some equipment she always carries with her and the rest fits into a case on wheels that is almost liftable. While working she wears a camera vest so she can keep her hands free (*see right, bottom*). She travels without an assistant, which means that in addition to doing the setups and shooting, she must do all the coordination with plant personnel or other contacts. An on-site contact is essential; she needs someone who has the authority to ask people to stop work and pose and who understands how various jobs are performed so that the scene looks authentic when photographed.

Gervais says that she tries to get the people that she photographs involved in the process so that they feel relaxed and at ease. "Most people are hams when they loosen up, and that can really help me. When I am adjusting my lighting, I make a Polaroid photograph and give that to them. I ask their opinion of how they would make it better. People don't like to be 'taken.' I always tell them, 'I am not taking a photograph of you, I am *making* one, and we are going to construct it together.'"

She feels that the fact that she is a woman can help when people are nervous about being photographed. When they have been expecting a male photographer and a 5′2″ female arrives instead, she at least has their attention. "People tend to watch what I am doing very closely. I often get comments like, 'It is really interesting to watch you work.' They may be reserved, but they usually don't feel threatened anymore."

Gervais likes going to places that she wouldn't see otherwise, like the oil fields in the Arctic or the drilling rigs at sea. Another satisfaction is the essence of photographic illustration itself: solving the problem of how to interpret a concept photographically (*see illustrations, above right and opposite*).

LOIS GERVAIS: *Geothermal Energy*, 1977

PETE NEWMAN: *Lois Gervais*, 1983

To illustrate the concept of geothermal energy (energy from the earth), Lois Gervais started with a piece of oiled, black, textured vinyl that resembled a rock surface. In it she mounted the faceplate of a wall outlet with sockets that she had painted red. Underneath she placed a chunk of dry ice in a covered paper cup with a straw coming through the lid, positioning the top of the straw so that it fed into one of the sockets. When she added water to the cup, the dry ice forced a steamy-looking vapor out of the straw. She sprinkled on some water to simulate condensed steam, and lit the whole setup with electronic flash. Gervais credits this shot, which she conceived on her own, as being one of the factors that caused Atlantic Richfield to hire her.

For a brochure promoting one of Atlantic Richfield Company's analytical labs, Lois Gervais combined a long exposure to record the computer screen with a flash exposure for the rest of the scene. First, she composed the picture with the camera on a tripod. She selected the lens aperture she needed to get enough depth of field to have the entire scene sharp —f/16. Then, using Polaroid film, she tested for the exposure time that the screen would need at that aperture—6 min. Finally, she adjusted her flash distance and power so that it would give a correct exposure for the overall scene with the camera lens set to f/16. The combined exposure was made on 35mm transparency film.

LOIS GERVAIS: *Bioengineering Technician*, 1982

Cultural Research: Carl Fleischhauer

Whether he is making a photograph of a buckaroo roping a calf in Nevada (*opposite page*) or of a man showing his blue tick hound in Georgia (*right*), Carl Fleischhauer has two possible goals. He looks for images that have visual impact and appeal, but, even more important, he seeks to collect and record information about how people live. Fleischhauer is a photographer and folklife specialist for the American Folklife Center at the Library of Congress in Washington, D.C. His work there satisfies his long-term interest both in photography and in folklife—traditional arts, skills, and customs that are passed down from one generation to the next. "I don't think of myself as purely a maker of images," he says. "I think of myself as a person who is curious about culture."

The American Folklife Center coordinates activities related to folk culture, such as working with the Illinois State Art Council to survey ethnic arts in Chicago neighborhoods or with the National Park Service to document traditional life along the Blue Ridge Parkway. Fleischhauer works with teams that may include several folklorists, an anthropologist, an archaeologist, an ethnomusicologist, and others. Folklorists can be interested in all sorts of things. For instance, one project on cowboy life in northern Nevada documented shoeing a horse, branding-iron designs, bunkhouse construction, saddles, storytelling, and local history.

Fleischhauer's work is somewhat like photojournalism, except that he usually covers a subject more completely than a photojournalist would. For example, he records every step in shoeing a horse rather than making just one or two pictures of the process. He photographs details, such as the types of corn cribs or church pews in a region. He takes overall shots to provide a con-

text for more specialized information. He photographs other members of the team at work, such as one of the folklorists conducting an interview, as a way of showing how material is gathered.

Fleischhauer often photographs people in their homes, and to do this effectively he has to gain their confidence and cooperation. "One mark of a professional is to be able to enter a situation and find a way to make the pictures you want. You have to feel confident and show it. If you are, people are comfortable with you. If you are uneasy, which is natural, you won't build confidence in response. This is not necessarily a natural gift, but a skill that you can work on and improve."

As an agency of the Library of Congress, the American Folklife Center makes the photographs and other materials it gathers accessible to anyone. Consequently, there are some things the center does not record, such as illegal activities. Some people continue to make moonshine whiskey very much the way their grandparents did, but Fleischhauer does not incriminate them by photographing it. Furthermore, even if an activity is legal, some people might not choose to bring it forward. "We want to find out how the people themselves value parts of their lives," he says, "and which parts they choose to present to strangers."

In addition to photographing, Fleischhauer writes, edits, supervises the organization and documentation of all the center's photographs, and, for some projects, hires freelance photographers. The pay for freelancers is not high, and because prints are available free from the Library of Congress, the photographers get no income from later sales of stock photographs. However, the work will live as part of the library's collections, and that has a value of its own.

CARL FLEISCHHAUER: *Carlton Lupo and a Blue Tick Hound, Irwin County, Georgia,* 1977

Luther A. Bailey, sometimes known as "Lying" Bailey, told about one of his hound dogs on the track of a very fast raccoon. "He struck this durn coon and that coon went right out and across the open field. And they just looked like he was going, going to catch that coon every minute. He was just biting at him. Woof, woof. And he quit. And he never did bark no more. I took my lantern and went out across there, see could I find him, find out what was wrong. That dog was laying out there dead. And do you know—that coon was running so fast until them rings on his tail slipped off from his tail and went over that dog's neck and choked him to death." (Story collected as part of the South-Central Georgia Folklife Project, 1977)

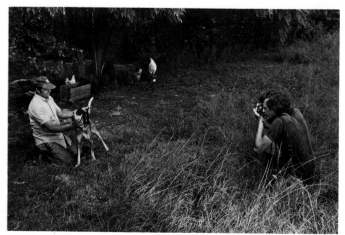

HOWARD W. MARSHALL: *Carl Fleischhauer at Work,* 1977

CARL FLEISCHHAUER: *Roping a Calf, Paradise Valley, Nevada,* 1978

Carl Fleischhauer photographed cattle branding in northern Nevada for an American Folklife Center project. The photograph above was used on the cover of a book on the project, Buckaroos in Paradise. (Buckaroo is the local term for a cowboy, from the Spanish vaquero, cowperson. The Paradise is Paradise Valley, Nevada.) The picture was made inside a corral but looks like a trail drive because of the dust being kicked up. "I knew at the time that the picture would have impact," Fleischhauer says, "beyond the information it gave about branding activities."

Industrial Photography: Matt Weinberg

To Matt Weinberg, the most interesting part of his job is working out a way to record what someone else needs to see. Weinberg is part of the Photographic Services Department at Santa Barbara Research Center, a subsidiary of Hughes Aircraft Company. SBRC designs, develops, and manufactures infrared sensing components and electro-optical systems used in weather satellites and other advanced systems.

Typically, an engineer who is working on a system comes to Weinberg's department to request photographic assistance, such as seeing a particular component in an extreme enlargement or examining its reaction under stress. The camera is the last thing Weinberg brings out because first he has to understand exactly what the engineer needs. Only then can he devise a way to record that information photographically.

Among the techniques at Weinberg's command is photography using infrared and ultraviolet radiation. For example, you can detect hairline cracks too small to be seen even with a microscope if you immerse an object in fluorescent dye, wash off the dye, and then expose the object to ultraviolet radiation. Dye will seep into cracks or other faults and fluoresce under ultraviolet radiation to reveal any damage on film. Critical examination of this kind is vital for certain satellite components in which even the slightest defect can disrupt functioning.

Weinberg also makes high-speed still photographs (to stop motion) and high-speed motion pictures (to slow down motion). One satellite component oscillates at a very high speed and in space is subjected to rapid temperature changes from extremely hot to extremely cold. Weinberg made high-speed motion pictures at various temperatures to test how the component

would perform in space. If you project movie film slower than the rate at which you expose it, any motion on the film will appear slower than normal. The normal projection rate for 35mm film is 24 frames per second; Weinberg has shot film as fast as 5,000 frames per second for such tests, and even faster speeds are possible.

Weinberg frequently makes photomacrographs (greatly enlarged photographs made with a camera lens) and photomicrographs) even greater enlargements made with a microscope). Scanning electron microscopes are available for extreme enlargements, as much as 300,000× life size.

Weinberg goes to the component if the component cannot come to him. One satellite had a problem deep in its core, and to photograph it he had to work inside the clean room in which the satellite was being assembled. After donning clean-room garb, including a jumpsuit that covered him from head to toe, he and his equipment were vacuumed off for dust. He was scanned with ultraviolet light, being checked for even the smallest dust particle, and then particle counters within the room kept further tabs on the cleanliness of the operation.

In high school, Weinberg became fascinated with photography the first time he saw a black-and-white image come up on a piece of printing paper. A broad technical training in photography gave him the background he needed for his job. He is pleased to have a job that pays him to do exactly what he likes to do—take more pictures. His advice to any photography student: "Shoot pictures—as many as you can. To be really good you have to have a lot of experience, about 50,000 pictures' worth. It is important to have the pride in your work that makes you try to do better every time."

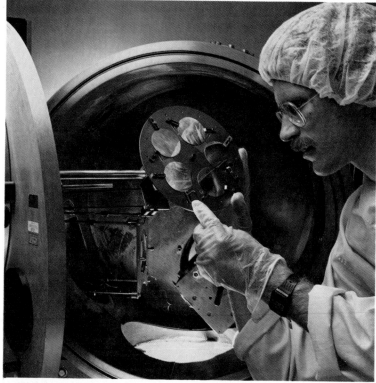

MATT WEINBERG: *Engineer Loading Vacuum Chamber*, 1983

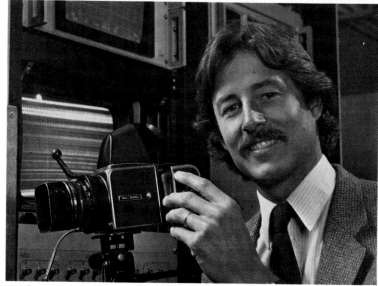

DOUG STELCK: *Matt Weinberg at Work*, 1984

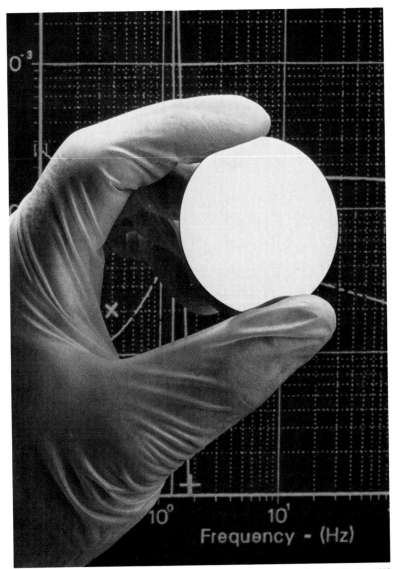

MATT WEINBERG: *Disc with Scratch-Resistant Coating,* 1983

In an experiment to develop a scratch-resistant material for high-tech applications, an engineer (opposite page, top) loads five sapphire discs into a holder prior to putting them into a vacuum chamber where they will be coated with a diamondlike carbon substance. The coated disc has a mirrorlike surface that appears very smooth (this page, left). Extreme magnification lets engineers study the textured surface of the coating (this page, right) and any flaws (arrow).

Surface of disc magnified 50 ×

Surface of disc magnified 200 ×

23

Showing Your Work to Editors and Others

Suppose you decide to show your work to a potential client, an agency, or a gallery. What kind of work should you show? Every editor and agent below said that you should tailor your portfolio to fit the needs of individual clients. For example, if you take your work to a magazine, look at recent issues and show them the kind of work that they publish. Editors and others have different expectations regarding the presentation of pictures for viewing. Call ahead to find out what people want.

Mel Scott, Assistant Picture Editor, Life. "The worst and commonest mistake," Scott says, "is to pad a portfolio. Show your absolute best, not your whole life's work. Don't show one great landscape with ten mediocre ones; the bad ones will only dilute the impact of the great one." He says that photographers should show him the kinds of pictures that the magazine uses. *Life* is now a monthly magazine that publishes very little news, so there is no point in showing him news pictures. Professionalism is important; Scott's day is tightly scheduled, so he expects photographers to arrive on time.

Scott files a 3 × 5 card for every photographer he sees and then uses that file as a source of names when editors or others come to him looking for a photographer. He often passes names on to others, so he says not to be discouraged if no work comes right away.

Julia Scully, Editor, Modern Photography. Scully looks at portfolios at weekly meetings with Andy Grundberg, Senior Picture Editor (*right*), and Howard Millard, Picture Editor (*center*). *Modern*'s audience consists of advanced amateurs, so she looks first to see if work would be interesting to readers, then considers its quality—both technically and aesthetically. "Sometimes the basic technical craft isn't there. People don't seem to know that they don't know how to print." Consistency is important; Scully likes to publish work from portfolios that exhibit strength, not the one good print in an otherwise weak portfolio. She suggests, incidentally, that photographers avoid overwrought titles like Autumn Splendor or Modern Madonna. Material should be easy to view, preferably unmounted prints or slides in trays or view sheets.

John Hair, Art Director, Pan Am Clipper. This monthly magazine is the one you find on the airplane in the pocket of the seat in front of yours. Hair is looking for evocative photographs that capture the essence of a place without looking like a postcard or snapshot view. He wants variety in a story, everything from a shot that conveys the overall feeling of a city to a close-up of the local food. Rather than a straightforward story on a place, he wants some kind of a tie-in or concept; for example, an exotic railroad trip that you get to via Pan Am.

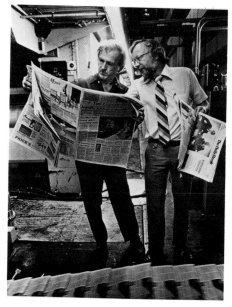

Bob Lynn, Graphics Director, The Virginian-Pilot and The Ledger-Star, Norfolk, Virginia. Lynn (*above, right*) is in charge of photography and graphics for all editions of these newspapers. When he opens a portfolio, he hopes he will find surprises, not clichés or even good but standard imagery. "I want someone who can see ordinary events in a different way or who can capture ironies in human behavior that others don't see." He suggests that photographers show only work of which they are especially proud. People often try to prove to him that they can shoot sports, spot news, general features, and every other photojournalism category, and as a result they include lesser pictures; when they do, he wonders if they can tell good work from bad. "If you don't have it, don't show it."

Brigitte Barkley, Foreign Correspondent, Geo (West Germany). Although this German magazine is similar in style to the English-language *Geo,* the two magazines publish different stories. German *Geo* maintains an office in New York, where Barkley's job is to screen material before submitting it to the main office in Hamburg. Barkley wants to see a story, not individual pictures. "I want to see how you think. How you would cover a story. You should be able to tell me that story and define it clearly." Too many photographers say they can do a story but don't show her that they can. "Find something that interests you and go out and do it. That's what I want to see."

Michael Quackenbush, Managing Picture Editor, Image Bank. This stock agency maintains a large library of pictures that are sold mostly to advertisers but also for editorial use. Quackenbush says that stock sales used to be resales from assignment work, but now many photographers shoot specifically for stock. He wants to see a good selection of work, about 300 original transparencies in view sheets. He says that the best-selling pictures are those with a direct approach to an easily perceived subject: a colorful sunset, a city skyline, a family having a picnic. However, there is also a market for less conventional imagery.

Advertising sales are usually generic: general views rather than ones that are tied to a specific situation. Travel advertisers want pictures that immediately convey the idea of vacation or tourism, such as a man and woman in bathing suits strolling on a tropical beach. Sales for corporate annual reports might be a factory silhouetted against the sky or a scene of two engineers conferring over a blueprint.

Editorial sales are more often linked to specific places and subjects. Instead of a generic photograph of luxury goods for sale, an editor might need a photograph of Saks Fifth Avenue or Neiman-Marcus. Instead of a sunset, the request might be for the St. Louis Arch at sunset.

Anne Edmonson, Production Editor, Gamma-Liaison. Publications make most of the purchases from this agency —current news, politics, feature stories, and personalities, as well as stock pictures. Edmonson says she does not want to look at a portfolio that contains hundreds of pictures—some tear sheets of published work, a few contact sheets with every shot on the roll to show how a photographer covers a story, about 60 slides, and some black-and-white prints are enough. Ideally, a portfolio should show a range of work. A news event can demonstrate that a photographer won't lose control in a fast-moving situation. A business portrait can show that the photographer can handle lighting. But, Edmonson's advice is, "Don't fake it. Edit down the material to your best, so that you feel confident with what you show."

———————

The following galleries sell to collectors of vintage and contemporary fine photographs.

Lee D. Witkin, The Witkin Gallery, Inc., New York. When Witkin opens a portfolio, he hopes to find images that he hasn't seen before. "It's hard to be new, but I am at least looking for a different point of view, a new twist, or some sign of a unique vision." Presentation is important because it is a sign that the photographer values the work. He wants to see 25 to 35 fine prints, matted or presented in an aesthetically pleasing way.

Witkin says that photography as an art requires a tremendous commitment. "Work takes time to evolve, and you can't skip the starting stage." He suggests that photographers get feedback from as many people as possible. "You don't have to follow everybody's advice, but at least consider if their remarks apply to you."

Brent Sikkema, Vision Gallery, Boston. Sikkema says that he makes notes of work he sees, asks for a résumé, and then files that material. Many people use his files, such as curators of group shows, so the names of people he sees often get passed on to others. Sikkema does not accept a photographer the first time he looks at a portfolio; instead he wants to see work over a period of time. "If I say your work is interesting and that I want to follow it, it's not a put-off." Many photographers make the mistake of being impatient, according to Sikkema. "Don't be discouraged and don't be afraid to go back six months or a year later, even if you got little response the first time."

Tiana G. Wimmer, Daniel Wolf, Inc., New York. This gallery looks for artists with an individual and unique style, something that Wimmer feels comes only with maturity. "Beginners are often disappointed not to get immediate recognition, but they need time for growth." Wimmer wants to see 20 prints maximum, matted and packed in a standard portfolio box. Showing too many prints makes it look as if you cannot edit your work properly. Unmounted prints stuffed in a box that printing paper comes in makes the work appear less significant. Wimmer says you should show your best prints but realize that as you take them around, they will become worn.

Student Photographers at Work

Following is the work of the nine finalists in the juried selection of student work conducted for this edition of *Photography*. Any person who at the time of the selection was enrolled in an undergraduate course in photography was eligible to enter. The judges making the final selection were Judy Dater, photographer and teacher (*see page 343*); Bruce Davidson, photographer (*see pages 2–3 and 64*); and Beaumont Newhall, whose work in the history of photography has shaped much of modern perception of the subject.

Like the entries submitted for the second edition of this book, the work submitted this time was diverse in style and wide-ranging in subject matter. The judges' choices reflect that diversity.

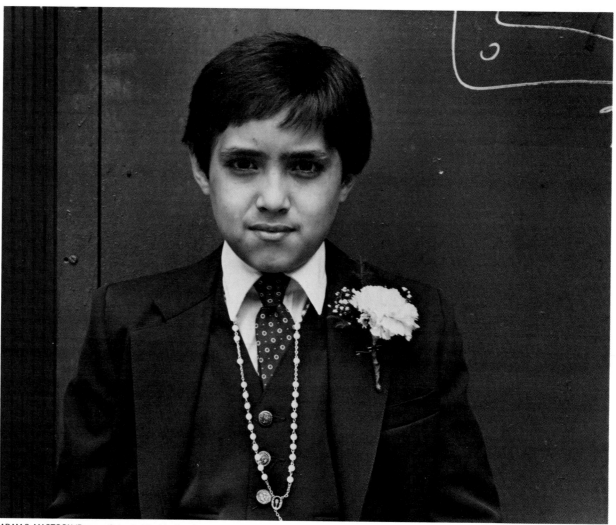

ADAM S. MASTOON (Parsons School of Design, New York, New York): *Untitled*, 1983

A photograph can seem to be quite straightforward at first but become increasingly complex the more one looks at it. Above, the direct stare and frontal posing of the boy, even the flat wall behind him, seem to hold no secrets. The boy is immaculately dressed in adult style with a flower and rosary as further evidence of the specialness of the occasion. He is a little man, dutifully playing his role—except that the longer one looks at his expression, the more difficult it becomes to say what he might be feeling and the more he seems to be keeping his opinions to himself. The marking on the wall behind him is equally cryptic.

ANDREW B. COGAN (Harvard University, Cambridge, Massachusetts): *Sheep Crossing*, 1982

The tonality of a photograph, the way it reproduces the light and dark tones of a scene, can add to the mood of an image. Above, this soft and delicate print blends sky, clouds, grass, and sheep into an integrated whole. The man silhouetted against the brighter sky stands a bit apart, both literally and tonally.

The apparent bleakness of this industrialized rural crossroads is made appealing by the intricacy of the fine detail and the careful balance of the photograph. Vertical lines repeat, square shapes repeat, X-shapes repeat—and all the forms circle around the empty central intersection.

JOHN W. EDWARDS (East Tennessee State University, Johnson City, Tennessee): *New Street, Johnson City, Tennessee*, 1982

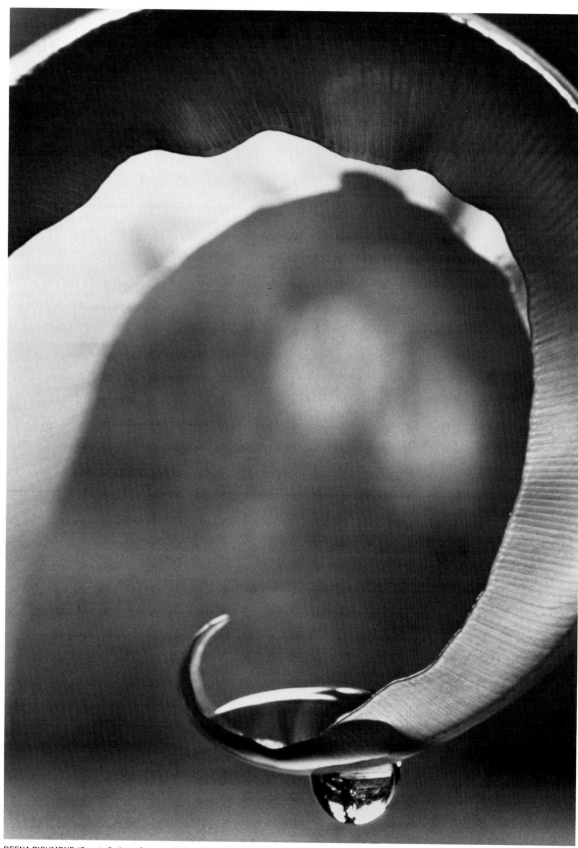

DEENA RICHMOND (Cuesta College, San Luis Obispo, California): *Bird's-Nest Fern*, 1982. Original in color

Pictures are affected by other images nearby. The result can be a jarring conflict or, as with the two pictures here, an interesting play of contrasts and similarities. The scale seems large in both images, even though the actual sizes of the subjects are vastly different. The roundness of one photograph is pleasantly echoed in the other.

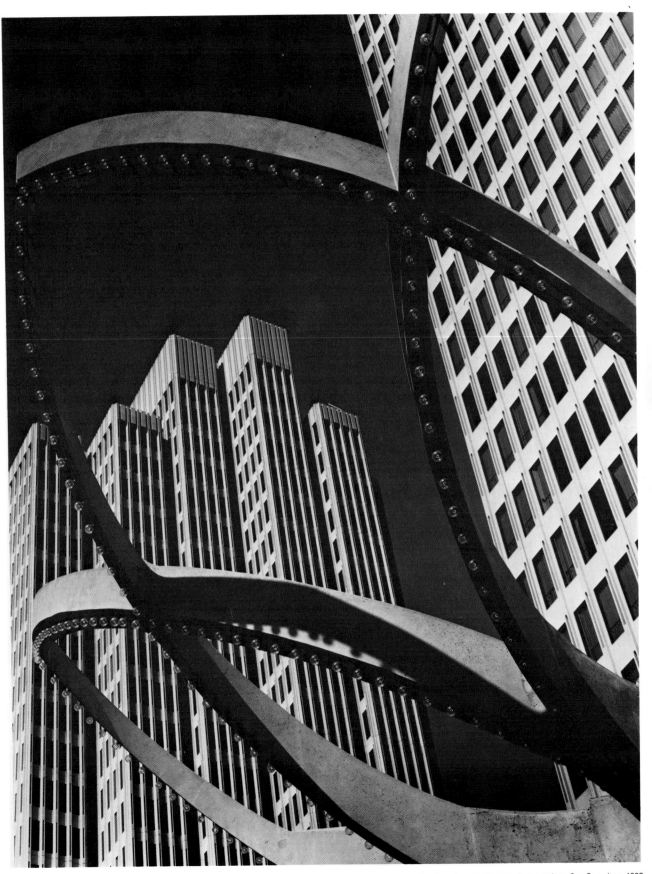

STEPHEN J. CARNEY (City College of San Francisco, San Francisco, California): *Embarcadero, San Francisco,* 1982

SCOTT FORBES (Tyler School of Art, Philadelphia, Pennsylvania): *Untitled, Waterford, Virginia,* 1982. Original in color

Left, two women engage in a communication that is as perfectly stereotyped as their outfits and hairstyles. Above, two women engage in a dramatized posing of a personal but ambiguous communication.

I was once able to make a perfect zabaglione on a kerosene stove by the light of an oil lamp in a Virginia cabin!

TOBY L. GREENBERG (Tyler School of Art, Philadelphia, Pennsylvania): *Afternoon Chat,* 1983. Original in color

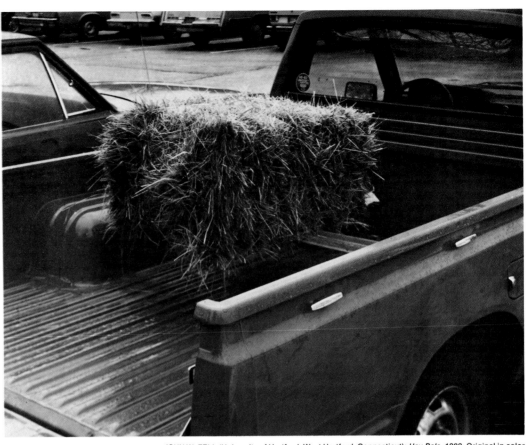

JOHN W. FELL (University of Hartford, West Hartford, Connecticut): *Hay Bale*, 1983. Original in color

On this page, two more mysteries. Above, the hay bale seemingly floats above the bed of the truck, quirkily defying gravity. Below, the woman in the photograph is oddly responsive to the creeping menace of the spilled ink. Both pictures call into question the assumption that a photograph does not lie.

BIL ROCKWELL (Western Connecticut State University, Danbury, Connecticut): *Untitled Final #1*, 1983

SARA FACIO: *Looking at Life, Colonia, Uruguay,* 1963

2
Camera

Why do you need to know how a camera works? Much of camera design today is based on one of the earliest camera slogans—"You press the button, we do the rest." Automatic, electronic, and computerized modern cameras try to make picture taking as easy as possible by choosing the shutter speed or aperture for you or by presetting the focus. But they can make choices for you only up to a certain point. Do you want to freeze the motion of a speeding car or let it race by in a blur? Bring the whole forest into sharp focus or isolate a single flower? Exaggerate the size and strength of a man or show him dwarfed by the cement and steel of his environment? These are decisions that only you can make, and the more pictures you take the more you will want to make these decisions deliberately rather than leave them to chance. The time you spend learning what camera equipment can do and how to control its effects will be more than repaid whether you make a snapshot, a portrait, a commercial illustration, a news photograph, a personal statement about the world, or any other kind of photograph.

◀ *Argentine photographer Sara Facio took this picture of Uruguayan children crowding the window of an old house to watch passing tourists. Even when you know the circumstances, the photograph has its own life. The glass window seems to become the surface of the print, and the girl's fingers press against that surface. The frame of the window shown within the frame of the photograph also anchors the window at the surface of the print. The children are talking and laughing, but we can't hear them. Their expressions, as well as the doll's, seem unconnected, as do the disembodied heads and the hand at the top of the frame. All these elements contribute to the dreamlike quality of the picture.*

The Anatomy of a Camera

All **cameras** are basically alike. Each is a box with a piece of film in one end and a hole in the other. The hole is there so that light can enter the box, strike the light-sensitive surface of the film, and make a picture. Every camera from the most primitive to the most sophisticated works this way. The job is always the same: to get light onto film to form an image. The differences are in how well and how easily this is done.

The basic parts of a camera are shown opposite. First, there is a **viewing system,** a sighting device that enables the user to aim the camera accurately at the subject. The hole that admits light to the camera—the **aperture**—is adjustable, by a device called a diaphragm, which controls the amount of light that enters. A **lens** collects the light and projects an image onto the film. A movable screen—the **shutter**—keeps all light out of the camera until the moment you want to take the picture. Pressing a button opens the shutter for an instant, just long enough to admit enough light to make a satisfactory image on the film. There is a device for moving the exposed film out of the way and replacing it with unexposed film. Finally, a **focusing mechanism** moves the lens back and forth so that it can project sharp images of objects at various distances.

All cameras except the very cheapest have all these features in some form. Why then are there so many different kinds of cameras? The reason is that cameras are asked to do many different things under such a wide variety of conditions that they have become specialized. While a bulky view camera is ideal for taking architectural photographs, it is not as good as a smaller camera for taking unposed pictures of people on a crowded street.

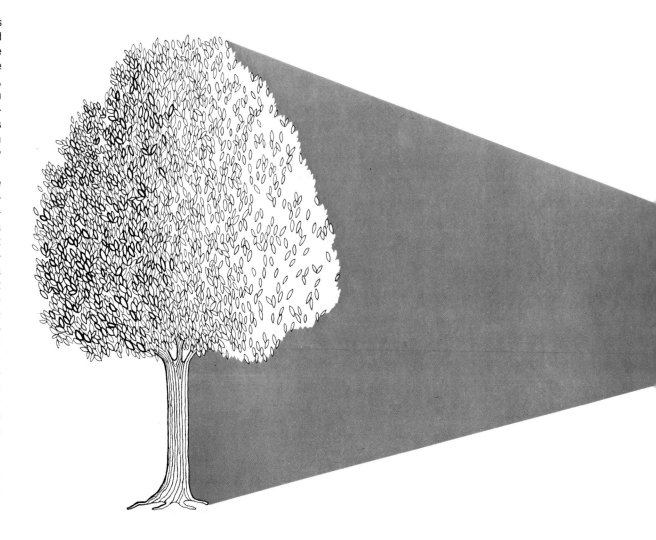

All cameras fit into one of four main categories according to the viewing system they use. Cameras with viewfinders and small single-lens reflex cameras are generally used at eye level; you put them up to your eye and use them as a direct extension of your vision into the scene in front of you. Viewing with the somewhat larger twin-lens reflex camera is usually done by looking down onto a ground-glass screen. The largest camera, the view camera, provides the most precise—and the slowest—viewing and composition.

The next few pages describe these four types of cameras in more detail. Understanding how they work will help you decide which type is best for you.

A | **The viewing system** *shows the scene the picture will cover, through a set of lenses (left) or the picture-taking lens itself.*

B | **The film** *receives the image of the object being photographed and records this image on its light-sensitive surface.*

C | **The film advance** *winds film from one spool to another in cameras using film rolls or cartridges. In cameras that use sheets of film, there is a slot admitting one sheet at a time.*

D | **The camera body,** *a box that houses the various parts of the camera, protects the film from all light except that which enters through the lens when a picture is taken.*

E | **The diaphragm,** *a light-control device usually made of overlapping metal leaves, forms an adjustable hole, or aperture. It can be opened to let more light pass through the lens or partially closed—stopped down—to restrict the passage of light.*

F | **The shutter,** *the second light-control device, is a movable, protective shield that opens and closes to permit a measured amount of light to strike the film. The shutter mechanism, a complicated one on adjustable cameras, is represented here schematically as a light-proof curtain with an opening that admits light when the opening passes by the lens.*

G | **The lens** *focuses the light rays from a subject and creates a reversed, upside-down image on the film at the back of the camera.*

H | **The focusing control** *moves elements of the lens back or forth to create a sharp image on the film. The gear-wheel-and-track system shown here shifts the whole camera front; more commonly the lens alone moves by turning like a screw.*

The Major Types of Cameras
View Camera

In a view camera, the light comes directly from the subject, through the lens, and falls on a ground-glass viewing screen (a) at the back of the camera. The image that the photographer sees comes directly from the lens, so it is reversed and upside down, as the upper bird photo shows. Otherwise it is identical to what will appear on the film (lower photo). As an aid in composing pictures, the ground glass of this camera is etched with a square grid of hairlines.

One of the oldest basic designs for a camera—direct, through-the-lens viewing and a large image on a translucent viewing screen—is still in use today. A **view camera** is built somewhat like an accordion, with a lens at the front, a **ground-glass** viewing screen at the back, and a flexible **bellows** in between. You focus by moving the lens, the back, or the entire camera forward or back until you see a sharp image on the ground glass.

Advantages of the view camera: The image on the ground glass is projected by the picture-taking lens, so what you see is exactly what will be on the negative; there can be no parallax error (as in a rangefinder camera, *opposite*). The ground glass is large, and you can examine it with a magnifying glass to check sharpness in all parts of the picture. The film size is also large (4 × 5, 5 × 7, 8 × 10 inches or larger), which produces sharp detail. The camera parts are adjustable, and you can change the position of lens and film relative to each other so that you can correct problems of focus or distortion.

Each picture is exposed on a separate piece of film, so you can give negatives individual development.

Disadvantages: The most serious are the bulk and weight of the camera and the necessity of using a tripod. Second, the image projected on the ground glass is not very bright, and to see it clearly you must put a **focusing cloth** over both your head and the back of the camera. Finally, the image appears reversed and upside down on the viewing screen. You get used to this, but it is disconcerting at first.

Rangefinder Camera

In a **rangefinder camera** the scene to be photographed is viewed through a peephole (the **viewfinder**) equipped with a simple lens system that shows an image approximating what the picture will be. Cameras with this type of viewfinder (except the least expensive ones) include a device called a **coupled rangefinder** (*page 41*) that shows when the picture is in focus. Most models use 35mm film; a few use other sizes.

Advantages of the rangefinder: A camera with a combined rangefinder-viewfinder is compact, lightweight, and fast handling. Compared to a single-lens reflex camera, it has fewer parts that move during an exposure, so it tends to be somewhat quieter and less subject to vibration during operation, and to work reliably, even with long, hard use. Good-quality models provide excellent focusing, particularly at low light levels where other viewing systems do not function as well.

Disadvantages: Because the viewfinder is in a different position than the lens that exposes the negative, the camera suffers from an inherent defect called **parallax** (*left*) that prevents you from seeing exactly what the lens sees. The closer the subject to the camera, the more evident the parallax. A high-quality camera like the one shown here automatically corrects for parallax except when the subject is within a few feet of the camera. Because complete correction is difficult at close range, sighting through the viewfinder is awkward for carefully composed close-up work. In addition, even when the edges of the picture are fully corrected for parallax, the alignment of objects within the picture will always be seen from slightly different angles by the viewfinder and the taking lens, which exposes the film. Also, the images seen through a poor-quality viewfinder can be small and difficult to focus.

In a rangefinder camera, light from the subject goes through a viewfinder to the eye and through another lens to the film (cutaway, center). The difference between these two viewpoints creates parallax. Even though the viewfinder covers the whole bird (broken lines in diagram at left), the lens does not (solid lines) and the bird's head will be cut off in the picture. Better-quality rangefinder cameras correct for parallax to match the views (above), except for subjects that are very near.

Reflex Cameras

Single-Lens Reflex

The best way to see what the camera sees is to look right through the camera lens itself. This way you can frame the subject precisely and see how much of the scene, from foreground objects to distant background, will be sharp. You cannot evaluate sharpness with a viewfinder, which produces a sharp image of everything it sees, but you can with a **single-lens reflex camera.** This camera has a **mirror** and **pentaprism** (*diagram, left*) to let you use the lens for composing and focusing. Most cameras take 35mm film, but medium-format sizes for 2¼-inch film are also popular.

Advantages of the single-lens reflex: It eliminates parallax and so is excellent for close-up work. It is easy and quick to focus. Since the viewing system uses the camera lens itself, it works equally well with all lenses—from fisheye to supertelephoto; whatever the lens sees, you see. An exposure meter built into the camera is usually designed to view through the lens so that you can see the area the meter is measuring.

Disadvantages: A single-lens reflex is heavier and larger than a rangefinder camera that uses the same size film; however, newer compact models have been considerably reduced in weight and size, so this is not as significant as it was with older models. The camera is relatively complex, with more components that may need repair. Its moving mirror makes a comparatively loud click during exposure, especially in medium-format models; this is a drawback if you are stalking wild animals or self-conscious people. When the mirror moves up during exposure, it momentarily blacks out the viewing image, also a distraction in some situations. And the motion of the mirror and shutter may cause vibrations that make the camera more difficult to hold steady at slow shutter speeds, although better models all but eliminate vibration.

The viewing system of a single-lens reflex camera is built around a mirror (a). Light coming in through the camera lens is reflected by this mirror (hence the name, reflex) up to a viewing screen, then usually through a five-sided pentaprism that turns the inverted image around so it appears the correct way to the eye. When a picture is taken, the mirror swings up momentarily (b), permitting light to strike the film at the back of the camera. The image viewed through the lens with a pentaprism is virtually identical with the image produced on the film (bird pictures at right).

Twin-Lens Reflex

A twin-lens reflex has separate viewing and picture-taking lenses stacked one over the other. The lower lens conducts light to the film. The upper one, coupled to the lower for focusing, conducts light to a mirror (a) set at a 45° angle, where it is reflected upward to a ground-glass viewing screen (b). Like all mirror reflections, the image appears reversed left to right, as shown in the top photo. The top photo also shows a grid of hairlines, etched on the viewing screen, that can be used to align elements in the scene.

The **twin-lens reflex camera,** like the single-lens reflex camera, uses a mirror that reflects an image of the scene upward onto a viewing screen. But its mirror is fixed, and there is one lens to expose the film and another one for viewing. The lenses are coupled mechanically so that when one is focused sharply, the other is also.

A twin-lens reflex camera combines characteristics of the larger view camera and the smaller rangefinder camera.

Advantages of the twin-lens reflex:
The fixed mirror means simple, rugged construction and quiet operation, and the relatively large ground glass makes viewing easy. Because you usually look into this camera from the top, you can lower it to waist level or even place it on the ground for photographing from a low angle, an awkward position for an eye-level viewfinder. The camera gives you a medium-format film size for a relatively low price.

Disadvantages: The principal problem is parallax—the viewing lens does not see exactly the same picture as the taking lens. Some twin-lens reflexes have automatic parallax correction, but not for objects at very close range and not for the alignment of objects within the picture. The image projected on the viewing screen is reversed left to right, which can make it difficult to follow moving objects. The larger size of the twin-lens reflex makes the camera somewhat cumbersome, and it is awkward to use at eye level. Lenses are not interchangeable on all models.

Focusing Systems

Ground-Glass Viewing Screen

All cameras with movable controls have some means of showing you when a subject is sharply focused. With a **ground-glass viewing screen,** light from the camera lens hits a pane of glass that is etched, or ground, to be translucent. This ground glass creates a surface on which a viewer, looking at it from the other side, can see an image (*above*) and focus it. The image on a ground glass is not as bright as that in a viewfinder; in dim light you may not be able to see readily whether the image is sharp.

A **coupled rangefinder** (*opposite*) may be easier to use in dim light because you only have to line up a double image, or two parts of a split image. The focusing mechanism of the lens is coupled with the rangefinder so that they focus at the same time.

A **microprism** focusing aid may accompany a ground glass or split image, especially on a single-lens reflex camera. A central spot or collar around the split image shimmers or appears broken when the subject is unfocused.

Don't confuse the function of a rangefinder with that of a viewfinder. The viewfinder shows the view the camera will take. The rangefinder (usually built into the viewfinder) finds the range or distance of an object and shows when it is sharply focused.

In this reflex camera a mirror reflects the image from the lens upward onto a ground-glass screen. Since the ground glass at the top and the film at the back of the camera are the same distance from the lens, the image that falls on the screen will be sharp only when the lens is also focusing the image sharply on the film plane. At left, above, the focusing knob on the left side of the camera is incorrectly set at 25 ft, producing an unclear image of a toy soldier 15 ft away. But when the knob is set for 15 ft (above right) the image the photographer sees is sharply defined.

Coupled Rangefinder

A rangefinder operates by superimposing two images of the same subject as seen from different angles (diagram, below). One image passes through a viewfinder (on the left side of the camera shown here); the other image is reflected by a rotating prism (right side of camera) and is superimposed on the viewfinder image. The movement of the prism is mechanically linked to the focusing movement of the lens. If the subject is not in focus, the viewfinder will show a split image; part of the flower stem will be to the left of where it belongs (top photograph). This happens because that part has been deflected by the rotating prism.

When the image is sharply focused, the rotating prism is turned to the correct angle to superimpose its image directly over the viewfinder image so that the two images appear to be one. As with other cameras, the subject-to-camera distance is indicated in feet or meters on a band on the lens barrel so that the lens can also be focused by measuring the distance from subject to camera and then turning the lens to the appropriate distance.

The Shutter as a Controller of Light

To expose film correctly, so that your picture is neither too light nor too dark, you need to control the amount of light that enters the camera. Two controls make this possible: the shutter, described here, and the aperture (*pages 46–47*).

The **shutter** controls the amount of light by the length of time it remains open. Each shutter setting is half (or double) that of the next one and is marked as the denominator of the fraction of a second that the shutter remains open: 1 (¹⁄₁ or one second), 2 (½ second), 4 (¼ second), and so on through 8, 15, 30, 60, 125, 250, 500, and on some cameras 1000, 2000, and 4000. You may find a different sequence on older equipment: 1, 2, 5, 10, 25, 50, 100, 250. B or bulb setting keeps the shutter open as long as the release button is held down. T or time setting opens the shutter with one press of the release, closes it with another.

There are two principal types of shutters: the leaf shutter (*this page*) and the focal-plane shutter (*opposite*). Each type has its own advantages and draw-

A leaf or between-the-lens shutter is generally located in the lens itself (a). It consists of a number of small overlapping metal blades powered by a spring. When the shutter release is pushed, the tension on the spring is released and the blades open up and then shut again in a preset amount of time. In the examples at right, the blades are just beginning to swing open at (1) and very little light is hitting the film. At (2), with the shutter open farther, the blades are almost completely withdrawn, and at (3) light pours in. Then the blades begin to close again, admitting less and less light (4, 5). The total amount of light admitted during this cycle produces the fully exposed photograph (6).

The amount of light that enters a camera, like the amount of water that pours from an open faucet into a glass, depends on how long the flow of light continues. If a glass is filled halfway in 2 sec, it will be filled to the top in 4 sec. In the same way, if the shutter is left open twice as long, the film will be exposed to twice as much light.

Leaf Shutter

1

2

3

4

5

Focal-Plane Shutter

backs. A **focal-plane shutter** is built into the camera body itself—just in front of the film, or focal, plane—while a leaf shutter is usually located between the lens elements. Interchangeable lenses for a camera with a focal-plane shutter are therefore less expensive since a shutter mechanism does not have to be built into each lens. One drawback to the focal-plane shutter is that it cannot be used with electronic flash at fast shutter speeds. Usually the maximum speed with flash is 1/60 or 1/125 second with 35mm cameras, even slower with larger formats. This is because at faster shutter speeds the slit in the focal-plane shutter does not completely uncover the film at any one time; before the first part of the shutter is fully open, the second part starts to close (*right*). Also, since the slit exposes one end of the film frame before the other, objects moving rapidly parallel to the shutter may be distorted; this is rare, but it can happen. Finally, every time you open the camera to load or unload film, the delicate shutter curtains are exposed; touching them can cause damage.

A **leaf shutter** is quieter than a focal-plane shutter and can be used with flash at any shutter speed. But since the leaf shutter has to open, stop, and then reverse direction to close again, most have top speeds of 1/500 second. The focal-plane shutter has a simpler mechanism that moves in one direction and permits speeds of up to 1/4000 second.

The focal-plane shutter is located directly in front of the film (a). The shutter consists of two overlapping curtains that form an adjustable slit or window. When the shutter is released, the window moves across the film, exposing the film as it moves. The series at left shows how the film is exposed at fast shutter speeds. The slit is narrow and exposes only part of the film at any one time. Picture (6), below, shows the effect of the entire exposure, with all sections of the film having received the proper amount of light. At slow shutter speeds, one edge of the slit travels across the film until the film is completely uncovered; then the other edge of the slit travels in the same direction, re-covering the film. The shutter shown here moves from side to side across the length of the film. The Copal Square type of focal-plane shutter moves from top to bottom across the film.

The Shutter as a Controller of Motion

 1/30 second

 1/500 second

A blurred image can occur when an object moves in front of a camera that is not moving, because the image projected onto the film by the lens will move. If the object moves swiftly or if the shutter is open for a relatively long time, this moving image will **blur** and be indistinct. But if the shutter speed is increased, the blur can be reduced or eliminated. You can control this effect and even use it to advantage. A fast shutter speed can freeze a moving object, showing its position at any given instant, whether it be a bird in flight or a football player jumping for a pass. A slow shutter speed can be used deliberately to increase the blurring and accentuate the feeling of motion.

The effects of varying shutter speed and camera movement are shown above. In the picture at far left the bicycle moved enough during the relatively long ⅟₃₀-second exposure to leave a broad blur on the film. In the next photograph a shutter speed of ⅟₅₀₀ second stopped the motion so effectively it is

hard to tell whether the bicycle was moving at all. A moving subject may vary in speed and thus affect the shutter speed needed to stop motion. For example, at the peak of a movement that reverses (such as the peak of a jump just before descent), motion slows, and even a relatively slow shutter speed will record the action sharply.

The amount of blurring in a photograph, however, is not determined simply by how fast the object itself moves. What matters is how far an image actually travels across the film during the exposure. In the third photograph, with the rider moving directly toward the camera, the bicycle remains in virtually the same position on the film. Thus, there is far less blurring even at ⅟₃₀ second. A slow-moving object close to the camera, such as a bicycle 10 feet away, will cross more of the film and appear to blur more than a fast-moving object far away, such as a jet in flight. A telephoto lens magnifies objects and makes them appear closer to the camera; it

will blur a moving subject more than a normal lens used at the same distance.

The photograph at far right shows the effect of **panning.** The camera was moved in the same direction the bicycle was moving. Since the camera moved at about the same speed as the bicycle, the rider appears sharp while the motionless background appears blurred. Successful panning takes both practice and luck. Variables such as the exact speed and direction of the moving object make it difficult to predict exactly how fast to pan. Decide where you want the object to be at the moment of exposure, start moving the camera a few moments before the object reaches that point, and follow your motion through as you would with a golf or tennis stroke. The longer the focal length of the lens, the less you will need to pan the camera; with a telephoto lens, a very small amount of lens movement creates a great deal of movement of the picture image. (*Focal length is explained on page 62.*)

1/30 second

 1/30 second, camera panned

The diagram at left shows how the direction of a moving object affects the amount of blur that will result. When the object is traveling parallel to the plane of the film (first arrow), all the movement is recorded on the film. If it is moving at an angle to the film (second arrow), less left-to-right movement will be recorded and, as a result, less blur. When the object moves directly toward the camera (third arrow), there is no left-to-right movement at all and hence a minimum of blur. When the camera is panned or moved in the same direction as the object (right arrows), the object will be sharp and the background blurred.

The Aperture as a Controller of Light

Changing the size of the **aperture,** the lens opening through which light enters the camera, can adjust the exposure, the amount of light that reaches the film. The shutter speed changes the length of time that light strikes the film; the aperture changes the brightness of the light.

The aperture works like the pupil of an eye; it can be enlarged or contracted to admit more light or less. In a camera this is done with a **diaphragm,** a ring of thin, overlapping metal leaves located inside the lens. The leaves are movable; turning the aperture ring on the lens rotates the leaves out of the way so that most of the light reaching the surface of the lens passes through. A turn in the opposite direction will close the diaphragm until the aperture becomes very small and so allows less light to pass (*see opposite*).

Aperture sizes are measured on a scale of numbers called **f-stops.** On early cameras the aperture was adjusted by individual metal stop plates that had holes of different diameters.

The term "stop" is still used to refer to the aperture size, and a lens is said to be "stopped down" when the size of the aperture is decreased.

The standardized series of numbers commonly used on the f-stop scale runs as follows: f/1.4, f/2, f/2.8, f/4, f/5.6, f/8, f/11, f/16, f/22, f/32, f/45, f/64. The largest of these, f/1.4, admits the most light. Each f-stop after that admits half the light of the previous one. A lens that is set at f/4 admits half as much light as one set at f/2.8 and only a quarter as much as one set at f/2. The variation over the full range of f-stops is large; a lens whose aperture is stopped down to f/64 admits less than 1/2000 of the light that comes through a lens set at f/1.4.

No lens is built to use the whole range of apertures. A general-purpose lens for a 35mm camera, for example, might run from f/1.4 to f/22. A camera lens designed for a large view camera might stop down to f/64 but open up only to f/5.6. The widest possible aperture at which a particular lens design will function well may not be a full stop from a standard setting. So a lens's f-stops may begin with a setting such as f/3.5, f/4.5, or f/7.7, then proceed in the standard sequence.

Lenses are often described as **fast** or **slow.** These terms refer to how wide the maximum aperture is. A lens that opens to f/1.4 opens wider and is said to be faster than one that opens only to f/2. (In the same way, the faucet on the left in the diagram below is said to be running faster than the faucet on the right.)

The term **stop** is used to refer to a change in exposure, whether the aperture or the shutter speed is changed. To give one stop more exposure means to double the amount of light reaching the film (either by opening up to the next larger aperture setting or by doubling the exposure time). To give one stop less exposure means to cut the light reaching the film in half (stopping down to the next smaller aperture setting or halving the exposure time). More about f-stops is explained on pages 48–51 and 74–77.

The flow of light into a camera can be controlled by aperture size just as the flow of water into a glass can be controlled by the faucet setting. Here a faucet running wide open for 2 sec fills a glass. If it runs half shut, it fills only half a glass in that time period. The same is true for light. In a given length of time, an aperture opened to any f-stop admits half as much light as one opened to the next larger f-stop. Thus the aperture setting controls the rate at which light enters the camera—in contrast to shutter setting, which controls how long the light flow continues.

F-stops are marked on a movable ring on the outside of a lens. In the lens below, they go from f/2.8 to f/22, with the actual size of the apertures shown in the seven circles. To select an f-stop on this lens, the ring is turned until the desired setting is opposite a white arrow. You can set the ring exactly on an f-stop or partway in between. Turning the ring adjusts the diaphragm inside the lens. Here the camera is set at f/8. Each f-stop setting lets in half (or double) the light of the next setting. The effect of decreasing the light by stopping down is shown in the diagrams at left, in which the circles are the same size as the actual apertures below. It takes four circles the size of an f/5.6 aperture to equal the size of a circle at f/2.8. Notice that the lowest f-stop numeral (2.8) lets in the most light. As the f-stop numerals get larger (4, 5.6, etc.), the aperture size and light admitted decrease.

2,8   4   5,6   8   11   16   22

f=80mm

The Aperture as a Controller of Depth of Field

aperture setting: f/2

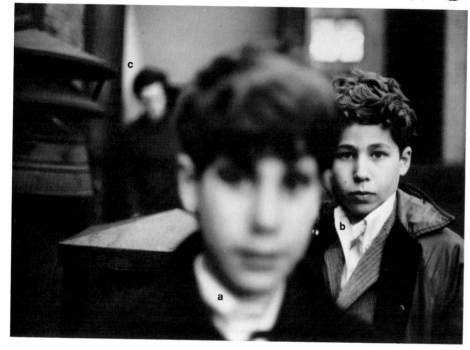

a b c

depth of field: 1 foot

distance (feet)

depth-of-field scale (f-stops)

aperture (f-stops)

A change in aperture size affects the sharpness of the image as well as the amount of light entering the camera. As the aperture decreases in size, more of the background and foreground in a given scene becomes sharp. The area of acceptable sharpness in a picture is known as the **depth of field**. (*See also pages 72–77.*)

The two large photographs shown on these pages were taken under identical conditions but with different aperture settings. In the photograph above, the diaphragm was opened to its widest aperture, f/2, and the lens was focused on the boy (b) about seven feet away (*see side view of the photographer and his subjects, above right*). The resulting photograph shows a shallow depth of field; only the middle boy (b) is sharp, while both the boy in front (a) and the

man behind (c) appear out of focus. Using a small aperture, f/16, gives a different picture (*opposite page*). The lens is still focused on the middle boy but the depth of field is now great enough to yield sharp images of the other figures as well.

With a view camera or a single-lens reflex, checking depth of field is relatively simple. A view camera views directly through the lens. As the lens is stopped down, the increasing depth of field is shown on the ground-glass viewing screen. A single-lens reflex camera also views through the lens. Most models automatically show the scene through the widest aperture, and so with the least depth of field. But some also provide a **depth-of-field preview button** that stops down the lens so you can see the depth of field at the

At the widest setting, f/2, marked by the bottom ring, the depth of field on this lens when focused at 7 ft is barely deep enough to include the middle boy (b) (see side view of scene, above). The bracketing marks—that is, the vertical lines—on the center ring, when read against the camera's distance scale on the top ring, indicate that at f/2 on this lens only objects slightly more than 6 ft but less than 8 ft from the lens will be sharp in the photograph. If depth of field is shallow, as it is here, a lens can be sharply focused and still not produce a picture that is sharp enough.

When the lens is closed down to its smallest aperture, f/16, almost the entire scene before the camera becomes sharp at the same focusing distance of 7 ft. The photographer can check this on the depth-of-field and distance scales. For, as the bracketing marks for f/16 show, everything between 5 ft and 13 ft will now be sharp.

aperture to which you have set the camera. However, in very dim light or at a very small aperture, the image may be too dark to be seen clearly once the lens is stopped down.

Examining depth of field is somewhat more difficult with a twin-lens reflex camera or a camera with a viewfinder. A twin-lens reflex shows the scene only at the widest aperture of the viewing lens. There is no way to stop it down to check depth of field at other apertures. Through a viewfinder, objects at all distances appear equally sharp.

A **depth-of-field scale** is a way to predict depth of field in place of or in addition to visually checking through the lens. This scale often appears printed on the lens as paired numbers that bracket the distances of the nearest and farthest points of the depth of field.

As the lens is focused and the f-stop set, the scale shows what part of the picture will be in focus and what part will not.

The lens shown on these two pages has such a scale. The bottom row of numbers shows the f-stops. The top row shows the distance from the lens to the object on which it is sharply focused. The middle row shows the nearest and farthest distances within which objects will be sharp at various apertures. (This lens shows the distances only in feet; many lenses also show them in meters.) The greatest distance on the lens appears as the symbol ∞. This **infinity** mark stands for all distances at that point or farther from the lens. When the camera is focused on infinity, all objects at that distance or farther will be in sharp focus.

Using Shutter and Aperture Together

The quantity of light that reaches a piece of film inside a camera depends on a combination of aperture size (f-stop) and length of exposure (shutter speed). In the same way, the water that flows from a faucet depends on how wide the valve is open and how long the water flows. If a 2-sec flow from a wide-open faucet fills a glass, then the same glass will be filled in 4 sec from a half-open faucet.

Both shutter speed and aperture affect the amount of light that enters the camera. To get a correctly exposed negative (one that is neither too light nor too dark), you have to find a **combination of shutter speed and aperture** that will let in the right amount of light for a particular scene and film. (Chapter 5, Exposure, tells in detail how to do this.) But shutter speed and aperture also affect sharpness, and in this respect they act quite differently: shutter speed affects the sharpness of moving objects; aperture affects the sharpness from near to far.

Once you know any single combination of shutter speed and aperture that will let in the right amount of light, you can change one setting as long as you change the other—in the correct direction. Since each aperture setting lets in twice as much light as the next smaller size, and each shutter speed lets in half as much light as the next slower speed, you can use a larger aperture if you use a faster shutter speed or a smaller aperture if you use a slower shutter speed. The same amount of light will be let in by an f/22 aperture at a 1-second shutter speed, f/16 at ½ second, f/11 at ¼ second, and so on.

The effects of such combinations are shown in the three photographs at right. In each, the lens was focused on the same point, and shutter and aperture settings were balanced to admit the same total amount of light into the camera. But the three equivalent exposures resulted in three very different photographs.

In the first picture, a small aperture produced considerable depth of field that rendered background details sharply; but the shutter speed needed to compensate for this tiny aperture had to be so slow that the rapidly moving flock of pigeons appears only as indistinct ghosts. In the center photograph, the aperture was wider and the shutter speed faster; the background is less sharp but the pigeons are visible, though still blurred. At far right, a still larger aperture and faster shutter speed sacrificed almost all background detail, but the birds are now very clear, with only a few wing tips still blurred.

A small aperture (f/16) produces great depth of field; in this scene even distant trees are sharp. But to admit enough light, a slow shutter speed (⅛ sec) was needed; it was too slow to capture the pigeons in flight.

f/16	f/11	f/8	f/5.6	f/4	f/2.8	f/2

Each combination here of f-stop and shutter speed produces the equivalent exposure (lets in the same amount of light) but produces differences in depth of field and motion.

1/8	1/15	1/30	1/60	1/125	1/250	1/500

A medium aperture (f/4) and shutter speed (1/125 sec) sacrifice some background detail to produce recognizable images of the birds. But the exposure is still too long to freeze the motion of the birds' wings.

A fast shutter speed (1/500 sec) stops the motion of the pigeons so completely that the flapping wings are frozen. But the wide aperture (f/2) needed gives so little depth of field that the background is now out of focus.

Keeping the Camera Steady

Even with the finest camera and lens, you won't be happy with the pictures you take if you don't keep the camera steady enough during exposure. Too much camera motion during exposure will cause problems ranging from a slight lack of sharpness to hopeless blurring. But how much camera movement is too much? That depends partly on how much the image is enlarged, since any blur is more noticeable in a big enlargement. It also depends on the shutter speed and the focal length of the lens. The faster the shutter speed, the less you have to worry about camera movement. The longer the focal length of the lens, the more movement becomes apparent because longer lenses magnify objects—and camera movements—more.

As a general rule, if you are **hand-holding** a camera, use a shutter speed that is faster than the focal length of the lens: 1/60 second or faster with a 50mm lens, 1/250 second or faster with a 200mm lens, and so on. When hand-holding, squeeze the shutter release gently and smoothly. If you can, brace your body in some way—put your back against a wall or your elbows on a table, fence, or other object (see *opposite, top left*).

Putting the camera on a **tripod** and using a **cable release** to trigger the shutter is the best way to prevent camera movement (*opposite, right*). Be sure the tripod is sturdy enough for the camera; if you balance a large, heavy camera on a flimsy, lightweight tripod, your camera can end up on the floor. Miniature tripods are sometimes useful; their very short legs can be steadied on a table, car fender, or even against a wall. A monopod (single-leg support) or a hand grip gives extra stability if you have to keep moving, for example, along a football sideline.

holding an eye-level viewing camera

For a vertical picture, some people hold an eye-level camera with the film advance lever down (left). Your right hand supports the camera, the right index finger works the shutter release, and the right thumb advances the film. The left hand adjusts focus and f-stops. You may prefer to have the film advance lever up (right). Support the camera on the heel of your left hand, with fingers free to adjust focus and f-stops.

holding a waist-level viewing camera

The bigger viewing screen of a large-format reflex camera lets you focus with your eye some distance from the screen (left). To shoot over a crowd (right) try holding the camera at arm's length, upside down.

To steady an eye-level camera, press one arm (or preferably both) against your body. Keep the camera strap around your neck or wound around one wrist to guard against dropping the camera.

Cradling the camera in both hands, with elbows against sides, is a standard position for working with a large-format reflex camera. Your entire body helps steady the camera, which is held close to the eye for precise composition and focusing.

holding a camera with a long lens

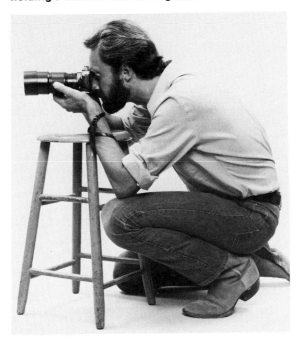

With a long lens, such as this 200mm one, attached to your camera, try to find some extra support such as a stool, chair, or other steady object to brace yourself against. Kneeling, you can brace your elbow on one knee.

Place yourself in as stable a position as possible when kneeling without any additional support (left). For a standing shot with a long lens (right) tuck your elbow firmly against your ribs to hold camera and lens steady. Particularly when using a long lens and slow shutter speed, be careful to squeeze the shutter release gently to avoid jerking the camera.

using a tripod

A tripod is the best way to prevent unwanted camera movement. Camera height is adjusted by raising or lowering the tripod legs or center shaft; camera angle is adjusted by tilting or swiveling the tripod head. Some tripods have a center shaft that can be removed and reversed; the tripod head and camera then hang upside down and the camera can photograph from a low angle.

A cable release lets you trigger the shutter release without jarring the camera. Leave a little slack in the cable when releasing it, instead of pulling it taut. Choose a release that fits your camera; some fit over, most screw into the shutter release button.

Choosing a Camera

Choosing a camera will be easier if you first decide what you want it for—what kind of pictures you want to take—then think about which basic camera design best fits your needs.

If your picture taking consists of occasional snapshots of family, friends, or sightseeing views, then an inexpensive, nonadjustable camera like the Kodak Instamatic will be satisfactory. You simply aim it at the subject by looking through a viewfinder window and then push the shutter release to make the exposure; the focusing distance, aperture, and shutter speed are all preset. But the very simplicity of this type of camera limits the things you can do with it, and as soon as you begin to be more than casually interested in photography your needs outstrip the camera's potential.

If you are a photography student, a serious amateur, or just someone who would like to learn more about photography, you will want an adjustable camera. Unless you have a specialized need (for stereo or panoramic photographs, for example) you will probably choose one of the five basic designs shown and described at right.

Once you have decided on a basic design and are ready to buy, **shop around** to compare prices, accessories, and service. Try handling various cameras; if you wear glasses, make sure you can see the entire image. You may be able to find a good used camera at a considerable saving. But look over used equipment carefully: avoid cameras with dents, scratched lenses, rattles, or gouged screw heads that could indicate a home repair job. If a dealer is reputable, you will be able to exchange a camera, new or used, if your first roll of film is unsatisfactory. Examine that first roll carefully for scratches, soft focus, or other signs of trouble.

Rangefinder cameras have a viewfinder for sighting and a rangefinder for focusing the image. Interchangeable lenses are available for more expensive models, although not in as great a variety as for single-lens reflex cameras. Most use 35mm film; a few are designed for larger roll-film sizes. The rangefinder has long been a favorite with photojournalists, who value its eye-level viewing, quick focusing even at low light levels, light weight, small size, durability, and quiet operation. It is an ideal camera for any fast-moving situation that requires the photographer to seize, as Henri Cartier-Bresson said, the "decisive moment." Canon, Konica, Leica, and Minolta are some of the 35mm brands. Plaubel makes medium-format models.

Disadvantages include some parallax error, which is unavoidable in viewfinder sighting, especially at close range. It is also impossible to evaluate depth of field visually through a viewfinder. This type of camera is not your best choice if you want to make extreme close-ups, align objects within the picture precisely, experiment with special filters or other optical effects, or preview the image for other reasons.

Single-lens reflex cameras offer the greatest variety of interchangeable lenses plus options such as through-the-lens metering, automatic exposure, and motorized film advance. Since these cameras view directly through the lens, you get an exact view of the scene, an advantage with close-ups, microphotography, or other work where you want to see in advance exactly how the image will look. New designs are compact and increasingly automated.

Most single-lens reflex cameras use 35mm film, although a few are designed for larger film sizes. The 35mm format produces a rather small negative, 1 × 1½ inches (24 × 36 mm). It is quite possible to make large-size, high-quality enlargements from 35mm negatives, but you need carefully exposed and processed negatives to do so. Many types of film, both black-and-white and color, are available in 35mm, and this format also has the advantage of being relatively inexpensive.

The single-lens reflex is the most popular camera when a buyer moves beyond snapshot level. Many brands are available, including Canon, Konica, Leica, Minolta, Nikon, Olympus, Pentax, Rollei, and Yashica.

The larger single-lens reflex cameras using 2¼-inch film are popular with photographers who want a negative larger than 35mm plus the versatility of a single-lens reflex—fashion or advertising photographers, for example. Not only are lenses interchangeable but camera-backs are as well; you can expose part of a roll of black-and-white film, remove the camera-back, and replace it with another loaded with color film. Size, weight, and noise of operation are all greater than with a 35mm single-lens reflex and so is the price. Most cameras make a 2¼-inch-square (6 × 6 cm) negative; a few models have a rectangular format such as 2¼ × 2¾ inches (6 × 7 cm). Bronica, Hasselblad, Pentax, and Rollei are some of the brands.

Twin-lens reflex cameras are more limited than single-lens reflexes. Most do not have interchangeable lenses (with the exception of the Mamiya), although supplementary lenses are available for close-up or long-range work. What you see on the ground-glass viewing screen is almost—but not exactly—what you get on the negative, since the viewing lens is separate from the taking lens.

What you do get is a relatively large negative (2¼ inches square) and durability for a reasonable price. The twin-lens reflex camera is good for portraits, landscapes, better-quality snapshots, and similar fairly conventional photographic situations. But don't expect it to be as fast as a rangefinder or as flexible as a single-lens reflex. Many manufacturers have ceased making twin-lens reflexes, but used models are still available. Yashica and Mamiya continue to market new cameras.

View cameras give the utmost in control over the image, even control over the apparent shape and perspective of objects (*see pages 291–306*). The large-size negatives (4 × 5 inches and larger) make prints of maximum sharpness and minimum grain. Ordinarily, each picture is shot on a separate sheet of film, but roll film and Polaroid film adapters are available. The view camera is unsurpassed for architectural work, product photography, studio work—anything where the photographer's first aim is carefully controlled, technically superior pictures. What you sacrifice are automatic features (there aren't any), size and weight (enough to make a tripod a necessity), and speed of operation (slow). Burke and James, Calumet, Cambo, Deardorff, Linhof, Omega, Plaubel, Sinar, Toyo, and Wista are among the brands.

The press camera is the hand-held cousin of the view camera, designed so it can be used without being mounted on a tripod. Once widely used by press photographers, it has been replaced in recent years by 35mm cameras.

ANDRE KERTÉSZ: *On Martinique*, 1972

Uncontrolled light rays, shown reflected from two points—the subject's pipe and the bottom of his coat—travel in straight lines in almost all directions toward a sheet of film placed in front of the subject. Rays from the pipe strike the film all over its surface and so do rays from the coat; they never form an image of pipe or coat at any place on the film. The result is not a picture but totally exposed film.

◄ *On the island of Martinique, an anonymous figure looks out over an anonymous ocean. Glass, sky, ocean, and railing divide the scene in a geometry of angles and gray shapes that the eye takes pleasure in comparing and measuring. The print is relatively grainy, echoing the granularity of the glass. The scene is quite understandable—we have all seen figures or shapes behind translucent glass—but the picture invites other associations. Landscapes by the surrealist painter René Magritte come to mind, and one imagines that just out of sight a giant rock is floating across the sky.*

Light must be shaped and controlled so that our eyes or our cameras can form images of objects. You can't simply place a square of sensitized film in front of a man and hope that an image of him will appear on the film. The rays reflecting off the man would hit the film in a random jumble, resulting not in a picture but in a uniform exposure over the entire surface of the film. For simplicity's sake, the drawing at left shows only a few rays coming from only two points on the man, his pipe and his coat tip, but their random distribution over the entire film makes it clear that they are not going to produce a useful image. The rays from the pipe, for example, will hit the film all over its surface, never creating in any one place an image of the pipe. What is needed is some sort of light-control device in front of the film that will select and aim the rays, putting the pipe rays where they belong and the coat rays where *they* belong, resulting in a clear picture.

All photographic lenses do the same basic job: they collect light rays coming from a scene in front of the camera and project them as images onto a piece of film at the back. This chapter explains how this happens and how you can use variations in lens size, lens aperture, and subject distance to make the kinds of pictures you want.

Why Lenses Are Needed
A Pinhole to Form an Image

Although all the light rays reflected from an object cannot produce an image on a flat surface, a selection of rays can. Suppose there is a barrier with a small hole in it, like that in the drawing below. All but a few rays from each point are deflected by the barrier. Those few rays that do get through, traveling in straight lines from object to film, can make an image.

For example, the few rays from the man's pipe that get through the hole all fall on a certain spot near the bottom of the film. Only that one spot on the film registers an image of a pipe. Similarly, rays from the coat, the shoes, the ear, the hat brim—from every point on the man—travel to other specific points on the film. Together they form a complete image, but one that is inverted. Everything that was at the top of the man appears at the bottom of his image on the film and everything at the bottom appears at the top. Similarly, left becomes right and right becomes left.

The image-making ability of the pinhole was first put to use—long before the invention of photography—as part of the **camera obscura,** a darkened room whose only light source is a small hole in one wall. Light rays coming through the hole form on the opposite wall an image of the scene outside. The camera obscura is, in fact, a room-sized primitive camera. Shrink the room down to shoebox size, reduce the hole to ¹⁄₅₀ inch (0.5 mm) in diameter, place a piece of film at the end opposite the hole, and it will make a recognizable

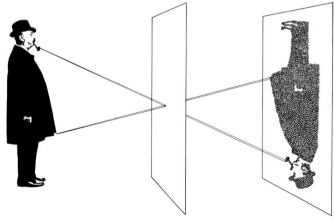

To take this picture of a fence and barn in California, photographer Ansel Adams replaced the lens of an ordinary camera with a thin metal disk pierced by a pinhole with ¹⁄₅₀-inch diameter. The film was exposed for 6 sec. The way the pinhole produced an image is illustrated in the diagram at left. Only a few rays of light from each point on the subject can get through the tiny opening, and these strike the film in such tight clusters that blurring is reduced to a minimum. The result is a soft but acceptably clear photograph.

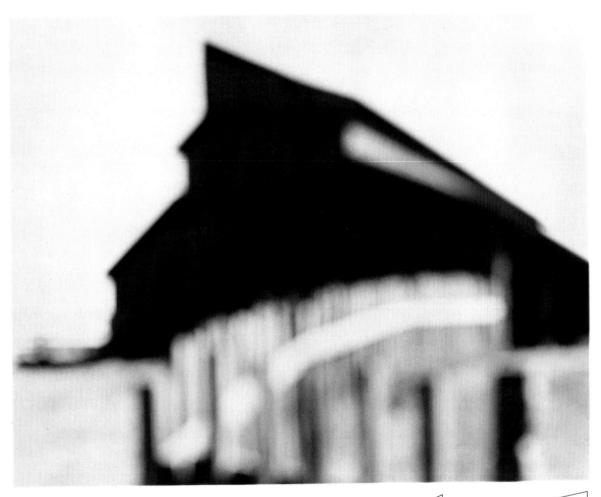

For a second photograph of the same scene, Adams increased the size of the opening to ⅛ inch, which meant reducing the exposure time to ⅕ sec. The result is an extremely out-of-focus picture. As shown in the diagram at right, the larger hole permits a greater number of rays from each point on the subject to enter the camera. These rays spread before reaching the film and are recorded as large circles. Because of their size, these circles tend to run into one another, creating an unclear image.

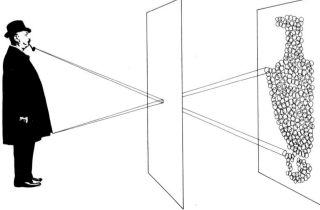

picture; the photograph opposite was made with such a camera. The trouble with this **pinhole camera** is its tiny opening, which admits so little light that very long exposures are needed to register an image on the film. If the hole is enlarged appreciably, the picture it makes becomes much less sharp, like the photograph on this page. Why this happens is explained in the two drawings.

The image in the drawing on the opposite page is actually composed of a great many tiny circles known as **circles of confusion.** This is because the hole, small though it is, actually admits a cluster of light rays. Coming at slightly different angles, these rays continue through the hole in slightly different directions. They fan out, and when they hit the film they cover a small circular area on it. If the hole in the barrier is made larger (*drawing below*), a larger cluster of light rays will get through to the film and cover a wider circle. The larger the circles are, the more they will overlap their neighbors and the less clear the picture will be.

To get sharp pictures, the circles of confusion should be as small as possible. But the only way to achieve that with a pinhole camera is to use a very small opening, which admits little light and requires long exposure times. To admit more light and to make a sharper picture, a different method of image formation is needed. That is what a lens provides.

A Lens to Form an Image

Four centuries ago a Venetian noble-man named Daniele Barbaro found a new and better way to convert light rays into images in the camera obscura of his day. He enlarged the opening of his room-sized camera obscura and fitted into it a convex **lens** taken from the spectacles of a farsighted man. To his delight, the lens projected images superior to those previously supplied by the simple pinhole opening.

Several hundred years later, with the advent of photography, this discovery proved even more significant. For not only can a camera with a lens provide sharper images than a pinhole camera, but it admits enough light to take a picture in a fraction of a second.

Most modern photographic lenses are based on the convex lens, the type used by Barbaro. Thicker in the middle than at the edges, the convex lens can collect a large number of light rays from a single point on an object and refract, or bend, them toward each other so that they converge at a single point (*diagram, right*). This point of convergence, the **focal point,** falls on a surface called the **focal plane.** In a camera, a strip of film is stretched across the focal plane, which is now the **film plane.** The film records an image formed by light rays from an infinite number of points on the object, focused by the lens into an infinite number of tiny circles of confusion.

How does a lens **refract** (bend) light to form an image? When light rays pass from one transparent medium, such as air, into a different transparent medium, such as water or glass, the rays may be bent, or refracted. Look at the shape of a spoon half submerged in a glass of water and you will see a common example of refraction: rays of light reflected by the spoon are bent by the water and glass so that part of the spoon appears displaced.

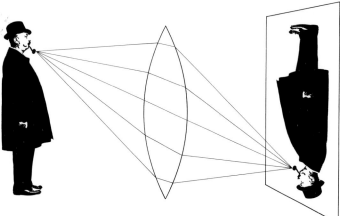

Photographed this time through a convex lens, Ansel Adams's barn scene is as good as—or better than—the one on page 58 taken with a pinhole camera. Its exposure time, instead of being 6 sec, was only 1/100 sec. This is because the lens is much bigger than a pinhole and thus admits far more light. The diagram at left shows how the lens handles all this light by collecting many rays reflected from a single point and redirecting them to a corresponding single point on the film or focal plane.

For refraction to take place, light must strike the new medium at an angle. If it is perpendicular to the surface when it enters and leaves the medium (*diagram, 1*), the rays pass straight through. But if it enters or leaves at an oblique angle (*2*), the rays will be bent to a predictable degree. The farther from the perpendicular they strike, the more they will be bent.

When light strikes a transparent medium with a curved surface, such as a lens, the rays will be bent at a number of angles depending on the angle at which each ray enters and leaves the lens surface. They will be spread apart by concave surfaces (*3*) and directed toward each other by convex surfaces (*4*). Rays coming from a single point on an object and passing through a convex lens (the simplest form of camera lens) will cross each other—and be focused —at the focal point.

A modern compound lens, as this cutaway view shows, is usually a single convex lens sliced in two with some other lens elements placed in between to correct the aberrations or focusing defects that in any single lens affect the sharpness and sometimes the shape of the image. The front half of the convex lens (a) has a 2-piece element of special color-correcting glass (b) behind it. Farther back is another color-correcting element (c) and finally the back half of the convex lens (d). The use of optical glass manufactured with certain chemicals, such as fluoride, also improves lens performance.

How refraction works is shown in the diagram (right) of beams of light passing through four glass blocks. The beams, entering from the left, strike the first block head on and are therefore not refracted. But the next block has been placed at an angle, so that the rays are refracted, resuming their former direction on the other side. The concave surfaces of the third block spread the beams apart, but the last block—a convex lens like the basic light-gathering lenses used in cameras— draws the rays back together so that they cross each other at the focal point.

Types of Lenses
Lens Focal Length

Since most cameras can be used with interchangeable lenses, a photographer can choose which lens to buy or use. The most important way lenses differ is in their **focal length.** Focal length is the distance between the lens (technically, from its rear nodal point) and the focal plane when the lens is focused on infinity (a far distance from which light reaches the lens in approximately parallel rays). A lens is often described in terms of its focal length (a 50mm lens, a 12-inch lens) or its relative focal length (short, normal, or long).

Focal length controls **magnification** (the size of the image formed by the lens) and **angle of view** (the amount of the scene shown on a given size of film). The effect of focal length on magnification is diagrammed at right. A lens of short focal length bends light sharply. The rays of light focus close behind the lens and form a small image of the object (*top diagram*). The longer the focal length, the less the lens bends the light rays, the farther behind the lens the image is focused, and the more the image is magnified (*bottom diagram*). The size of the image increases in proportion to the focal length; if the subject remains at the same distance from the lens, the image formed by a 25mm lens will be half as big as that from a 50mm lens.

A lens of long focal length forms a larger image of an object, so it includes on a given size of film less of the scene in which the object appears. If you make a circle with your thumb and forefinger and hold it close to your eye, you will see most of the scene in front of you. If you move your hand farther from your eye, the circle will be filled by a smaller part of the scene: you have decreased the angle of view seen through your fingers. In the same way, the longer the focal length, the smaller the angle of view seen by the lens.

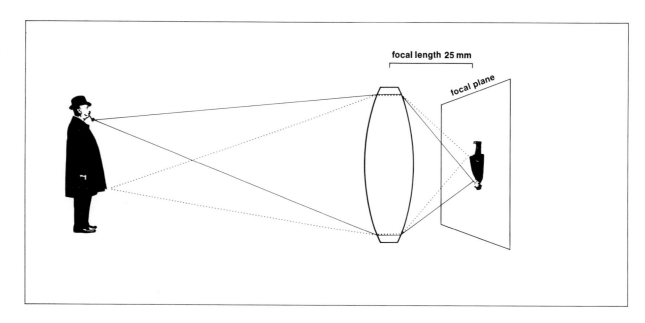

focal length 25 mm

focal plane

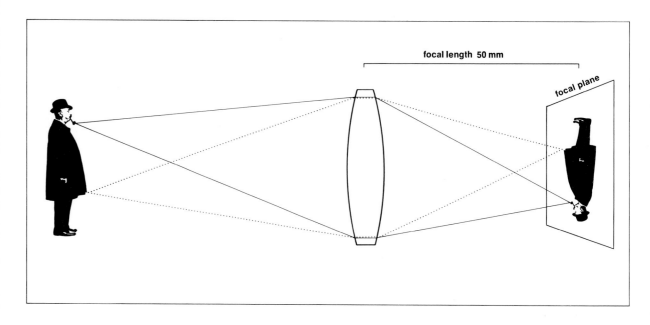

focal length 50 mm

focal plane

7.5mm fisheye

28mm

50mm

105mm

135mm

300mm

500mm

1000mm

1000 mm — 2½°
500 mm — 5°
300 mm — 8°
135 mm — 18°
105 mm — 23°
50 mm — 47°
28 mm — 75°
7.5 mm — 180°

The diagram above shows the angle of view of some of the lenses that can be used with a 35mm camera. The examples at left show the effect of increasing focal length while keeping the same lens-to-subject distance: a decrease in the angle of view and an increase in magnification. Since the photographer has not changed position, the sizes of objects within the scene remain the same in relation to each other.

The Normal Lens

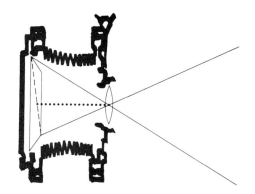

If the focal length of a lens (dotted line) is about the same as the diagonal measurement of the film (broken line), the lens is considered to be of normal (or standard) focal length for that film size. It collects light rays from an angle of view of about 50°—the same as the human eye—and projects them onto the film within the same angle. A normal focal length lens for a 4 × 5 camera is 150 mm. An 80mm lens is normal for a camera using 2¼ × 2¼-inch film; a 50mm lens is normal for a 35mm camera.

Bruce Davidson used a 50mm lens on his 35mm camera for the picture at right, part of a photo essay on a Brooklyn teenage gang, the Jokers.

BRUCE DAVIDSON: *The Brooklyn Gang,* 1959

You can create significantly different effects simply by switching to a lens of a different focal length (*see page 63*), but one of the greatest of modern photographers almost never changed lenses. Henri Cartier-Bresson, who once described the camera as "an extension of my eye," usually did his work with a **normal-focal-length lens,** also called a standard-focal-length lens— one that approximates the impression human vision gives. In his picture opposite, the angle of view is about the same as what the eye can see clearly from one position, and the relative size of near and far objects seems normal.

But a lens that is a normal focal length for one camera can be a long focal length for another camera. Film size determines what will be a "normal" focal length. The larger the size of the film format, the longer the focal length of a normal lens for that format. A camera using 35mm film takes a 50mm lens as a normal focal length; a camera using 4 × 5-inch film requires a 150mm lens. Usage varies somewhat: for example, lenses from about 40mm to 58mm are also referred to as normal focal lengths for a 35mm camera.

A lens of normal focal length has certain advantages over lenses of longer or shorter focal length. Most normal lenses are faster, that is, they open to a wider maximum aperture, and so can be used with faster shutter speeds or in dimmer light than lenses that do not open as wide. They often are less expensive, more compact, and lighter weight.

Though a 50mm lens is called normal for a 35mm camera, that doesn't necessarily mean it is the one you will usually want to use on your camera. Some photographers habitually use a shorter focal length because they want a wide angle of view most of the time; others prefer a longer focal length that narrows the angle of view to the central objects in a scene. If you have a 35mm camera, a 50mm lens is a good focal length to start with, but the lens that turns out to be normal for you will be a matter of personal preference.

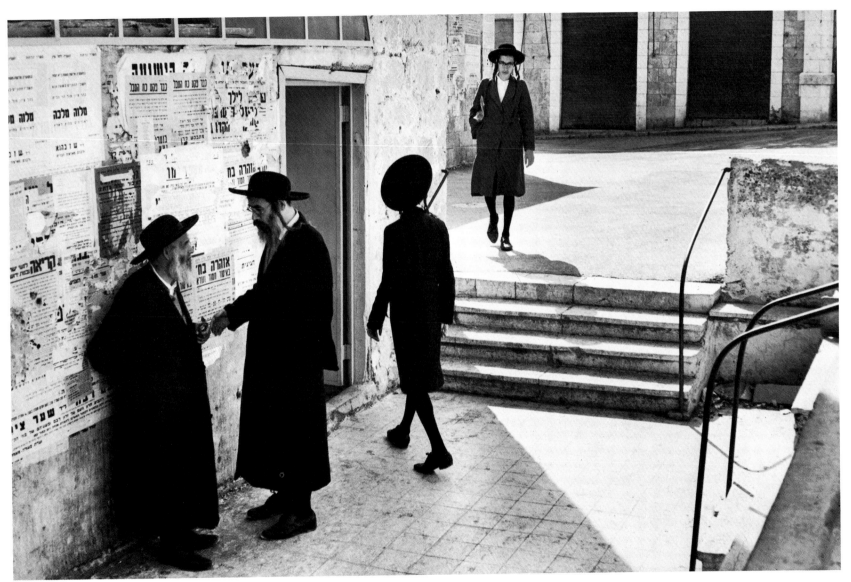

HENRI CARTIER-BRESSON: *Jerusalem*, 1967

This photograph of Hasidic Jews in Jerusalem shows Henri Cartier-Bresson's characteristic use of a normal-focal-length lens. The photographer was at a medium distance, so all four figures appear to be of normal size and perspective relative to each other. There is no distortion of perspective as there might have been had a shorter lens been used up close or a longer lens been used from far away. Most of the scene is sharp because at a medium distance a normal-focal-length lens provides considerable depth of field.

The Long Lens

A lens is considered long for a camera if its focal length (dotted line) is appreciably greater than the diagonal of the film format (broken line). It then collects light over an angle that is narrower than that covered by human vision, producing an enlarged view of a restricted area. For a 35mm camera, a popular and useful long focal length is 105 mm; for a 2¼ × 2¼ reflex the comparable focal length is 150 mm; and for a 4 × 5 view camera, about 300 mm.

A moderately long lens (such as an 85mm or 105mm lens on a 35mm camera) used at least 6 ft from the subject (above left) makes a better portrait than a shorter lens used close to the subject (above right). Compare the sizes of nose, chin, and hand in the pictures. Photographing a person at too close a lens-to-subject distance makes features nearest the camera appear too large and gives an unnatural-looking roundness to the head.

A **long-focal-length lens** provides an enlarged image of an object. Its angle of view is narrower and its magnification greater than that of a normal lens. Long lenses are excellent for situations where you cannot or do not want to get close to the subject, as in the picture opposite, where the photographer seems to be in the middle of the action even though he is standing on the sidelines. Long lenses make it possible to photograph birds and animals from a distance. They are excellent for portraiture; most people get self-conscious when a camera is too close to them and their expressions become artificial. A long lens also avoids the kind of distortion that occurs when shorter lenses used close to a subject exaggerate the size of whatever is nearest the camera —in a portrait, usually the nose (*above*).

There are also subtler qualities that can be exploited when you use a long lens. Because a long lens has less depth of field, objects in the foreground or background can be photographed out of focus so that the sharply focused subject stands out clearly and powerfully. Also, a long lens can be used to create an unusual perspective in which objects seem to be closer together than they really are (*see opposite and page 80*).

Long lenses have some disadvantages, and the longer the lens the more noticeable the disadvantages become. Compared to a lens of normal focal length, they are somewhat heavier, bulkier, and usually more expensive. Because of their shallow depth of field, they must be focused accurately. They usually do not open to a very wide aper-

ture; a maximum aperture of f/4 is typical for a 200mm lens. And they are difficult to use for hand-held shots since they magnify lens movements as well as the subject. The shutter speed for a medium-long lens, such as a 105mm lens on a 35mm camera, should be at least ¹/₁₂₅ second if the camera is hand-held; otherwise camera movement may cause blurring. A tripod or some other support is even better.

Photographers commonly call any long lens a **telephoto,** or tele, although not all long lenses are actually of telephoto design. A true telephoto does not require full focal length distance from lens to film plane. A **tele-extender** or teleconverter contains an optical element that increases the effective focal length of a lens. It attaches between lens and camera like an extension tube.

WALTER IOOSS, JR.: *Giants' Defense*, 1963

This photograph of the New York Giants' defense line stopping Number 33 also shows two characteristics of the long lens. Although the photographer was standing on the sidelines, a 400mm lens on his 35mm camera includes only a 6° angle of view, magnifying the image to fill the frame with action. The long lens also seems to compress the space, making the players appear to be in even more of a crunch than they actually are.

The Short Lens

In the diagram above, the focal length of the lens (dotted line) is about ⅔ of the film diagonal (broken line). This makes it a wide-angle lens; it produces a viewing angle of 75°, or about 50 percent more than the eye could see clearly if focused on the same subject. The focal length of a commonly used wide-angle lens for a 35mm camera is 28 mm; for a 2¼ × 2¼ reflex it is 55 mm, and for a 4 × 5 view camera, 90 mm.

The exaggerated size of the model's hand, her rapidly receding arm, and her unnaturally undersized body were all created by photographing an average-size model with the camera close to her outstretched fingertips. This kind of apparent distortion is a result of the short distance from lens to subject and is easy to achieve—intentionally or otherwise—with a wide-angle lens, which can be focused very close to a subject.

A wide-angle lens is useful for photographing in ▶ confined areas, whether a small room or the president's helicopter. There is some distortion of the arm closest to the camera, but it is partly shadowed and not as noticeable as the model's arm in the photograph at left. During President Ford's term in office, David Kennerly was his personal photographer and had access to him during many informal moments. This particular moment pairs a serious president with a well-known symbol of America, the Washington Monument. The pairing is almost too obvious; the photograph may have been unposed but somehow has an edge of contrivance to it. One imagines Kennerly saying, "Could we circle around the monument one more time, Mr. President?"

A **short-focal-length lens** shows more of a scene than a normal lens used from the same position. This is of special importance if you are physically prevented (as by the walls of a room) from moving back as much as necessary to take the picture with a normal lens. The short lens (commonly called a **wide-angle lens** or sometimes a **wide-field lens**) increases the angle of view and thus reduces the size of the image compared to the image formed by a normal lens.

Wide-angle lenses also have considerable depth of field. A 24mm lens focused on an object 7 feet away and stopped down to f/8 will show everything from 4 feet to infinity in sharp focus. News photographers or others who work in fast-moving situations often use a moderately wide lens, such as a 35mm lens on a 35mm camera, as their normal lens. They don't have to pause to refocus for every shot because

so much of a scene is sharp with this type of lens. At the same time it does not display too much **distortion,** which is the wide-angle lens's other main characteristic.

Pictures taken with a wide-angle lens can show both real and apparent distortions. Genuine aberrations of the lens itself such as curvilinear distortion are inherent in extremely curved or wide elements made of thick pieces of glass, which are frequently used in wide-angle lenses. While most aberrations can be corrected in a lens of a moderate angle of view and speed, the wider or faster the lens, the more difficult and/or expensive that correction becomes.

A wide-angle lens can also show an apparent distortion of perspective, but this is actually caused by the photographer, not the lens. An object that is close to a lens (or your eye) appears larger than an object of the same size

that is farther away. Since a wide-angle lens can be focused very close to an object, it is easy to get this kind of exaggerated-size relationship (*photograph, above*). The cure is to learn to see what the camera sees and either minimize the distortion, as in the photograph at right, or use it intentionally. More about how to control perspective and apparent distortion is on pages 78–81.

A lens of very short focal length requires some design changes for use in a single-lens reflex camera, because the lens is so close to the film plane that it gets in the way of the mirror used for viewing. A retrofocus (reversed-telephoto) lens solves this problem with a design that is the reverse of that of a telephoto lens. The result is a lens of very short focal length that can be used relatively far from the film plane and out of the way of the viewing mirror.

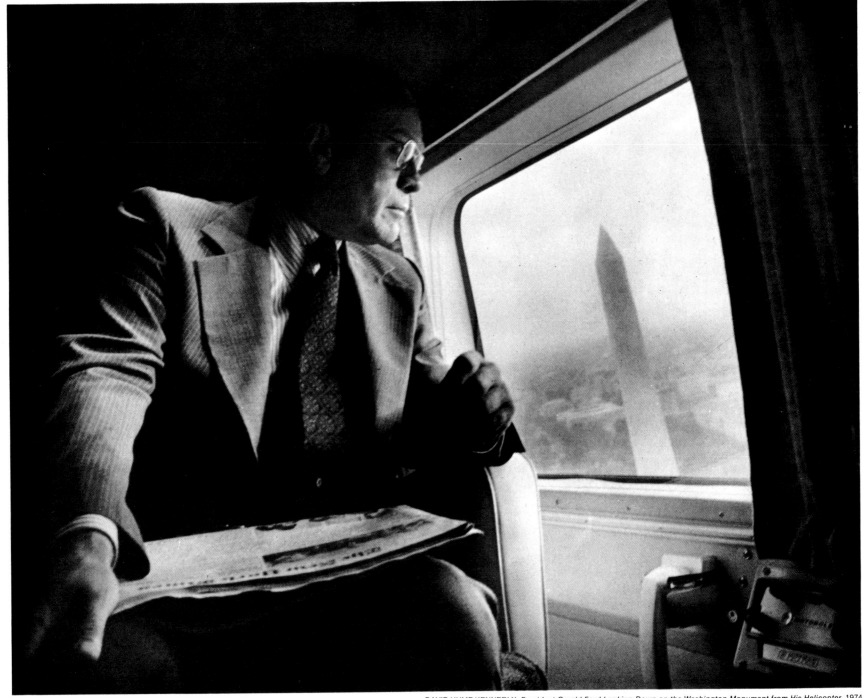

DAVID HUME KENNERLY: *President Gerald Ford Looking Down on the Washington Monument from His Helicopter,* 1974

Special-Purpose Lenses

JOHN NEUBAUER: *Le Champignon,* 1979

A macro lens is useful for photographing very close to a subject without having to use other accessories such as extension tubes (more about close-ups on pages 198–203). When you photograph close to a subject, depth of field is very shallow—only a narrow distance from near to far will be sharp. Here, to make the photograph sharp, the photographer sliced and positioned the mushrooms so that their front surfaces lined up evenly, parallel to the film plane.

For the widest of wide-angle views, consider the **fisheye lens** (*opposite*). It is not a lens for every situation, but it can produce startling and effective views. Its angle of view and depth of field are enormous—and so is its barrel distortion, an optical aberration that bends straight lines into curves at the edges of an image.

A **catadioptric lens** or **mirror lens** is similar in design to a reflecting telescope, incorporating curved mirrors as well as glass elements within the lens. The result is a long-focal-length lens that is much smaller and lighter than a lens of equivalent focal length that uses only glass elements. A cat lens has a fixed aperture, usually rather small—f/8 or f/11 is typical. And the front mirror in the lens has the unusual effect of caus-

ing out-of-focus highlights to take on a donut shape rather than the usual disc shape produced by an ordinary lens.

A **zoom lens** can be used at a variety of focal lengths. It works by having some of its optical elements movable in relation to one another; this changes the focal length and therefore the size of the image. It is convenient to be able to frame the image merely by zooming to another focal length rather than by changing camera position or changing lenses. A zoom lens is particularly useful for making color slides, since cropping the image later is not easy. But it is necessary to weigh the convenience of a zoom lens against its disadvantages, among which are increased cost, size, and weight and somewhat decreased image quality and speed. The greater

the zooming range, the more these disadvantages increase. The best prices and sharpest images are found over a modest zooming range, from 35mm to 70mm, for example.

A **macro lens** is useful for extremely close shots such as that of the mushrooms above. It is usually a lens of normal focal length built into a lens barrel that can be extended extra far for focusing at very close range. It is corrected for the aberrations that occur at close focusing distances. The lens is occasionally called, somewhat inaccurately, a *micro* lens.

Aberrations may be deliberately introduced in a **soft-focus lens,** sometimes called a portrait lens, to produce an image that will soften details such as facial wrinkles.

This "crystal-ball" view of a high-school student body and faculty was shot from directly overhead with a 7.5mm fisheye lens, which can take in an enormously wide viewing angle of 180°. Although it gets everybody into the picture, it sacrifices a great deal in perspective; those at the edge of the picture are tiny compared to those at the center. The round format adds to the visual meaning of the picture, forming a school world into its own global shape.

ROBERT PACKO: *Fisheye View*, 1968

Focus and Depth of Field

When part of a picture is sharp and part out of focus (or soft), a viewer looks first at the sharply focused area. In the picture opposite, your eyes are immediately drawn to the woman—the photographer has made her the most important part of the photograph. In another situation, however, a photographer might want to have the entire scene sharp (*photograph this page*). What exactly is sharpness and how much can it be controlled?

When you focus a lens, done by rotating the focusing ring or knob, you are moving the lens nearer to or farther from the film. The closer an object is to a lens, the farther the lens has to be from the film in order to focus that object sharply. So, in theory, a lens is able to focus on only one distance at a time, and all other distances will be less sharp. If your lens is focused on an object 10 feet away, everything else at a distance of 10 feet will be sharp, but anything nearer or farther than 10 feet will not be as sharp.

However, in most cases, objects within a certain depth in the scene appear to be sharp. The acceptably sharp area in a photograph, the **depth of field**, includes the **plane of critical focus,** that part of the scene on which you focused, plus portions of the scene in front of and behind that plane that are also sharp.

Think of a subject as being composed of an infinite number of tiny points lo-cated at various distances from the lens. When a single subject point is critically focused, it appears in the image as a point. But since a lens can focus on only one distance at a time, another point located in front of or behind the critically focused one will not be focused entirely sharply. The lens will cause it to appear not as a point, but as a very small disc, a **circle of confusion.** The farther that points are from the sharply focused distance, the larger the circles—and the more out of focus that part of the image will be. But, if the circles are small enough, the eye will see them as points, and that part of the image will appear to be sharp; it will be within the depth of field.

Depth of field can be shallow, with only a narrow band across the scene appearing to be sharp, or it can be deep, with everything sharp from near to far. To a large extent, you can control just how much will be sharp (the next pages tell how). There are no definite limits to the depth of field; objects gradually change from sharp to soft the farther they are from the sharply focused area (*photograph opposite*).

In general, the more a print is enlarged, the less sharp it appears. But sharpness is also affected by viewing distance: a mural-size print placed high on a wall and viewed at a distance of 20 feet may appear sharp even though the same print viewed up close may not.

MARGARET BOURKE-WHITE: *American Woolen Co., New England,* 1935

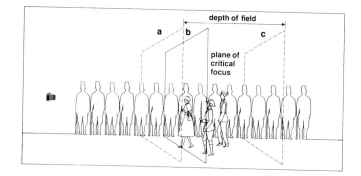

Imagine the distance on which you are focused to be like a pane of glass parallel to the camera, stretching across the scene in front of you. Everything at this distance (the plane of critical focus) will be sharp in the photograph. In front and in back of the plane lies the depth of field, the area that will be acceptably sharp in the photograph. The farther from the plane of critical focus that objects are, the less sharp they will be. Notice that the depth of field is unevenly distributed. At normal shooting distances, about ⅓ of the depth of field lies in front of the plane (toward the camera), and about ⅔ lies behind it (away from the camera).

depth of field

a   b   c

plane of
critical
focus

The depth of field—the area in a scene in which objects appear sharp—can be deep or shallow. In the photograph above, everything is sharp from the nearest woman to the farthest spindle. In the photograph opposite, the depth of field includes only a few soldiers, the princess, and the officers, while other parts of the scene are increasingly out of focus the farther they are from the plane of critical focus.

MARK KAUFFMAN: *Princess Margaret Inspecting King's African Rifles, Mauritius,* 1956

Controlling Depth of Field

There are several ways to control the depth of field, the distance between the nearest and farthest points in a scene that appear sharp in a photograph. If you want to increase the depth of field so that more of a scene is sharp, setting the lens to a small aperture is almost always the first choice. This is the case even though you have to use a correspondingly slower shutter speed to maintain the same exposure, which can be a problem if you are photographing moving objects. You can also increase the depth of field by changing to a shorter focal length lens or stepping back from the subject, but that will change the picture in other ways as well (*opposite*). To decrease the depth of field and make less of the scene sharp, use a wider aperture or a longer lens, or move closer to the subject.

Why does a lens of longer focal length produce less depth of field than a shorter lens used at the same f-stop? The answer relates to the diameter of the aperture opening. The **relative aperture** (the same f-stop setting for lenses of different focal lengths) is a larger actual opening on a longer lens than it is on a shorter lens. For example, f/8 on a 50mm lens is an aperture of larger diameter than f/8 on a 28mm lens. The diagram below shows why this is so. Since at the same f-stop setting, the aperture diameter of the longer lens is larger than that of the shorter lens, the circles of confusion for the longer lens will also be larger and the image will have less depth of field.

The smaller the aperture, the greater the depth of field. *Here the photographer focused on the mooring buoy. Near right: with a wide aperture, f/2, the depth of field was relatively shallow; only objects that were about the same distance from the lens as the mooring buoy are sharp; other objects that were nearer or farther are out of focus. Far right: only the aperture was changed, to a much smaller one— f/16. Much more of the scene is now sharp. Changing the aperture is usually the easiest way to change the depth of field.*

◄ *Any f-stop, for example f/8, requires a larger aperture diameter for a longer-focal-length lens than for a shorter lens. The two lenses, left, are both set at f/8, but the actual opening in the 50mm lens (bottom) is larger than the opening in the shorter 28mm lens (top). As focal length increases, the amount of light that reaches the film decreases. Therefore, a long lens will form a dimmer image than a short lens unless more light is admitted by the lens.*

The sizes of the aperture openings are adjusted so that at a given f-stop the same amount of light reaches the film no matter what the focal length of the lens. The f-stop number, also called the relative aperture, equals the focal length of the lens divided by the aperture diameter:

$$f\text{-}stop = \frac{lens\ focal\ length}{aperture\ diameter}$$

If the focal length of the lens is 50mm, at f/8 the actual diameter of the aperture will be 6.25 mm:

$$8 = \frac{50}{6.25}$$

For a 28 mm lens, at f/8 the actual diameter of the aperture will be only 3.5 mm.

$$f/8 = \frac{28}{3.5}$$

The diagrams, by actually lining up eight aperture-sized circles and fitting them into the focal length of each lens, show the larger aperture diameter for the longer focal length.

The shorter the focal length of the ▶ lens, the greater the depth of field. *Near right: with a 200mm lens, only two gravestones are sharp. Far right: with a 35mm lens set to the same aperture and focused on the same point as the previous shot, a bigger section of the cemetery is now sharp. Notice that changing the focal length changes the angle of view (the amount of the scene shown) and the magnification of objects in the scene. The kind of picture has changed as well as the sharpness of it.*

The greater the distance from the ▶ subject, the greater the depth of field. *Near right: with the lens focused on the horse about 5 ft away, only a narrow band from near to far in the scene is sharp. Far right: stepping back to 15 ft from the horse and refocusing on it made much more of the scene sharp. Stepping back has an effect similar to changing to a shorter focal length lens: more of the scene is shown.*

less depth of field

more depth of field

wider aperture

smaller aperture

longer focal length

shorter focal length

closer to subject

farther from subject

Using Depth of Field

How much of a scene should be sharp? You won't always want everything to be sharp. A distracting background is much less conspicuous if it is soft and out of focus instead of crisply detailed. But something that obviously should be sharp but isn't can be equally distracting. Pages 74–75 present basic techniques for controlling depth of field. Some other techniques are shown here.

When you want to be able to shoot rapidly, **zone focusing** lets you set the depth of field in advance of shooting. This is useful if you can predict approximately where, although not exactly when, action will take place. It is also useful if you want to be relatively inconspicuous; for example, when photographing strangers on the street. To zone focus, use the depth-of-field scale on your lens to prefocus and to find the f-stop you will need to use in order to get adequate depth of field. Everything photographed within the near and far limits of that depth of field will be acceptably sharp; the precise distance at which something happens will not be important because the general area will be sharp (*see illustration, below*).

Sometimes you will want maximum depth of field, with everything sharp from the foreground to the far distance. When a scene extends into the distance, you may find that you rather automatically focus on a far part of the scene. In photographic terms, you have focused on **infinity,** which, depending on the lens, extends from about 40 feet or so to as far as the eye can see. (Infinity is marked ∞ on the lens distance scale.)

But for maximum depth of field in a scene that extends to a far distance, don't focus on infinity. Instead, turn the focusing ring so that the infinity mark falls just within the farthest limits of the depth of field for the f-stop you are using. You are now focused on a distance that is closer to the lens than infinity (the **hyperfocal distance**). Everything from the infinity distance and farther will still be sharp, but more of the foreground will be in focus (*see illustration, opposite*).

ELLIOTT ERWITT: *Sunday in Hungary,* 1964

— **distance scale**

— **depth-of-field scale**

— **aperture ring**

Zone focusing is a way of using a lens's depth-of-field scale so you can be ready to shoot without focusing before every shot. Suppose the nearest point you want sharp is 7 feet away and the farthest is 15 feet away. Turn the focusing ring until those distances on the distance scale fall opposite a matched pair of f-stops on the depth-of-field scale. If you set your lens aperture to that f-stop, objects between the two distances will be in focus. Here, the two distances fall opposite a pair of f/5.6's. With this lens set to f/5.6 or a smaller aperture (f/8 or f/11), everything between 7 feet and 15 feet will be sharp. No further focusing need be done as long as the action stays between these distances.

PHOTOGRAPHER UNKNOWN: *Upper area of Mendenhall Glacier, Alaska, 1968*

For maximum depth of field in a scene that extends to the far distance—infinity, in photographic terms (marked ∞ on the lens distance scale), don't focus on the infinity mark, as has been done with the lens at left. With this lens, if the aperture is f/8 and the lens is focused on infinity, everything from 20 ft to infinity will be sharp.

Instead, set the distance scale so that the infinity mark lines up opposite your f-stop on the depth-of-field scale (lens, right). Now, with the lens still set to f/8, everything from 10 ft to infinity will be sharp.

Perspective

It is vital to learn to see things the way the camera sees them, since the camera image can appear surprisingly different from reality. A long lens used far from the subject gives a so-called **telephoto effect**—on page 73, for example, the line of soldiers seems compressed, with the soldiers in impossibly close formation. A short lens used close to the subject produces what is known as **wide-angle distortion**—on page 68 it apparently stretches a human form to unnatural proportions. See also the photographs on pages 80 and 81.

Those photographs seem to show distortions in **perspective**—in the relative size and depth of objects within the image. Actually, perspective is controlled not by lens focal length but by the lens-to-subject distance.

How perspective changes when lens-to-subject distance is changed is shown at right. The photographs in the top row were taken from the same distance but with lenses of different focal lengths. The shortest lens produced the widest view of the room and the smallest image of the woman; the longest lens gave the narrowest view, an enlargement of part of the original picture. The perspective remains the same: the woman's head is bigger but so is everything else—pillows, ivy, the building across the street.

The photographs in the lower row were all taken with the same lens placed progressively closer to the woman. With decreasing lens-to-subject distance, the size of the woman increases relative to the size of the objects behind her. Since the brain judges depth in a photographed scene mostly by comparing the size of objects, the depth seems to increase as the camera moves closer. Compare the illusion of depth in the pictures at far right, top and bottom.

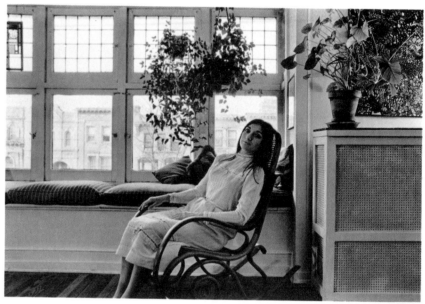

Three views of a woman, each shot from 15 ft, show how lenses of different focal lengths change image size but not perspective. Angles of view are reduced as larger images of the subject, (S) in the diagram, fill the film. The first picture was taken with a short-focal-length lens (angle aa'), the next with a normal lens (angle bb') and the third with a long lens (angle cc').

These pictures show how changes in distance affect image size and perspective as well. A decreasing lens-to-subject distance enlarged foreground images more than background ones to give three different perspectives.

Using Perspective

ANDREAS FEININGER: *Cemetery, New York, 1948*

You can exaggerate the perspective, the impression of depth in a photograph, simply to add impact to an image or to communicate an idea visually. What is known as telephoto effect seems to compress the objects in a scene into a crowded mass. It occurs when a long-focal-length lens is used far from a subject. Left, the tombstones in a New York cemetery appear to be as densely packed as the current residents of New York City are.

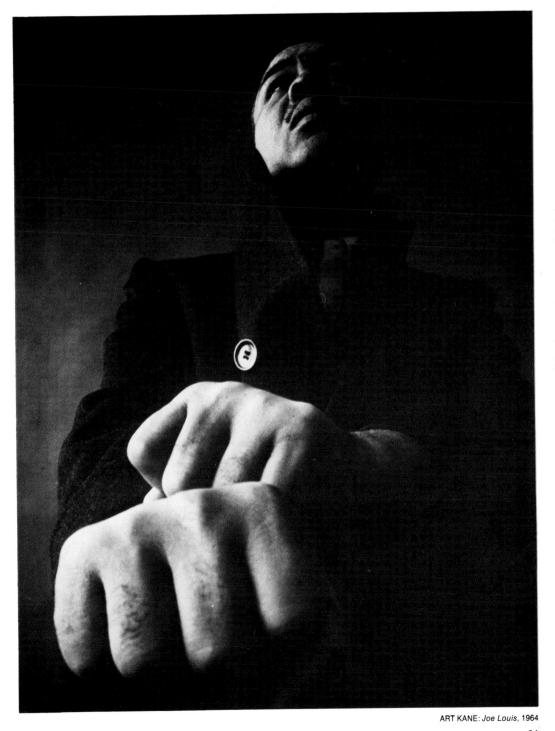

A short-focal-length lens used up close increases the apparent size of the part of the subject that is closest to the camera, producing what is called wide-angle distortion. Like telephoto effect (shown opposite), this is caused by the distance of the lens to the subject, not by the lens itself. Right, the fists that brought the world heavyweight championship to Joe Louis are emphasized in this brooding portrait taken after the fighter had lost his title and fallen on hard times.

ART KANE: *Joe Louis,* 1964

Getting the Most from a Lens

ghosting

A modern compound lens is a complex structure of glass and metal designed to give precise focusing and a sharp image. Lens performance can be assisted or hindered by how you handle and care for a lens.

Stopping down the lens aperture often improves the image by eliminating rays from the edges of the lens where certain aberrations occur. Even a well-designed lens may have some aberrations that were impossible to overcome in manufacture. This is especially so if it is a zoom, extremely wide-angle, or telephoto lens or if it has a very wide maximum aperture or is used very close to the subject.

There is a limit to the improvement that comes with stopping down. As light rays pass across a sharp, opaque edge, like the edge of the diaphragm opening, the rays bend slightly. As the lens is stopped down and the aperture becomes smaller, this edge bending or diffraction can cause a point of light to appear as a blurred circle and the whole image to appear very slightly less sharp. The optimum aperture at which most lenses perform best is two or three f-stops stopped down from the widest aperture. This is enough to minimize aberrations but not enough to cause noticeable diffraction. Of course, in a particular situation you may prefer the increased depth of field that results if the lens is stopped down all the way.

Ordinarily you will want to avoid **flare** —the reflection and scattering of light within the lens and camera—although it is sometimes deliberately used for a special effect. **Ghosting** (right, top) occurs when you include a strong light source, such as the sun or a bright bulb, in the picture. Ghosting is difficult to cure since its cause is within the picture itself. Sometimes you can change your position so that some object comes between the lens and the light source. Even when the light source is not actually in the picture, light rays hitting the front surface of the lens at an angle can scatter within the lens and cause an overall **fogging** of the image (right, bottom).

Avoid flare by using a **lens shade** or lens hood. This will block any light outside the lens's angle of view that might be shining at an angle on the lens surface. Be sure the lens shade is matched to the focal length of the lens you are using. The shorter the focal length of the lens, the wider the angle the lens sees and the wider the shade must be to avoid becoming part of the scene itself and **vignetting** or blocking the light from the edges of the image (opposite).

Lens coatings also reduce flare. Since some reflection and scattering of light take place at every glass-to-air surface of the lens, including those within the lens, manufacturers coat lens surfaces with a very thin layer of a metallic fluoride. This coating helps reduce reflections and subsequent flare. The coatings are extremely thin—as little as 0.0001 mm—and relatively delicate. Treat them with care when cleaning the lens.

A clean lens performs better than a dirty one. Dust, grease, and drops of moisture all scatter the light that passes through a lens and soften the sharpness and contrast of the image. However, although a lens should be kept clean, too frequent or too energetic cleaning can produce a maze of fine scratches or rub away part of the lens coating. See box, page 85, for how to keep your lens and camera in peak condition.

fogging

Stray light bouncing around inside the lens caused the two effects seen above. Top, the photographer included the bright sun directly in the image. Light reflecting from the various lens elements caused multiple images in the shape of the lens diaphragm, as well as star points (streamers of light around the sun itself). Although it was not actually in the picture below, the sun caused flare in the image by shining at an angle on the front glass surface of the lens. To prevent this type of flare use a lens shade the right size for your lens. Too narrow a shade will vignette the image (see opposite, above).

vignetting

light streaks

double exposure

Troubleshooting Camera and Lens Problems

All photographers occasionally encounter problems with their pictures, sometimes owing to equipment failure, sometimes to human failure. If your negatives don't look the way you expected, you may find the solution on the chart below. See also Troubleshooting Negative Problems (page 151), Printing Problems (page 181) and Flash Problems (pages 286–287).

Dark streaks in negative, light in print

Cause: Exposure to unwanted light before film is developed and fixed. Sections of streaks across the width of the film are caused by opening the back of a loaded camera. A damaged camera-back or bent film cassette can cause light streaks along one edge of the film (illustration, center), as can opening the developing tank before the film is completely fixed. Either type of streak can be caused by loading the camera in bright light.

Prevention: Until the film has been developed and fixed, the only light striking the film should come through the camera's lens. One roll of light-struck film is an accident; repeated problems are more likely equipment failure.

Vignetting (image obscured around the edges)

Cause: A lens shade or filter or combination of them that extended too far forward of the lens front, obscuring part of the image (illustration, top). In large-format cameras, this can be caused by a lens with inadequate coverage of the film format (see page 292).

Prevention: Lens shades are made in sizes to match lens focal lengths. Use the correct size shade for your lens. Check for vignetting if you are using a wide-angle lens with both a filter and lens shade. The filter can move the lens shade just far enough forward to be seen.

Double exposures

Entire roll double exposed.

Cause: The same roll of film was run through the camera twice.

Prevention: Rewind an exposed roll of film, including the film leader, entirely back into the film cassette. If part of the leader hangs out, you may later mistake an exposed roll for an unexposed one.

One frame double exposed.

Cause: Probably the film rewind button was inadvertently pushed, which would let you expose some or all of the same frame twice (see illustration, bottom).

Prevention: Check the way you grip the camera. It is difficult to push the rewind button without intending to do so, but it is possible.

Frames frequently overlap.

Cause: Probably a failing film-advance mechanism.

Prevention: Camera repair.

Static marks, dark in the negative, light in the print

Cause: A motorized camera winding film rapidly on a very cold, dry day can cause lightning-like marks on the film. In the darkroom, pulling roll film rapidly away from its paper backing can cause static that appears as stars or other shapes.

Prevention: When humidity is extremely low, avoid snapping the film advance lever forward or otherwise moving the film extremely rapidly. In the darkroom, unwind film in a smooth, even manner.

No picture at all

Image area and edges of film (except for film frame numbers) are both clear.

Cause: Film was not exposed to light. If the entire roll of film is blank, an unexposed roll may have been processed by mistake. If you are sure you took pictures with the film in the camera, it probably did not catch on the film-advance sprockets and so did not advance from frame to frame. If only some frames are blank, the lens cap could have been left on during exposure, the flash failed to fire, the shutter failed to open, or the mirror in a reflex camera failed to move out of the way of the film.

Prevention: Check for equipment failure if this is a recurring problem.

Image area of film is very dark, edges are clear (except for film frame numbers).

Cause: Massive overexposure of film in the camera. In very bright light, the aperture failed to stop down, shutter failed to close, shutter mistakenly set to B, or exposure calculated using much too low a film speed.

Prevention: Check for equipment failure if you are sure you set in the correct film speed.

Image area and edges of film are both very dark.

Cause: The entire roll of film was accidentally exposed to light—for example, by turning on the room lights after the film had been spooled onto the developing reel but before it was put into a light-tight developing tank.

Image area and edges are both clear. Film frame numbers do not show.

Cause: The film was put into fixer before it was developed.

Prevention for both of the above: Try not to do it again.

Choosing Lenses

- brand name
- speed (widest f setting)
- focal length (millimeters)
- manufacturer and location
- serial number

- distance scale (feet)
- distance scale (meters)
- depth-of-field scale (f-stops)
- aperture setting (f-stops)

Learn to read the information about a lens that is marked on it. On its front (top photograph) are its brand (Xenon), its speed (maximum aperture of f/1.9), its focal length (50 mm), its maker's name and location (Schneider, Kreuznach, Germany), and its serial number (9939322). Distance, depth of field, and aperture scales are marked on the side of the lens.

Since buying a lens can involve a considerable investment of money, it pays to invest a little time in deciding exactly what lenses you need.

The "speed" of a lens affects its price. Lenses made by reputable manufacturers can be assumed to be reasonably good. And yet two lenses of the same focal length, perhaps even made by the same company, may vary widely in price. This price difference probably reflects a difference in the speed of the lens. One will be faster—it will have a wider maximum aperture and admit more light than the other. The faster and more expensive lens can be used over a wider range of lighting conditions than the slower one but otherwise may perform no better. It may, in fact, perform less well at its widest aperture because of increased optical aberrations.

Following are some guidelines for **buying camera lenses.**

1. If you are getting a camera with interchangeable lenses, start with a normal lens. (This is the one that ordinarily comes with the camera anyway.) Don't buy more lenses until you feel a strong need to take the different kinds of pictures that other focal lengths can provide.

2. Get your lenses one at a time and think ahead to the assortment you may someday need. Begin by buying lenses in increments of more or less two times the focal length; for example, a good combination for a 35mm camera is a 50mm normal lens for general use, a 28mm wide-angle lens for close-in work, and a 105mm long lens for portraits and for magnifying more distant subjects. Be wary of ultra-wide-angle (24mm or below) and extra-long (above 200mm) lenses. They may be considerably more expensive than the less extreme types and are so specialized that their usefulness is limited. Adjustable-

length zoom lenses are popular, although they are more expensive and may not produce as critically sharp an image as conventional lenses.

3. Don't spend money on extra-fast lenses unless you have unusual requirements. A couple of extra f-stops may cost you an extra couple of hundred dollars. With modern high-speed film, a lens that can open to f/2.8 is adequate in all but the dimmest light.

4. Consider a secondhand lens. Many reputable dealers take used lenses in trade, and they may be bargains. But look for signs of hard use, such as a dented barrel, scratched lens surface, or a slight rattling that may indicate loose parts, and be sure to check the diaphragm to see that it opens smoothly to each f-stop over the entire range of settings.

5. Test your lens. The only sure way is to take pictures with it in your own camera at various f-stops, so insist on a trial period or a return guarantee. If you plan to buy several lenses eventually, a good investment is a standardized test chart that can give an accurate reading of a lens's sharpness.

6. A lens shade is a very desirable accessory to attach to the front of the lens to prevent flare (see page 82). Buy one that is matched to the focal length of the lens; too wide a shade is inefficient, too narrow a shade will cut into the image area (see vignetting, page 83).

Cameras and lenses are rugged, considering what precision instruments they are. Commonsense care and a little simple maintenance will help keep them running smoothly and performing well.

Protect from dust and dirt. *The best way to keep equipment clean is to not get it dirty in the first place. Cases and bags protect cameras and lenses from bangs and scratches as well as keep them clean. Keep a cap on the lens when it is not in use, and if you take a lens off a camera, protect both front and back lens surfaces either by placing the lens in a separate lens container or by capping both ends. Sand is a particular menace; clean the camera well after using it on the beach.*

Protect from moisture. *Most modern cameras are packed with electronic components that can corrode and malfunction if exposed to excessive humidity or moisture, especially salt water. On a boat or at the beach, keep equipment inside a case when it is not in use. If you use it where salt spray will get on it, wrap it in a plastic bag so just the lens pokes out.*

Protect from temperature extremes. *Excessive heat is the worst enemy. It can cause parts to warp, lubricating oil inside the camera to get where it shouldn't be, and film to deteriorate. Avoid storage in places where heat builds up: in the sun, inside an auto trunk or glove compartment on a hot summer day, or near a radiator in winter.*

Excessive cold is less likely to cause damage but can make batteries sluggish. If you photograph outdoors on a very cold day, keep your camera warm inside your coat until you are ready to use it. Moisture can condense on a camera, just as it does on eyeglasses, if metal or glass that has gotten cold outdoors meets warm, humid air when it comes indoors. Keep a cold camera wrapped up until it comes to room temperature.

Protect during storage. *If you won't be using the camera for a while, release the shutter, make sure the meter is off, and store in a clean, dry place. If humidity is high, ventilation should be good to prevent a buildup of moisture on electronic components. Cock and release the shutter once in a while; it can become balky if not used for long periods of time. For long-term storage, remove batteries to prevent possible damage from corrosion.*

Batteries *provide the power for a camera's metering system, viewfinder readout, automatic functions, and sometimes the shutter. Check the battery strength regularly (see manufacturer's instructions).*

How to clean a lens. *Gently. Blow or gently brush any dust particles from the lens surface. Be especially careful with granular dirt, like sand, which can scratch the lens surface badly. To clean grease or water spots from the lens, wad a clean piece of camera lens tissue into a loose ball and moisten it with a drop or two of lens cleaner solution. Don't put drops of solution directly on the lens. They can seep along the edges of the lens to the inside. Wipe the lens gently with a circular motion. Dry it by wiping gently with another clean piece of wadded lens tissue. Don't use any products designed for cleaning eyeglasses.*

How to clean a camera. *If you are cleaning the lens or changing film, also check inside the camera for dust that can settle on the film and cause specks on the final image. Blow or gently dust along the film path, particularly around the winding mechanisms, but be careful not to damage the shutter curtain in the body of the camera or the film pressure plate on the camera-back. The shutter curtain is particularly delicate, and it is best not to touch it at all unless absolutely necessary.*

Professional care *is recommended for all but basic maintenance. Never lubricate any part of the camera yourself or disassemble anything for which the manufacturer's manual does not give instructions. Cameras are more difficult to put back together than they are to take apart.*

film size used by camera				
	35mm	2¼ × 2¼ inch	2¼ × 2¾ inch	4 × 5 inch
short focal length	35mm or shorter	55mm or shorter	75mm or shorter	90mm or shorter
normal focal length	50mm	75mm, 80mm	100mm	150mm (6 inch)
long focal length	85mm or longer	120mm or longer	150mm or longer	250mm (10 inch) or longer

The chart at left gives some typical focal lengths for cameras using various sizes of film. Focal lengths are sometimes stated in inches, sometimes in millimeters. There are approximately 25 mm to an inch.

CHARLES HARBUTT: *Blind Boy, New York City*, c. 1960

The spectrum contains heat as well as light, and you can feel the sun even if you can't see it. Charles Harbutt's photograph is an interesting picture even without the title. But the words add a poignant meaning that greatly strengthens the photograph; without the words there is no clue that the child can't see.

This picture is one of a series Harbutt made of children at The Lighthouse in New York City, an institution for the blind. Harbutt had noticed that every day the boy used his hands to feel for the warmth created by the rays of sunlight that threaded the narrow space between two buildings each afternoon at about the same time.

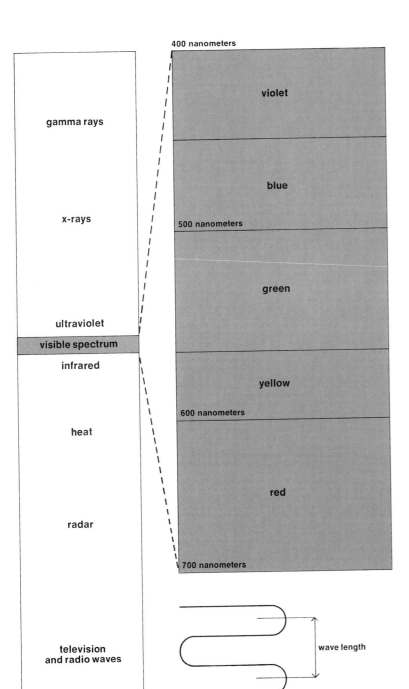

400 nanometers

violet

blue

500 nanometers

green

yellow

600 nanometers

red

700 nanometers

gamma rays

x-rays

ultraviolet

visible spectrum

infrared

heat

radar

television
and radio waves

wave length

The light that we see and that we use to form an image on film is only a small part of a tremendous range of energy called the **electromagnetic spectrum** (*diagram, left*), which also includes X-rays, heat, radar, and television and radio waves. This energy can be described as waves that spread from a source in the same way that ripples spread when a stone is dropped in a pond of water. The waves can be measured; the distance from crest to crest (wavelength) ranges from 0.000000001 millimeter for some gamma rays to six miles for some radio waves.

The human eye is sensitive to a very small group of waves near the middle of the spectrum whose wavelengths range from about 400 nanometers (billionths of a meter) to 700 nanometers. When waves in this **visible spectrum** strike the retina of the eye, the brain senses light; each wavelength or combination of wavelengths produces the sensation of a different color, and a mixture of all the wavelengths produces colorless or "white" light. For most purposes, films are manufactured to be sensitive to about the same range of wavelengths that the eye sees.

Making an Image in Silver

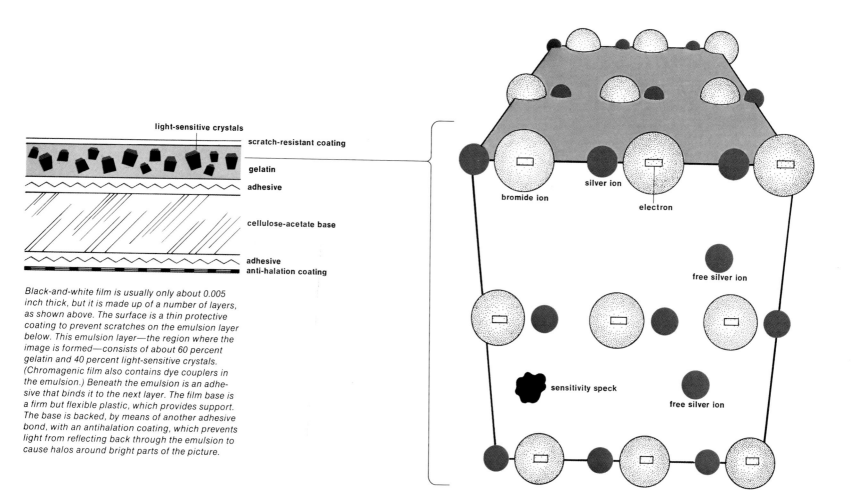

light-sensitive crystals
scratch-resistant coating
gelatin
adhesive
cellulose-acetate base
adhesive
anti-halation coating

Black-and-white film is usually only about 0.005 inch thick, but it is made up of a number of layers, as shown above. The surface is a thin protective coating to prevent scratches on the emulsion layer below. This emulsion layer—the region where the image is formed—consists of about 60 percent gelatin and 40 percent light-sensitive crystals. (Chromagenic film also contains dye couplers in the emulsion.) Beneath the emulsion is an adhesive that binds it to the next layer. The film base is a firm but flexible plastic, which provides support. The base is backed, by means of another adhesive bond, with an antihalation coating, which prevents light from reflecting back through the emulsion to cause halos around bright parts of the picture.

bromide ion
silver ion
electron
free silver ion
sensitivity speck
free silver ion

The process that creates a picture on a piece of film involves a reaction between light and the **silver-halide** crystals spread through the gelatin of the **emulsion** layer. Each crystal is a compound of silver plus a halogen such as bromine, iodine, or chlorine, held together in a cubical arrangement by electrical attraction. If a crystal were a perfect structure lacking any irregularities, it would not react to light. However, a number of electrically charged silver ions are out of place in the structure and are free to move about to help form an image. The crystal also contains impurities, such as molecules of silver sulfide, that play a role in the trapping of light energy.

As shown in the diagrams on the opposite page, an impurity—called a sensitivity speck—and the out-of-place silver ions build a small collection of uncharged atoms of silver metal when the crystal is struck by light. This bit of metallic silver, too small to be visible even under a microscope, is the beginning of a latent image. But developing chemicals use the latent image specks to build up **density,** an accumulation of enough metallic silver to create a visible image.

A **chromagenic film** is somewhat different from the conventional silver film described above. A chromagenic emulsion contains dye couplers as well as silver halides. During development, the presence of silver that has been exposed to light leads to a proportional buildup of dyes. The original silver is then bleached out, leaving the dyes to form the visible image. (*See page 92 for more about chromagenic film.*)

A silver bromide crystal (above) has a cubic structure somewhat like a jungle gym, in which silver (small balls) and bromine (large balls) are held in place by electrical attraction. Both are in the form of ions—atoms possessing electrical charge. Each bromide ion has an extra electron (small box)—that is, one more electron than an uncharged bromine atom, giving it a negative charge; each silver ion has one electron less than an uncharged silver atom and is positively charged. The irregularly shaped object in the crystal represents a "sensitivity speck." In actuality, each crystal possesses many such specks, or imperfections, which are essential to the image-forming process (diagrammed at right).

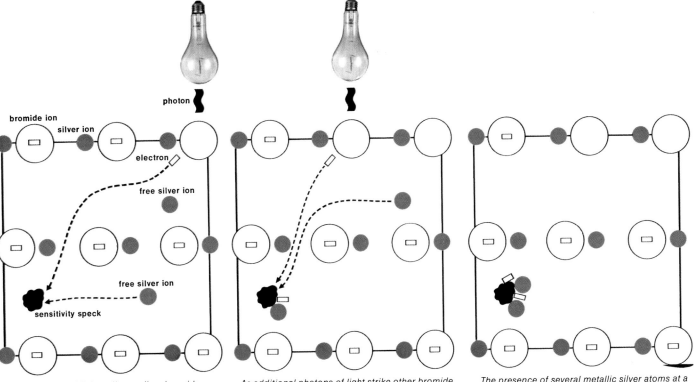

When a photon of light strikes a silver bromide crystal, image formation begins. The photon gives its energy to a bromide ion's extra electron, lifting it to a higher energy level. Then the negatively charged electron can roam the structure of the crystal until it reaches a sensitivity speck. There its electrical attraction pulls a positively charged free silver ion to it.

As additional photons of light strike other bromide ions in the crystal and release electrons, more silver migrates to the sensitivity speck. The electrons join up with the silver ions, balancing their electrical charges and making them atoms of silver metal. However, if the crystal were examined through a microscope at this stage, no change would be seen.

The presence of several metallic silver atoms at a sensitivity speck constitutes a latent image—an invisible chemical site that will serve as the starting point for the conversion of the whole crystal to silver during development. The developer enormously magnifies the slight chemical change caused by light energy and creates the visible photographic image.

A conventional black-and-white negative is formed when millions of exposed crystals are converted to silver metal by the developer. The result is a record of the camera's view in which the film areas struck by the most light are darkened by metallic silver, while the areas struck by no light remain transparent after processing, since they contain no silver. The intermediate areas have varying amounts of silver, creating shades of gray.

A chromagenic negative has dye couplers as well as silver in the emulsion. When the couplers are activated during development, they produce an image in visible dyes. The original silver is then bleached out.

MINOR WHITE: *Negative Print of Feet*, 1948

When this very ordinary scene was printed as a negative image, the feet became not quite real. They seem to float above the surface of the floor, as if the subject is stepping off into space. The skin tones resemble an X-ray, so that one looks not just at the feet but into them. The diagonal lines of the floorboards add a visual tension to the picture, repeating at an angle the rectangular shape of the print format.

Characteristic Curves: How Films Respond to Light

The more light that reaches film, the denser with silver (or dyes), and so the darker, the developed negative will be. The pictures opposite were all taken at the same aperture and shutter speed. As more and more light bulbs shine on the head of Buddha, the negatives (*bottom row*) become darker. The negatives are the opposite of their positive prints (*top row*); the darkest parts of the negative are the lightest in the print.

The response of a particular film to light can be diagrammed as its **characteristic curve,** which shows to what degree silver density increases as the amount of light reaching the film increases. The graph on the next page represents the characteristic curve for the film used in taking those pictures.

The curve shows graphically something you can also see if you look closely at the pictures—the density of the negatives did not increase in exact proportion to the amount of light reaching the film. Although the light was doubled for each exposure, the negative densities increased slowly for the first few exposures (the **toe** of the curve), increased more rapidly for the middle exposures (the **straight-line** portion), then leveled off again for the last exposures (the **shoulder**).

Here the characteristic curve plots seven different pictures. But imagine the seven pictures as all part of the same scene, each representing an object of a different tone ranging from a dark, shadow area (*Buddha at left*) to a brilliant, highlight area (*Buddha at right*). If you take a picture of such a scene, the film will record different densities depending on the lightness or darkness of the various objects *and* on the portion of the characteristic curve in which they fall.

In the straight-line portion of the curve, an increase in light will cause a proportionate increase in density, but in the toe and shoulder portions an increase in light will cause a much smaller increase in density. This means that in the straight-line portion, tones that were different in the original scene will look that way in the final print. The tonal separation will be good for these areas and the print will seem to represent the scene accurately.

When film is **underexposed,** it receives too little light. The tones move toward the toe of the curve, where only small increases in silver density occur. With considerable underexposure, shadow areas and midtones are thin, tonal separation poor, and detail lost. Only light areas of the original scene are on the straight-line portion and show good tonal separation and detail. Tones are reversed in the positive print, so a print will tend to be too dark.

When film is considerably **overexposed,** it receives too much light. The tones move too much toward the shoulder of the curve. Midtones and bright values are too dense with silver; they "block up" without tonal separation, and details again are lost. Only the shadow values show tonal separation and detail. A print will tend to be too light.

Exposure is not the only process that affects the density of a negative. The developer used and the time and temperature of development also affect density, especially for bright areas in the original scene. The Zone System is one method used by some photographers for controlling densities in a negative by making adjustments in exposure and development (*pages 313–325*). Some adjustments can also be made to an image during printing, but a very thin or very dense negative will never make a print with the richness and clarity of a print made from a properly exposed negative with good tonal separation.

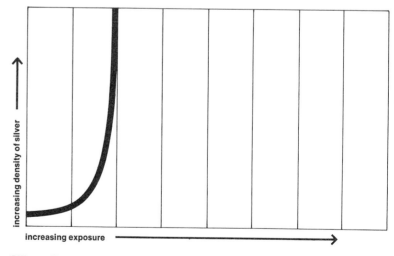

Different films have different characteristic curves. The negative above, made with high-contrast film, consists of two tones, maximum black and maximum white. High-contrast film has a curve that rises almost straight up. Silver density increases rapidly in the negative so that tones above a certain light level are recorded as very dense areas; they will appear in a print as white. Tones below a certain light level are recorded mostly as clear areas in the negative; they will appear in a print as black. Compare this to the curve for the normal-contrast film at right, in which density increases gradually and many midtones are produced.

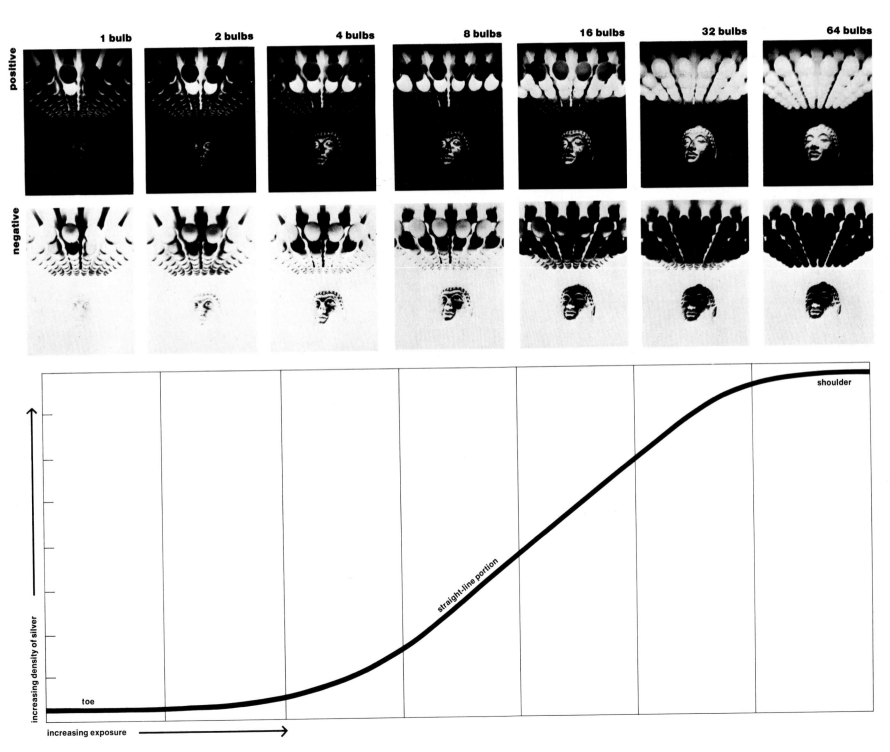

positive

1 bulb   **2 bulbs**   **4 bulbs**   **8 bulbs**   **16 bulbs**   **32 bulbs**   **64 bulbs**

negative

shoulder

straight-line portion

increasing density of silver

toe

increasing exposure

Choosing a Film

What **film speed** do you need? The faster a film, the less light is required to produce an image; therefore, faster film can be used in dimmer light or with faster shutter speeds or smaller apertures. Faster films tend to produce grainier pictures (*see opposite*), so theoretically you will get the best results by selecting the slowest film usable in each situation. In practice, however, it is inconvenient and unnecessary to work with several types of film. Some photographers use a moderately fast film, such as ISO/ASA 400, for almost all their work. One type of film may not be enough, but two—a slow, fine-grain one and a fast one—are enough for most photographers.

Storage and handling affect film performance. Heat affects any film badly, so don't leave film where temperatures may be high, such as in a car's glove compartment on a hot day or near a heater in winter. Film keeps well in the refrigerator or freezer if it is in a moisture-proof wrapping. Let it warm to room temperature before unwrapping it so that moisture does not condense on the surface.

When buying film, check the expiration date on the side of the film package; there is a steady decline in quality and speed after the expiration date. Make sure that the dealer has refrigerated the film if that is recommended by the manufacturer, as it is for professional color film and infrared film.

Load and unload your camera out of strong light and put exposed film where strong light won't reach it. Light can ruin your pictures by fogging them with unwanted exposure if the light leaks around the edges of the film spool or into the light-trap opening out of which the film feeds. Airport security X-ray machines can also fog film, so ask to have film examined by hand rather than passing it through the machine.

Types of Film

Negative film. *Produces an image on the film in which the tones (or colors) are the reverse of those in the original scene—light areas in the scene are dark in the negative, dark areas are light. Later the negative is printed, usually onto paper, to make a positive image, with tones the same as in the original scene.*

Reversal film. *Produces a transparency, a positive image on the film, with tones (or colors) the same as those in the original scene. Most reversal films are color, but a few black-and-white films can be given reversal processing. Color reversal film often has "-chrome" in its name (Ektachrome, Fujichrome), and professional photographers often refer to a color transparency, especially a large-format one, as a chrome. A slide is a transparency mounted in a cardboard holder so it can be inserted in a projector for viewing.*

Instant films. *Used in cameras like the Polaroid SX-70 or Kodak's Kodamatic cameras. For more about instant films, see pages 102–103 and 256–257.*

High-contrast film. *Produces two tones, a clear film base and a very dense deposit of silver (see illustration, page 90, and pages 208–213).*

Infrared film. *Responds to infrared wavelengths that the human eye cannot see (see pages 100–101).*

Color film. *More information in Chapter 10, Color, pages 220–257.*

Chromagenic films. *These black-and-white films (such as Agfapan Vario-XL and Ilford XP1) produce a dye image rather than a silver one. They have great exposure latitude, which means that you can expose individual frames on the same roll of film at different film speeds and get printable negatives in all cases, unlike a roll of conventional film, which should be exposed at a single film speed. Frames exposed at about ISO/ASA 100 will have finer grain, but frames on the same roll of film can be exposed at speeds as high as ISO/ASA 1600. Unfortunately, the film must be developed as if it were a color negative (in Kodak's C-41 chemistry or Agfa or Ilford versions of the same process), which is not as simple or as inexpensive as conventional black-and-white development.*

Professional films. *The word "professional" in a film name (Kodachrome 64 Professional Film) means that the film is designed for professional photographers, who often have exacting standards, especially for color balance, and who tend to buy film in large quantities, use it up quickly, and process it soon after exposure. The most significant difference is in color film, particularly color reversal film. Kodak manufactures its professional color films so that they are at optimum color balance when they reach the retailer, where*—*if the retailer is competent—the film will be refrigerated.*

Kodak makes its nonprofessional color films for a typical "amateur" or "consumer," who would be more likely to accept some variation in color balance, buy one or two rolls at a time, and keep a roll of film in the camera for days, weeks, or longer, making exposures intermittently. Thus Kodak nonprofessional color films do not have to be refrigerated unless room temperatures are high. In fact, they are manufactured to age to their optimum color balance sometime after they reach the retailer and after room-temperature storage.

Format. *The size of film to buy naturally depends on the size your camera accepts.* **35mm film** *is packaged in cassettes and produces up to 36 1 × 1½-inch negatives. Some 35mm films can be purchased in 100-foot rolls and then loaded into separately purchased cassettes. This reduces the cost and, if you use a great deal of film, can be worthwhile.* **Roll film** *is wound around a spool and is backed with a separate strip of paper to protect it from light. (The term "roll" is also used in a general sense to refer to any film that is rolled rather than flat.) 120 roll film makes 12 2¼ × 2¼-inch negatives or, in certain cameras, 10 2¼ × 2¾ or 8 2¼ × 3¼ negatives. Some cameras accept 220 roll film, which has paper only on the end, reducing the thickness of the roll so that twice as much film can be loaded on the roll.* **Sheet film** *or* **cut film** *for use in view cameras is made in 4 × 5-inch and larger sizes. It is packed 10 or more sheets to a box and must be loaded in a film holder before use.*

Film speed. *The higher the number in a given rating system, the faster the film—the less light it needs for a correct exposure. There are several rating systems. An* **ASA** *rating (commonly used in the United States) doubles each time the speed of the film doubles. A film rated at ASA 200 is twice as fast as ASA 100 film. The ASA 200 film requires only half the exposure that the slower ASA 100 film does to produce the same negative density. A* **DIN** *film speed rating, used in Europe, adds 3 to the rating each time the film speed doubles: ASA 100 equals DIN 21, ASA 200 equals DIN 24, and so on.*

An **ISO** *rating combines ASA and DIN: for example, ISO 100/21°. A shortened version uses only the first part of the combined rating: for example, ISO/ASA 100. Don't worry too much about this numerical soup; almost all film and equipment sold in North America uses the ASA or short ISO rating, which are identical.*

Slow films are about ISO/ASA 50 (DIN 18) or less; medium-speed films about ISO/ASA 100 (DIN 21); fast films about ISO/ASA 400 (DIN 27); ultra-fast films ISO/ASA 1000 (DIN 31) or more.

ISO/ASA 32 film speed

ISO/ASA 400 film speed

ISO/ASA 1000 film speed

The segments above were enlarged from three different photographs similar to the one above, right. Each photograph was made on a film of a different speed. The segments show how graininess increases as film speed increases.

Unfortunately, the faster the film, the more visible its **grain**—to the extent that very fast films reproduce shades of gray not as smooth tones but as distinct specks that can obscure detail. Fast films (which contain larger silver halide crystals) produce coarser grain than slower films (which have smaller crystals), because when the faster films are developed, they yield larger bits of silver or, in the case of color or chromogenic films, dyes.

The relationship between speed and graininess can be seen in enlarged segments of photographs such as those on the left. Films of different speeds were used for the negatives from which the enlargements were made. Each increase in speed also increased graininess. If maximum sharpness and minimum graininess is your desire, select the slowest film that the situation will permit. Extreme grain is not always something to be avoided; it can occasionally be used for a special effect. (*See page 108.*)

Graininess is particularly obvious in areas of uniform tone, such as the sky, and it becomes even more apparent when a picture is greatly enlarged. Grain is also affected by the film developer, the printing paper, and the type of enlarger used. Graininess is increased when the negative is overexposed (except with chromagenic films, which *decrease* graininess with overexposure). If you have persistent problems with grain, check the temperatures of your developing solutions; if they vary from each other more than a few degrees, grain can increase sharply.

Certain film and developer combinations enhance fine grain; for example, Kodak Technical Pan 2415 film used with Technidol LC developer produces extremely fine grain and high resolution of detail. The film lets you make very big enlargements without loss of quality, so much so that an enlargement from a 35mm frame of film can look as if it were made from a 4 × 5-inch negative.

For Maximum Detail, Slow and Medium-Speed Films

A **slow film,** ISO/ASA 50 or less, is useful when you want to show very fine detail or want to enlarge a negative considerably with a minimum of grain. A slow film has very small silver halide crystals and a thin emulsion, both of which increase its ability to render detail sharply. (A thin emulsion reduces the internal reflection of light among the crystals, reflections that blur edges and decrease apparent sharpness.)

The film is slow because smaller crystals yield less silver, and so the film requires more light to build up printable silver density. If you have bright sunlight or enough artificial light to illuminate the subject, however, or if you can make a long enough exposure, this will not be a problem.

A **medium-speed film,** around ISO/ASA 100, has larger grain than slow film but maintains good sharpness. Since the film is of moderate speed, you may be able to use a relatively fast shutter speed and hand-hold the camera, whereas a slower film may require a tripod to hold the camera steady during a longer exposure of the same scene. The extra film speed can be important if there are moving objects in the scene.

Medium-speed and fast films have less tonal contrast than slow films and thus may be better for photographing subjects that have both deep shadows and bright highlights.

Medium-speed film is an excellent all-around film, able to handle all but the dimmest light, capable of photographing fast-moving subjects, and producing finer grain than faster films. However, manufacturers have been steadily improving the grain of fast films, so medium-speed film seems destined for a reduced role in the future.

Imogen Cunningham made a number of close-ups ▶ of plant forms in the 1920s. Commonplace objects such as flowers and leaves were photographed in heroic terms, oversize and isolated in the picture and explored for their design and structure, not as strictly botanical specimens. Edward Weston's Pepper No. 30 (page 377) is a similar image. The photograph at right has a gently expressed voluptuous quality. Cropping into the graceful curves of the petals enfolds the viewer in the photograph much as the petals enfold the cone of the stamen and pistil. The light shines through the petals as well as on them and they are luminous with delicate tones of gray. Fine gradations of tonality are usually rendered best with slower films.

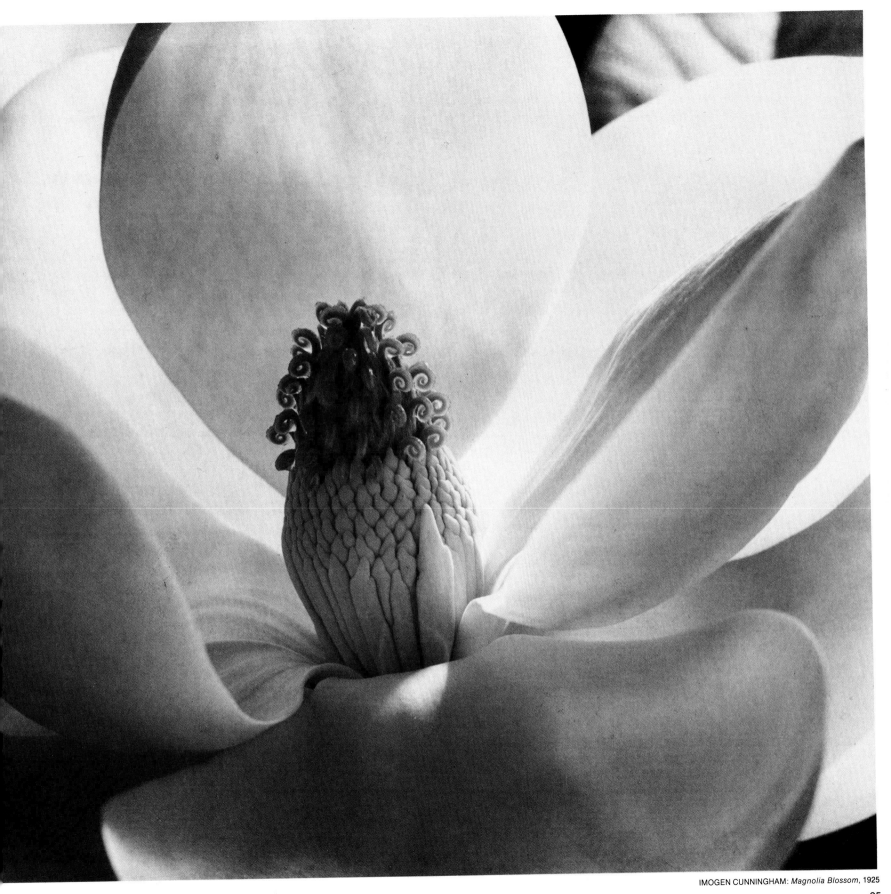

IMOGEN CUNNINGHAM: *Magnolia Blossom*, 1925

When Speed Is Essential

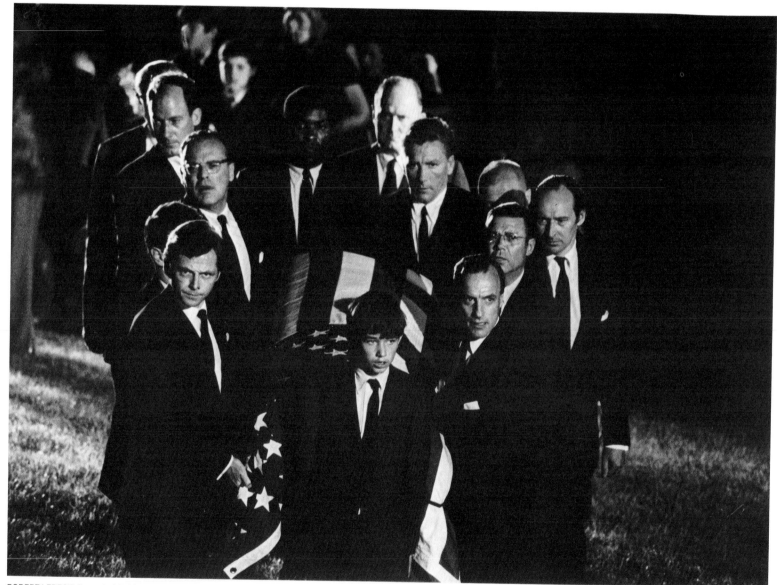

ROBERT LEBECK: *Funeral of Robert Kennedy,* 1968

A **fast film,** about ISO/ASA 400 or higher, is an asset when photographing in dim light. Because a fast film needs less light to produce a printable image, it makes photography easier indoors, at night, or in other low-light situations. If you "push" a fast film, you can increase

even more the speed at which you shoot it. Expose the film as though the film speed is higher than the one designated by the manufacturer, and then give the film special development (*see page 148*). The picture above, taken at the funeral of Senator Robert F. Ken-

nedy, was pushed so it could be shot on Tri-X film rated at ISO/ASA 1000 instead of the standard ISO/ASA 400.

A fast film is useful for stopping motion. Since it requires less light than a slower film, you can use a faster shutter speed, which will show a moving sub-

JAMES DRAKE: *World Series*, 1963

ject sharper than a slow shutter speed will. In the photograph above, the photographer used a 1000mm lens from high up in the press box at Yankee Stadium. A lens of this extremely long focal length typically has a maximum aperture of only about f/8. But because the photographer was using high-speed film, he was still able to use a fast enough shutter speed to stop umpire, ballplayers and hat in mid-play.

A fast film may show increased grain and loss of image detail, especially if you are using an ultrafast film (ISO/ASA 1000 or higher) or if you push the film during development, but the advantages of fast film often outweigh its disadvantages.

How Black-and-White Film Sees Color

Different types of black-and-white film react differently to colors in a scene (*see illustrations at right*). Colors are produced by specific wavelengths of light, and silver halide crystals (the light-sensitive part of photographic emulsion) do not respond equally to all wavelengths.

The first photographic emulsions responded only to the shorter wavelengths of light, from ultraviolet through blue-green. In 1873, **orthochromatic film** was introduced. It had a dye added to the emulsion that extended the response to green and yellow wavelengths. In a way that is still not completely understood, the dye absorbs these slightly longer wavelengths and transfers their energy to the silver halide crystals.

Panchromatic film was a further improvement, and it is now used for almost all ordinary photography. Dyes enable the film to record all colors seen by the human eye, although the film's response is still not exactly like that of the eye. Panchromatic film is still slightly more sensitive to short wavelengths (bluish colors) than to long wavelengths (reddish colors). Sometimes in a print, blue sky may appear too light or red apples may have almost the same tone as green leaves. This final imbalance can be corrected with filters (*pages 104–107*) if desired.

Special dyes have also been devised to make films respond to invisible infrared wavelengths in addition to all the visible colors, with unusual and often beautiful results (*far right and following pages*).

In a photograph made on orthochromatic film, some of the fruits and vegetables above come out looking darker than they would to the human eye because the film responds only to shorter wavelengths—toward the violet end of the spectrum (above)—and is insensitive to reddish colors. The orange, red pepper, and apple (upper right) and the red onion (lower left) all appear unnaturally dark.

When panchromatic film is used, the tones of red-dish objects are more natural in appearance because the film records almost all colors, red through violet and into the ultraviolet (above), that are seen by the eye. The egg looks even whiter than it does in the orthochromatic picture because it has added the light energy of the longer wavelengths to its blend of reflected colors.

Infrared film records visible colors as well as some longer wavelengths that are not visible. Although most natural objects strongly reflect infrared rays, there is no consistent relationship between the color of an object and the amount of infrared rays that are reflected. In the picture above, only the avocado (upper left) and the mushrooms do not reflect infrared strongly; thus they appear darker than the other objects.

Infrared Film: Seeing Beyond the Visible

Infrared film can produce hauntingly beautiful black-and-white photographs, giving the world a strange appearance —the sky dark, the clouds fleecy, and the green foliage unexpectedly luminous. This sort of transformation was made in the picture at right, taken on infrared film with a red filter placed over the lens. Infrared color film produces interesting color variations but not always with such visually appealing results as black-and-white infrared film.

Infrared films are sensitive to invisible infrared wavelengths that are just slightly longer than the visible waves of red light. These "near-red" waves, emitted copiously by the sun and incandescent bulbs, often create unusual photographic effects because they are not always absorbed or reflected in the same amounts as visible light. When a deep-red filter on the lens is used to block most visible wavelengths, so that the photograph is taken principally with infrared waves, these effects become particularly evident.

The leaves and grass in the picture came out snowy white because they reflected infrared waves very strongly. (The leaves are blurred because of their motion during the exposure.) Water particles in clouds also reflect infrared waves strongly, making the clouds seem a brilliant white. But the sky turned out black, because its blue light, mainly in the short-wavelength range, was largely blocked by the deep-red filter.

Sometimes photographers use infrared film and a filter for long-distance views on hazy days. Haze is caused by the scattering of visible light by very small particles of water and smoke in the air—an action that does not affect infrared radiation. Instead of being scattered by these particles, infrared waves reflected off the scenery can pass right through them as if they did not exist; a hazy scene photographed with infrared film thus looks perfectly clear.

Using Infrared Film

Storage. *Exposure to heat will fog infrared film with unwanted exposure. Buy infrared film only if it has been refrigerated by the dealer, and keep it under refrigeration yourself as much as possible.*

Handling. *Even slight exposure to infrared radiation will fog the film, so load and unload the camera in total darkness, either in a darkroom or in a changing bag (a light-tight cloth sack into which you put your hands, the camera, and the film).*

Focusing. *A lens focuses infrared wavelengths slightly differently than it focuses visible light; so if you focus sharply on the visible image, the infrared image will be slightly out of focus. With black-and-white film, focus as usual, then rotate the lens barrel very slightly forward as if you were focusing on an object just a little closer. Most lenses have a red indexing mark on the lens barrel to show the adjustment needed. Make this correction if depth of field is very shallow, for example, if you are using a long-focal-length lens at a wide aperture or if you are focusing on a point very close to the lens. But the difference is so slight that you don't need to adjust for it otherwise; the depth of field will be adequate to keep the image sharp, even if the critical focusing point is slightly off. No adjustment is necessary with color infrared film.*

Filtration. *See manufacturer's instructions. Kodak recommends a #25 red filter for general use with black-and-white infrared film. This increases the infrared effect by absorbing the blue light to which the film is also sensitive. Kodak recommends a #12 minus-blue filter for general use with color infrared film.*

Exposure. *Infrared wavelengths are not accurately measured by ordinary light meters, whether built into the camera or hand-held. Kodak recommends the following manually set trial exposures for average, front-lit subjects in daylight.*

Kodak High-Speed Infrared black-and-white film used with #25 filter: distant scenes—1/125 sec at f/11; nearby scenes—1/30 sec at f/11.

Kodak Ektachrome Infrared color film used with #12 filter: 1/125 sec at f/16.

After making the trial exposure, make at least four additional exposures: ½ stop more exposure, 1 stop more, ½ stop less, and 1 stop less.

Minor White often saw the sublime in the ordinary, ▶ *and here infrared film with its altered tonalities aids in the expression of a landscape that becomes a dreamscape. The perspective of the converging lines of road and trees funnels the eye down the road to the dark mountains beyond. The brightness of the foliage increases the contrast with the dark road. The repeated shadows of the trees reinforce the depth in the scene as the distance between them apparently diminishes. There is no sure way to make a landscape like this happen out of a road lined with trees, no matter what film you use. The landscape itself has to cooperate. White often put forth his basic rule of composition: let the subject generate its own composition.*

MINOR WHITE: *Road and Poplar Trees, Upstate New York*, 1955

Instant-Print Film

In the ordinary photographic process, film is exposed, later developed to produce a negative, and then, even later, printed to make a positive. **Instant-print film,** however, gives you a visible image almost at once. The Polaroid Land film diagrammed at right has both a negative emulsion and positive paper in one package. After the picture is exposed, the negative and positive are tightly sandwiched together by being pulled between two metal rollers. The image is transferred from the negative to the positive by chemicals at the center of the sandwich.

Polaroid makes instant materials in many formats. In addition to pack film, individual sheets of 4 × 5-inch or 8 ×

10-inch film can be used (with a special film holder) in a view camera. Polaroid instant 35mm transparency film can be exposed in any 35mm camera and then, using a special processor, be completely processed in about three minutes to make color or black-and-white slides. (*See pages 256–257 for more about instant color films.*)

Instant film is often used by professional photographers to make a quick check of a setup. An exposure can be made and evaluated on the spot to avoid a mistake when the picture is taken with standard film. Many photographers also use Polaroid film as an end product.

Polaroid Land film in pack form consists of a box containing flat sheets of negative and positive materials that is snapped into the back of the camera. First, the picture is exposed (above). The negative is then turned upside down to meet the positive paper. This is done by pulling on a white tab (below).

When the white tab is pulled, the exposed negative turns upside down and is brought close to the steel rollers (the positive paper has not yet moved). Next, a yellow tab is pulled, drawing both the negative and the positive through the rollers and breaking the pod of chemicals in the process (below). The chemicals are thus spread evenly within the sandwich to develop and fix the picture.

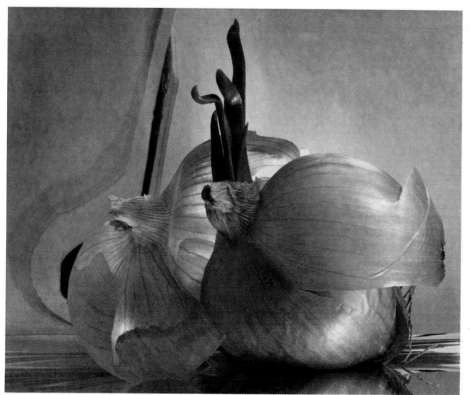

ALAN ROSS: *Onion,* 1976

◀ *Instant-print materials can produce extraordinarily beautiful images. Polaroid Polapan Type 52 4 × 5 film has very fine grain and a very smooth gradation of tones. An original Type 52 print can have a subtle luminosity that is almost impossible to achieve with conventional black-and-white materials. The reproduction at left only hints at the quality of the original.*

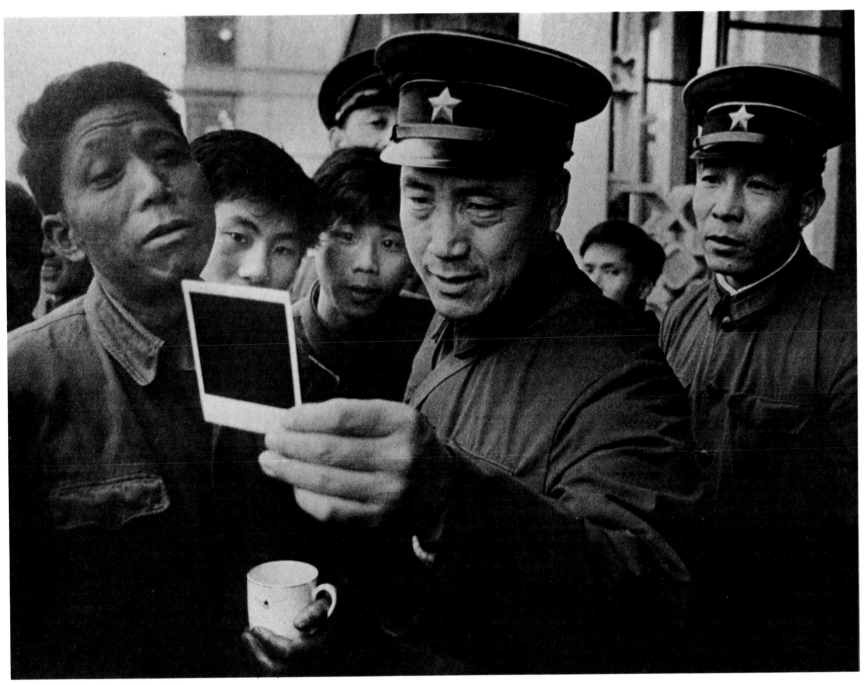

JOE WRINN: *Their First Polaroid, Canton, 1979*

The special pleasure of instant photography: a group of Chinese soldiers in Canton sees for the first time a Polaroid SX-70 picture as it develops its image. The Polaroid is of the soldiers themselves, taken by a Western tourist just a few moments before. This scene has a naturalness and ease that is not always easy to get when the photographer is obviously a foreigner. The soldiers have forgotten the photographer and become engrossed in the instant magic of the instant picture—objects taking shape, colors brightening and getting richer while they watch.

Using Filters

Attach a filter to the front of a lens, and you change the light that reaches the film. The name—*filter*—describes what most filters do: they remove some of the wavelengths of light reflected from a scene and so change the way that the scene looks in a photograph.

Colored filters let you control the relative lightness and darkness of tones in a black-and-white photograph. They absorb light of certain colors and thus make objects of those colors appear as darker tones of gray. The more light the filter absorbs, the less light reaches the film, and the darker those colors will appear to be. It is easier to predict the effect of a colored filter if you think of it as subtracting (and darkening) colors, not adding them. For example, if you look through a red filter, it seems to tint the entire scene red, but it isn't adding red, it is removing blue and green; consequently, blue and green objects will appear darker.

A colored filter absorbs its **complementary color,** the color or colors opposite it on a color wheel (*see color wheel illustrated on page 248*): a yellow filter absorbs blue, a green filter absorbs red and blue, and so on. A colored filter can appear to lighten objects of its own color, but this is because it makes other colors darker, and by comparison, objects that are the color of the filter seem lighter. You will need to increase the exposure for a filtered scene; page 107 tells how to do this.

Correction filters are colored filters designed to correct the response of film so that it shows the same relative brightnesses that the human eye perceives. For example, film is more sensitive to blue and ultraviolet wavelengths than the eye is. A blue sky photographed without a filter can look too light in a black-and-white photograph, almost as light as clouds that appeared at the scene to be much lighter. A yel-

low or red filter, which absorbs blue, darkens the blue part of the sky so that clouds stand out (*see illustrations on next page*).

Contrast filters are colored filters that change the relative brightness of colors that would otherwise be too similar in tone in black and white. To the normal human eye, red apples contrast strongly against a background of green leaves, but in black and white the apples and leaves can reproduce as almost the same gray tone. A green filter, which absorbs red, darkens the apples so that they look more natural (*see illustrations, right*).

Neutral-density filters absorb a quantity of all wavelengths of light. They reduce the overall amount of light that reaches the film while leaving the color balance unchanged; they can be used with either black-and-white or color film. Their purpose is to increase the exposure needed for a scene, so that you can use a slower shutter speed (to blur motion) or a larger aperture (to decrease depth of field).

A **polarizing filter** absorbs wavelengths that are vibrating in certain directions. It can be used with either black-and-white or color film to remove reflections, darken skies, and intensify colors (*see page 106*).

In addition to filters that absorb light, certain **lens attachments** can be used for special effects. A cross-screen attachment causes streamers of light to appear to radiate from bright lights such as light bulbs. A soft-focus attachment softens details and makes them slightly hazy.

Some photographers leave a clear or nearly clear filter, like a 1A or UV, on a lens simply to protect the lens surface from dirt or accidental bumps. It is much cheaper to replace a damaged filter than a damaged lens.

Colors that appear very different to the eye can be confusingly similar in tone in black and white, such as the red apples on the green leaves, above. A colored filter can correct this by absorbing certain colors and making those colors darker in a black-and-white print.

A green filter *#58, used to take the picture below, absorbs much red light, making the red apples darker than the leaves, a natural-looking appearance.*

One of the most common uses for a filter in black-and-white photography is to darken a blue sky. Colored filters work for this purpose only when the sky is actually blue. They do not darken the sky on an overcast or hazy day.

Without any filter, the sky in this photograph appears very light, with clouds barely visible. Black-and-white film is very sensitive to blue and ultraviolet light; this often causes skies to appear too light in a black-and-white photograph.

A yellow filter #8 absorbs some of the sky's blue light, making the sky in the picture at right appear somewhat darker than it does above.

A red filter #25 absorbs nearly all blue as well as green light, making the sky in the picture at right much darker than it normally appears and also darkening foliage. Shadows, too, appear darker than in the unfiltered view, because they are illuminated largely by blue light from the sky that the red filter blocks.

A Polarizing Filter to Reduce Reflections

Reflections from a shiny surface can be a distracting element in a photograph. With a **polarizing filter,** you can remove or reduce reflections from water, glass (*top right*), or any smooth surface except metal. This is possible because light waves ordinarily vibrate in all directions perpendicular to their direction of travel. But light reflected from nonmetallic smooth surfaces has been polarized—the light waves vibrate in only one plane.

A polarizing filter contains submicroscopic crystals lined up like parallel slats. Light waves that are parallel to the crystals pass between them; waves vibrating at other angles are blocked by the crystals (*diagram, right*). Since the polarized light is all at the same angle, the filter can be turned so as to block it.

To use a polarizing filter, look through it and rotate it until the unwanted reflection is reduced as desired (*bottom right*). Then place the filter in the same position over the lens. (With a single-lens reflex or view camera, the filter can be adjusted while it is in place over the lens.) Because of the partial blockage of light by the filter, the exposure must be increased by one to two stops.

Tiny particles of dust and water in the atmosphere also reflect light and can make a distant scene look hazy. A polarizing filter will decrease such reflections, darken the sky, and make a distant scene look more distinct and more vividly colored. It is the only filter that will darken the sky in a color picture without changing the color balance.

The photograph at top was taken without any filter. The reflection in the window was removed in the picture below by adjusting a polarizing filter (or polarizer) over the lens. The drawing shows how the polarizer works. It is adjusted to pass only those light waves (black) oriented parallel to its picketlike aligned crystals and to screen out all other light waves (gray) angled across the pickets.

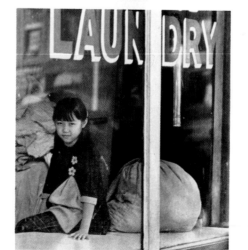

reducing reflections from shiny surfaces

reflecting surface

35°

reducing reflections from atmosphere

90°

▲
A polarizing filter used to block reflections from a shiny surface like glass or water is most efficient at an angle of about 35° to the reflecting surface (top diagram). Directly in front of the surface, the filter has little or no effect. A polarizing filter can be used to darken a blue sky and to reduce haze by blocking light reflected from particles in the atmosphere. In this case, the filter works best when you are taking pictures at approximately a right angle to the sun (bottom diagram).

Since filters absorb part of the light from a scene before it reaches the film, exposures must be increased or the film will be underexposed. A **filter factor** gives the approximate number of times that the exposure must be increased. The factor for tungsten light (from light bulbs) is different from the factor for daylight because tungsten (except for special blue bulbs) emits more red wavelengths than daylight does.

The factor tells *how many times* the exposure must be multiplied. A factor of two means the exposure must be doubled (the next widest f-stop or the next slowest shutter speed). A factor of four requires four times the exposure (two f-stops wider or two shutter speeds slower, or one f-stop wider plus one

shutter speed slower). When using two filters together, such as a polarizing filter (factor of 2.5) and a red #25 filter (factor of eight), the factors are multiplied, not added. The factor for the above combination is 20.

If you have a camera that meters through the lens, such as a single-lens reflex camera, the metering system will automatically increase the exposure when the filter is on the lens because it reads the light after it has been filtered. With a hand-held meter or a camera that does not meter through the lens, you can let the meter do the arithmetic for you by dividing the filter factor into the film speed and then using that film speed setting instead of the regular one. For example, suppose you are

using a film rated at ISO/ASA 100 with a yellow filter (factor of two): 100 ÷ 2 = 50. Set the film speed dial on the meter or the camera to 50, instead of 100.

Filters are made of gelatin or of glass in various sizes to fit different lens diameters. **Gelatin filters** are taped to the front of the lens or placed in a filter holder. They are inexpensive and come in many colors, but they easily acquire scratches and fingerprints that cannot be cleaned off. Handle them by the edges only. **Glass filters** screw or clamp onto the front of the lens. They are convenient to use and much sturdier than gelatin but are more expensive. The chart below lists filters for black-and-white film. See page 229 for filters used with color film.

Filters for Black-and-White Film

number or designation	color or name	physical effect	practical use	factor with black-and-white panchromatic film	
				daylight	tungsten
8	yellow	Absorbs ultraviolet and blue-violet	Darkens blue sky to bring out clouds. Increases contrast by darkening bluish shadows. Reduces bluish haze.	2	1.5
15	deep yellow	Absorbs ultraviolet, violet, and most blue	Lightens yellow and red subjects such as flowers. Darkens blue water and blue sky to emphasize contrasting objects or clouds. Increases contrast and texture and reduces bluish haze more than #8 filter.	3	2
25	red	Absorbs ultraviolet, blue-violet, blue, and green	Lightens yellow and red subjects. Darkens blue water and sky considerably. Increases contrast in landscapes. Reduces bluish haze more than #15 filter. Used with infrared film.	8	6
11	yellowish-green	Absorbs ultraviolet, violet, blue, and some red	Lightens foliage, darkens sky. For outdoor portraits, darkens sky without making light skin tones appear too pale. Balances values in tungsten-lit scenes by removing excess red.	4	3
47	blue	Absorbs red, yellow, green, and ultraviolet	Lightens blue subjects. Increases bluish haze.	8	16
1A or UV	skylight / ultraviolet	Absorbs ultraviolet	More often used in color photography but also has some effect on black-and-white films. Eliminates ultraviolet that eye does not see but that film will record as haze or decreased contrast in mountain, marine, or aerial scenes.	1	1
ND	neutral density	Absorbs equal quantities of light from all parts of the spectrum	Increases required exposure so camera can be set to wider aperture or slower shutter speed. Comes in densities from 0.01 (⅓ stop more exposure) to 1.00 (3⅓ stops more exposure).	varies with density	
	polarizing	Absorbs light waves traveling in certain planes relative to the filter	Reduces reflections from nonmetallic surfaces, such as water or glass. Penetrates haze by reducing reflections from atmospheric particles. Darkens sky at some angles.	2.5	2.5

if factor is	1	1.2	1.5	2	2.5	3	4	5	6	8	16	32
increase exposure (stops)	0	⅓	⅔	1	1⅓	1⅔	2	2⅓	2⅔	3	4	5

Using Light and Film

MAX WALDMAN: *Actor Robert Lloyd in the role of the Violent Inmate in Marat/Sade,* 1966

Certain photographs are enhanced by the use of a film that emphasizes grain, which can add a gritty or theatrical quality to a picture. Max Waldman made many pictures of theater and dance works. He often isolated a performer, using dramatic gestures and lighting to convey the essential quality of a movement or emotion.

Waldman did not reveal the method by which he achieved the extreme graininess that was characteristic of his work, but a similar effect can be obtained with a film such as Kodak Recording Film 2475. This coarse-grained 35mm film, often used for surveillance work, has a film speed of ISO/ASA 1000. Extended development increases the film speed—and the grain. Printing on high-contrast paper exaggerates the grain even more.

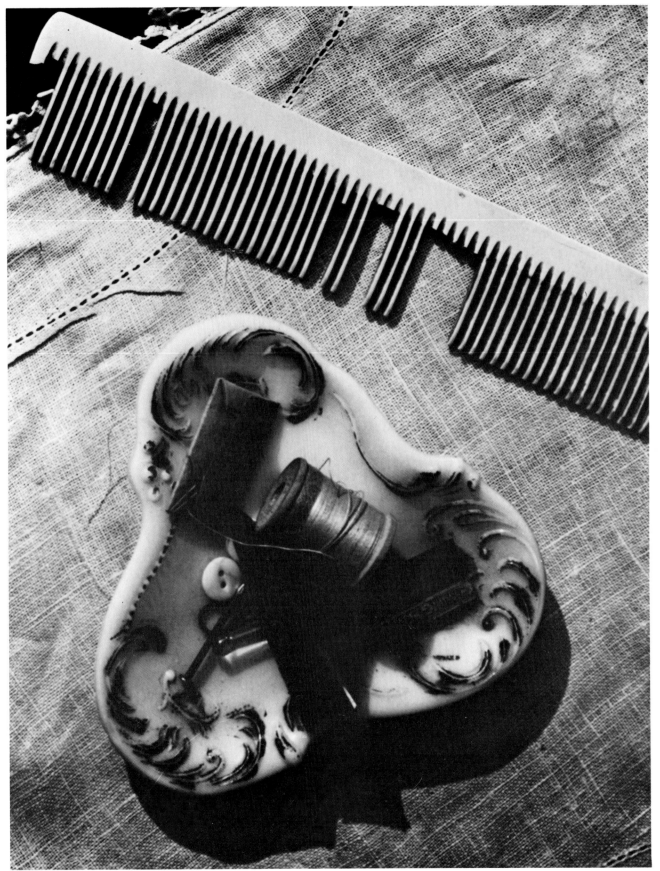

Grain is minimized and detail is kept crisp if extreme enlargements are not made. One reason photographers use large-format films, 4 × 5 inches or larger, is for the image clarity possible with a contact print (the same size as the negative) or a moderate enlargement. Right, an enlargement from a 4 × 5 negative. Wright Morris grew up in the Midwest and returned there intermittently. In his book The Home Place, he combined photographs and text about the rural and small town life he had known.

WRIGHT MORRIS: *Comb on Dresser, Home Place,* 1947

HIROSHI SUGIMOTO: *Cabot Street Cinema, Beverly, Massachusetts,* 1978

5
Exposure

Most black-and-white films have a tolerance, or latitude, for a certain amount of exposure error; they allow for a range of exposures all of which will produce satisfactory negatives. However, the best prints, especially if enlargements are made, are produced from properly exposed negatives. Greatly overexposed negatives are difficult to print and produce grainy and unsharp prints. Badly underexposed negatives show no detail in the shadows—something that cannot be remedied when the negative is printed. Reversal films, especially color transparency films, have very little latitude; underexposure or overexposure of only one stop makes a distinctly inferior slide.

Cameras, especially 35mm cameras, have become increasingly automated in recent years, with built-in meters to measure the intensity of the light and with electronic circuitry to recommend lens aperture and shutter-speed settings, or even to set the lens and shutter automatically. But personal judgment is still important. Equipment is programmed for "average" conditions, so you may have to change the recommended settings if you are photographing a backlit scene, a snowy landscape, or other non-average situation. This chapter tells when you can rely on automatic equipment and when you need to override it.

One of the best cures for exposure problems is experience. The most expensive meter or camera, complicated exposure strategy, or detailed charts will never replace the sureness you will have when you photograph something for the second—and, even better, the third or fourth—time.

◀ *Hiroshi Sugimoto photographs movies—but not in the usual way. He sets up his 8 × 10 view camera, mounted on a tripod, in a theater balcony. He positions the camera with the lens more or less equidistant from all points in the image, so that the photograph is symmetrical and evenly focused from edge to edge. The movie is the main source of light, and its length determines the exposure time. The photograph, in effect, shows the whole movie all at once. This is what we see at the movies, but translated into another time frame.*

How Exposure Meters Work

An **exposure meter,** commonly called a light meter, is an essential piece of equipment because it enables you to produce consistently accurate exposures. Meters built into the camera are popular because they are so convenient. Yet many photographers still prefer a separate hand-held meter when they want greater control over exposure. A hand-held meter makes it easy to move close to various parts of the scene and take light readings of specific areas.

The light-sensitive part of an exposure meter is a **photoelectric cell.** A selenium or silicon cell converts the energy of light into electrical energy that moves a needle across a gauge or provides digital readout or other information. The stronger the light the stronger the current and the more the needle or other indicator responds. A cadmium sulfide (CdS) cell acts as a resistor; it lets more or less current from a small battery pass to the gauge depending on the amount of light that strikes the cell.

Selenium cell meters have the simplest design and, since they generate electricity directly, have no batteries to wear out. But they are relatively insensitive at low light levels. Since CdS meters are sensitive over a wider range of light levels than selenium, they can be used in very dim light, can be made small enough to be built into a camera, and can be used to measure a very narrow angle. However, they tend to creep slowly to the correct reading when going from bright to dim light or vice versa. Silicon or gallium cells have all the advantages of CdS and, in addition, react quickly at all light levels.

Light meters differ in the way they are used to measure light. Most hand-held meters and all those built into cameras are **reflected-light meters;** they measure **luminance,** the light reflected from

(or emitted by) the subject. The meter is pointed at the subject—or at the particular part of the subject the photographer wants to measure at close range—and the reading is made. The light-admitting opening of such meters is restricted by a hood, baffle, or faceted lens so that the angle of view of the meter approximates that of a normal camera lens, about 30° to 50°. In a variation of this type of meter, a spot meter (*page 122*), the angle may be reduced to as little as one-half degree so that readings of very small areas can be made.

Incident-light meters are hand-held. They have a much wider angle of view (about 180°) and measure **illuminance,** the light incident on (falling on) the subject from one side. This wider angle is made possible by a translucent dome of white glass or plastic placed over the light-measuring cell to diffuse the light. An incident-light meter is pointed not toward the subject but toward the camera from the position of the subject, so that it receives the same light as is falling on the subject.

Since each type has advantages under certain conditions, some, such as the one shown on the opposite page, are designed to make both reflected and incident readings. When the sensing cell is open to direct light, it is a reflected-light meter; when the dome-like diffuser is slid into position over the sensing cell, it becomes an incident-light meter.

Most meters are designed to measure a continuously burning source of light, such as a tungsten lamp or the sun. **Flash meters** measure the output from the brief burst of light from electronic flash. **Color meters** measure the color temperature of light rather than its brightness and are used to determine the filtration needed when a specific color balance is required.

A reflected-light meter can be hand-held (left) or built into a camera (right) and is aimed at a subject to make a reading. It measures the luminance (commonly called the brightness) of a subject, here, the light reflected from the man's coat.

An incident-light meter is faced toward the camera from the position of the subject. It measures the light falling on a subject as seen from the direction of the camera.

incident-light diffuser

light opening

lens

cadmium sulfide cell

gauge 1 2 3 4 5 6 8 9 10

battery

ASA
400

LIGHT SCALE

aperture (f-stop)
speed (fractions of a second)

6

7

8

9

10

32

22

16

11

8

5.6

4

2.8

2

4

8

15

30

60

125

250

500

1000

An exposure meter measures the light and then for a given film speed computes shutter speed and f-stop combinations. All meters are calibrated on the assumption that the average of all the tones in any scene will equal a middle-gray tone. This is true for most scenes—but not all of them. Moreover, the meter doesn't know what it is reading or how light or dark you want the subject to be in the photograph. For these reasons, you sometimes have to override the meter's recommended exposure settings. The following pages contain more details about how and when to do this.

Measuring the light. The meter at left is set to measure reflected light. The domed diffuser, used to make an incident reading, has been slid away from the opening over the light-sensitive cell. How much light strikes the cell determines how much current reaches the needle that moves across the measuring gauge.

The numbers on an exposure meter gauge are one stop apart: each number indicates a light level twice as high as the preceding number. In this case, the reading is slightly over 7—about twice the light level at 6, about half the level at 8.

Film speed. The speed of the film being used must be set into the meter. Here the center knob is turned until an ISO/ASA rating of 400 is shown in the small window near the center of the dial.

Computing the exposure. To convert the light measurement into an exposure setting, the large outer dial of this meter is turned until its arrow points to the number indicated by the gauge needle. This matches apertures (f-stops) with shutter speeds at the bottom of the dials to recommend an exposure for the light intensity measured; f/32 at 1/4 sec, f/22 at 1/8 sec or any other combination shown would give the same exposure. Here the dial shows the shutter speed in fractions of a second: 1/8 sec is shown on the dial as 8, 1/4 sec is shown as 4, and so on. The shutter-speed dial continues on into full seconds, minutes, and, on some meters, hours of exposure time. Some meters provide a direct digital readout of shutter speed and f-stop combinations, light intensity measured in foot-candles, or other data.

Batteries. Some hand-held meters and all meters built into cameras are battery powered. Check batteries regularly (see manufacturer's directions for how to do this). A worn-down or exhausted battery can give an inaccurate reading and eventually will cease functioning altogether.

Built-in Meters

The rings drawn on the picture below indicate the way most built-in meters give different emphasis to different parts of an image in gauging light. The meter is center-weighted, that is, made 100 percent responsive to light reflected from the area of the scene inside the central ring; response falls off sharply from there outward. At each surrounding ring, the meter's responsiveness is reduced by half.

Most photographers, even those professionals who used to feel that only hand-held meters were accurate enough for critical metering, now on some assignments use exposure meters built into cameras. **Built-in meters,** like hand-held, reflected-light meters, measure the light reflected or produced by objects in their view and then calculate an exposure setting.

To use a built-in meter, you look through the camera's viewfinder while pointing the meter at the scene or at the part of the scene that you want to meter. The viewfinder shows the area being metered, and most viewfinders also display shutter speed and/or aperture settings (*right, bottom*). An automatic camera contains circuitry that sets the shutter speed or aperture for you based on the meter reading (*see opposite page*).

Most built-in meters are **center-weighted:** the meter averages all the light in the scene but weights its average to give more emphasis to the area at the center of the viewfinder than to the surrounding area. This system is based on the assumption—usually correct—that the subject is in the center of the scene. A center-weighted meter can give an inaccurate reading if the subject is at the side of the frame, for instance, or if the subject does not fill the central area and the surroundings are much lighter or darker than it is.

There are also scenes that can cause any reflected-light meter to produce the wrong exposure. All such meters are designed to indicate exposure for scenes including both very light and very dark areas in a more or less equal balance that averages out to a middle gray tone. If a scene is uniformly light (such as a snow scene), the meter still calculates an exposure as if it were reading middle gray. The result is not enough exposure and a photograph that is too dark. The opposite can happen with a uniformly dark scene (such as a display of black velvet): too much exposure and a photograph that is too light. The following pages tell how to interpret such a scene and how to set your camera accordingly.

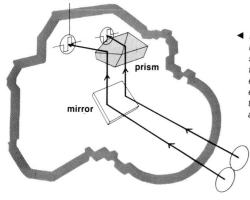

photoelectric cell

prism

mirror

◀ In this single-lens reflex camera with a built-in meter, light enters through the camera lens, strikes the angled mirror, and is reflected upward to the prism. Photoelectric cells are mounted on either side of the eyepiece and aimed at the prism; each measures light reflected from part of the picture area. The cells are interconnected to give an average reading of light reflected from the scene.

The viewing screen (above) of a 35mm single-lens reflex camera gives information from the built-in meter. With this camera, the number at top shows the lens aperture, f/8. The scale at right shows the shutter speeds, and the lighted dot indicates that at f/8, the meter has chosen a shutter speed of 1/125 sec. When the camera is set for manual operation, a lighted dot appears next to "M," with another dot next to the recommended shutter speed to be set manually. If the arrow at the top of the scale lights up, the scene is too bright for exposure at the chosen aperture. A lighted arrow at the bottom shows need for exposure longer than 1 sec. The center circles are focusing aids.

Overriding Automatic Exposure

memory lock

backlight button

film speed dial

exposure compensation dial

manual mode

Automatic exposure works well much of the time, but for some scenes you will want to alter the exposure set by the automatic circuitry. You may want to increase the exposure to lighten one picture or decrease the exposure to darken another. All cameras have one or more of the following means of allowing you to do so. See the manufacturer's instructions.

Manual mode. *An option on many automatic cameras. You adjust both shutter speed and aperture settings to lighten or darken the picture as you wish.*

Exposure compensation dial. *Moving the dial to +1 or +2 increases the exposure one or two stops and lightens the picture (some dials say ×2 or ×4 for comparable settings). Moving the dial to −1 or −2 (×½ or ×¼ on some dials) decreases the exposure one or two stops and darkens the picture.*

Backlight button. *May be on the camera if an exposure compensation dial is not. Depressing the button adds a fixed amount of exposure (usually one to one and a half stops) to lighten a picture. It cannot be used to decrease exposure. As its name indicates, it is useful for backlit scenes in which the main subject is against a much lighter background.*

Memory lock. *Available on a few of the more expensive cameras. The switch temporarily locks in a shutter speed and aperture combination. You meter the most important part of the scene, lock in the settings, then step back to photograph the entire scene at that exposure.*

Film speed dial. *Even if a camera has no other means of changing the exposure, you can always reset the film speed dial. The camera then responds as if the film needs more (or less) light than it really does. To lighten a picture, decrease the film speed: Halving an ISO/ASA film speed (for example, from 400 to 200) increases the exposure by one stop. To darken a picture, increase the film speed: doubling the film speed (for example, 400 to 800) decreases the exposure by one stop. Remember to reset the film speed dial to the normal rating when you are done.*

Many cameras today come equipped with **automatic exposure.** If your camera is an automatic one, a meter built into the camera measures the brightness of the scene in your viewfinder. Electronic circuitry within the camera automatically calculates an exposure that would be correct for an average scene and then adjusts shutter speed, aperture, or both, based on the speed of the film you are using. The basic modes of automatic exposure are listed in the box below. Your camera may operate in only one of these modes or in several. See the manufacturer's instruction book for details.

For most scenes (those with an average distribution of light and dark tones), automatic exposure works easily and well. There are, however, some scenes for which it will operate easily but not so well: for example, if a subject is against a much lighter or darker background. At those times, you will have to override the automatic mechanism to get the exposure you want. Various means to do this are listed at left; your camera has at least one of them. See pages 116–117 for how to meter an average scene, pages 118–121 and 124–125 for how to spot a nonaverage scene and what to do about it.

Exposure Modes

Aperture-priority automatic. You select the aperture and the camera adjusts the shutter speed.	You set aperture	f/5.6	f/8	f/11
	Camera adjusts shutter speed	1/250 sec	1/125	1/60
Shutter-priority automatic. You select the shutter speed and the camera adjusts the aperture.	You set shutter speed	1/250 sec	1/125	1/60
	Camera adjusts aperture	f/5.6	f/8	f/11
Programmed (fully) automatic. The camera adjusts both shutter speed and aperture based on a built-in program. In some models, the camera selects the fastest possible shutter speed; in others, the camera goes to slower shutter speeds rather than opening the lens to the widest aperture.	Camera adjusts aperture	f/5.6	f/8	f/11
	Camera adjusts shutter speed	1/250 sec	1/125	1/60
Manual. You set both shutter speed and aperture. The camera's built-in meter still can be used to calculate the correct settings.	You set aperture	f/5.6	f/8	f/11
	You set shutter speed	1/250 sec	1/125	1/60

How to Meter
An Overall Reading for an Average Scene

How do you get a good exposure—that combination of f-stop and shutter speed that lets just the right amount of light reach the film, so that your picture is not underexposed and too dark or overexposed and too light? For many scenes, the correct exposure is easy to calculate: you use a reflected-light meter to make an **overall reading** of the brightness of objects in the scene (*opposite, left and center*). If you have an incident-light meter, you make a reading of the overall brightness of light falling on the scene (*opposite, right*).

An overall reading works very well for metering average scenes, where light and dark tones are of more or less equal distribution and importance, especially if the scene is evenly illuminated, either by light that is coming from behind the camera or by light that is evenly diffused over the entire scene. But a meter is only a measuring device—it cannot interpret what it reads, nor does it know whether a scene is average or if you want the subject to be light or dark. So in some cases you have to think for the meter and override the settings it recommends. The following pages will tell when to do so.

A **reflected-light meter** (built into the camera or hand-held) acts as if the scene it is metering is middle gray. It averages all the tones in its angle of view and then calculates a combination of f-stop and shutter speed that will produce middle gray in a print. The assumption is that the average of all the tones from light to dark in a scene will be a middle gray, so an exposure for middle gray will be approximately correct for the entire scene. This method actually does give a good exposure in a large number of situations.

A reflected-light meter averages the luminances in a scene—the light reflected or produced by all the objects in the meter's angle of view—so you have

to make sure that the meter is reading only the light you want it to read. If your meter is built into the camera, you can see in the viewfinder the area that the meter is reading. Some hand-held meters have a small viewfinder through which you look at the scene, but if yours does not, you can estimate the area the meter is covering. For most reflected-light hand-held meters, the angle is 30° to 50°, about the coverage of a normal focal length lens.

You may get a deceptively high reading (and subsequently a too-dark picture) if the scene contains very light areas like a bright sky or light sources like the sun or a lamp. Your reading may be too low (and the resulting picture too light) if a very large dark area surrounds the subject. See pages 118–119 for how to handle such scenes.

Since an **incident-light meter** reads only the light falling on a subject, its reading does not include surrounding dark or light areas. An incident-light meter is preferred by many commercial photographers to balance the illumination in studio setups where lights can be arranged at will. It is also quick and easy to use and therefore useful in fast-moving situations. However, it cannot measure the actual luminances of different objects in a scene and it cannot give an exposure for an object that is itself emitting light, such as a neon sign or a lamp.

To use an incident-light meter, point it in the direction opposite from the one the lens is pointing (*see opposite, right*). This aligns the meter so that it receives the same amount of light as is falling on the subject as seen from camera position. Move close enough to the subject so that you do in fact read the same light that is falling on it. Indoors, for example, don't take a reading near a sunny window if your subject is standing in a dark corner.

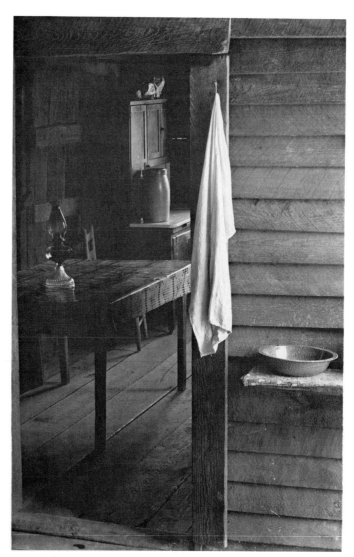

WALKER EVANS: *Hale County, Alabama*, 1936

Exposure meters are designed on the assumption that the scene you are metering contains an "average" distribution of tones from light to dark. A meter reading of the overall scene produces a good exposure if this, in fact, is so, and if light and dark areas are of more or less equal importance. You can make an overall reading with a meter built into the camera or one that is hand held (see opposite).

using a meter built into a camera

1 | Set the film speed dial of the camera to the ISO/ASA rating of the film you are using.

2 | Set the exposure mode of the camera, if you have a choice: (a) aperture-priority automatic, (b) shutter-priority automatic, (c) programmed automatic, or (d) manual.

3 | Look at the scene through the camera's viewfinder and activate the meter.

4a | In aperture-priority automatic operation, select an aperture small enough to give the desired depth of field. The camera will adjust the shutter speed. If your subject is moving or if you are hand-holding the camera, check the viewfinder readout to make sure that the shutter speed is fast enough to prevent blur. The wider the aperture you select, the faster the shutter speed that the camera will set. (Remember that a wide aperture is a small number: f/2 is wider than f/4.)

4b | In shutter-priority automatic operation, select a shutter speed fast enough to prevent blur. The camera will adjust the aperture. Check that the aperture is small enough to produce the desired depth of field. The slower the shutter speed you select, the smaller the aperture will be.

4c | In programmed automatic operation, the camera will adjust both shutter speed and aperture.

4d | In manual operation, you select both shutter speed and aperture. You can use the camera's built-in meter or a hand-held meter to calculate the settings.

using a hand-held, reflected-light meter

1 | Set the meter to the ISO/ASA rating of the film you are using.

2 | Point the meter's photoelectric cell at the subject from the direction of the camera. Activate the meter.

3 | Line up the number registered by the meter's indicator needle with the arrow on the calculator dial. (Not necessary with meters that automatically provide shutter-speed and f-stop combinations.)

4 | Choose one of the combinations of shutter speed and f-stop shown on the calculator dial or provided as digital readout, and set the camera accordingly. Any combination shown by the meter lets in the same amount of light and produces the same exposure.

using an incident-light meter

1 | Set the meter to the ISO/ASA rating of the film you are using.

2 | Point the meter's photoelectric cell away from the subject, in the opposite direction from the camera lens. Activate the meter. You want to measure the amount of light falling on the subject, so make sure that the meter is in the same light as the subject. For example, don't shade the meter if your subject is sunlit.

3 | Line up the number registered by the meter's indicator needle with the arrow on the calculator dial. (Not necessary with meters that automatically provide shutter-speed and f-stop combinations.)

4 | Choose one of the combinations of shutter speed and f-stop shown on the calculator dial or provided as digital readout, and set the camera accordingly. Any combination shown by the meter lets in the same amount of light and produces the same exposure.

Metering Scenes with High Contrast

Although a simple overall reading works well much of the time, it does not work for some scenes. The most common situation in which overall metering does not work is **a subject against a much lighter background,** for example, outdoors with a bright sky in the background. Suppose you are using a reflected-light meter, either built into the camera or hand-held, to meter such a scene. If you meter the scene overall, the bright sky will increase the entire reading too much. The meter will calculate an exposure for a very light scene and as a result underexpose the main subject.

Preventing this type of deceptive reading is easy: if a subject is against a much lighter background, such as a bright sky, a very light wall, or a bright window indoors during the day, move in close enough so that you are metering mostly the main subject rather than the lighter background. Set the aperture and shutter speed from the up-close reading before you move back to take the picture (*this page and opposite, top*). Similarly, try not to include light sources, such as the sun or a lighted lamp, in a meter reading. And make sure that light is not shining directly onto a reflected-light meter's cell because this will inflate the reading also.

If you are metering a landscape, cityscape, or other distant scene, tilt the camera or meter down to exclude most of a bright sky from the reading; the lower reading will give a more accurate exposure for the land elements in the scene (*opposite, bottom*). Of course, if your main subject is the sky itself, such as a cloud formation, take your reading directly from the sky.

Less common, but sometimes a problem, is **a subject against a much darker background,** especially if the subject occupies only a small part of the image. Metering such a scene overall with a re-flected-light meter would produce a reading that is too low and an overexposed and too-light picture. Prevention is the same: move in close to meter mostly the main subject.

How do you use an automatic camera to expose a picture with a background much lighter or darker than the subject? You can't simply meter the scene up close and then step back to take the picture. The camera will automatically recalculate the exposure from farther away, including the light or dark background that you want to exclude from the metering. You can change from automatic to manual operation, if that is possible with your camera, so that you can set both shutter speed and aperture yourself. Or use one of the other means of overriding automatic exposure described on page 115.

Suppose you want to use an automatic camera's exposure compensation dial, backlight button, or film speed dial, which let you change the exposure by a fixed amount. How much should you change it? First meter the scene as you want to shoot it, then meter with the background excluded. Count the number of stops difference between the two readings as shown by the viewfinder readout and adjust the exposure accordingly. Every change from one shutter speed to the next or from one f-stop to the next counts as one stop.

If you are using an incident-light meter to determine the exposure for a scene that has both brightly lit and shaded areas, decide whether the light or dark areas are more important. If shaded areas are more important, make your reading in the shadows or with the meter shaded by your body or hand. If brightly lit areas are more important, make a reading with the meter held so that the cell is lit in the same way as that part of the scene.

Metering from up close gives good results when contrast is high and the most important part of the scene is much darker or much lighter than its surroundings. With a meter built into a camera, move in until the main subject fills the viewfinder (be careful not to block the light on the subject). Make the reading, set the shutter speed and aperture, then move back to the original position to take the picture. With an automatic camera, set the camera for manual operation or override the automatic exposure (see page 115).

With a hand-held, reflected-light meter, move in close enough to meter mostly the main subject, but not so close that you block the light. A spot meter (page 122), which reads a very narrow angle, can be used to meter a small part of a scene from farther away.

	chemicals needed	procedure	
preparation		Mix the chemical stock solutions needed and dilute to working strength. Carefully follow manufacturer's recommendations for development time and temperature.	Ideally, the developer should be exactly at the recommended temperature, with the other solutions no more than 1 or 2 degrees different. See page 130 for more on mixing and storing chemicals.
loading film		In total darkness, load film onto developing reel. Put reeled film into empty, dry tank and close with light-tight cover.	
water presoak (optional)		Before adding developer, fill tank with plain water at the same temperature as the developer. Agitate gently for one minute, then drain and fill tank with developer. Extend development time by 10 percent to compensate for the time it takes for the water that has soaked into the emulsion to be replaced by developer.	Although this optional step is commonly used, Kodak reports some possible problems. The advantages are that the water washes off any dust that may be on the negative, and it wets the emulsion uniformly, which in some cases may help prevent uneven development or air bells. However, Kodak not only doesn't recommend presoaking of roll films, it warns that in some cases (such as with Technical Pan 2415 film) a presoak can *cause* uneven development.
development	Use a developer suitable for film. All-purpose developers (such as Kodak D-76 or HC-110, Ilford ID-11, Ethol TEC or UFG, Edwal FG7) work well for most uses. High-energy developers (such as Acufine and Diafine) are useful for film exposed at low light levels (*see page 148*). Fine-grain developers (such as Kodak Microdol-X, Ilford Microphen, and Edwal Super 20 and TEC) produce finer grain but with some loss in contrast and apparent sharpness. Sometimes dilution can be varied to adjust grain or sharpness; see manufacturer's data.	Begin development by rapping the bottom of the tank on a hard surface to dislodge air bubbles. Thereafter, agitate once every 30 sec by inverting the tank 5 times, with each inversion taking about 1 sec. Shortly before development time is over, pour out developer through pouring opening of cover. DO NOT REMOVE COVER UNTIL FILM IS FIXED.	
stop bath	Some photographers use a plain water rinse for a stop bath; others prefer a dilute solution of acetic acid (about 1 oz 28% acetic acid per quart of water). An indicator-type stop bath changes color when it is exhausted, but some photographers simply mix the stop bath fresh each time.	Quickly fill tank through pouring opening with stop bath. Replace cap over pouring opening and agitate for 30 sec. Pour out.	
fixing	Fresh fixer will process about 25 rolls of film per quart of working solution. The age of the solution also affects its strength. An inexpensive testing solution is available that indicates when fixer should be discarded.	Fill tank through pouring opening with fixer. Agitate for 30 sec, then at 1-min intervals for the recommended time.	The tank cover can be removed about halfway through the fixing process.
washing aid (optional)	A washing aid (also called hypo neutralizer or clearing agent) promotes more effective washing in less time than washing in water alone. Discard after about 10 rolls of film have been treated per quart of working solution (or as directed).	Rinse in running water for 30 sec, then follow manufacturer's data for treatment. With Kodak Hypo Clearing Agent: 2-min immersion with agitation for first 30 sec, then occasional agitation thereafter.	
washing	A wetting agent, such as Kodak Photo-Flo, is an optional treatment that helps prevent water spots, especially in hard-water areas. Mix with distilled water.	Wash 30 min (much less if a washing aid is used; follow manufacturer's data). Then immerse in a wetting agent for 30 sec without agitation.	Water should run at least fast enough to completely fill the container several times in 5 min. Dump water several times as well.
drying		Hang to dry in dust-free place with clip on bottom of film to prevent curling. When dry, cut film into convenient lengths and store in negative envelopes.	

How Developer and Fixer Affect a Negative

Photo supply stores sell a variety of developers that only need to be dissolved in water; all the chemicals have been added in the proper amount. But a general knowledge of developer chemicals is useful background information since you may sometimes mix a developer from a formula.

The most important ingredient in any developer formula is the **reducing agent,** also called the developing agent. Its job is to free metallic silver from the emulsion's crystals so it can form the image. These crystals contain silver atoms combined with halides such as bromine in light-sensitive compounds, in this case silver bromide. When struck by light during an exposure, the silver bromide crystals undergo a partial chemical change. The exposed crystals (forming the latent image) provide the developing agent with a ready-made working site. The reducer cracks the exposed crystals into their components: metallic silver, which stays to form the dark parts of the image (*see pictures, this page*), and bromine, which unites chemically with the developer. In a chromagenic film, the silver is later replaced by dyes, but the original silver development is the same.

Some reducing agents are used alone, but often two together assist each other. Many formulas consist of a combination of the compounds Metol and hydroquinone (called M.Q. formulas). The Metol improves film speed and tonal gradation while the hydroquinone increases density and contrast. Some other reducing agents are glycin and para-aminophenol (in fine-grain formulas) and phenidone (like Metol but less irritating to the skin).

Since most reducing agents work only in an alkaline solution, an alkaline salt such as borax or sodium carbonate is usually added as an **accelerator.** Some developers are so active that they will develop the unexposed as well as the exposed parts of the emulsion, thus fogging the negative; to prevent this, a **restrainer,** usually potassium bromide, is added to some formulas. The bromide that is released by the reducing agent from the silver bromide crystals also has a restraining effect. Finally, since exposure to oxygen in the atmosphere causes a developer to lose its effectiveness, a **preservative** such as sodium sulfite may be added to prevent oxidation.

undeveloped silver bromide crystals

developed 10 seconds

developed 1 minute

Electron microscope pictures of emulsions show how exposed crystals of silver bromide (magnified 5,000×) are converted to pure silver during development. At first (top) the crystals show no activity (dark specks on some crystals are caused by the microscope procedure). After 10 sec, parts of two small clusters (arrows) have been converted to dark silver. After a minute, about half the crystals are developed, forming strands of silver. In the bottom picture all exposed crystals are developed; undeveloped crystals have been removed by fixer solution, and the strands now form the negative image.

developed 5 minutes and fixed

not enough fixing

normal fixing

too much fixing

After the developer has done its work, the image on the negative is visible but very perishable. If exposed to light, the entire negative will turn dark. To prevent this, the **fixer** sets the image permanently on the film.

The fixing agent is needed because the negative image contains leftover crystals of silver bromide. These crystals were part of shadow areas in the image, so were not exposed, but they are still light sensitive and, if allowed to remain, will darken the negative (*above left*). The fixer prevents this by dissolving these crystals out of the emulsion.

The active agent in fixer is sodium thiosulfate. (The early name for this substance was sodium hyposulfite, and **hypo** is still a common name for fixer.) Ammonium thiosulfate, a fast-acting

fixer, can also be used. A **hardener** is generally part of the fixer solution. This prevents the film emulsion from becoming so soft or swollen that it is damaged during the washing that follows fixing.

Follow fixer instructions carefully. If used correctly, the fixer dissolves only the unexposed crystals of silver bromide and does not affect the metallic silver making up the image itself. But if the film is left too long in the fixer the image will eventually bleach (*above right*).

Ordinarily, however, the danger is not too much fixing but too little. If the film is not left in the fixer long enough, if it is not agitated during fixing, or if the fixer is exhausted, silver bromide crystals are left undissolved and will later darken the film.

How Time and Temperature Affect Development

The longer the developer is allowed to act on the film, the greater the number of crystals converted to metallic silver and the darker the negative becomes (*opposite page, left column*). But the pictures show that the **density** of silver in the image did not increase uniformly. Increasing the development time caused a great deal of change in those parts of the negative that received the most exposure (the bright areas in the original scene—sky and house roofs). It caused some changes in those areas that received moderate exposure (the midtones—grass and side of large house), but only a little change where the negative received the least exposure (the shadow areas—trees and windows). In any negative, lengthening or shortening development time has a marked effect on **contrast**—the relationship between light and dark tones.

Development time controls contrast and density because of the way that film emulsion is constructed. The crystals of silver bromide that will develop into the negative image lie both on and below the surface of the emulsion. As exposure increases, the number of exposed crystals and their depth in the emulsion also increase. When the developer goes to work, it gets at the surface crystals immediately but needs extra time to soak into the emulsion and develop the crystals below the surface, as illustrated in the photomicrographs on this page. Thus the total amount of time the developer is allowed to work determines how deeply it penetrates and how densely it develops the exposed crystals, while the original exposure determines how many crystals are available to be developed. See pages 144–145 for examples of how exposure and development time both affect the negative.

The rate of development changes during the process, as is shown in the examples opposite (*left column*). During the first seconds, before the solution has soaked into the emulsion, activity is very slow; the strongest highlights have barely begun to show up (*top*). Soon the solution soaks in enough to develop many of the exposed crystals; during this period a doubling of the development time will double the density of the negative (*center*). Still later, after most of the exposed crystals have been developed, the pace slows down again so that a tripling, or more, of the time adds proportionately less density than it did before (*bottom*).

Developer temperature also affects the rate of development. Most photographic chemicals and even the wash water take longer to work as their temperatures drop. All solutions work faster at higher temperatures, but at around 80° F (27° C), the gelatin emulsion of the film begins to soften and becomes very easily damaged. The effects of temperature on the rate of development are shown on the opposite page.

Time-and-temperature charts that accompany films and developers show the recommended development times at various temperatures—the higher the temperature, the shorter the development time needed (*see chart at right*). The temperature generally recommended is 68° F (20° C); this temperature combines the most efficient chemical activity with the least softening of the film emulsion and is a practical temperature to maintain in the average darkroom. Higher temperatures may be recommended with very dilute developers. A higher temperature can be used when the tap water is very warm, as it is in many areas during the summer.

developed for 2 minutes **developed for 5 minutes** **developed for 15 minutes**

Grains of silver, enlarged about 2,500× in this cross section of film emulsion, get denser as development is extended. Grains near the surface (top) form first and grow in size. As developer soaks down, subsurface grains form.

KODAK TRI-X PAN FILM

KODAK Packaged Developers	Developing Times (in Minutes)*									
	SMALL TANK—(Agitation at 30-Second Intervals)					LARGE TANK—(Agitation at 1-Minute Intervals)				
	65°F 18.5°C	68°F 20°C	70°F 21°C	72°F 22°C	75°F 24°C	65°F 18.5°C	68°F 20°C	70°F 21°C	72°F 22°C	75°F 24°C
HC-110 (Dilution B)	8½	7½	6½	6	5	9½	8½	8	7½	6½
D-76	9	8	7½	6½	5½	10	9	8	7	6
D-76 (1:1)	11	10	9½	9	8	13	12	11	10	9
MICRODOL-X	11	10	9½	9	8	13	12	11	10	9
MICRODOL-X (1:3)	—	—	15	14	13	—	—	17	16	15
DK-50 (1:1)	7	6	5½	5	4½	7½	6½	6	5½	5
HC-110 (Dilution A)	4½	3¾	3¼	3	2½	4¾	4¼	4	3¾	3¼

*Avoid development times of less than 5 minutes if possible, because poor uniformity may result.
Note: Do not use developers containing silver halide solvents.

A time-and-temperature chart for development is provided by film manufacturers. 68° F (20° C), shown in boldface type, is the recommended temperature to be used with the developers listed on the left of the chart. The exception on this chart is with Microdol-X at high dilution, for which the recommended temperature increases to 75° F (24° C). A change in temperature of even a few degrees can cause a significant change in the rate of development and therefore requires a change in the development time. For best results all the solutions—developer, stop bath, fixer, and wash water—should be within a few degrees of each other.

negative developed for 45 seconds

negative developed at 40° F

negative developed for 7½ minutes

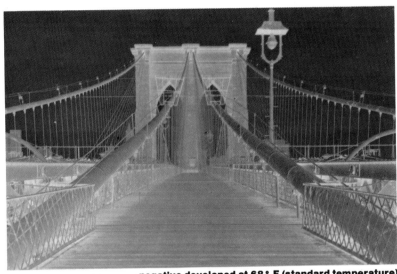

negative developed at 68° F (standard temperature)

negative developed for 30 minutes

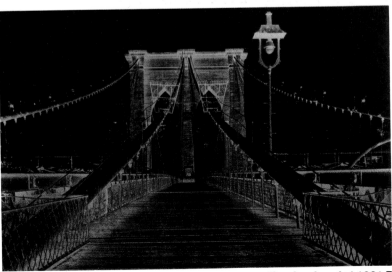

negative developed at 100° F

Exposure and Development: Under, Normal, Over

After developing a roll of film, how do you evaluate it? The negatives may look too pale and thin. Were they underexposed or could something have gone wrong in development so that the negatives were underdeveloped? They may look too dark and dense. Were they overexposed or overdeveloped? Comparing the negatives with those at the right will help in evaluating them. The pictures show a **ringaround sequence** of variations in exposure and development.

Notice that overdeveloping film that was underexposed will not produce a negative of normal density and contrast. Nor will underdeveloping cure mistakenly overexposed film. However, under- or overexposed negatives can be improved to a certain extent. By increasing development time, density can be added in the highlights and to a lesser extent in the midtones of a negative that would be too thin because of underexposure. By decreasing development time, density can be decreased —again mostly in the highlights, but somewhat in the midtones—in a negative that would otherwise be too dense from overexposure. But there is a price for this—a change in contrast and sometimes increased graininess, or a loss of detail and sharpness.

Underexposed, underdeveloped. *Little detail in shadow areas; highlights too thin. Overall very thin with low contrast.*

Underexposed, normally developed. *Little detail in shadow areas. Somewhat low contrast.*

One of the best ways to learn how a particular film-developer combination responds to variations in exposure and development is to make a series of negatives like these. You may find, for example, that the combination you are using has very little tolerance for errors in exposure. Or perhaps it increases contrast considerably with overdevelopment. Try the series under different lighting conditions—in soft, flat light in the shade or when the sky is overcast and in contrasty light on a brilliant, sunny day when there are deep shadows and bright highlights. The normally developed negatives were developed at the manufacturer's suggested time and temperature, the overdeveloped negatives for twice the suggested time, the underdeveloped negatives for half the time. The overexposed negatives were given 1½ stops more than the normal exposure, the underexposed negatives 1½ stops less.

Underexposed, overdeveloped. *Little detail in shadow areas; highlights of normal density. Excessive contrast.*

Normally exposed, underdeveloped. *Good shadow detail. Overall reduction in contrast.*

Overexposed, underdeveloped. *Average density. Low overall contrast. Some loss of sharpness in highlights noticeable in an enlargement.*

Normally exposed, normally developed. *Good separation in all tonal values. Prints on normal contrast paper. Normal grain for film.*

Overexposed, normally developed. *Highlights too dense. Density increased overall. Grain increased. Some loss of sharpness in an enlargement.*

Normally exposed, overdeveloped. *Good shadow detail; too much density in highlights. Excessive contrast.*

Overexposed, overdeveloped. *Lack of separation in highlights. Excessively dense. Quite grainy. Distinct loss of sharpness in an enlargement.*

The Importance of Proper Agitation and Fresh Solutions

The purpose of **agitation** (as in *step 10, page 135*) is to move the solution inside the developing tank so that a steady supply of fresh chemicals reaches the emulsion at regular intervals. Agitation is vital while the film is in the developer and is also important during later processing stages. Too little or too much agitation can cause problems, as shown in the pictures below.

Inadequate agitation in the developer causes the chemicals next to the emulsion, after performing their share of the chemical reaction, to stop working and form a stagnant area where development activity slows down and eventually stops. Exhausted chemicals are also heavier than the rest of the solution and will slowly sink to the bottom of the tank, causing what is called bromide drag—streaks of uneven development

as the exhausted chemicals slide down the surface of the film (*below left*).

Too much agitation creates problems even more often than too little agitation. In addition to general overdevelopment, turbulence patterns force extra quantities of fresh developer along the edges of the film, causing uneven development (*below right*).

To avoid these problems, agitate gently at regular intervals. A pattern often recommended is to agitate for 5 out of every 30 seconds. Follow the manufacturer's directions if another pattern is recommended for a specific product. If possible, agitate in two or more different directions during each agitation period. This avoids setting up a repetitive pattern of flow across the face of the film. If you are developing one reel of film in a two-reel tank, put in

an extra empty reel so that the loaded one does not bounce up and down excessively.

You may be tempted some day to try to process one or two more rolls or sheets of film in **exhausted developer or fixer** rather than remixing fresh solutions, but doing so is a mistake, as shown on the opposite page. A properly exposed negative can be damaged or completely ruined because the chemicals in the solutions are exhausted from overuse or aging. Prevention is easy enough: never use exhausted developer or fixer. Developer manufacturers specify how much film may be processed per quart of solution and, usually, how long the solution can be stored. Fixers can be checked for strength with an inexpensive testing solution.

An exhausted developer produces underdeveloped negatives; there is just not enough active developing agent left to build up density. With partially exhausted developer, details, particularly in shadow areas, may be weakened, but with greater exhaustion the image is all but lost (opposite, left). Damage may be worse than that caused by underdevelopment because impurities in the exhausted solution may stain the negative.

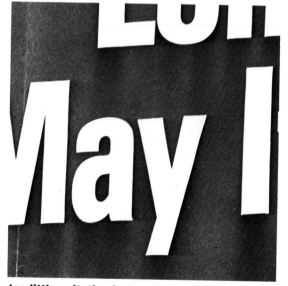

too little agitation in developer

too much agitation in developer

An exhausted fixer produces a negative (opposite, left) that seems overdeveloped compared to a normal one. The solution is unable to dissolve unexposed silver bromide crystals from the negative. These leftover crystals turn dark and increase density in the negative. As shadow areas (in the model's hair, for example) darken, the overall image grows flat; details such as individual strands of hair are obscured and a grayish density fogs the entire negative, even clouding unexposed borders.

The photographs above show some of the problems caused by poor agitation of film during development. Above left, the film was not agitated enough. Exhausted chemicals from dense areas of the negative (the white letters in the positive print shown here) slid down the surface of the film, causing streaks of uneven development below the letters. Above right, a roll of film was agitated too much and too vigorously. Fresh developer forced along the spirals of the developing reel caused the edges of the film to be overdeveloped (denser in the negative) and consequently lighter in the print.

developer exhaustion

negative developed in
exhausted solution

negative developed in
fresh solution

Film can fade or turn yellow if it is not thoroughly washed after fixing. The cause of this damage is the fixer itself. The fixing solution contains dissolved sulfur compounds that tarnish the silver image of the negative if they are not removed. It is exactly the same kind of reaction that causes silverware to tarnish. The unexposed silver compounds that are dissolved in the fixer will tarnish too. Worse still, the tarnish often becomes soluble in the moisture in the air, gradually causing the negative image to dissolve and fade.

Another cause of damage to negatives—one that shows immediately—is careless drying (*shown below*). Just-washed film is delicate and easily scratched. Dust clings to wet film, sometimes implants itself in the emulsion, and can be impossible to remove even with rewashing.

Careful washing and drying is worth the effort involved. Water for washing must be clean, near the temperature of the earlier solutions, and kept constantly moving across the surface of the film to flush away fixer that has soaked in. Dump the water and refill the tank often; fixer is heavier than water and accumulates at the bottom of the tank. Although much of the fixer can be washed away with water alone if the film is washed long enough, it is best to use a **washing aid** (also called hypo neutralizer or clearing agent). In addition to working more efficiently than plain water, it greatly reduces washing time and avoids the swelling caused by a long washing period.

Damage during drying is even easier to avoid. Handle the film as little as possible while it is wet and hang to dry in a clean place free from drafts and temperature changes.

fixer exhaustion

negative fixed in
exhausted solution

negative fixed in
fresh solution

carelessly handled negative

normal negative

Special Development Techniques

A standard developer used at the time and temperature recommended by the manufacturer will generally give good results. But you may encounter special situations for which you want to depart from the standard procedure.

One common situation arises when the light is too dim for a reasonably fast shutter speed, even with the aperture wide open. In that case, you can **push** the film—shoot at a higher-than-normal film speed rating and then adjust the development accordingly. You can either increase the development time or temperature so that it is greater than normal, or use a special high-energy developer such as Acufine, Diafine, or Microphen. Some developers can be used at concentrations that permit shooting at higher-than-normal film speeds—Edwal FG7 diluted 1:3, for example. (*See chart at right.*)

Generally, increasing the development time by 50 percent will let you double the film speed rating—for example, letting you shoot an ISO/ASA 400 film at ISO/ASA 800, an increase of one stop. Kodak recommends this as the maximum practical increase. However, depending on your purpose, you may find that even more of an increase produces satisfactory results.

Push processing does not actually increase the film speed. You are, in effect, underexposing and overdeveloping the film. The pictures on pages 144–145 show that this produces a negative with more contrast than a normally exposed, normally developed negative. You can expect a certain loss of detail in shadow areas when compared to a normal negative. Actually, this is caused by too little exposure and not by the increased development; the exposure simply was not great enough for the shadow details to register on the film. In addition, the print will probably be grainier and somewhat less sharp than a print from a

Push Processing

film (ISO/ASA 400) and developer	to double film speed to 800	to quadruple film speed to 1600
Agfapan Rodinal	17½ min at 68° F (20° C) (diluted 1:100)	18½ min at 68° F (diluted 1:50)
Ilford HP5 Microphen	8 min at 68° F	9½–12 min at 68° F
Kodak Tri-X Pan D-76	12 min at 68° F	13 min at 75° F (24° C)
HC-110 (diluted 1:15)	6 min at 68° F	8 min at 68° F

Also try high-energy developers, such as Acufine. Specifications are suggestions only; for best results make your own tests.

When taking pictures in dim light, many photographers deliberately underexpose the film—that is, they assume its film speed is double or even quadruple the normal rating—and then compensate by giving it special treatment during development. This is called "pushing." It can be done as the chart above shows: by increasing development time in a normal developer; by increasing temperature in a normal developer; or by switching to a high-energy developer. Pushing film is a valuable technique, but it increases graininess and contrast and decreases shadow detail. This is not very serious if the film speed is doubled. Beyond that, quality begins to fall off fast, especially with small negatives (see prints at right).

normal exposure and development

film pushed to four times normal ASA

high-contrast scene, regular development

Low-Contrast Development

Two-bath development: D-23 and Kodalk

First bath: D-23
  Mix in the order given:

Water 125° F (52° C)	750 cc (24 oz)
Metol (Kodak Elon)	7.5 gm (0.25 oz)
Sodium sulfite (desiccated)	100 gm (3.25 oz)
Water to make	1000 cc (32 oz)

Second bath: 1% Kodalk solution

Kodalk Balanced Alkali	10 gm (0.3 oz)
Water to make	1000 cc (32 oz)

Bring solutions to 68° F (20° C). Place film in first bath and agitate continuously for first 30 sec, then for 5 out of every 30 sec. Remove film from first bath and place gently, without agitation, in second bath. When developing roll film, invert reel in second bath after 15 sec (this helps prevent uneven development).

For moderate reduction of contrast:
  First bath: 6 min   Second bath: 3 min
For greater reduction of contrast, shorten the time in the first bath:
  First bath: 4 min   Second bath: 3 min

Water-bath development: D-76 and water

First bath: Kodak D-76 full strength
Second bath: plain water

Bring solutions to 68° F (20° C). Round 1: place film in developer and agitate continuously for 30 sec, then for 5 out of every 30 sec. After 1 min, place film gently, without agitation, in water.

Round 1:

Developer	1 min
Water	2 min

Round 2 (and additional rounds):

Developer	30 sec
Water	2 min

Increasing the number of times round 2 is repeated will raise the overall density of the negative without unduly increasing the contrast. Reverse the reel on each round when developing roll film.

When photographing in high-contrast situations you can reduce the contrast of the negative by using a two-bath or water-bath developer. In the two procedures above, the negative is partially developed in the first solution. In the second solution, the shadow areas continue developing while the highlight areas quickly exhaust the available developing agents and stop development. The result is reduced density in the highlights and reduced contrast. The times given above are suggestions only.

high-contrast scene, low-contrast development

normal negative (compare the two prints at right); the greater the enlargement, the more this is noticeable. But these disadvantages are offset by the increase in the working film speed.

Development time can be changed to adjust the contrast of the negative. The contrast of a flat scene (where the important highlight areas meter within two or three stops of the important shadow areas) can be strengthened by increasing the development time. If you think a scene will be too flat, you can try exposing it normally and then developing it for one and one-half times the normal development time. Excessive contrast in a scene (bright areas meter six or more stops from dark ones) can be reduced by decreasing the development time to about two-thirds the normal time. See also information on the Zone System (*pages 313–325*).

Two-bath development and **water-bath development** both decrease contrast (*see box at left*). In the first bath of the two-bath method, the film emulsion absorbs developing agents that are activated in the second bath, an alkaline solution. But the developing agents are quickly exhausted in the highlight areas and, since there is no new developer to replace them, stop working. The developing agents in the shadow areas continue working longer because there are not so many exposed silver bromide crystals to use them up. The result is a compensating effect—the shadows receive more development than the highlights and contrast is reduced. In water-bath development, the film is partially developed in the first solution, then transferred to a tank of plain water.

For two-bath or water-bath development to work, the emulsion must be relatively thick or it will not absorb enough developer. A thick-emulsion film like Tri-X responds better than a thin-emulsion film like Panatomic-X.

Intensification and Reduction

A completely processed negative (*top right*) that is too dense or too thin to make an acceptable print can sometimes be improved. Thin negatives can be made darker (*middle right*) by a process called intensification. A very dense negative can be thinned down (*bottom right*) by a solution called a reducer (not the same as the reducing agent in film developer). The processes are relatively easy since they are carried out with regular room lighting. There are, however, disadvantages. Intensification increases grain—quite noticeably in an enlargement from a small negative. And both processes involve some danger of staining or otherwise ruining the negative. Unfortunately, the only negatives worth the trouble of intensification or reduction are usually so important that ruining them is worse than having a poor print. Making the best print you can before you treat the negative in any way is good insurance against total loss.

Intensification strengthens density by adding minute particles of another metal (such as chromium) on top of the silver that already forms the negative image. The amount of intensification is usually proportional to the existing amount of silver, which means that the denser (highlight) areas will be intensified more than the thinner (shadow) areas. The result is a greater separation between light and dark parts of the negative and an increase in contrast. Intensification improves a negative that is thin because of underdevelopment or moderate underexposure. It probably won't help a negative that is seriously underexposed, since it can't put back detail that isn't there in the first place.

Reduction decreases the density of a negative by dissolving some of the metallic silver that forms the image. A cutting or subtractive reducer removes approximately equal amounts of silver from all parts of the image and has little or no effect on contrast; it is useful for treating fogged or overexposed negatives. A proportional reducer decreases density in proportion to the existing amount of silver, thus reducing contrast; this is useful for a negative that has too much contrast because of overdevelopment. A super-proportional reducer removes much more silver from the dense areas than it does from the thin areas, thus reducing contrast without affecting the thinner areas of the negative; this would improve an overdeveloped negative of a contrasty subject.

You can purchase intensifiers and reducers or mix them yourself. Farmer's Reducer, for example, is a subtractive reducer, available in photo supply stores, that can be used either for allover reduction of negative density or for local reduction of smaller areas in negatives or prints. Many types of reducers and intensifiers, including Farmer's Reducer, can be mixed from formulas; the Photo-Lab-Index (*see Bibliography*) gives a number of these.

normally developed negative

underdeveloped negative

intensified negative

overdeveloped negative

reduced negative

film stuck together

not enough developer

reticulation

Troubleshooting Negative Problems

If spots, stains, or other ailments cause problems with your negatives, check below. You may find a simple way to prevent such problems from happening again. See also Troubleshooting Camera and Lens Problems (page 83), Printing Problems (page 181), and Flash Problems (page 286).

Opaque patches in negative (light in print) or clear in negative (dark in print)

Cause: *Winding two loops of film onto one loop of developing reel or squeezing the reeled film so that one loop remains in contact with another. This keeps chemicals from reaching the film emulsion at the point of contact. Most often the area will be totally unprocessed and opaque (see illustration, top). It will be clear if the film separates during fixing.*

Prevention: *Wind film on the developing reel carefully. If the winding doesn't proceed smoothly, unwind a few loops and start again.*

Crescent-shaped "cinch" marks, dark in the negative, light in a print

Cause: *Crimping or creasing the film while loading it onto the developing reel.*

Prevention: *Handle film with care, especially if you have trouble loading it onto a developing reel and have to reel it on and off several times. Bow the film just enough to feed it onto the reel but not so much that the film buckles. Spotting can improve a print that shows marks.*

Every frame on the roll only partially developed, with part lighter than rest of negative image, darker in print.

(May not be developed at all if you use a developing tank that is not inverted during agitation.)

Cause: *Not enough developer to cover film (see illustration, center).*

Prevention: *Check amount of developer needed to cover reel (or reels, in a tank that holds more than one) or fill tank to overflowing when you add developer.*

Small, round clear spots in negative, dark spots in print

Cause: *Air bells—bubbles of air on surface of film.*

Prevention: *Tap the tank vigorously at start of development period (see page 135, step 10).*

Reticulation (image appears crinkled or cracked overall)

Cause: *Extreme variations in temperatures of processing solutions, such as very warm developer and very cold fixer (see illustration, bottom). Less-extreme variations can cause increased graininess.*

Prevention: *Keep all solutions, from developer to wash, at or within a few degrees of the same temperature.*

Faint, watery looking marks

Cause: *Uneven drying or water splashed on film during drying.*

Prevention: *Treat film in a wetting solution, such as Kodak Photo-Flo, just before hanging up to dry. Don't let water from one roll of film drip onto another when hanging to dry. Rewashing the damaged film or spotting the print may help.*

Specks, scratches, fingerprints

Cause: *Dust and dirt, careless handling (see page 147).*

Overdeveloped areas around sprocket holes, dark on film, light in print

Cause: *Too much agitation in developer (see page 146).*

Uneven, streaky development

Cause: *Too little agitation in developer (see page 146).*

Thin-looking, too-light negative

Cause: *Probably underexposed film but could be exhausted developer (see pages 146–147), developer time too short, or temperature too low (see pages 142–143). Pages 144–145 show the effects of changing exposure versus development.*

Dense-looking, too-dark negative

Cause: *Probably overexposed film but could be developer time too long or temperature too high (see pages 142–143). See also pages 144–145.*

Cloudy look to negative overall

Cause: *Inadequate fixing (see pages 141 and 146–147), possibly old, light-struck, or X-ray-damaged film.*

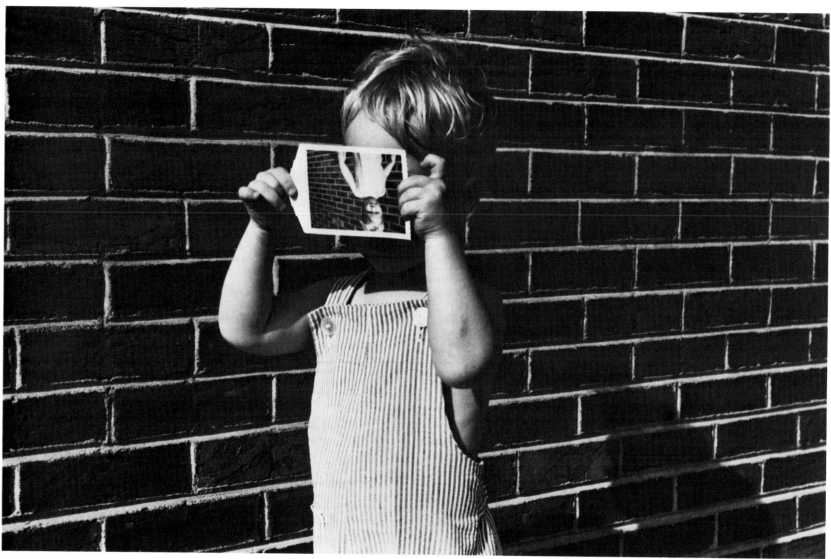

KEN JOSEPHSON: *Matthew*, 1965

Kenneth Josephson often plays with what he calls the "special reality of photographs." Here a child is transforming a picture of himself into a camera so that he can play photographer. Josephson, in addition to making a charming photograph of a child, brings to our attention some grown-up make-believe. We often unthinkingly look at photographs as if they were substitutes for reality, so that a picture of Michael Jackson, for example, replaces seeing the performer in person. But when the photograph of this child replaces part of his face, it becomes more difficult to ignore that both are abstractions: the picture of the boy is no more real than the picture of the snapshot of the boy.

152

7

Printing the Positive

negative

positive

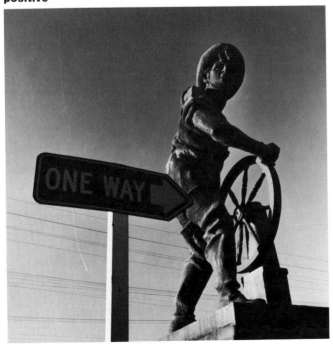

Printmaking is one of the most pleasurable parts of photography. Unlike film development, which requires rigid control, printmaking lends itself to leisurely creation. During printing you make a number of decisions that determine how the print will look. Mistakes are inevitable at first, but a wrong choice can be easily corrected by simply making another print.

Like film, printing paper is coated with a light-sensitive emulsion containing crystals of silver atoms combined with bromine or chlorine atoms or both. Light is passed through the negative and onto the paper. After exposure, the paper is placed in a developer where chemical action converts into metallic silver those crystals in the emulsion that have been exposed to light. A stop bath halts the action of the developer; a fixer removes undeveloped and unexposed crystals; finally the print is washed and dried.

The negative is a reversal of the tones in the original scene. Where the scene was bright, the negative contains many dense, dark grains of silver. These dense areas hold back light from the paper, prevent the formation of silver in the paper's emulsion, and so create a bright area in the print corresponding to the bright area in the scene. Where the scene was dark, the negative is thin or even clear. It passes much light to the paper so that dark silver is formed in the emulsion, resulting in a dark area in the print. Compare the illustrations on this page.

The Darkroom

1 | **enlarger**

2 | **printing paper**

3 | **contact-printing frame**

4 | **enlarger timer**

5 | **antistatic cleaning cloth**

6 | **dodging and burning-in tools**

7 | **negatives**

8 | **antistatic cleaning brush**

9 | **magnifier**

10 | **printing-paper easel**

Darkrooms are usually set up with dry and wet sides, although printmaking procedures vary somewhat depending on whether you are using your own equipment or sharing facilities in a school.

On the **dry side** (*materials shown above*), photographic paper is exposed to make a print. Cleanliness as well as dryness is important because chemical contamination can create even more problems in printing than in negative development. A typical printing session involves trips from enlarger to developing trays and back again, and traces of chemicals can end up where they don't belong, causing streaks, spots, and other problems.

The commonest problem on the dry side is **dust.** Every dust speck on your negative produces a white spot on your print. Remove dust with an antistatic brush or a rubber air blower. Handle negatives by their edges to avoid fingerprints. If cleaning a negative is necessary, use a liquid film cleaner. Dust and fingerprints on enlarger lenses or condensers decrease the contrast and detail in a print. Clean them as you would a camera lens (*page 85*).

11 | **three 8 × 10 trays,
one 11 × 14 washing tray**

12 | **blotters or other means
of drying**

13 | **safelight**

14 | **safelight filter**

15 | **chemical solutions**

16 | **graduate**

17 | **timer**

18 | **washing siphon**

19 | **sponge**

20 | **squeegee**

21 | **developer tongs**

22 | **stop bath—fixer tongs**

On the **wet side** of the darkroom (*materials shown above*), the exposed paper is processed in chemicals similar to those used for developing negatives. See page 171 for a summary of the process.

Printing paper is developed under **safelight,** not ordinary room light. The paper is sensitive to only a portion—usually the blue end—of the light spectrum. A safelight produces enough light for you to see what you are doing, but not so much that the paper becomes fogged with unwanted exposure. A suitable safelight for most papers is a 15-watt bulb in a fixture covered with a light amber filter (such as a DuPont S-55X or Wratten OC) placed at least four feet from working surfaces. Check the manufacturer's instructions if you use any special-purpose papers; safelight filters vary for different materials.

A safelight is not bright enough for you to judge accurately the quality of a print after it has been developed and fixed. You will want to do that under ordinary room light. If you carry a wet print away from the wet side of the darkroom, put it in an empty tray so it doesn't drip.

The Enlarger: Basic Tool of the Printmaker

An **enlarger** can produce a print of any size—larger, smaller, or the same size as a negative, so it is sometimes more accurately called a projection printer. Most often, however, it is used to enlarge an image. Although an enlarger is a relatively simple machine, it is a vital link in the photographic process; the best camera in the world will not give good pictures if they are printed by an enlarger that shakes when touched, has a poor lens, or tends to slip out of focus or alignment.

An enlarger operates like a slide projector mounted vertically on a column. Light from an enclosed lamp shines through a negative and is then focused by a lens to expose an image of the negative on printing paper placed at the foot of the enlarger column. Image size is set by changing the distance from the enlarger head (the housing containing lamp, negative, and lens) to the paper; the greater the distance, the larger the image. The image is focused by changing the distance between the lens and the negative. The exposure time is controlled by a timer. To regulate the intensity of the light, the lens has a diaphragm aperture with f-stops like those on a camera lens.

An enlarger should spread light rays uniformly over the negative. It can do this in several ways. In a **diffusion enlarger,** a sheet of opal glass (a cloudy, translucent glass) is placed beneath the light source to scatter the light evenly over the negative. In a **condenser enlarger,** lenses gather the rays from the light source and send them straight through the negative. Sometimes a combination of the two systems is used (*see diagrams, right*).

Condensers must be matched to negative and lens for even illumination. Depending on the enlarger, this is done by changing the position of the negative or condensers or by using condensers of different sizes.

The most noticeable difference between diffusion and condenser enlargers is in contrast. A diffusion enlarger produces about one grade less contrast than a condenser enlarger (*see pages 172–177 for more about contrast*). A diffusion system has the advantage of minimizing faults in the negative such as minor scratches, dust spots, and grain by lessening the sharp contrast between, for example, a dust speck and its immediately surrounding area. Some photographers believe that this decreasing and smoothing of contrast can also result in a loss of fine detail and texture in a print, especially when a negative is greatly enlarged; however, many photographers find no evidence to support this. Many modern enlargers combine characteristics of both systems.

The focal length of the **enlarger lens** must be matched to the size of the negative, as shown in the chart at right. If the focal length is too short, it will not cover the full area of the negative, and the corners will be out of focus or, in extreme cases, vignetted and too light in the print. If the focal length is too long, the image will be magnified very little unless the enlarger head is raised very high.

The **light source** in an enlarger is usually a tungsten or quartz-halogen bulb, although in some diffusion enlargers a cold-cathode or cold light source (fluorescent tubing) is used. Fluorescent light is usually not recommended for use with variable contrast papers (*pages 176–177*) or color printing papers. See page 240 for information on enlargers for printing color.

In a diffusion enlarger, a sheet of cloudy glass scatters light from the lamp in many directions so that the negative will be uniformly illuminated. Many light rays overlap, so contrast in the print is softened.

A condenser enlarger uses two lenses to collect light and to concentrate it directly on the negative. Light rays go straight through and produce increased contrast.

A combination diffusion-condenser enlarger offers a compromise. Condenser lenses collect light and focus it through the negative; a sheet of ground glass diffuses the light somewhat and eliminates excessive contrast.

negative size	focal length of enlarger lens
35 mm	50–63 mm
2¼ × 2¼ inches	75–80 mm
2¼ × 2¾ inches	90–105 mm
4 × 5 inches	135–160 mm

1 | **The enlarger head** *contains the main working parts: light source, negative carrier, and lens. It is cranked up or down to set the size of the image.*

2 | **The lamp** *supplies the light to expose the printing paper; it is usually a tungsten bulb similar to a household lamp. Some enlargers contain tubular fluorescent lamps, which give a more diffuse light.*

3 | **The condenser,** *a pair of convex lenses, spreads light uniformly over the negative. In some types of enlargers, a different system—a flat piece of diffusing glass used alone or in combination with a condenser—serves the same purpose (see diagrams on opposite page).*

4 | **The negative carrier,** *which holds the negative flat and level, fits into an opening between the lens and condenser.*

5 | **A diaphragm,** *an adjustable opening like that in a camera lens, controls the amount of light passing through the lens.*

6 | **The lens** *bends light rays passing through the negative to form an enlarged image.*

7 | **The focusing control** *moves the lens up or down to focus the projected image. The type shown here—a geared wheel and track shifting a bellows-mounted lens—is common, but other kinds are used.*

8 | **The supporting column** *holds the enlarger head out over the base-board and printing paper and serves as a rail on which the head can be moved up or down.*

9 | **The height adjustment** *raises or lowers the entire enlarger head to set the image size. Instead of the geared wheel and track shown in the drawing, some enlargers have a clamp that slides on the supporting column and is tightened to hold the enlarger head at the desired position.*

10 | **The counterbalance** *compensates for the weight of the enlarger head, permitting it to be raised or lowered effortlessly.*

11 | **The baseboard** *is the foundation supporting the whole unit; it also holds the easel on which printing paper is placed.*

Printing Papers

The difference between matte and glossy surfaces is revealed in two prints of an architectural photograph. The picture at right, above, reproduced to show a matte effect, scatters reflected light and produces less intense blacks than the glossy print at left.

Black-and-white printing papers vary in texture, color, contrast and other characteristics (*see box, opposite*). Choices are extensive, but rather than buying a different type of paper every time, start with one type and explore its capabilities before trying others.

Many photographers prefer to use a smooth-surfaced, glossy paper because it has the greatest tonal range and brilliance. Prints are seen by reflected light, and a rough or matte finish scatters light and so decreases the tonal range between the darkest blacks and the whitest highlights.

Resin-coated (RC) papers require much less washing time than **fiber-base papers.** They are often used in school darkrooms and are also popular for contact sheets and general printing. However, many photographers do not use RC papers for their better prints because they prefer the tonality and surface quality of fiber-base papers. The latter are also better for long-term archival preservation, a factor primarily of interest if prints are sold to museums and photographic collectors.

Paper storage is important because stray light fogs paper, giving it an overall gray tinge. Time and heat do the same. Store paper in a light-tight box in a cool, dry place. Open a package of paper only under darkroom safelight. Most papers last about two years at room temperature, considerably longer if kept refrigerated.

Characteristics of Black-and-White Printing Papers

Photographic characteristics

Printing grade. *The contrast of the emulsion.* **Graded papers** *are available in packages of individual contrast grades ranging from grade 0 (very low contrast) through grade 5 (very high contrast). Grade 2 or 3 is used to print a negative of normal contrast. With* **variable-contrast papers,** *only one kind of paper is needed; contrast is changed by changing filtration on the enlarger. The range of contrast is not as great with variable-contrast papers as with graded papers—about the equivalent of grades 1 to 4 can be produced. See pages 172–177 for more about contrast.*

Speed. *The sensitivity of the emulsion to light. Papers designed solely for contact printing are slow—they require a large amount of light to expose them properly. Papers used for enlargements are faster since only a rather dim light reaches the paper during the projection of the image by the enlarger. Enlarging papers are also commonly used for contact prints.*

Color sensitivity. *The portion of the light spectrum to which the emulsion is sensitive. Papers are sensitive to the blue end of the spectrum; this makes it possible to work with them under a yellowish safelight. Variable-contrast papers are also somewhat green sensitive, with contrast being controlled by the color of the filter used on the enlarger. Panchromatic papers are sensitive to all parts of the spectrum; they are used to make black-and-white prints from color negatives.*

Latitude. *The amount that exposure or development of the paper can vary from the ideal and still produce a good print. Most printing papers (especially high-contrast papers) have little exposure latitude; even a slight change in exposure affects print quality. This is why test strips (pages 166–167) are useful in printing. Development latitude varies with different papers. Good latitude means that print density (darkness) can be increased or decreased somewhat by increasing or decreasing development time. Other papers have little development latitude; changing the development time to any extent causes uneven development, fogging, or staining of the print.*

Premium papers. *A few papers, which cost more than conventional papers, contain extra silver in the emulsion plus paper base whiteners. These papers are capable of producing richer blacks, cleaner whites, and a greater tonal range, but it takes some experience to utilize their capability fully. Brands include Agfa Portriga Rapid, Ilford Ilfobrom Galerie, Kodak Elite, Oriental New Seagull, and Unicolor Exhibition.*

Physical characteristics

Texture. *The surface roughness of the paper. Ranges from smooth to fine grain to rough. Some finishes resemble canvas, silk, or other materials. Smoother surfaces reveal finer details and any graininess of the negative more than rougher surfaces do.*

Gloss. *The surface sheen of the paper. Ranges from glossy (greatest shine) to lustre (medium shine) to matte (dull). Fiber-base glossy papers can be ferrotyped (page 188) for maximum sheen; resin-coated glossy papers air-dry to a very high sheen. The dark areas of glossy papers appear blacker than those of matte papers; therefore the contrast of glossy papers appears greater. Glossiness shows the maximum detail and grain in a print. Very high gloss (as from ferrotyping) can cause distracting reflections.*

Paper base tint. *The color of the paper stock. Ranges from pure white to off-white tints such as cream, ivory, or buff.*

Image tone. *The color of the silver deposit in the finished print. Ranges from warm (brown-black) to neutral to cold (blue-black). Can be emphasized by the print developer used; a developer that helps produce a noticeably warm or cold tone indicates this on the package.*

Weight. *The thickness of the paper stock. Fiber-base papers are available in single weight and double weight. Single-weight papers are suitable for contact sheets and small prints. Double-weight papers are easier to handle during processing and mounting of large prints. RC papers come in a medium-weight base that is between single and double weight.*

Size. *8 × 10 inches is standard. You can cut this into four 4 × 5-inch pieces for small prints. Some commonly available precut sizes include 4 × 5, 5 × 7, 11 × 14, 14 × 17, 16 × 20, and 20 × 24 inches. (Comparable European sizes range from 8.9 × 12.7 cm to 50.8 × 61 cm.)*

Resin coating. *A water-resistant coating applied to some papers. Resin-coated (RC) papers absorb very little moisture, so processing, washing and drying times are shorter than for fiber-base papers. They also dry flat and stay that way, unlike fiber-base papers, which tend to curl. Too much heat during drying or mounting RC papers can damage the surface; see manufacturer's directions.*

How to Process Prints
The Contact Sheet: A Whole Roll at Once

A **contact sheet** or **proof** is useful when you want to choose a negative to enlarge. In contact printing, negatives are pressed against a sheet of photographic paper and the two are exposed to light. The result is a print that is the same size as the negative.

Don't be tempted to skip the contact printing stage and select a negative to be enlarged by looking at the film itself. Pictures are often difficult to judge as negatives, and small size compounds the difficulty with 35mm negatives. If you made several shots of the same scene, they may differ only slightly from one another, so make contacts carefully enough to compare similar pictures. A contact print of a 35mm negative is too small for you to judge sharpness critically, but you will be able to make a first assessment of sharpness as well as of exposure, lighting, and other factors.

Contact sheets are easy to make. An entire roll (36 negatives of 35mm film or 12 negatives of 2¼ × 2¼ film) fits on a single sheet of 8 × 10 paper. The contact sheet then becomes a permanent record of negatives on that roll. The procedure for making a contact print shown on the following pages uses an enlarger as a light source. Another method uses a contact printer—a box containing a light and having a translucent surface on which the negatives and paper are placed.

1 │ set out trays and tongs

Four trays are needed—one each for developer, stop bath, and fixer plus one filled with water to hold prints after fixing until they are ready for washing. If you use tongs, you will need two pairs: one for the developer and one for stop bath and fixer. Do not interchange them. See page 171 for information about chemicals.

2 │ prepare the solutions

Solution temperatures are not as critical as in film development. Manufacturers often recommend about 68° F (20° C) for the developer, 65° to 75° F (18° to 24° C) for stop bath and fixer.

3 │ assemble the negatives

Collect the negatives to be printed. If you have used care in handling and storing them, they will be free of fingerprints and mostly free of dust.

4 | dust the negatives

Remove any dust from negatives with an antistatic brush or compressed air. There should be no fingerprints, but remove them if necessary with film cleaner.

5 | identify the emulsion side

Film curls toward the emulsion, which has a duller sheen than the film base. The emulsion side must face the paper during printing.

6 | clean the contact frame

Clean the printing-frame glass with water or cleaner sold for this purpose. A plain sheet of glass can be used if a printing frame is not available; tape the edges for safety.

7 | prepare to insert negatives

Open the cover of the contact frame all the way, taking care to keep your fingers from leaving marks on the glass; they may show on the print. Make sure no dampness remains from cleaning.

8 | place the negatives in the frame

In this printing frame, strips of negatives snap under clips on the glass cover. Face the emulsion side away from the glass, toward the paper.

9 | position the enlarger head

Switch on the enlarger lamp and raise the enlarger head until the light that is projected covers the entire contact frame. Switch the lamp off.

10 | adjust the lens aperture

Open the diaphragm on the enlarger lens to f/8 as a trial exposure. After developing and evaluating the print, you may need to change to another setting.

11 | set the timer

For an 8 × 10 test print of negatives of average density, turn the timer pointer to 5 sec as a starting point for a correct exposure.

12 | take a sheet of paper from the box

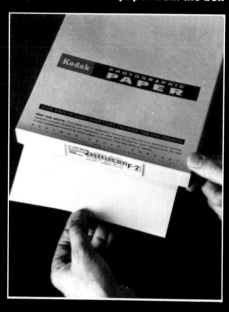

With room lights off and safelight on, remove from its box a sheet of printing paper, contrast grade 2. Close the box to keep out stray light.

13 | identify the emulsion side

Paper emulsion must face the negatives. The emulsion side is shinier and, with glossy papers, smoother than the backing side. Fiber-base paper curls toward emulsion; RC paper curls little.

14 | insert the paper into the frame

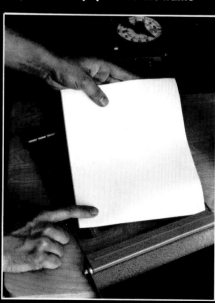

Slide the paper into the slot on the hinged side of the glass lid, making sure that the emulsion side of the paper faces the negatives.

15 | close the frame lid

Holding the printing paper in place with a finger, close the glass lid of the frame. Its weight holds it shut and presses negatives against paper.

16 | make the exposure

After placing the frame under the enlarger, press the timer button, the timer shown provides power to the enlarger and automatically turns the enlarger lamp off after the exposure.

17 | withdraw the paper

Take the printing paper out of the frame, but leave the negatives in place, ready for another attempt if the first print is not good.

18 | begin processing

Slip the paper smoothly into the developer, emulsion side up, immersing the surface quickly. Agitate the print by rocking the tray or with the tongs.

19 | conclude development

Develop for the time recommended for the developer—usually about 2 min. Lift the paper out by a corner with the tongs and let it drain into the tray.

20 | transfer to stop bath, then fixer

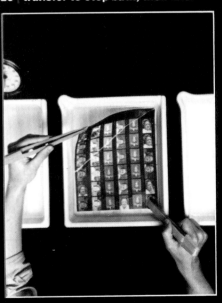

Agitate in stop bath 30 sec (5–10 sec for RC paper). Fix for 5–10 min (2 min for RC paper), agitating occasionally. View by white light after 2 min.

21 | evaluate the print

If print is too light, make another giving more exposure; if too dark, give less exposure. If okay, wash and dry (steps 57–59) after fixing.

Preparing the Negative for Enlargement

Personal judgments *count the most when selecting negatives for enlargement when you have many shots of the same scene. Which had the most pleasing light? Which captured the action most dramatically? Which expressions were the most natural or most revealing? Which is the best picture overall?*

Technical points *should be considered as well. For example, is the negative sharp? With a magnifying glass examine all parts of the contact prints of similar negatives to check for blurring caused by poor focusing or by movement of the camera or subject. If the negative is small—particularly if it is 35mm—even seemingly slight blurring in the contact print will be quite noticeable in an 8 × 10-inch enlargement because the defects will be enlarged as well. Extreme underexposure (shown on the contact as pictures that are very dark) or extreme overexposure (pictures that are very light) will make the negative difficult or even impossible to print successfully. Minor exposure faults, however, can be remedied during enlargement. Use a light-colored grease pencil to mark the contact sheet as a rough guide for cropping.*

22 | select a negative for printing

Under bright light, examine the processed contact sheet with a magnifying glass to determine which negative you want to enlarge.

23 | extract the negative carrier

Lift up the lamp housing of the enlarger and remove the negative carrier—usually two sheets of metal that hold the negative between them.

24 | insert the negative

Place the negative over the window in the carrier and center it. The emulsion side must face down when the carrier is put in the enlarger.

25 | clean the negative

Before printing, hold the negative at an angle under the enlarger lens with the lamp on so that the bright light reveals any dust; brush it off. Dust may be easier to see with room lights off.

26 | replace the negative carrier

Tilt the lamp housing and place the negative carrier in position. Switch off room lights so that you can see the image clearly for focusing.

Open the enlarger's aperture to its largest f-stop to supply maximum light for focusing. The enlarger lamp should be on.

Insert a piece of white paper under the masking slides of the easel. Paper shows the focus more clearly than even a white easel surface.

Adjust the movable masking slides on the easel, first to hold the size of paper being used (in this case, 8 × 10 inches) and later to crop the image.

30 | arrange the picture

31 | focus the image

32 | refine the focus

Raise or lower the enlarger head to get the desired degree of image enlargement, adjusting the easel as needed to compose the picture.

Focus by turning the knob that raises and lowers the lens. Don't shift the enlarger head except to readjust size if this is necessary.

A magnifier helps to make the final adjustments in focus. Some types magnify enough for you to focus on the grain in the negative.

Making a Test Print

The best way to tell how long to expose an enlargement is to make a **test print**. This will look like a striped version of the final print (step 43, opposite). The strips are sections of the print, each strip exposed under the enlarger longer than its neighbor to the left. The test print is judged for density and contrast (pages 172–173). A full-sized sheet of printing paper is used here, but a smaller strip of paper placed across an important area is usually enough.

Time, rather than aperture setting, is generally changed when adjusting the exposure. If the negative is badly overexposed or underexposed, however, change the lens aperture to avoid impractically long or short exposure times. The method shown here exposes each strip 5 sec longer than its neighbor and produces strips exposed for a total of 5, 10, 15, 20, and 25 sec. Some photographers use a method that doubles the exposure for each strip and so produces a greater range of tones. For example, exposing the strips for 2½, 2½, 5, 10, and 20 sec gives total exposures of 2½, 5, 10, 20, and 40 sec.

Make the exposure with the lens stopped down a few stops from its widest aperture. This gives good lens performance plus enough depth of focus to minimize slight errors in focusing the projected image.

33 | close down the aperture

When focus is sharp, reduce the aperture of the enlarger lens to about f/11. The relatively small opening offsets slight focusing errors.

34 | insert printing paper

With room lights and enlarger lamp off, slip a piece of contrast grade 2 or 3 printing paper, emulsion side up, under the easel's masking slides.

35 | set the timer

Set the timer by turning its pointer to 5 sec. This test print will receive a series of 5 exposures of 5 sec each.

36 | first exposure

Cover four-fifths of the printing paper with a piece of cardboard and press the button to expose the uncovered section for 5 sec.

37 | second exposure

Slide the cardboard to cover only three-fifths of the paper and press the button. The timer makes another 5-sec exposure automatically.

...ove the cardboard and expose again. The first ...ction has now been given 15 sec of exposure, ...e second 10, and the third 5.

Make two more 5-sec exposures in the same manner, first revealing four-fifths of the paper, then exposing the entire sheet.

Take the paper from the easel for development. It will now have strips bearing 5 different exposures that range from 5 to 25 sec.

| **develop the test**

42 | transfer to the stop bath

43 | select the best exposure

Evaluate the test print carefully. Before making the final print, examine the test under ordinary room light. Darkroom safelight illumination makes prints seem darker than they actually are. Details on how to judge a test print appear on pages 172–173.

Exposure. Is one of the exposures about right—not too dark or too light? Or should an entire series of longer or shorter test times be made?

Contrast. Is the test print too contrasty, with inky black shadows, harsh white highlights, and little detail showing in either? Or is the print too flat—muddy and gray with dingy highlights and dull shadows? If you change print contrast, the printing time may change, so make another test print for the new contrast grade.

Dodging and burning in. Most prints require some local control of exposure, which you can provide by holding light back (dodging) or adding light (burning in). See page 178 for more information.

Recheck the focus. Set the timer to the exposure indicated by the test, insert fresh paper in the easel, and press the button for final exposure.

Dodging, or blocking light during part of the exposure, lightens areas that would otherwise print too dark. Often, shadow areas are dodged.

46 | burn in, if necessary

47 | develop the print

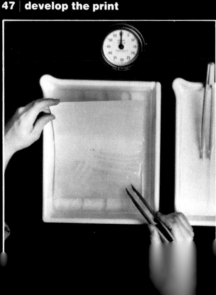

48 | agitate gently

49 | complete development

If the print develops too rapidly or too slowly, process for the standard time anyway. Then examine the print and change exposure as needed.

50 | drain off developer

Hold the print above the tray for a few seconds so that the developer solution, which contaminates stop bath, can drain away.

51 | transfer to the stop bath

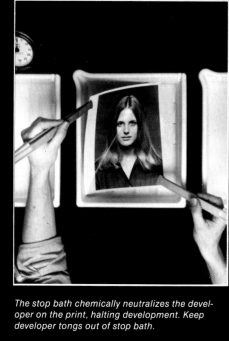

The stop bath chemically neutralizes the developer on the print, halting development. Keep developer tongs out of stop bath.

52 | agitate

Keep the print immersed in the stop bath for 30 sec (5–10 sec for RC paper), agitating it gently. Use stop bath–fixer tongs in this solution.

53 | drain off stop bath

Again lift the print so that solution can drain into the stop-bath tray. Don't let stop-bath solution splash into developer.

54 | transfer to the fixer

Slip the print into the fixer and keep it submerged. The same tongs are used for stop bath and fixer, which are compatible solutions.

55 | agitate

Agitate the print occasionally while it is in the fixer. Room lights can be turned on after about 2 min and the print examined.

Take time again at this point to evaluate the print. Don't be discouraged if the print is less than perfect on the first try. Often several trials must be made.

Exposure and contrast. Could the print be improved by adjusting the exposure or contrast? It is not always possible to tell from a test strip how all areas of the print will look. Skin tones are important if your print is a portrait. Give more exposure if skin tones look pale and washed out. Beginners tend to print skin tones too light, without a feeling of substance and texture.

Dodging and burning in. Examine the print again for areas that could be improved by dodging or burning in. Often several trials are needed to get all the tones just where you want them.

56 | remove the print

After fixing, transfer the print to the washing tray. Follow manufacturer's fixing recommendations or the image may fade and stain.

57 | wash

Wash for 60 min in running water; much less time is needed if a washing aid is used. RC papers need no washing aid and only 4 min washing.

58 | remove the surface water

Place the print on a clean, overturned tray or sheet of glass or plastic and gently squeegee off most of the water from front and back.

59 | dry

A blotter roll is one way to dry fiber-base papers. You can dry RC papers simply by placing them face up on a clean surface. See page 188.

	chemicals needed	procedure	tips for better prints
preparation		Mix the chemical stock solutions needed. Dilute to working strength and adjust temperature as recommended by manufacturer. (*See page 130 for information on mixing and storing chemicals.*) **Resin-coated (RC) paper** needs less fixing, no washing aid, and less washing than fiber-base papers; see manufacturer's instructions.	Temperature control is less critical for black-and-white printing than for negative development. 65°–70° F (18°–21° C) is ideal; 60°–75° F (16°–24° C) is acceptable. Below 65° F, chemicals take longer to work. Above 70° F, the developer more quickly fogs or grays the highlights, and the paper emulsion softens and is more easily damaged.
development	Use a developer suitable for papers. Neutral or cold-tone developers such as Acufine Printofine or Kodak Dektol produce a neutral or blue-black tone when used with neutral or cold-tone papers. Warm-tone developers such as Kodak Selectol increase the brown-black tone of warm-tone papers. Discard developer if it turns dark after 15 or 20 prints have been processed per quart of working solution, or at the end of a printing session.	After exposing the paper, slip it quickly and completely into the developer. Development times can range from 45 sec to 2 min (see manufacturer's directions). Agitate gently and constantly with tongs or by rocking the tray. If two or more prints at a time are processed, rotate individual prints from bottom to top of the stack in the tray.	Do not cut short the development time to salvage a print that darkens too rapidly; uneven development and mottling will result. If the print is too dark, make another with less exposure. Development time for some papers can be extended to slightly darken a too-light print, but this can also cause staining. If the print is too light, make another with more exposure.
selective development		You can darken part of a print during development by breathing on the area while holding the print out of the tray, or by pulling the print out of the tray, rinsing it with water and gently swabbing the area to be darkened with cotton dipped in warm or concentrated developer.	Prints kept too long out of the developer will stain. Darkening individual areas by burning in during exposure works better.
stop bath	Stop-bath solution. Discard after about 20 prints have been treated per quart of working solution or when a testing solution indicates exhaustion. An indicator-type stop bath is useful because it turns dark when exhausted.	Agitate prints in stop bath for 30 sec (5–10 sec for **RC paper**). Agitation during the first few seconds is important.	Drain developer from print for a few seconds before putting print into stop bath. This will help keep the stop bath fresh. Also avoid getting stop bath or fixer into the developer; use developer tongs only in developer tray, stop bath–fixer tongs only in those trays.
fixing	Fixing solution. Rapid fixer is similar but faster acting. Fixer with hardener helps prevent softening of print when water temperatures are high. Discard after about 20 prints have been fixed per quart of working solution or when a testing solution indicates exhaustion.	Fix for 5 to 10 min, agitating several times. If several prints are in the fixer at one time, agitate more often and rotate individual prints from bottom to top of the stack. If fixer becomes exhausted during a printing session, refix all prints in fresh fixer. **RC paper** fixes in 2 min.	The most complete and economical fixing uses two trays of fixer. Fix the print in the first tray for half the fixing time. Then transfer the print to the second tray for half the fixing time. When the fixer in the first tray is exhausted, replace it with the solution from the second tray. Mix fresh fixer for the second tray.
holding until wash		After fixing, place prints in a large tray filled with water until the end of the printing session. Gently run water in tray or dump and refill frequently. Wash **RC paper** promptly for best results; total wet time should not exceed 10 min.	Remove prints promptly from fixer at the end of the fixing time or they will take longer to wash and may bleach or stain.
washing aid (optional)	Washing-aid solution. Discard after about 10 prints have been treated per quart of working solution (or as directed).	Rinse prints in running water for about 5 min (or as directed). Then agitate prints in the washing aid solution for the time indicated by the manufacturer —usually just a few minutes. Do not use a washing aid with **RC paper.**	While using a washing aid with fiber-base paper is optional, it is a very good practice. Prints treated with a washing aid will be washed cleaner of residual chemicals than untreated prints and in much less time.
washing		If a washing aid is used first, wash 5 to 10 min (or as directed). Otherwise, wash for at least 1 hr. Adjust the water flow or dump and refill the tray so that the water changes once every 5 min. Wash **RC paper** 4 min; agitate and change water frequently.	If several prints are washed at one time, they must be separated or circulated so that fresh water constantly reaches all surfaces. Some print washers do this automatically. In a tray, it must be done by hand.
drying		Sponge or squeegee off excess water. Fiber-base paper can be dried on racks, on a heated dryer, or between blotters. **RC paper** dries well on racks.	See page 188 for more about drying and optional glossing of prints.

171

How to Judge a Test Print

Prints are judged for density and contrast. The goal during printing is usually to make a **full-scale print**—one that has a full range of tones (rich blacks, many shades of gray, brilliant whites) and a realistic sense of texture and substance (*opposite page, top*). You may deliberately depart from this goal at times, but first learning how to make a full-scale print will give you control over your materials so that later you can produce whatever kind of print you want. A test print like the one at near right helps in evaluating a print and deciding how to improve it. Do all your judging under ordinary room light because prints look darker under safelight.

Density refers to the overall darkness or lightness of the print (*opposite, bottom left*). It is controlled primarily by the amount of exposure given the paper—the greater the exposure, the greater the density of silver produced and the darker the print. Exposure can be adjusted either by opening or closing the enlarger lens aperture or by changing the exposure time.

Contrast is the difference in brightness between light and dark areas within the print (*opposite, bottom right*). A low-contrast or flat print seems gray and weak, with no real blacks or brilliant whites. A high-contrast or hard print seems harsh and too contrasty: large shadow areas seem too dark and may print as solid black; highlights, very light areas, seem too light and may be completely white; texture and detail are missing in shadows, highlights, or both. The contrast of a print is controlled mainly by the contrast grade of the paper used or, with variable contrast paper, by the printing filter used (*see the following pages*).

Begin by judging the density. With some experience, you can judge both density and contrast at the same time, but it is easier at first to adjust them in two steps. Examine the test print for an exposure that produced highlights of about the right density, especially in areas where you want a good sense of texture. If all strips in the test seem too light, make another set of strips with more exposure by opening the enlarger aperture two f-stops. If all seem too dark, make a test with less exposure by stopping down two f-stops.

Then check the contrast. When the highlights seem about right in one strip, examine the shadow areas. If they are too dark (if you can see details in the negative image in an area that prints as solid black), your print is too contrasty. Make another test print on a lower-contrast paper. If your shadow areas are too light and look weak and gray, your print does not have enough contrast. Make another test on a higher-contrast paper. If you are printing a portrait, the skin tones are important. Adjust the exposure so that the brightest skin area is about the right density, and then, if necessary, adjust the contrast.

When one of the tests looks about right, expose the full image using the exposure and contrast that you chose. It can be difficult to predict from a single strip in a test exactly how an entire print will look, so judge the density and contrast of the print overall. Examine the print for individual areas you may want to darken or lighten by burning in or dodging (*pages 178–179*). Prints, especially on matte-finish papers, tend to "dry down," or appear slightly darker when dry. Experience will help you take this into account when printing.

Black and white test patches can help you judge a print. To evaluate the density and contrast of a print, you need standards against which to compare the tones in your print, since the eye can be fooled into accepting a very dark gray as black or a very light gray as white. As much as one full grade of contrast can be involved, enough to make the difference between a flat, dull print and a rich, brilliant one. Two small pieces of printing paper, one developed to the darkest black and the other to the brightest white that the paper can produce, are an aid when you are first learning how to print as well as later when you want to make a particularly fine print.

By placing a black or white patch next to an area, you can accurately judge how light or dark the tone actually is. As a bonus, the black patch indicates developer exhaustion; the developer should be replaced when you are no longer able to produce a black tone in a print as dark as the black patch no matter how much exposure you give the paper. The white patch will help you check for the overall gray tinge caused by safelight fogging.

Make the patches at the beginning of a printing session when developer and fixer are fresh. Cut two 2-inch-square pieces from your printing paper. Use the enlarger as the light source to make the black patch. Set the enlarger head about a foot and a half above the baseboard. The patch should be borderless, so do not use an easel. Expose one patch for 30 seconds at f/5.6; do not expose the other. Develop both patches with constant agitation for the time recommended by the manufacturer or for 2 minutes. Process as usual with stop bath and fixer. Remove promptly from fixer after the recommended time, then store in fresh water. To avoid any possible fogging of the white patch, cut and process the paper in a minimum amount of safelight.

2½ seconds

5 seconds

10 seconds

20 seconds

40 seconds

Many photographers make test prints like the one above to help them judge the density (darkness) and contrast of a print. The exposures on this print range from 2½ to 40 sec. First, the exposure is chosen that renders the highlights (in the lightest area you want to retain detail) at the right density. Then the shadow values are examined: if they appear neither too dark and harsh nor gray and flat, then the contrast of the print is correct.

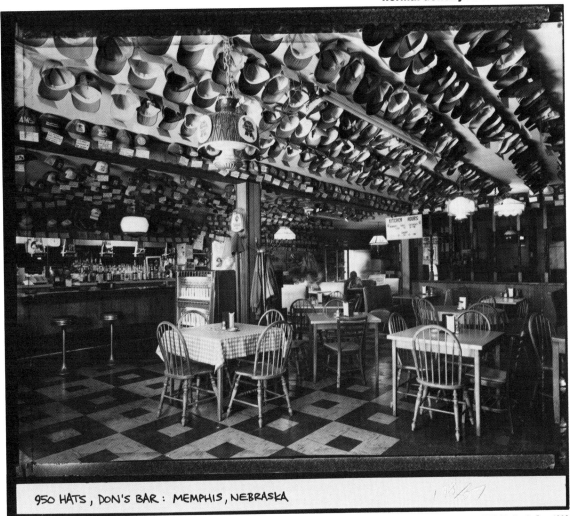

950 HATS, DON'S BAR : MEMPHIS, NEBRASKA

JIM STONE: *Don's Bar*, 1983

A full-scale print of normal density and normal contrast, with texture and detail in the major shadow areas and important highlights, is shown at left. Decreasing the exposure produced a lighter print; increasing the exposure gave a darker version (below left). Printing the same negative on a lower-contrast grade of paper produced a flat print; printing on a higher-contrast grade made a contrasty print (below right).

This photograph was made on Polaroid Type 55 4 × 5 film, which produces both a positive print and a high-quality negative. Stone later reprints the negative in a 5 × 7 glass negative carrier so that the entire edge of the negative shows.

density

too light　　　　　　　　　　　　　　**too dark**

contrast

too flat　　　　　　　　　　　　　**too contrasty**

Papers That Control Contrast
Graded-Contrast Papers

Contrast—the relative lightness and darkness of areas in a scene—is important in any photograph. Frequently you will want normal contrast—a full range of tones from black through many shades of gray to pure white. Sometimes, however, you may feel that a particular scene requires low contrast—mostly a smooth range of middle grays (such as a scene in the fog). For another scene (perhaps a fireworks display) you may want high contrast—deep blacks and brilliant whites and limited detail in between.

By the time you are ready to make a print, the contrast of the negative has been set, mostly by the contrast in the subject itself, the type of film, and the way it was developed. But you can adjust the contrast of the final print with the contrast grade of the printing paper. As shown on the opposite page, a paper of normal contrast produces a print of normal contrast from a negative of normal contrast. A paper of high contrast increases the contrast; a paper of low contrast decreases it. This can help when printing a problem negative. A high-contrast paper increases contrast for scenes that may be too flat, such as those shot in dull light. A low-contrast paper decreases contrast, and can soften too-harsh shadows and highlights.

These changes are caused by responses in the paper emulsion. With a paper of high contrast, only a small increase in exposure is needed to cause a relatively great increase in density in the paper emulsion. A low-contrast negative has relatively small differences between its thinnest and densest areas. If it is printed on a high-contrast paper, however, these small differences are enough to produce relatively large differences in lightness and darkness in the print, and therefore more contrast.

The reverse is true for a paper of low contrast. A large increase in exposure produces only a relatively small increase in print density. A high-contrast negative has great differences between its thinnest and densest areas; printed on a low-contrast paper, these differences become only moderate in the final print.

Other factors besides the printing paper affect contrast: the enlarger, the surface finish of the paper, and the type of paper developer (Kodak Selectol Soft, for example, lowers contrast). But the basic way of changing contrast in a print is to use a different contrast grade of paper.

There are two ways to do this. You can use a variable-contrast paper (*see pages 176–177*), with which you alter the contrast by changing the filtration of the enlarger light. Or you can use a **graded-contrast paper,** each grade of which has a fixed contrast. Many photographers prefer to work with graded papers, even though you have to purchase each contrast grade separately. Graded-contrast papers are available in grades 0 and 1 (low or soft contrast) through grade 2 (normal or medium contrast), grade 3 (often the normal contrast grade for 35mm negatives), and grades 4 and 5 (high or hard contrast). Not all papers are made in all contrast grades and not all manufacturers use the same grading system, so some experimentation may be needed with a new brand of paper.

Contrast is the relative lightness or darkness of ▶ different parts of a scene. Depending on the contrast grade of the printing paper used, a print will show more, less, or about the same amount of contrast as is present in the negative. Compare the range of tones in the three prints at far right. The normal print contains small areas of black and white plus a wide range of gray tones. A low-contrast print has tones that cluster mostly around middle gray. A high-contrast print has large areas that are strongly black or brilliantly white but has relatively few gray tones in between.

How can you tell if your negative is of normal contrast? There are laboratory instruments—densitometers—that measure contrast, but there is also an old rule of thumb. Lay the negative over the type on this page. The negative has normal contrast if you can barely read the type through the highlights and if the shadows have visible detail.

low-contrast negative

normal-contrast negative

high-contrast negative

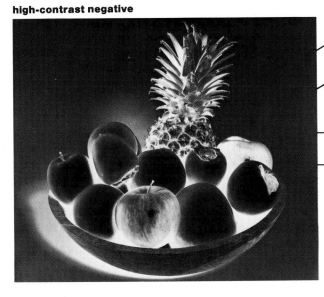

normal-contrast paper

high-contrast paper

paper

low-contrast

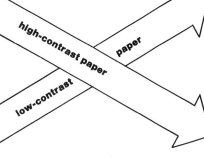

normal-contrast paper

high-contrast

low-contrast paper

paper

normal-contrast paper

low-contrast print

normal contrast print

high-contrast print

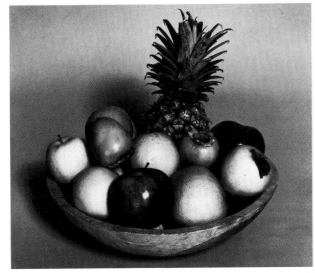

Variable-Contrast Papers

number 1 filter

number 1½ filter

number 2 filter

number 2½ filter

You can use a single paper with adjustable contrast instead of stocking paper in several contrast grades. A **variable-contrast paper** is coated with two emulsions. One, sensitive to yellow-green light, yields low contrast; the other, sensitive to blue-violet light, produces high contrast. You vary the degree of contrast by inserting appropriately colored filters in the enlarger (*far right*). The filter affects the color of the light that reaches the printing paper from the enlarger light source and thus controls contrast. If you have a dichroic enlarger head, used for color printing, you can dial in the filtration. However, depending on the enlarger, you may get more consistent and satisfactory results using separate filters.

An advantage of variable-contrast paper compared to graded-contrast paper is the convenience and economy of working with only one kind of paper. You can get a range of contrast out of one package of paper and a set of filters instead of having to buy several different packages of paper. Furthermore, you can change the contrast in different parts of a photograph by printing them with different filters (*shown at right*).

The three versions at right of a New Hampshire mill scene show how variable-contrast paper lets you print different parts of a scene using different degrees of contrast. In the version made with a number 3 filter (upper right), the water and sky seem too contrasty; in the version made with a number 1 filter (bottom right), the mill is too dark and flat.

The final print (opposite page) was made by exposing the mill with the number 3 filter while shielding the water and sky, then exposing the water and sky with the number 1 filter while shielding the mill. It is tricky to blend the lines where the different areas of contrast meet, but when done successfully it achieves a balance of contrast impossible with paper of a single contrast grade.

number 3 filter

number 3½ filter

number 4 filter

◄ Variable-contrast paper can produce different degrees of contrast by filtering the light from the enlarger, as shown in the series of pictures at left. This particular filter set has seven filters. The contrast range is approximately equal to paper grades 1 through 4—rising by half steps. The number 2 filter produces contrast equal to a grade 2 paper.

Two ways of inserting filters in enlargers are shown below. A filter holder can be attached below the enlarger lens, and a gelatin filter slipped into the holder (top). Some enlargers have a filter drawer (bottom) between the lamp and the negative; an acetate filter is used here. This latter system is preferable. Since the filter is above the lens, it interferes less with the focused image.

Dodging and Burning In

◀ *Dodging (far left) holds back light during the basic printing exposure to lighten an area. Burning in (center) adds light after the basic exposure to darken an area. Flashing (near left) exposes part of the print to direct light and adds an overall dark tone wherever the light strikes the paper.*

You can give different exposures to different parts of a print by dodging and burning in. Often, the overall density of a print is nearly right, but part of the picture appears too light or too dark—an extremely bright sky or a very dark shadow area, for example.

Dodging lightens an area that prints too dark. That part of the print is simply shadowed during part of the initial exposure time. A dodging tool is useful; the one shown above on the left is a piece of cardboard attached to the end of a wire. Your hand (*opposite page*), a finger, a piece of cardboard, or any other appropriately shaped object can be used. Dodging works well when you can see detail in shadow areas in the negative image. Dodging of areas that have no detail or dodging for too long merely produces a murky gray tone in the print.

Burning in adds exposure when part of a print is too light. After the entire negative has received an exposure that is correct for most areas, the light is blocked from most of the print while the area that is too light receives extra ex-

posure. A large piece of cardboard with a hole in it (*above center*) works well. A piece of cardboard can be cut to an appropriate shape (*opposite page*), or your hands can be used—cupped or spread so that light reaches the paper only where you want it to.

If you want to darken an area considerably, try **flashing** it—exposing it directly to white light from a small penlight flashlight. Unlike burning in, which darkens the image, flashing fogs the paper: it adds a solid gray or black tone. Tape a cone of paper around the end of the penlight so it can be directed at a small area. Devise some method to see exactly where you are pointing the light. Either do the flashing during the initial exposure or add the flashing afterward with the enlarger light on and an orange or red filter held under the lens. The filter prevents the enlarger light from exposing the paper but lets you see the image during the flashing.

Keep the dodging or burning tool, your hands, or the penlight in constant motion. Move them back and forth so that the tones of the area you are work-

ing on blend into the rest of the print. If you simply hold a dodging tool, for example, under the light source, an outline of the tool will be printed on the paper.

Many prints are both dodged and burned. Depending on the print, shadow areas or dark objects may need dodging to keep them from darkening so much that important details are obscured. Sometimes shadows or other areas are burned in to darken them and make distracting details less noticeable. Light areas may need burning in to increase the visible detail. Skies are often burned in, as they were on the opposite page, to make clouds more visible. Even if there are no clouds, skies are sometimes burned in because they may seem distractingly bright. They are usually given slightly more exposure at the top of the sky area than near the horizon. Whatever areas you dodge or burn, blend them into the rest of the print so that the changes are a subtle improvement rather than a noticeable distraction.

This photograph of a Maine inlet was dodged to lighten certain areas and burned in to darken others. The exposures for the test print (top left) ranged from 3 to 18 sec. The dark rock showed the best detail and texture at an exposure of about 6 sec, the water looked best at about 9 sec, and the sky needed about 18 sec of exposure to bring out detail in the clouds. The photographer gave the print a basic exposure of 9 sec, while dodging the rock for 3 sec (top right). Then the sky was burned in for another 9 sec while the rock and water were shielded from light with a shaped cardboard mask (above). In order to blend the tones of the different areas, the photographer's hand and the cardboard mask were kept moving during the exposures.

179

Cropping

ARNOLD NEWMAN: *Igor Stravinsky*, 1946

Arnold Newman is famous for portraits that use graphic and symbolic elements to suggest what a person does. One of his best-known photographs is of the composer Igor Stravinsky, a portrait that Newman cropped to its essentials. Newman knew what he wanted to do, but, just starting out at the time, he didn't have the focal length lens he needed. He moved back until he had what he wanted in the frame, then cropped the photograph later. Newman says that the image "echoed my feelings about Stravinsky's music: strong, harsh, but with a stark beauty of its own." (Page 259 shows Newman at work.)

Eventually you must make a decision about **cropping**—what to leave out and what to include along the edges of a photograph. Some photographers prefer to crop only with the camera; they use the ground glass or viewfinder to frame the subject, and do not change the cropping later. Most photographers, however, do not hesitate to crop while printing if it improves the image.

Sometimes cropping improves a picture by eliminating distracting elements. Sometimes a negative is cropped to fill a standard paper size; square negatives may be cropped so that when enlarged they fit a rectangular format. Cropping can direct the viewer's attention to the forms and shapes as the photographer saw them.

Enlarging a very small part of a negative can create problems because the greater the enlargement, the more grain becomes noticeable and the more the image tends to lose definition and detail. But within reasonable limits, cropping can improve many photographs.

To help you decide how to crop a picture, make two L-shaped guides and place them over the photograph to try various croppings, as shown at right. Think of the photograph as a window and notice how the edges of the frame cut or encircle the objects in the picture. You can experiment to some extent on the contact sheet although the image there is small, but you will probably want to refine your cropping when you enlarge the image. Making an enlargement of the entire negative before doing any cropping can be useful because there may be potentials in the print you would not otherwise see.

Two L-shaped pieces of paper laid over a photograph can help you visualize different croppings.

Troubleshooting Print Problems

If you have a technical difficulty with your prints, you may find the cause of the problem and its prevention below. See also Troubleshooting Camera and Lens Problems (page 83), Negative Problems (page 151) and Flash Problems (page 286).

White specks or small spots

Cause: *Dust on the negative, printing-frame glass, or glass negative carrier. Fuzzy-edged spots may be due to dust on enlarger condensers.*

Prevention: *Dust these surfaces carefully before printing. Improve the print by darkening the spots with dyes (see page 189).*

Black specks or small spots

Cause: *Dust deposited on the film prior to exposure.*

Prevention: *Dust the inside of the camera. With sheet film, dust holders carefully and load film in a dust-free place. The spots can be etched or bleached to remove them (see page 189).*

Dark scratch lines

Cause: *Scratches on negative emulsion caused by rough handling. If scratches can be seen only on the print, not on the negative, the cause is abrasion of print emulsion.*

Prevention: *Handle film with extreme care and avoid cinching roll film, sliding sheet film against a rough surface, or otherwise abrading film in any way. Check the film path in the camera for grit or unevenness. Prevent abrasion of print emulsion by handling paper with greater care. If print tongs are used, don't slide them across the print surface; even light pressure can mark the surface of the print. Grip paper with tongs in the print margin so tong marks can be trimmed off if necessary.*

Light scratch lines

Cause: *Hairline scratches on the backing side of the negative.*

Prevention: *More careful handling or storing of the negative. An already scratched negative can be improved somewhat by a light coating of oil. An oily "scratch remover" is sold for this purpose. You can also rub your finger on your nose or forehead to pick up a light coating of oil. Then gently smooth the oil over any fine scratches that are visible. This should at least partially improve the next print by filling in the scratch. It works only with scratches that print as white. The oil attracts dust, so wipe the negative clean and store carefully.*

Mottled, mealy, or uneven print development

Cause: *Too little time or inadequate agitation in print developer. Use of exhausted developer.*

Prevention: *Develop prints with constant agitation in fresh developer for no less than the minimum time recommended by the manufacturer.*

Fingerprints

Cause: *Touching film or paper emulsion with greasy or chemical-contaminated hands. Fingerprints on negative will appear oversized in an enlarged print.*

Prevention: *Rinse and dry hands after they have been in any chemical solution. Be particularly careful to clean print fixer off hands before handling another piece of printing paper. Hold film and paper by edges.*

Fading of prints

Cause: *Prints that look faded immediately after washing were bleached by a too-strong or too-warm fixer or by too long a time in the fixer. Later fading is caused by inadequate fixing or washing.*

Prevention: *Review the recommended fixing and washing procedure (page 171), and follow it carefully.*

Yellowish stains

Cause: *Any number of processing faults—too long a time in the developer, exhausted or too-warm developer, contamination of developer with fixer, exposure of paper to air during development by lifting it out of developer too often, exhausted stop bath or fixer, delay in placing print into fixer, inadequate agitation or too short a time in fixer, inadequate washing. Inadequate fixing also causes brownish-purple stains.*

Prevention: *Review processing techniques on page 171 and information about contamination on page 130.*

Overall gray cast in highlights or paper margins

Cause: *Fogging of print by light leaking into darkroom from outside, by stray light from enlarger, by too strong a safelight, by too long or too close an exposure to a proper safelight, by storage of paper in a package that is not light tight, by too much time in developer, by room light on too soon after print is placed in fixer.*

Prevention: *Check all of the above. Fogging affects highlights first, so prints may be reduced in brilliance before the cause becomes apparent in a definite tinge in print margins. This is because the light from very slight fogging may be too weak by itself to cause any visible response in the paper's emulsion. But when added to the slight exposure received by the highlights, it may be enough to make them grayish. Compare highlights that should be pure white in the print with the white test patch described on page 172.*

Only part of negative image can be focused at any one time

Cause: *Negative carrier of enlarger not parallel to baseboard or easel.*

Prevention: *Stopping down the lens may produce enough depth of focus to bring the image into acceptable focus, but aligning the enlarger is better.*

Entire print out of focus, sharp negative image

Cause: *Vibration of enlarger during exposure.*

Prevention: *Eliminate the source of vibration. Placing the paper in the easel can be enough to make a wobbly enlarger vibrate; pause a few seconds before exposure to let it come to a rest. Lightly press the button that starts the exposure, don't hit it. Avoid touching the enlarger during exposure.*

Part of the print out of focus, sharp negative image

Cause: *In contact printing, due to poor contact between negative and paper. In enlarging, due to negative buckling caused by heat generated during a long exposure time.*

Prevention: *In contact printing, even out or increase the pressure on the sandwich of glass, negative, paper, and backing. In enlarging, use a glass negative carrier, a cold-light enlarger, or a shorter exposure time.*

Toning for Color and Other Effects

Toning can be used to change the color of a print and to produce several other effects as well. Immersing a print in certain chemical toner solutions causes a distinct change in the color of the silver image, ranging from shades of sepia (yellowish-brown), brown, red, or orange to blue or bluish-green. Most toners combine with the silver to form silver-based compounds. The darker the silver deposit in the original print, the deeper the toned color will be.

Most toners help increase the life of a print. The silver in an image can deteriorate in much the same way that a piece of silver jewelry tarnishes. A toner in- creases the stability of the silver by combining it with a more stable substance, such as selenium. **Toning for intensification** is done with a selenium toner. For this purpose the print color is changed very little—just enough to remove the slight color cast present in most prints and to leave a neutral black image. In selenium toning the density of the dark areas of the print increases, which also increases the richness and brilliance of the print. You can easily see the effect by comparing a toned print to a similar, untoned one. A procedure for toning prints for intensification is described at the right.

GEORGE A. TICE: *Grasses with Iris, Saddle River, New Jersey, 1968*

Toning Black-and-White Prints

Paper and development. *Changes during toning depend not only on the toner but on the type of paper, type of developer, development time, even print exposure time. Sepia toners lighten a print slightly, so start with a slightly dark print. Bluish toners containing ferric ammonium citrate darken a print, so start with a slightly light print. Test the effect of a toner on your particular combination of paper and chemistry.*

Fixing and washing. *Prints will stain if they have not been properly fixed and washed before toning. Two fixing baths are recommended (see page 171). After fixing, prints are usually ready to be toned after a rinse in running water, use of a washing aid, then a 10-min wash.*

Tips. *As a color comparison, keep an untoned print in a tray of water nearby. Changes due to residual chemicals may take place after a print has been removed from the toner, so if your dried prints look overtoned, remove prints from toner just before they reach the tone you want.*

Caution. *Use gloves or tongs to handle prints in any toner. Use toners only in a well-ventilated area; fumes released during processing may smell bad or even be toxic if ventilation is inadequate. Read and follow manufacturer's instructions carefully.*

How to Tone for Intensification

The formula for a selenium toner given here deepens blacks and produces a rich, neutral black image. The formula incorporates a washing aid, which eliminates its use as a separate step.

Mixing the solution. *Mix solution and store in a clean bottle. To tone 12 prints, pour out 1 qt solution and discard after use.*

> *4 liters (1 gal) freshly mixed washing aid (such as Ilford Ilfobrom Archival Wash Aid or Kodak Hypo Clearing Agent), at working strength*
> *200 cc (7 oz) selenium toner (such as Kodak Rapid Selenium Toner)*
> *75 gm (2.5 oz) Kodalk Balanced Alkali (for RC prints, which do not need a washing aid, use 4 liters of plain water and omit the alkali)*

Preparing to tone. *Develop prints for the recommended time and fix in a two-step fixing bath. Kodak recommends transferring prints directly from the fixer to the toning solution to prevent staining, but this is not always a workable procedure. Instead, prints can be rinsed thoroughly and held for up to 24 hr in a tray of water, or they can be completely washed and dried for later toning. Rinse the prints briefly in fixer just before toning.*

Set out three clean trays in a well-lighted area. Ideally, light should be similar to the conditions under which the print will be seen. A regular tungsten bulb will make the toning easier to see; a blue bulb will show the color under daylight viewing conditions. Place the prints in water in one tray, the toner at 75° F (24° C) in the middle tray, and water in the third tray—gently running, if possible.

Toning. *Place a print in the toning solution. Agitate constantly until a slight change is visible, usually within 3 to 5 min. Very little change is needed— just enough so the print looks neutral or very slightly purplish in the middle- gray areas when compared to an untoned print. Immediately rinse the print in the third tray, of clean water. Wash prints 30 min or longer.*

Archival Processing for Maximum Permanence

Archival Print Processing

Following is one standard procedure for archival processing. Ilford has developed another method that shortens processing times considerably. Details can be found with Ilfobrom Galerie printing paper.

Paper. *Use a fiber-base paper. RC papers are not recommended for archival processing because of the potential instability of the polyethylene that coats them.*

Exposure and development. *Expose the print with a wide border—at least 1 inch around the edges. Develop for the full length of time in fresh developer at the temperature recommended by the manufacturer.*

Stop bath. *Agitate constantly for 30 sec in fresh stop bath.*

Fixing. *Use 2 baths of fresh fixer. Agitate constantly for 4 min in each bath. You can agitate a print in the first bath and store it in gently running water (or in several changes of water) until a number of prints have accumulated. Then all prints can be treated for 4 min in the second bath by constantly shuffling one print at a time from the bottom to the top of the stack.*

Protective toning. *Use the selenium toner formula on page 182, which includes a washing aid. If no change in image tone is desired, reduce the selenium to 40 cc per 4 liters (1⅓ oz per gal) and treat prints 3 to 5 min.*

Washing. *Rinse toned prints several times. Wash at 75°–80° F (24°–27° C). Separate the prints frequently if the washer does not. Ideally, the water in the washer should be completely changed every 5 min. Wash until the prints test acceptably free of hypo (see test procedure below), which will take 30 min to 1 hr or longer, depending on the efficiency of the washer.*

Testing for hypo. *Mix the hypo test solution below. Cut off a strip from the print's margin and blot dry. With a dropper, place a drop of test solution on the strip and allow to remain for 2 min. Blot off the excess and compare the stain that appears with the Kodak Hypo Estimator, an inexpensive series of comparison patches that is available from some camera stores or from Eastman Kodak, Rochester, N.Y. The stain should be lighter than the lightest test patch.*

Kodak formula HT-2, residual hypo test solution
750 cc (24 oz) distilled water
125 cc (4 oz) 28% acetic acid (3 parts glacial acetic acid diluted with 8 parts distilled water)
7.5 gm (¼ oz) silver nitrate
distilled water to make 1000 cc (32 oz)

Drying and mounting. *Dry on fiberglass drying screens. Leave unmounted or slip print corners into white photo corners (used for snapshot albums) attached to mounting stock, then overmat. An archival-quality mounting stock is available in art supply stores; ask for 100% rag, acid-free boards. Separate prints with sheets of 100% rag, acid-free paper.*

How long does a photograph last? Some very early prints, particularly platinum prints that were produced around the turn of the century, have held up perfectly. Platinum paper has a light-sensitive coating that contains no silver and produces an extremely durable and very beautiful image in platinum metal (*see page 184*). Other photographs not nearly so old have faded to a brownish yellow, their scenes lost forever.

Conventional prints, which have a silver-based image, have a long life if they are processed in the ordinary way with even moderate care. But today, many museums and individuals are collecting photographs, and, understandably, they want their acquisitions to last as long as possible.

Archival processing provides maximum permanence for fiber-base silver prints. Resin-coated (RC) paper is not recommended for archival purposes. Archival processing is not very different from the customary method of developing, fixing, and washing. It is basically an extension of the ordinary procedures and involves a few extra steps, some additional expense, and careful attention to the fine details of the work.

Archival processing eliminates residual chemicals, those that washing alone cannot remove entirely. Among the substances that are potentially harmful to a print are the very ones that create the normal black-and-white image: salts of silver, such as silver bromide or silver chloride. During development, the grains of silver salts that have been exposed to light are reduced to black metallic silver, which forms the image; but unexposed grains are not reduced and remain in other parts of the print in the form of a silver compound. If not removed, they will darken when struck by light and will darken the image overall. The chemical used to remove these unexposed grains is fixer, or hypo as it is sometimes called, which converts them into soluble compounds that can be washed away.

Fixer, however, must also be removed. It contains sulfur compounds, which if allowed to remain in a picture will tarnish the metallic silver of the image just as sulfur in the air tarnishes a silver fork. Also, fixer can become attached to silver salts and form complex compounds that are themselves insoluble and difficult to remove. When these silver-fixer complexes decompose, they produce a brown-yellow sulfide compound that may cause discoloration.

Protective toning coats the silver in the image with a compound of selenium, sepia, or gold. This acts as a shield against external contaminants, such as the sulfur that may be present in air pollution. Selenium toner is used most often. Sepia is more stable but turns the image brown. Gold toners used to be recommended for maximum protection but are much more expensive than selenium, and there is now some evidence that they are not as effective as once believed. One method of archival processing is summarized at left. See the Bibliography for more information.

Platinum Prints: Beauty and Permanence

Platinum printing has produced some of the most beautiful and stable photographic images. Platinum paper has a light-sensitive coating that produces an image of platinum metal instead of silver. Platinum's subtle gradations of tone give unsurpassed clarity and depth. And because platinum is chemically stable, the prints are extremely long lasting. Images produced around the turn of the century, when the platinum process was originally popular, still retain their exquisite richness and delicacy of detail.

The main disadvantage of platinum prints is cost. Platinum is more expensive than silver. Among the minor disadvantages is that the paper is not very sensitive to light, which means that only contact prints, and not enlargements, can be made.

Interest in platinum printing has increased in recent years (along with interest in a related process, palladium printing) because of its remarkable tonal range, which can only be hinted at in book reproduction (*see page 373*). Although you have to coat the paper yourself, platinum printing is surprisingly easy. An introduction to the process is given here, demonstrated by George Tice (*photograph, page 182*), who often prints in platinum. For more detailed references, see the Bibliography.

1 | mix the solutions

Use a balance scale to weigh the chemicals for the stock solutions, then prepare as explained in box, right. Tack the paper to a board. Dampen the brush in water, squeeze dry.

2 | sensitize the paper

Working in subdued light (dim tungsten light is best), pour the sensitizer down the center of paper and spread evenly with the brush, stroking side to side, then up and down.

Platinum Printing

Negative. *You will need a negative of the same size that you want your final print to be. If your original is too small, make an enlarged continuous-tone negative on Kodak Professional Direct Duplicating Film SO–015. Ideally, the negative should have a long density scale, that is, it should print well on the softest contrast grade of silver paper.*

Paper. *Use a top-quality 100% rag paper such as Crane's Kid Finish AS 9111.*

Brush. *A soft brush about 2 inches wide is used to spread the sensitizing solution over the paper. If the bristles are set in metal, avoid contacting the metal with the sensitizing solution.*

Light source. *You will need a bright source of light that is high in ultraviolet rays, such as a sunlamp or sunlight. A sunlamp is more predictable than sunlight, but it takes longer—about 25 min versus about 1 min for bright, midsummer sun.*

Chemicals. *Available from chemical supply houses or from Photographers' Formulary, Box 5105, Missoula, Montana 59806.*

Test strips. *Unless you have unlimited funds, use a trimming from the coated paper for a test strip before you make a full-size print.*

Sensitizing solution. *Prepare three stock solutions, storing each in an amber, dropper-capped bottle. These quantities will coat about 30 8 × 10-inch prints.*

Solution 1: 0.5 gm oxalic acid, 8 gm ferric oxalate, dissolved in 30 ml (1 oz) 125° F (52° C) distilled water. Lasts about 6 months.

Solution 2: 0.5 gm oxalic acid, 8 gm ferric oxalate, 0.1 gm potassium chlorate, dissolved in 30 ml (1 oz) 125° F (52° C) distilled water. Lasts about 6 months.

Solution 3: 7 gm potassium choroplatinite dissolved in 37 ml (1¼ oz) 125° F (52° C) distilled water. Lasts indefinitely.

Just before using, combine desired quantities of the three stock solutions in a small glass. Proportions depend on the contrast desired in the print. These quantities will coat one 8 × 10-inch print plus test strips.

	lowest contrast	moderately low contrast	average contrast	moderately high contrast	highest contrast
Solution 1	22 drops	18 drops	14 drops	10 drops	0 drops
Solution 2	0 drops	4 drops	8 drops	12 drops	22 drops
Solution 3	24 drops	24 drops	24 drops	24 drops	24 drops

Developer. *Mix 454 gm (1 lb) potassium oxalate in 1.4 liters (48 oz) warm water. The developer lasts indefinitely and may even improve with age.*

Clearing solution. *Mix 30 ml (1 oz) hydrochloric acid (37%) into 1.8 liters (60 oz) water. (Caution: Always add acid to water, not water to acid.) Set out three separate trays of clearing solution. After processing a few prints through all three baths, discard the first bath. Make the second tray the first bath, and the third tray the second bath. Fill the empty tray with fresh solution, and make it the third bath.*

Tips. *Avoid contact of the sensitizing solution with metal; mix, store, and use chemical solutions only in glass or plastic containers. The surface of the print becomes rather delicate during processing, so process one print at a time, or at most two prints back to back.*

Caution. *Rubber gloves or tongs are recommended for processing; repeated contact with developer or clearing bath can cause skin problems.*

3 | dry the sensitized paper

Hang by a corner to dry in a dark place. You can speed the drying with warm (not hot) air from a blow dryer. The dried surface will be pale yellow.

4 | prepare to expose

Print as soon as the paper is dry. Trim paper to size and assemble in a printing frame so light can pass through the glass and negative to the coated side of the paper. Close the frame.

5 | make the exposure

Expose under a sunlamp or in sunlight. Adjust the frame so it is evenly lit; then, if using a sunlamp, move away to avoid exposure of your skin and especially your eyes.

6 | develop the print

Agitate the print in the developer for about 1 min under normal room lights. Extra development will not darken the print; development ceases when chemical reaction is complete.

7 | clear residual chemicals

Agitate the print for 5 min in each of three successive clearing baths of dilute hydrochloric acid. The final bath should remain clear. If it does not, agitate the print in a fourth bath of fresh solution.

8 | wash and dry the print

Wash for 30 min in a tray with a siphon or in an archival washer. Adjust water flow for a complete change of water every 5 min. Air-dry. If necessary, flatten in dry-mount press at low heat.

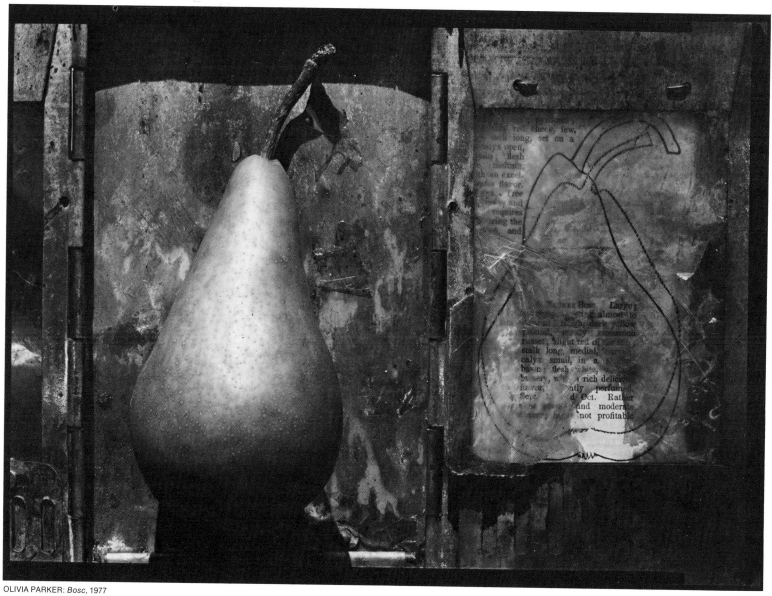

OLIVIA PARKER: *Bosc*, 1977

8

Finishing and Mounting

Although much pleasure lies in taking pictures, the real reward lies in displaying and viewing the results. Yet many photographers never seem to finish their images; they have a stack of dogeared workprints but few pictures they have been willing to carry to completion. Properly finishing and mounting a photograph is important because it tells viewers the image is worth their attention. And you yourself will see new aspects in your photographs if you take the time to complete them.

Finishing a photograph requires several steps, some of them optional. All prints are eventually dried; the most important precaution is to dry them in a way that does not stain or otherwise damage them. Most prints need some spotting—minor repair of small white or black specks caused by dust.

Mounting a print on a stiff backing protects it from creases and tears and prevents curling of fiber-base papers. Dry mounting, using a special dry-mount tissue, is the most common method; when heated, the tissue attaches the print to the backing in a perfectly smooth bond. An overmat can also be cut to help protect the photograph. Your choice of mounting materials depends on the degree of permanence you want for a print. The gelatin, silver, and paper in a photographic print can be seriously damaged by contact with materials like masking tape, which deteriorate in a relatively short time and generate destructive by-products in doing so.

The best-quality and longest-lasting materials are the most expensive. Acid-free, archival-quality mounting stock (sometimes called *museum board*) is free of the potentially damaging acids usually present in paper. It is sold by better art supply stores or companies that specialize in archival-quality photographic materials. Less expensive but still good-quality stock can be found in most art supply stores. It won't last for a hundred years but will make presentable mounting for your print. Avoid long-term contact of prints with ordinary cardboard, brown wrapping paper, brown envelopes, manila folders, and most cheap papers, including glassine. (Archivally minded photographers would say to avoid *all* contact of prints with such materials.) Also avoid attaching to the print pressure-sensitive tapes, such as masking tape or cellophane tape, brown paper tape, rubber cement, animal glues, and spray adhesives.

◀ *Olivia Parker's still life, opposite, pairs a real pear with its abstracted outline and verbal definition. As in this assemblage, Parker often incorporates aged or weathered objects, illustrations, and type into the constructions that she then photographs. Not shown here is the delicate color she gets from "split toning" her black-and-white prints. She selenium tones silver-chloride contact printing paper (such as Kodak AZO), removing the print from the toner when it combines silvery gray and brown colors rather than having an overall brown tone.*

Drying Your Prints

The goal in **drying prints** is to avoid damaging them and wasting all the effort that has gone into making them up to this point. The commonest source of trouble is that familiar enemy, contamination. One improperly washed print still loaded with fixer and placed on a dryer will contaminate every other print that is dried in the same position. And with contamination come stains—immediately or eventually. If blotters or cloths from heat dryers become tinged with yellow, they have been contaminated with fixer that was not completely washed from prints. Replace blotters and wash the dryer cloths, or they will contaminate other prints with which they come in contact. Wash fiberglass screening from time to time or whenever you suspect contamination.

The drying method can affect the surface gloss of the print. A glossy-surfaced, fiber-base (not RC) paper dried on a rack, in blotters, or on a heat dryer with the emulsion against the dryer cloth will dry to a semigloss finish. A high gloss can be obtained if a fiber-base glossy print is ferrotyped—dried with the emulsion pressed against a smooth metal plate, usually the hot metal drum or plate of a heat dryer (soaking the print first in a glossing solution helps prevent sticking and uneven drying). Do not ferrotype RC papers; use an RC glossy surface.

RC papers have a plasticlike coating that makes them resistant to water. Since water does not soak into the paper (as it does with fiber-base papers), RC prints dry well if surface water is simply sponged or squeegeed off and the print is placed face up on a clean surface such as a fiberglass screen. The process can be speeded by blowing the print with a blow dryer set at medium or low heat.

▲ Blotters may be used for print drying, provided the blotting material is the kind sold expressly for photographic use and has not been contaminated by previous use.

◄ This flat-bed electric dryer can be used to process two prints at once—one on each side. A cloth apron closes down over each print as it lies face up on the electrically heated metal surface. It is not recommended for RC prints.

The print is rolled into the rotary dryer by turning the large knob on the side. The cylinder's surface heats electrically while a cloth cover holds the print securely against the metal. It is not recommended for RC prints.

With a screen dryer, the prints are air dried at room temperature on contamination-resistant fiberglass screens—fiber-base prints face down, RC prints face up. You can make your own racks from wood frames covered with fiberglass screening purchased at a lumberyard or hardware store.

Spotting to Remove Minor Flaws

White specks, lines, or even large spots can be blended into the surrounding tones of the print by spotting with dyes that darken the area. The dyes are used straight from the bottle for the darkest areas, diluted with water for lighter ones.

etching

Small black specks or scratches can be removed by etching the surface of the print with a sharp blade until the darkened silver of the speck is removed. The roughened surface of the print is not objectionable if the speck is small and if you etch gently.

Your prints may have small imperfections that you would like to remove. Even after careful processing, it is almost impossible to produce a print without a few white specks caused by dust on the negative or paper during printing. Black specks or scratches can be very noticeable in a light-toned area. **Spotting** a print improves its overall appearance by removing these distracting marks. Most spotting is done after the print has been completely processed and dried; the exception is local reduction or bleaching, which is done while the print is still wet. Practice is essential with all these techniques; work on some scrap prints before you start on a good print.

White spots are removed by adding dye to the print until the tone of the area being spotted matches the surrounding tone (*top*). Liquid photographic dyes, such as Spotone, sink into the emulsion and match the surface gloss of unspotted areas. They are usually available in sets of at least three colors—neutral, warm (brown-black), and cool (blue-black)—so that the tones of different papers can be matched. Spotting colors packaged as dry pigments coated on small cards and watercolor paints tend to stay on top of the emulsion and may leave the spotted area duller than the rest of the print. You will need one or more soft, pointed brushes, size 00 or smaller (some people like a brush as small as size five zero, 00000), facial tissue to wipe the brushes, a little water, a small, flat dish to mix the colors, and a scrap print or a few margin trimmings to test them.

Pick up a drop of the neutral black on a brush and place it in the mixing dish. Spread a little on a margin trimming and compare the dye color to the color of the print to be spotted. If necessary, add some of the warmer or cooler dyes to the mixing dish until the spotting color matches the print. Spot first with undiluted dye in any completely black areas of the print. Dip the brush into the dye, wipe it almost dry, and touch it gently to the print. Several applications with an almost dry brush will give better results than overloading the brush and making a big blob on the print. Spread out the dye in the mixing dish and add a drop of water to part of it to dilute the dye for lighter areas. Since the dyes are permanent once they are applied to the print, it is safer to spot with a light shade of dye—you can always add more. Spot from the center of a speck to the outside so that the dye doesn't overlap tones outside the speck.

Etching can remove a small or thin black mark that obviously doesn't belong where it is, such as a dark scratch in a sky area. Gently stroke the sharp tip of a new mat knife blade or a single-edge razor blade over the black spot (*bottom*). Use short, light strokes to scrape off just a bit of silver at a time so that the surface of the print is not gouged. Etching generally does not work as well with RC papers as with fiber-base papers.

Local reduction or **bleaching** lightens larger areas. Farmer's Reducer (diluted 1:10) or Spot Off bleaches out larger areas than can be etched and also brightens highlights in a print. Prints are reduced while they are wet. Squeegee or blot off excess water and apply the reducer with a brush (used for this purpose only), a cotton swab, or a toothpick wrapped in cotton. If the print does not lighten enough within a minute or so, rinse, blot dry, and reapply fresh reducer. Refix the print for a few minutes before washing as usual. Do not use reducer in combination with toner.

How to Dry Mount

1 | **metal ruler**
2 | **mat knife**
3 | **tacking iron**
4 | **dry-mount tissue**
5 | **print**
6 | **mat board**
7 | **press**
8 | **paper for cover sheet**

Dry mounting is a fast method of providing a neat support for a print. Dry mounting uses dry-mount tissue, a thin sheet coated with an adhesive that becomes sticky when heated. The molten adhesive penetrates the fibers of both mounting board and print and forms a tight, perfect bond.

Dry mounting works best if two items are used: a small tacking iron to position the tissue on the board and print and a press to dry the materials and bond the print to the board. The press has a heating plate hinged to a bed plate; in it, the adhesive melts uniformly and is pressed into the board and print. For occasional mounting jobs, a household iron can be used, as on page 192.

Parts of the procedure are different (especially the temperatures used) depending on whether you are mounting a print made on fiber-base paper or one made on RC paper. Basically, though, the methods are alike.

All materials should be absolutely clean and dry. Even a small dirt particle trapped between print and board causes an unsightly and permanent lump in the print. The mount board, print, and cover sheet should be bone dry before mounting. A fiber-base print, the mount board, and a cover sheet are placed in a heated press to drive out any residual moisture. An RC print does not have to be heated since it will not have absorbed any atmospheric moisture.

There are various ways to mount a print. The print shown here is bleed mounted—trimmed so that the edges of the image are even with the edges of the mounting board. A common method is to mount the print with a wide border around the edges. Some photographers like a border that is the same width all around the print. Others prefer to have the side margins equal but the bottom margin slightly larger than the top.

1 | dry the materials

Heat the press to 200°–275° F (93°–135° C), or 180°–210° F (82°–99° C) for RC papers. Use the lowest setting that bonds print to mount. Predry mount board and print, with cover sheet on top, in press for 30 sec (do not predry RC prints).

2 | wipe materials clean

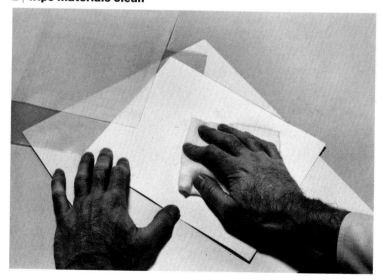

After the materials have been baked dry, let them cool for a few minutes, and then wipe away any loose dirt with a cloth; examine them for cleanliness under a strong light. Always use clean cloth, and take care not to grind dirt into materials.

3 | tack the mounting tissue to the print

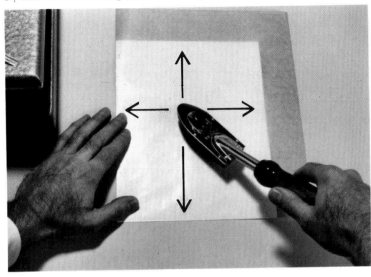

With the print face down and mounting tissue on top of it, tack the tissue to the print with a hot tacking iron by moving the iron from the center of the print to the sides. Do not tack at the corners.

4 | trim the mounting tissue

After placing a piece of smooth cardboard under the print, trim off the excess mounting tissue and a bit of the print margin, using the ruler as a guide. Press firmly on the ruler to prevent slipping. Don't cut into the image area of the print.

5 | attach mounting tissue and print to the board

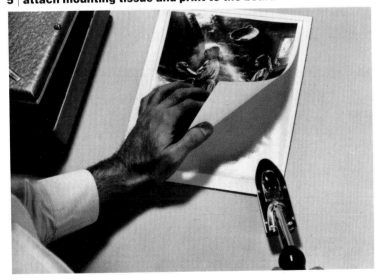

Position the print and tissue, face up, on top of the mount board. Slightly raise one corner of the print and tack the corner of the tissue to the board; tack the opposite corner next, then the remaining two. The tissue must lie flat to prevent wrinkles.

6 | mount the print

Put the sandwich of board, tissue, and print (with cover sheet on top) into the press. With RC prints, quickly open and close the press several times to drive out any moisture. Then clamp in the press for about 30 sec (or longer).

Dry Mounting with an Iron

If you are mounting a small print, a clothes iron can substitute for the mounting press and tacking iron. Clean the base plate well, empty it of water if it is a steam iron, and set the controls for synthetic fibers.

7 | trim the mounted print

Trim the edges of the mounted print with the mat knife. The blade must be sharp to make a clean cut. Several light slices often work better than only one cut. Press down firmly on the ruler so it does not slip—and be careful not to cut your fingers.

1 | tack the mounting tissue to the print

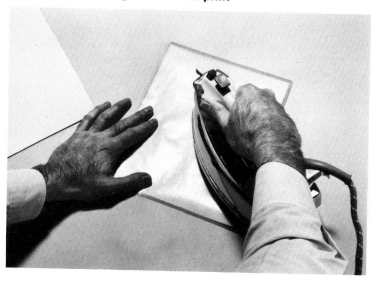

After drying the materials with the hot iron, use the tip to tack the mounting tissue to the back of the print. Don't press so hard as to crease or dent the print. Turn the print face up and trim away print margins and extra tissue with the ruler and mat knife.

8 | the finished print

The print above is bleed mounted, trimmed to leave no border. If you want a wide border of mounting board around the edges of the print, as at right, trim away the print margins and extra tissue before tacking down the print in step 5.

2 | seal the print to the mount board

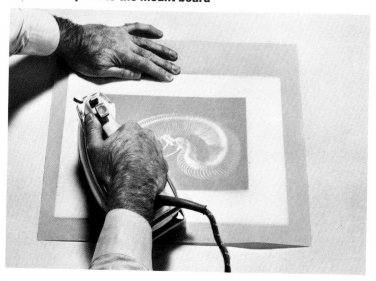

After positioning the print on the mount board, tack down the mounting tissue corners. Place a cover sheet over the print (tracing paper is shown, but heavier paper is better). Seal the print to the board with light strokes from the center outward.

Cutting an Overmat

1 | **T square**
2 | **metal ruler**
3 | **art gum eraser**
4 | **2 mat boards**
5 | **mat cutter**
6 | **single-edge razor blade**
7 | **print to be displayed**
8 | **pencil**

1 | measure the picture

Decide on cropping and measure the resulting image. This picture was cropped to 9⅜ × 5¾ inches. If the picture is not to be cropped, measure a fraction of an inch within the image area to make sure the print margin will not show.

2 | figure the dimensions

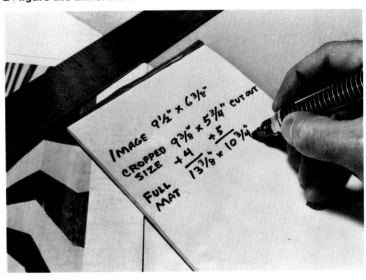

To find the size of the mat, add the dimensions of border and cropped image. Here the border is 2 inches on the sides and top and 3 inches on the bottom, requiring a mat 13⅜ × 10¾ inches. Cut two boards: one for backing, one for overmat.

An **overmat** provides a raised border around a print. It consists of a cardboard rectangle with a hole cut in it, placed over a print that has been mounted to a backing board. The raised border protects the surface of the print emulsion, which can be easily scratched by something sliding across it—such as another print. If the print is framed, it prevents the print emulsion from sticking to the glass in the frame. Damage can still occur with a matted print but is less likely. Since the overmat is replaceable, a new one can be cut and mounted without damage to the picture if the original mat becomes soiled. One of the great pleasures of photography is showing your prints to other people—but one of the great irritations is having someone leave a fingerprint on the mounting board of your best print. Prevent problems by handling your own and other people's pictures only by the edges.

It takes practice to cut the inner edges of an overmat with precision. It becomes easier after a few tries, so spend some time practicing with scrap board to get the knack of cutting perfectly clean corners. A mat cutter is a useful aid. A simple, heavy metal device designed to fit into the palm of the hand, it holds a knife blade that can be rotated to cut either a beveled (angled) or a perpendicular edge. Mat cutters, like the other tools and materials shown above, are available at most art or photographic supply stores. They are a worthwhile investment and can make the difference between a ruined board, cut freehand with an unbraced knife, and a perfectly cut mat.

3 | mark the mat board

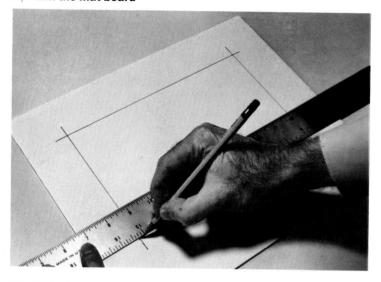

Mark the back of one board for the inner cut, using the dimensions of the image that will be visible. Measure with the ruler, but in drawing the lines use the T square firmly braced to align with the mat edge to be sure the lines are square.

4 | set the cutting blade

Insert the knife blade in the mat cutter, sliding it into the slot on the inner end of the movable bolt. Adjust the blade so that it extends far enough to cut through the board, then tighten, using the threaded knob on the bolt's outer end.

5 | cut the overmat

Get a firm grip on the mat cutter and brace it against the ruler. Cut each of the inside edges on a line, stopping short of the corners; finish the corners with the razor blade; do not cut too far, and take care to maintain the angle of the cut.

6 | position and attach the print

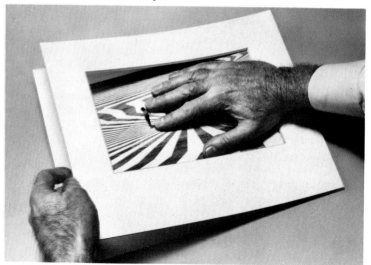

Ways of attaching the print to the backing board are shown at right. Slip the print between the backing board and the overmat. Align the print with the inner edge of the overmat. Then remove the overmat and attach the print.

7 | attach the overmat to the backing board

Hinge the overmat to the backing board with a strip of gummed linen tape (diagram below). Framing will hold the boards together without hinging. Handle any mounted print only by the edges. Use a gum eraser to clean the overmat if needed.

an overmatted print

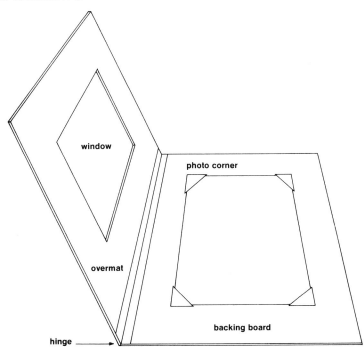

window

photo corner

overmat

backing board

hinge

attaching an overmatted print to a backing board

Materials. *Ideally, use archival-quality materials such as acid-free paper for the photo corners and gummed linen (Holland) tape or other pH-neutral tape for hinges. Less expensive but good-quality materials can be used when archival permanence is not required. If you value a print, do not hinge it with brown paper tape or pressure-sensitive tapes such as masking tape or cellophane tape. These products deteriorate with age and will damage a print.*

Dry mounting. *Before positioning the print (step 6, opposite) tack a piece of mounting tissue to the back of the print and trim off the excess. After positioning the print, tack the print to the board and then mount. See detailed instructions, pages 190–192.*

Cornering. *Photo corners, like the ones used to mount pictures in snapshot albums, are a convenient means of mounting. The corners are easy to apply and are hidden by the overmat. The print can easily be slipped out of the corners if you need to remove it from the backing. You can buy gummed photo corners or make your own (see below) and attach them to the backing board with a strip of tape.*

cut

crease

second fold

first fold

Hinging. *Hinging holds the print in place with strips of tape attached to the upper back edge of the print and to the backing board.*

print

hinge

backing board

A folded hinge is hidden when the print is in place.

A folded hinge can be reinforced by a piece of tape.

A pendant hinge is hidden if an overmat is used.

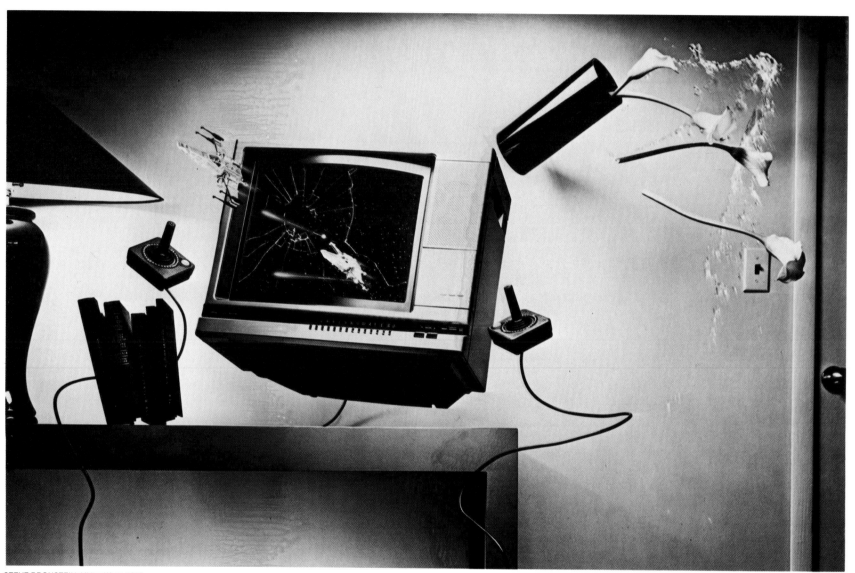

STEVE BRONSTEIN: *Video Wars*, 1982

Special Techniques

In addition to standard photographic procedures, you can create images using special equipment or techniques. This chapter shows some of these alternative ways of taking photographs or making prints.

Close-up photographs produce effects beyond simple magnification. Close-ups can show objects enlarged for scientific study, but there is also pleasure and magic just in seeing something larger and in greater detail than it is ordinarily seen.

You can also manipulate a photograph and radically change the image formed in the camera (or make a print entirely without a camera) in order to make a print that is more interesting or exciting to you or to express a personal viewpoint that could not be conveyed by conventional methods. There are many techniques besides those described in detail here; for example, nonsilver processes such as cyanotyping and photo silk screening (*page 216*) or multiple imagery (*pages 218–219*).

Ultimately, the success of a photograph depends not on the technique used but on your taste and judgment in fulfilling its potential—whether through a straight, full-scale black-and-white print or a manipulated image. Probably the main pitfall in manipulating a print is changing it merely for the sake of change instead of making alterations that actually strengthen the image. But you will never know what the possibilities are until you have used different techniques with your own images.

◄ *The ad agency for Mattel Electronics approached photographer Steve Bronstein with an idea they hoped would convey the excitement of home video games—a tongue-in-cheek ad to show that the games were so exciting they would even startle your TV set. The shoot began with getting the set built by a prop expert. The TV (gutted to reduce its weight) and the vase were suspended from the wall behind them. The flowers were hung from monofilament wire, which was later retouched out. Armature wire (which is sturdy but can be shaped) inside the game control cords gave them their wiggle.*

The set was lit from above by a bank of three 2400 watt/second strobes, a 1200 watt/second unit on the floor, another strobe inside the set to separate the screen from its frame, a light on the water to highlight it, and another inside the lamp.

The water was the most difficult part. The set builder filled a turkey baster with water, rigged it to the metal wringer of a sponge mop, and then hid the contraption behind the vase. When an assistant behind the set wall pulled a string, it closed the wringer, which squeezed the baster so the water spurted out, mostly into a pail positioned out of the frame. "It was a mess nevertheless," says Bronstein. "The smartest thing we did was to Scotchgard the set beforehand."

The World in Close-Up

If you want to make a large image of a small object, you can, at the simplest level, enlarge an ordinary negative. However, this is not always satisfactory because image quality deteriorates in extreme enlargements. A much better picture results from using **close-up techniques** to get a large image on the negative to begin with.

A close-up subject is focused closer than normal to the camera. This is done by fitting a supplementary lens over the front of the regular lens (*opposite*), by increasing the distance from lens to film with extension tubes or bellows inserted between the lens and the camera back (*page 200*) or by using a macro lens that is designed for close-up work (*pages 70 and 201*). Each method can focus a larger-than-normal image on the film (*diagram below*).

Working close up is somewhat different from working at normal distances. After roughly focusing and composing the image, it is often easier to finish focusing by moving the entire camera or the subject farther away or closer rather than by racking the lens in or out. During shooting, a tripod is almost a necessity because even a slight change in

lens-to-subject distance changes the focus. A highly magnified image readily shows the slightest camera movement, so a tripod also helps by keeping the camera steady.

Depth of field decreases as a subject is focused closer to the lens. Depth of field is very shallow at close working distances, so focusing becomes critical. A 50mm lens at a distance of about 12 inches from the subject has a depth of field of one-sixteenth inch when the aperture is set at f/4. At f/11 the depth of field increases—but only to one-half inch.

The depth of field is distributed differently, too. In a close-up it extends half in front and half behind the plane of focus. At normal working distances it is one-third in front and two-thirds behind the plane of focus.

Some cameras are better than others for close-up work. A single-lens reflex or view camera is good for close-ups, mostly because of its through-the-lens viewing. You can see exactly where the lens is focused and preview depth of field by stopping down the lens, an important ability with shallow depth of field. You can frame the image exactly

and see just how the subject relates to the background. Many single-lens reflex cameras have through-the-lens metering, which can solve some close-up metering problems (*see metering on page 202*).

Twin-lens reflex and rangefinder cameras are less convenient because it is difficult to see the image exactly as the lens does. If you have a twin-lens reflex, you can buy twin supplementary lenses that fit over the camera's viewing and taking lenses; a built-in prism changes the angle of the viewing lens so it sees the same area as the taking lens (although from a slightly higher point of view, which changes the relationship of subject to background). It is also possible to measure the distance from the center of the taking lens to the center of the viewing lens, then raise the tripod head exactly that much; a tripod accessory is available for this.

Rangefinder cameras are even harder to use since the rangefinder mechanism will not focus at very close distances and the viewfinder will not show the exact area being photographed. You may be able to buy an accessory close-up rangefinder attachment.

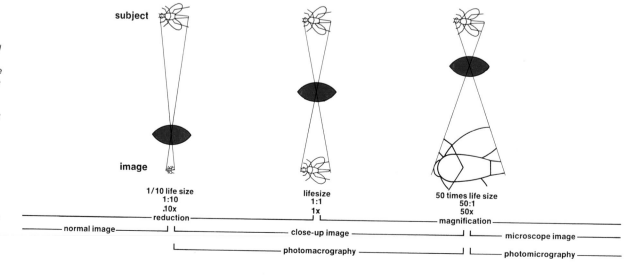

In normal photographic situations, the size of the image produced on the film is less than one-tenth the size of the object being photographed. Close-up images where the subject is closer than normal to the camera can range from about one-tenth to about 50 times life size. Beyond about 10 times life size, however, it is often more practical to take the photograph through a microscope. The relative sizes of image and subject are expressed as a ratio with the relative size of the image stated first: a 1:10 ratio means the image is one-tenth the size of the subject. Or the image size can be stated in terms of magnification: a 50× magnification means the image is 50 times the size of the subject. The magnification of an image smaller than life size (actually a reduction) is stated as a decimal: a .10 magnification produces an image one-tenth life size. The term photomacrograph (sometimes macrophotograph) refers to close-ups that are life size or larger. Pictures taken through a microscope are photomicrographs.

50mm lens alone

How supplementary lenses enlarge. Here, a cluster of petunias as seen by a 35mm camera with a 50mm lens. The lens, set at its closest focusing distance (about 18 inches), produces an image on the film about one-tenth life size. (The pictures here are enlarged slightly above actual film size.)

50mm lens and +1.5 diopter lens

With a +1.5 diopter supplementary lens, camera-to-subject distance is reduced to 15 inches for a larger image, about one-fifth life size.

50mm lens and +4.5 diopter lens

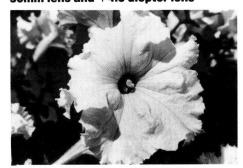

With +4.5 diopters, the distance is 10 inches to the flowers, and the image of a blossom is enlarged to about one-third life size.

lens hood   **supplementary lens**   **35mm SLR camera with 50mm lens**

Supplementary lenses let you make close-ups with any camera lens. They are magnifying glasses of varying powers that are attached to the front of regular lenses. Supplementary lenses enlarge an image in two ways: they add their own power to that of the regular lens, and they change the focusing distance of the regular lens so that it can move closer than normal to an object.

The power of a supplementary lens is expressed in **diopters,** an optical term used to describe both the focal length and the magnifying power of the lens. Thus a 1-diopter lens (expressed as +1) will focus on a subject one meter (100 cm, or 3.25 ft) away. A +2 diopter focuses at half that distance (50 cm) and magnifies twice as much; a +3 diopter focuses at 33 cm and magnifies three times as much, and so on. Lenses of varying diopters can be added to each other to provide greater magnification, as long as the stronger lens is attached to the camera first. Image quality tends to suffer, however, when more than one supplementary lens is used.

When a supplementary lens is attached to a camera lens set at infinity, the new focusing distance will be the focal length of the supplementary lens. This is true no matter which camera lens is being used. For example, with the lens at infinity a +2 lens will always focus on a subject 50 cm (19.5 inches)

away with a 50mm lens, a 135mm lens or any other lens—provided that the regular lens is set at infinity.

Image size, however, depends on the focal length of the camera lens. This happens because the degree of enlargement is determined by the diopter of the supplementary lens plus the magnifying power of the regular lens. Thus a +2 diopter gives a bigger image with a 135mm lens than with a 50mm lens. Also, a supplementary lens gives varying degrees of enlargement depending on the distance setting of the lens. With the lens set for a distance closer than infinity, an object can be brought into focus closer than the regular diopter distance to create an even larger image. Charts provided with the supplementary lenses give details.

Supplementary lenses are useful but have some problems. They do not change exposure readings, which is convenient. Also, they are small and inexpensive and can be used with any kind of camera, including those without interchangeable lenses. Because of their design, however, the lenses provide acceptable sharpness only when used with small apertures. Their surfaces, not bonded to the regular lens, may cause reflections and other aberrations. And overall sharpness decreases at +5 diopters or stronger.

How to Use Extension Tubes and Bellows

set of extension tubes

lens hood   **50mm lens**   **bellows**   **35mm SLR camera**

50mm lens on 35mm SLR camera

Some different degrees of magnification using extension tubes and bellows are shown in the pictures at left. Here, a view of some petunias taken with a 50mm lens alone. The image on the film is about one-tenth the actual size of the flowers. (The pictures are enlarged slightly more than the film size.)

50mm lens and full extension-tube set

A picture taken with a set of extension tubes inserted between the lens and the camera. This let the lens be focused closer to the flowers, which produced a life-size image of part of a single blossom. Increasing or decreasing the number of rings used in the tube set would produce greater or lesser magnification.

50mm lens reversed and extension tubes

Here the same extension tubes were used as above but with the 50mm lens reversed; the front end of the lens instead of the back was attached (with a reversing ring) to the tubes. At very close distances, many lenses perform better if reversed because of the asymmetrical design of the lens elements. Reversing also provides somewhat more magnification.

50mm lens and fully extended bellows

A picture taken with the reversed 50mm lens attached to a fully extended bellows. The lens was able to be focused so close that it showed just the center of a single flower magnified to five times life size.

Extension tubes and **bellows** are mounted between camera body and lens. They extend the lens farther from the film so the lens can be focused closer to the subject. The closer the lens comes to the subject, the larger its image size on the film. (Similarly, the closer you bring your eye to an object, the larger the object appears.) The main differences between extension tubes and bellows are in the ease with which they produce varying amounts of magnification and in their price.

Tubes are rings of metal. Most are rigid and extend the lens in predetermined, graduated steps depending on the length of each ring and how many of them are used. They are light, easily attached, and relatively inexpensive but not always as useful as bellows because they come in fixed lengths. A more expensive type of tube can be racked in or out like a lens barrel and so extended to variable lengths. A macro-converter is an extension tube with elements that optically improve sharpness when a conventional lens is used at close-up distances.

Bellows are made of a flexible material. They provide continuously variable magnifications over their entire extendable range. A good-quality bellows is a precision instrument, more expensive but more versatile than an extension tube.

Tubes and bellows maintain better optical quality than supplementary lenses. They provide a wide range of magnifications, including high-quality, larger-than-life-size images. Disadvantages are due to inserting them between lens and camera body. Tubes and bellows can be used only with cameras that have interchangeable lenses. Unless specifically designed for a particular camera, they will interrupt automatic exposure functions if the camera has them, which means that shutter speed and aperture must be adjusted manually.

55mm macro at medium distance

The magnifications produced by moving closer to a subject with a 55mm macro lens are shown at right. Here, the picture was taken from 5 ft away. The resulting image (slightly enlarged here) was about 1/25 life size.

55mm macro at closest distance, 10 inches

Setting the lens to focus as close as possible and moving the camera 10 inches from a flower produced an image one-half life size.

55mm macro with extension tube, 8 inches

Adding an extension tube, which moved the lens to only 8 inches from the flower, produced a life-size image.

70-150mm macro zoom lens

55mm macro lens   **extension tube**   **35mm SLR camera**

If you want to make close-ups, a **macro lens** is probably the most useful piece of equipment you can own. The lens barrel of a macro is constructed so it can be extended farther than normal, which lets you focus closer than normal to a subject. A 50mm macro lens without any accessories will focus as close as 9 inches and produce a one-half life-size image. The size of the image can be increased even more by inserting extension tubes or bellows between the lens and the camera body.

Macro lenses are optically corrected to prevent the aberrations that reduce sharpness at close focusing distances, so they give close-up images with edge-to-edge sharpness superior to that produced by lenses of conventional design. They also perform well when used for general photography. Macro lenses are available in several fixed focal lengths from 50mm to 200mm and as macro zoom lenses in focal lengths

such as 28–85mm and 70–150mm. Most macro lenses connect directly to the camera body, retaining connections with the camera's meter or any automatic features.

One inconvenience is that a macro lens's widest aperture is relatively small: f/3.5 is a typical maximum aperture for a 50mm macro. Adding an extension tube or bellows also cuts the amount of light reaching the film. This means that in dim light or with slow film, a relatively slow shutter speed must be used.

Macro zoom lenses are popular because they let you produce different degrees of magnification without moving the camera. However, many lenses sold as macro zooms would be more accurately called close-focusing zooms; they are not fully corrected for working up close, and unless tubes or bellows are added, produce an image no larger than one-third or one-quarter life size.

Close-Up Exposures: Greater than Normal

Two possible exposure problems arise when photographing close up. One is getting an accurate light reading in the first place and the other is adjusting that reading when the lens is extended farther than normal from the film.

The small size of a close-up subject can make metering difficult. The subject is usually so small that you can meter more background than subject and possibly get an inaccurate reading. A spot meter is one solution; it can read very small objects with great accuracy. Or you can make a substitution reading from a gray card (*page 123*). Another possibility is to use an incident-light meter to read the light falling on the subject. This will give a usable average exposure no matter what size the subject is.

An **exposure increase** is needed with bellows or extension tubes. As the distance between lens and film increases, the intensity of the light that falls on the film decreases and the image becomes dimmer. Therefore, to prevent underexposure in close-up photographs, the exposure must be increased. Accessory bellows and extension tubes come with charts for this purpose, or you can calculate the new exposure yourself. Whichever method you use, it's a good idea to bracket your exposures. First make the exposure you think is correct, then make one or two more with increased exposure.

You don't have to do any calculating if your camera has a through-the-lens meter that reads the light that actually reaches the film, as many single-lens reflex cameras do. If the object is magnified enough to fill the viewing screen (or that part of the screen that shows the area being read), the meter will calculate a corrected exposure by itself.

If you are using a hand-held meter, there are several ways to find the exposure increase needed. One way is to use

the dial of the meter, as shown in the diagrams at right. All the corrected f-stop and shutter-speed combinations are immediately readable on the dial.

If you want to do the arithmetic yourself, there are several formulas. Be sure the bellows extension (or the extension tube length) and the lens focal length are in the same units of measure—either in inches, centimeters, or millimeters (1 inch = 2.5 cm = 25 mm).

$$\frac{\text{indicated f-stop}}{\text{adjusted f-stop}} = \frac{\text{bellows extension}}{\text{focal length of lens}}$$

Meter the subject and choose an f-stop and shutter-speed combination. If the f-number indicated by the meter is f/16 at ⅛ sec, the focal length of the lens is 2 inches, and the distance from the lens diaphragm to the film plane measures 10 inches, then:

$$\frac{16}{x} = \frac{10}{2} \qquad 10x = 32 \qquad x = 3.2$$

The new exposure combination is f/3.2 (a slightly larger aperture than f/4) at the original shutter speed. Set f/3.2 opposite the shutter speed on the meter dial to read off equivalent combinations.

You can also calculate a bellows extension factor that tells how many times the exposure must be increased (similar to the method for changing exposures used with filter factors, *page 107*):

$$\text{factor} = \frac{\text{bellows extension}^2}{\text{focal length}^2}$$

$$\text{factor} = \frac{10^2}{2^2} = \frac{100}{4} = 25$$

Increase the exposure about 25 times (about 4½ stops).

When making a close-up, you need to increase the exposure because the lens is farther than normal from the film and produces a dimmer-than-normal image. If you are using a hand-held meter, first measure the bellows extension (or the extension tube length), the distance from the lens to the film.

Meter the subject and calculate an exposure as you normally would. Now find two numbers on the f-stop scale on the meter dial to stand for (1) the bellows extension measured above and (2) the focal length of the lens. Have both measurements either in inches or in metric units (1 inch = 2.5 cm = 25 mm). Here the bellows extension was 10 inches (25 cm) and the focal length of the lens was 2 inches (5 cm).

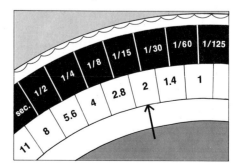

Move the number that stands for the focal length to the position occupied by the number that stands for the bellows extension. Read off the new f-stop and shutter-speed combinations.

A kohlrabi is a prosaic root vegetable, but in this close-up Ralph Weiss has shown it in an uncommon way. Isolating it against black separates it and causes the viewer to examine its shape in detail. There are no visual clues to its actual size (though the caption will tell you), and it is shown upside down from the way it grows: the photograph presents it as a visual experience rather than as something to eat. It becomes a sea creature, with trailing tentacles undulating through dark waters.

RALPH WEISS: *Kohlrabi,* 1966; magnified 0.6×, here enlarged to 3.4×

Special Printing Techniques
A Photogram: A Cameraless Picture

A **photogram** is a kind of contact print, made by placing objects, instead of just a negative, on a piece of light-sensitive material and exposing it to light. In the 1920s, about 80 years after the first camera photographs were made, photograms and other print manipulations such as solarization became popular with the painter-photographers Man Ray and László Moholy-Nagy, who sought to explore the "pure" actions of light in space. In Man Ray's Rayograph (as he named his photograms) at right, he used the Surrealist technique of combining unrelated objects.

Any object that comes between the light source and the sensitized material can be used. You can try two-dimensional objects like cut paper, three-dimensional ones, opaque objects that block the light completely, transparent or translucent objects like a pitcher or a plastic bottle that bend the light rays, objects laid on glass and held at different levels above the paper, moving objects, smoke blown over the surface of the paper during the exposure—the possibilities are limitless. All these objects are light modulators—they change the light on its way to the paper. Light can be added to the paper as well as held back: for example, a penlight flashed at the paper or suspended from a string and swung across the surface.

A photogram can be made on a piece of printing paper or on a negative that is then printed. Color photograms can be made by exposing color paper through different color filters or by using translucent, tinted objects to modulate the light.

MAN RAY: *Rayograph*, 1924

Here a simple photogram is being made by placing a piece of marsh grass on a sheet of high contrast (grade 5) printing paper. The head of the enlarger is positioned far enough above the base-board to light the paper completely. After exposure, the paper is developed, fixed, and washed in the usual manner to produce a life-size print of the grass. Experiment with different exposures—longer ones will penetrate some objects more and create a different effect.

Ordinarily a photographer uses a camera to select and frame a portion of an existing scene. But in a photogram, objects are arranged directly on light-sensitive material. The objects are transformed in shape or tonality and the photograph does not show them as they ordinarily look. The objects that are used are less important than what you see when you look at the picture.

◄ Man Ray arranged string, a toy gyroscope, and the end of a strip of movie film on a piece of photographic paper, then exposed the paper to light. The resulting image (opposite) is as open to interpretation as you wish to make it. You can see it simply as an assemblage of forms and tones. Or if you see the large black background as a person's head in silhouette (like the silhouetted head in the movie film), then the strip of film might be a dream seen by the internal gyroscope of the brain.

You can combine several layers to make a pho- ▶ togram or use just one. Jack Sal sandwiched together a matzo cracker and a piece of Kodak Studio Proof paper, a printing-out paper that darkens on exposure to sunlight or other light sources high in ultraviolet radiation. He put the two in his window for about a month, then fixed the paper like an ordinary print to prevent further darkening. The holes in the cracker appear large in the print because during the day the sun changed position in the sky and shone into the holes from different angles.

JACK SAL: *No Title,* 1978

A Sabattier Print—Part Positive, Part Negative

A **Sabattier print** is made by reexposing the paper to light during processing. This gives a print both negative and positive qualities and adds halolike Mackie lines between adjacent highlight and shadow areas (*see opposite*). The technique is commonly known as solarization, although, strictly speaking, **solarization** (which can look somewhat similar) takes place only when film is massively overexposed. The correct name for the phenomenon shown here is the Sabattier effect.

The unusual appearance of a Sabattier print results from a combination of effects. When the print is reexposed to light during processing, there is little effect on the dark areas of the print because most of the crystals there have already been exposed and reduced to black silver by the developing process. The bright areas, however, still contain many sensitive crystals that can respond to light and development. The bright areas therefore turn gray but usually remain somewhat lighter than the shadows. Between the light and dark areas, by-products remaining from the first development retard further development; these border regions remain light, forming the Mackie lines.

There are several ways to produce a Sabattier print. The simplest way, but the most difficult to control, is simply to turn on a light briefly while the print is in the developer. A procedure that gives much more control is described in the box at right.

Printing from a negative will give a positive image plus negative effects from the second exposure, as in the print opposite. You can also print from a positive color slide, which will give a negative image plus some positive effects. Black-and-white printing paper responds differently to colors in the slide: blue prints as black, yellow prints as white.

Making a Sabattier Print

Basic procedure

Materials needed. *A negative of normal to high contrast. Normal print processing chemicals. High-contrast paper (prints opposite were made with Agfa Brovira grade 6; other high-contrast papers such as Kodabromide grade 5 also work).*

First exposure. *Put negative in enlarger and focus. Expose a test print with a slightly lighter than normal series of test exposures. (Test print opposite left, received first exposures of 5, 10, 15, and 20 sec.)*

First development. *Develop for the standard time in normal developer.*

Rinse. *Wash in water for 30 sec to remove the surface developer. Do not use an acid stop bath. Remove excess water from the front and back of the print with a squeegee or soft paper towels. Handle gently to avoid scratching the fragile surface of the wet print.*

Second exposure. *Remove the negative from the enlarger. Stop down the aperture about two stops. Reexpose the test print in strips at right angles to the first exposures. (Test print, opposite left, was given second exposures of 5, 10, 15, and 20 sec.)*

Second development. *Develop for the standard time in normal developer.*

Finish processing. *Treat print with stop bath and fixer; wash and dry as usual.*

Final print. *Examine the test print and choose the square that gives the desired effect. Note the combination of exposure times, apertures, and development times. Make a print under these conditions.*

Variations

Set the enlarger slightly out of focus. This will broaden the Mackie lines without making the image noticeably out of focus. The Mackie lines will also be broader with a less contrasty negative.

Develop for less than the standard time. Remove the print quickly from the developer when the desired effect is visible.

Develop in a more dilute developer (if the normal dilution is 1:2, try 1:4, 1:10, or even greater dilutions to produce color shifts).

Develop in two different developers. A cold-tone developer for one development and a warm-tone developer for the other will give color shifts.

Some photographers report better results if the print is aged at this point in a dark place (a photo blotter book works well). Aging times vary from 15 min to a week.

See variations under first development.

Dodging or burning in during the first and/or second exposure will give different results. The Mackie lines can be lightened by bleaching. The reducing formula given by Ansel Adams in his book The Print *is recommended. You can also try local reduction or an overall immersion in Farmer's Reducer (diluted 1:10).*

This test for a Sabattier print was given first exposures of 5, 10, 15, and 20 sec (left to right). After a first development, the print was exposed again to light from the enlarger, but without the negative in place. The second exposures were 5, 10, 15, and 20 sec (bottom to top). The test was then developed again, fixed, and washed.

The exposures for the final print were chosen from the test print at left: a first exposure of 20 sec and a second exposure of 5 sec (the bottom right square of the test). The enlarger was deliberately set very slightly out of focus to broaden the Mackie lines, and the print was later bleached to lighten them.

Techniques Using High-Contrast Film

High-contrast materials can change a black-and-white picture in many ways. The pictures on the following pages show methods of using high-contrast materials to change the conventional portrait at right into a high-contrast print, a line sketch, a posterlike patch-work of grays, and finally color versions.

To start, the original negative is enlarged onto **lith film,** a high-contrast copying film sold under different trade names (Kodak Ultratec or Kodalith, Agfa Gevalith) for use in photo-offset printing. One of its properties is that it can convert the range of tones in an ordinary print into solid black and pure white. This produces a **dropout,** an image with only black or white areas and no intermediate gray tones. Because it eliminates middle grays, lith film can render invisible any slight smudges on a page of type that is being copied for a printing plate. The same property enables the graphic artist or photographer to convert any continuous-tone picture, made on ordinary film, into a pattern of black and white. And by altering the exposure time in the copying process, you can produce images with differing amounts of black—even to the extreme of a practically solid black silhouette pierced only by the brightest highlights.

Because lith film produces black-and-white transparencies, several can be superimposed in printing to achieve a range of effects. Lith film lends itself to various color-printing techniques, including the use of color printing paper. Step-by-step demonstrations of techniques using these materials appear on the following pages.

FRED BURRELL: *Portrait of Ann Ford,* 1971

To start off the printing processes shown on these pages, place the original negative within the enlarger's negative carrier, ready to be inserted in the enlarger for reproduction on high-contrast graphic arts (lith) film such as Kodalith Ortho Film 2556, Type 3. If the manufacturer describes the film as ortho or orthochromatic, it can be processed under red safelight; you will be able to see what you are doing and how the film is developing. Check the instructions.

The negative, projected onto the easel on the baseboard, is enlarged to fill an 8 × 10 sheet of film. The first reproduction will be a positive transparency and from that a negative will be contact printed. Try an exposure time of between 10 and 20 sec with the enlarger lens wide open; make a test strip to check the effects of different exposures—slight increases in exposure extend the dark areas.

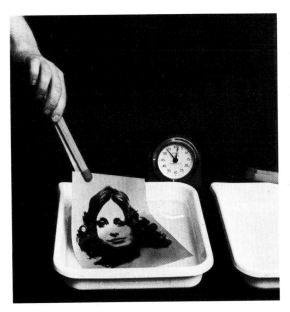

Process like a conventional photographic film but use a developer designed for lith film. Check the instruction sheet for development time—with Kodalith Developer it is about 2¾ min at 68° F (20° C) with constant agitation. Agitate in fresh stop-bath solution for about 10 sec. Then agitate in fresh fixer for about 4 min. Wash for 10 min in running water at 65°–70° F (18°–21° C).

To prevent water spots or streaks, gently draw a squeegee or sponge across each side of the wet positive—placed on the bottom of an upturned tray—to wipe off most of the water. Or treat in a wetting solution. Then hang the positive up to dry, after which a high-contrast negative can be made from it (following pages).

A negative can be produced from a positive transparency by using standard contact printing techniques (pages 160–163). First make sure the enlarger head is raised enough so the light will cover the contact frame. Then (above) clip the positive to the glass cover of a printing frame, emulsion side away from the glass. Insert, emulsion side up, an unexposed sheet of high-contrast copying film.

Try an exposure between 5 and 10 sec with the aperture wide open; a test strip will give an exact exposure. You may find in comparing the high-contrast positive to the high-contrast negative that the negative has dropped out more tones than the positive. If so, you can contact the negative onto another sheet of high-contrast film to make a positive that is an exact opposite of the negative: you'll need the positive if you want to make a line print.

Above are the high-contrast positive and negative transparencies, ready for use in the printing processes demonstrated on the following pages. They have no middle-gray tones, only black and white.

Check for pinholes—clear specks caused by dust on the film or by underexposure. Paint them out with a fine brush dipped in a gooey blocking-out material called opaque. Large areas can also be painted out, if desired. Black specks or large black areas can be removed with a strong solution of Farmer's Reducer, a chemical bleaching agent. A weak solution of Farmer's Reducer removes yellow processing stains.

To make a line print—an image composed of dark lines on a white background or white lines on a dark background—place the positive and negative over a light and carefully align them so that the two images overlap exactly. The result, looked at straight on, will be solid black. However, light can pass through the two copies at an angle, along the outlines of the paired images. Tape the copies together.

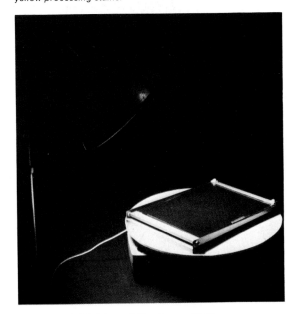

Put the sandwich into a printing frame with an unexposed sheet of film. A lazy Susan or a turntable rotates the frame so that light can come in from all sides at an angle. The light source shown is a 100-watt frosted bulb placed at a 45° angle 3 ft above a rotating turntable for a 15-sec exposure. You could also rotate the printing frame by hand under an enlarger.

The line picture, a thin black outline of the subject on clear film, resembles a pen-and-ink sketch. A thin sheet of acetate or of unexposed, fully processed film between the negative and positive would have made thicker lines. The line picture can be copied directly onto another sheet of high-contrast film to make a clear-line-on-black-background transparency. Either image can be printed on printing paper to make an opaque, white or black image.

A Posterization

The two positive images above were produced on high-contrast film from the same negative (right). The first, which has more dark area than the second, simply received more exposure.

Posterization gives an image with tones that look like the flat shades of poster paints. The image above was made from the three high-contrast copies at left: two positives plus a negative, each having different dark areas. The three were carefully aligned, then fastened with tape hinges (above left) so that each positive could be laid over or lifted away from the negative. The negative at the bottom of this stack was then taped on two sides to the enlarger baseboard. Printing paper was slipped under the untaped sides, and a piece of glass held all the sheets flat.

Three exposures were made. The first exposure, for 60 sec, was through all three copies and gave the black tones of the final print. Then the darker positive was flipped back, and an exposure of 1 sec was made through the lighter positive and the negative so as to start the dark-gray tone. An exposure of 1 sec through the negative alone produced the light gray and completed the dark gray. The exposures were determined by test strips.

The starting point for the color posterization shown above is much the same as for the black-and-white examples on the opposite page (high-contrast copies, one negative and two positives of unequal dark areas), but the line image shown on page 211 is also used. The color is introduced by filtering the light from the enlarger so it shines colored light through the copies onto a sheet of color printing paper.

For this posterization, the line print and the lighter positive were used for an exposure with a blue filter, to get yellow. The darker positive was added next and three exposures were made, through red, green, and blue filters, for 3, 5, and 6 sec, respectively. The resulting color, mixed with the yellow, gave the russet hue. The final exposure, with the negative copy added, was through a red filter and produced cyan, which gave the greenish cast that is most visible in the features of the face.

Prints from Office Copy Machines

(control panel diagram labels) stop print · start print · full color · magenta · cyan · yellow · on off · number of prints · color-contrast control · color-adjustment dials

Standard office **copy machines** can make excellent prints—but only if you exploit the graininess, contrast, and color variations inherent in their reproductions rather than seeking to imitate a conventional fine print. The instant feedback from the machines and their ability to alter images have made them popular with many photographers.

Black-and-white copiers are widely available and are inexpensive to operate. Some machines produce a more detailed photographic image than others do; try several different machines if you want to work extensively with one.

Color copy machines are available in commercial copy centers and are simple to use. Set a few dials, press a button, and out come opaque paper copies, in color, of transparencies, prints, or three-dimensional objects. Anything you can bring to the copier's document glass—including people—you can copy. You can display copies as is or make a transfer copy from which the image can be pressed onto another sheet of paper or onto cloth, for example onto a T-shirt. The adjustment dials and accessory equipment give considerable control over the image's color and even its shape, although the machines are not always as predictable as one might want.

The machine makes three passes to reproduce colors. The original is scanned three times through filters that separate the colors into the primary hues of magenta, cyan, and yellow. The machine applies corresponding layers of color toner during each of the three cycles. In copying a white area, for example, the machine withholds the colored toners, leaving the paper there blank. For black areas, the machine deposits full layers of toner in all three primary colors. To reproduce other colors, the machine deposits varying proportions of the primary colors.

Copying a Transparency

To make this natural-looking reproduction of a 35mm transparency, the slide was inserted in a slide projector attached to the machine, which projected it onto a plastic screen laid on the document glass. The button for full color was pressed. Then the start-print button was pressed to make the print. The color-adjustment dials can be readjusted—higher to intensify certain colors, lower to lessen them—if the normal setting proves to be unsatisfactory.

This copy of the same slide reproduced at left, but with colors that are muted, was made simply by turning all the color-adjustment dials down before the start-print button was pressed. This setting causes the machine to release all three pigments in lower quantities.

Copying Objects

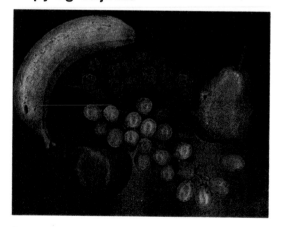

For this picture, real fruit was arranged on the document glass. When the lid over the document glass is up, the background comes out black—there was nothing in the spaces between the pieces of fruit to reflect light to the copier's lens, causing the machine to distribute full amounts of toner in all three colors in these spaces.

A rendition of the fruit with a light background was made by draping a white paper towel over the objects before copying them. During exposure, the machine withholds toner from any white area. So where the white towel touched the glass, the corresponding space on the print became white.

◄ The console of a typical color copier has various settings to control color. On this machine, the top button of the color-selection panel sets the machine for copying in full color; each lower button copies a black-and-white original in one primary color. Color is also controlled by three dials, marked 1 to 5, that vary the intensity of primary hues. The contrast control can be used to reduce contrast.

Copying a Copy

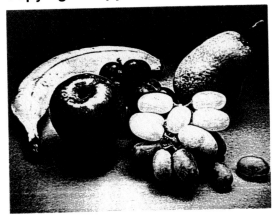

Contrasting colors and increased graininess are created by successive copying. For this example, a full-color copy was produced from the transparency used at left, then the copy was copied; this new copy again was copied. The effect is caused by slight fading and magnification that occur each time the image is reproduced; after one pass, these flaws are hardly visible, but each successive reproduction exaggerates them until the image begins to break down.

The color of an object can be altered by removing it during one or more of the passes. After the fruit was arranged on the glass, the banana was removed and a white paper towel placed over the copying area. Between the first and second passes, the towel was lifted and the banana put into position. The color of the banana in the final print is the result of toner distributed only during the second and third passes—yellow and cyan. Magenta is absent because none was distributed during the first pass.

ELLEN LAND-WEBER: *Eucalyptus Leaves and Hydrangea*, 1975

Ellen Land-Weber uses a copy paper from which the image can be transferred to another surface when heat and pressure are applied. She puts leaves, flowers, bits of seawood, and other materials on the machine's document glass and copies them, then cuts out parts of the resulting prints and transfers them to a large sheet of paper.

Using Special Techniques

Starry Night III. 1975, cyanotype with watercolors and applied stars

Blue Sky Variation and Erased, 1977, vandyke print with pencil and watercolors

BETTY HAHN

Taos Sky, 1979, lithograph

Starry Night Variation #2, 1977, silkscreen

As a starting point for work that incorporates various printing processes, hand coloring, and other techniques, Betty Hahn used a publicity photograph of those mythic heroes the Lone Ranger and Tonto. The cyanotype and vandyke processes, photographic printing processes invented in the 19th century, utilize light-sensitive iron salts to form the image. The lithograph and silk screen are traditional fine-art printmaking processes. Each print is enjoyable in its own right, but when the versions are placed together, the eye jumps back and forth among them comparing skies, colors, and other traces of the artist's intervention in the original photograph. A bonus is the cactus growing out of the Lone Ranger's head.

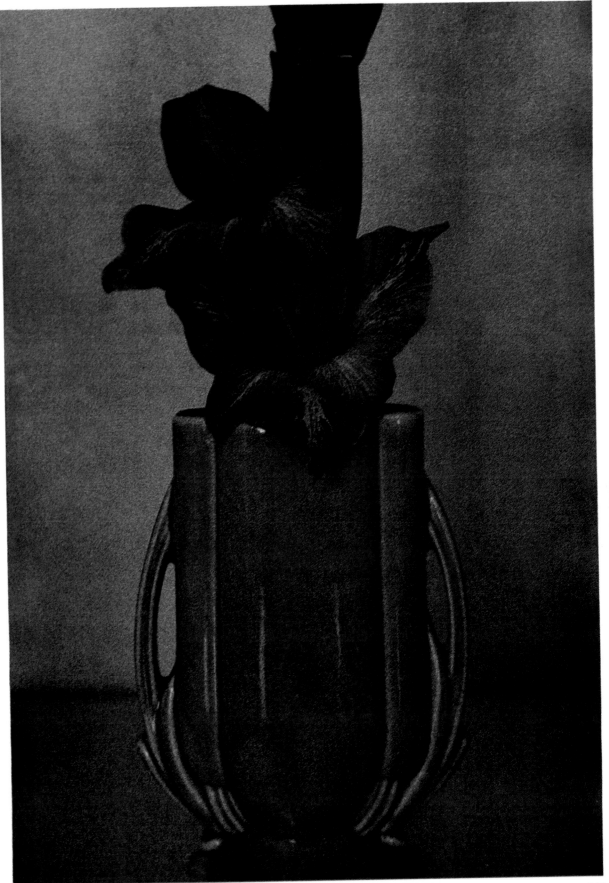

Sheila Metzner's carefully composed still lifes are stylized images in which the details of objects are reduced to broad masses and subdued tones. She begins with a 35mm color transparency. Prints are made by the Fresson Quadrichromie (four-color) process, in which layers of pigments in the three primary colors of cyan, magenta, and yellow, plus black, are transferred onto a single sheet to form the image. Details are softened by the graininess and mottle introduced during the printing process. Fresson printing is similar to carbon printing and other processes that were popular earlier in the century with Pictorialists, who liked the soft images that could be achieved with these printing methods.

SHEILA METZNER: *Painted Gladiola/Turquoise Vase*, 1980, Fresson print

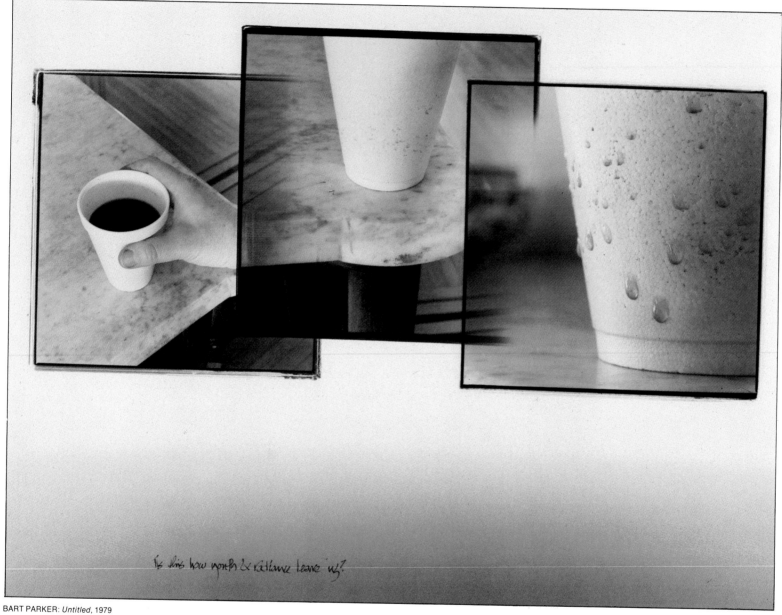

BART PARKER: *Untitled,* 1979

Multiple printing can join separate bits of reality together to form a new reality or to create a displaced one. Bart Parker combines views of commonplace objects to create an enigmatic statement. He often adds words to his images. The legend written at the bottom of this one, "Is this how youth & radiance leave us," seems to refer to the image but raises as many questions as it answers.

Jerry Uelsmann prefers postvisualization to pre-visualization. In the darkroom he prints various combinations of different negatives, experimenting and making discoveries as he goes. He may block out part of a scene, print in part of another one, and generally merge objects that do not seem to belong together into the same image. The result is a disquieting universe of real-looking but impossible dreamscapes.

JERRY N. UELSMANN: *Untitled*, 1982

RICHARD JEFFERY: *Melon Slice with Grapes,* 1968

10
Color

◄ *A realistic or, at least, pleasing color balance is important in food photography, where the intention is usually to appeal to the appetite by way of the eye. In this photograph the glistening highlights on the melon and the moisture on the grapes also help convey the mouth-watering succulence of the fruit.*

Color films take advantage of the fact that nearly all colors can be produced by mixing only a few basic or primary colors. Color films are made with three color-sensitive layers; each records the wavelengths of light in a different third of the spectrum. There are two basic types of color film. Color **negative film** is processed to be the opposite in colors and density of the original scene; then it is printed onto a sheet of sensitized paper to make a positive color print. **Reversal film** is processed so that the negative image produced in the camera is reversed back to a positive transparency with the same colors and density of the scene. Positive transparencies (such as slides) can be projected or viewed directly and can also be printed onto reversal paper to make a positive print.

The characteristics of color films are linked to film speed. Slow films appear sharper, have more delicate colors with subtler gradations, and have less apparent graininess. Faster films appear less sharp, with less color saturation and more apparent graininess. But even within the same speed range, different films produce different color balances. One film may have an overall reddish cast, while another may look slightly blue-green. These differences may be quite noticeable when reversal film is projected as a slide. If a print is made, however, the color balance can be adjusted.

Color: Additive or Subtractive

There are two ways to create colors in a photograph. One method, called additive, starts with three basic colors and adds them together to produce some other color. The second method, called subtractive, starts with white light (a mixture of all colors in the spectrum) and, by taking away some colors, leaves the one desired.

In **additive** mixing (*right*), the basic or primary colors are red, green, and blue lights (each providing about one-third of the wavelengths in the total spectrum). Mixed in varying proportions, they can produce all colors—and the sum of all three primaries is white.

In the **subtractive** method (*opposite page*), the primaries are cyan (a bluish green), magenta (a purplish pink), and yellow, the pigments or dyes that absorb red, green, and blue wavelengths, thus subtracting them from white light. These dye colors are the complementary colors to the three additive primaries of red, green, and blue. Properly combined, the subtractive primaries can absorb all colors of light, producing black. But, mixed in varying proportions, they too can produce any color in the spectrum.

Whether a particular color is obtained by adding colored lights together or by subtracting some light from the total spectrum, the result looks the same to the eye. The additive process was employed for early color photography. But the subtractive method, while requiring complex chemical techniques, has turned out to be more practical and is the basis of all modern color films.

In the additive method, separate colored lights combine to produce various other colors. The three additive primary colors are green, red, and blue. Green and red light mix to produce yellow; red and blue light mix to produce magenta; green and blue mix to produce cyan. When equal parts of all three of these primary-colored beams of light overlap, the mixture appears white to the eye. A color television produces its color by the additive system. The picture tube consists of green, red, and blue phosphors that can be mixed in various combinations to produce any color, including white.

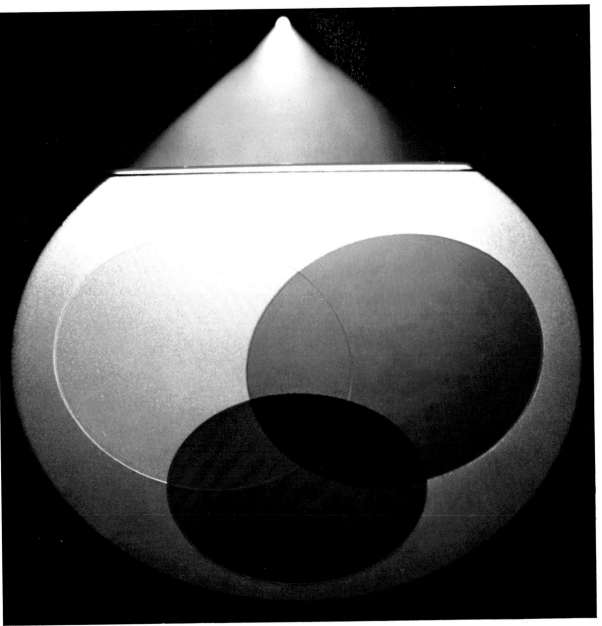

White light is a mixture of all wavelengths. In the subtractive process, colors are produced when a dye (as in paint or color photographic materials) absorbs some wavelengths and so passes on only part of the spectrum. Above, the three subtractive primaries—yellow, cyan, and magenta—are seen placed over a source of white light. Where two overlap, they pass red, green, and blue light. Where all three overlap, all wavelengths are blocked. At right, each subtractive primary transmits two-thirds of the spectrum and blocks one-third. Notice that the color often called blue is named cyan.

Color Photographs: Three Image Layers

A color photograph begins as three superimposed black-and-white negatives. Color film consists of three layers of emulsion, each layer basically the same as in black-and-white film but responding to only one-third of the spectrum. The top layer is sensitive to blue light, the middle layer to green light, and the bottom layer to red light. When this film is exposed to light and then developed, the result is a multilayered black-and-white negative.

The developer converts the light-sensitive silver halide compounds in the layers of emulsion to metallic silver. As it does so, the developer oxidizes and combines with **dye couplers** that are either built into the layers of emulsion or added during development. Three dye colors are formed—the subtractive primary colors of yellow, magenta, and cyan—one in each emulsion layer. The blue-sensitive layer of the film forms a yellow image, the green layer forms a magenta image, and the red layer forms a cyan image. A **bleach** then removes all the silver, and each layer is left with only a color image. This basic process is used in the production of color negatives, positive color transparencies (slides), and color prints (see illustrations, right and opposite).

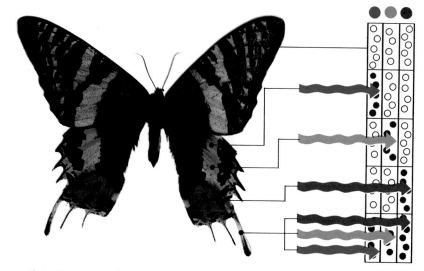

Color film consists of three layers of emulsion, each sensitive to blue, green, or red (as diagrammed above by color dots over a film cross section). During exposure, light of each color of the moth shown above produces an invisible latent image on the emulsion layer or layers sensitive to it. Where the moth is black, no emulsion is exposed; where it is white, all three layers are exposed equally. This results in three superimposed latent images.

During development of the film, each latent image is converted into a metallic silver negative image. Thus, three separate negative images indicate by the density of the silver they contain the amount of each primary color in the moth. The images are shown separately here but are, of course, superimposed on the film.

color negative

color transparency

color print

When exposed color negative film is developed, a colored dye is combined with each black-and-white negative image. The dyes are cyan, magenta, and yellow—the complements of red, green, and blue. The silver images are then bleached out, leaving three layers of superimposed negative dye images (shown separately above). The color negative also has an overall orange color or "mask" (top) to compensate for color distortions that would otherwise occur in printing.

The positive color image of a transparency or slide (top) is created in exposed film by a reversal process. After a first development, the emulsion is either exposed a second time to light or is treated with a chemical that produces the same effect. Silver is deposited by a second development to form black-and-white positive images in the emulsion. Dyes then combine with the metallic silver positive images to form three positive color images. In each layer the dye produced is the complement of the color of the light that was recorded there—yellow dye is formed in the blue-sensitive layer, magenta in the green-sensitive layer, and cyan in the red-sensitive layer. The black-and-white silver images are then bleached out, leaving the positive color images in each layer (shown separately, above).

When a beam of white light is projected through these superimposed color images, each of the colors of the moth is reproduced by the subtraction of the other colors from white light. To reproduce blue, for example, magenta and cyan dye images are formed, but no yellow image. The greens and reds of the light are subtracted by the magenta and cyan dyes, leaving only blue as visible color. Similarly, varying mixtures of dyes in the transparency produce the whole range of colors of the moth. Black is produced where all the colors of white light are subtracted by dyes, and white is produced where no color is subtracted.

The most common method of color printing uses paper with three emulsion layers like those in film. In a negative/positive printing process, the paper is exposed to light passed through a color negative. During development of the paper, three positive images are produced, each consisting of dye plus silver. The silver is then bleached out, leaving the color images. In a reversal process, light is passed through a positive transparency onto reversal paper; the result is a positive image.

The colors that appear in a color print are those reflected back to the eye from white light falling on the print. A blue spot on the moth, for example, looks blue in the print because cyan and magenta dyes in the emulsion layers of the paper absorb red and green wavelengths from the white light falling on the paper, and only blue wavelengths are reflected. The full-color image of the print (top) is a product of the colors subtracted from white light by the three superimposed dye images (shown separately, above).

Color Balance
Matching Film to the Light Source

Color films sometimes record colors that the photographer did not see when the shot was made. Though the picture may look wrong, the film is not at fault. Although a white shirt looks white both outdoors in daylight and indoors in artificial light, light from ordinary tungsten bulbs has a different **color balance**— more red wavelengths and fewer blue wavelengths—than daylight; thus the white shirt reflects more red light indoors than outdoors and has a golden cast. Color film records such subtle differences.

The balance of colors in light is measured as **color temperature** on the Kelvin scale. This scale is commonly used by physicists and serves as a standard comparative measure of wavelengths present in light (*see illustration, this page*).

Different color films are made for different color temperatures. **Daylight films** are balanced for a 5500K light source, and so give good results with the relatively high color temperature of midday light, electronic flash, and blue flashbulbs. **Indoor films** are balanced for incandescent light sources of lower temperatures. Most indoor films are **tungsten balanced**—designed specifically for light of 3200K color temperature, but producing acceptable results in any tungsten light. A few (**Type A**) films have a slightly different balance for use with 3400K photolamps.

Color balance is more important with reversal films than with negative films. With a color reversal film, transparencies (such as slides) are made directly from the film that was in the camera, and they have a distinct color cast if the film was not shot in the light for which it was balanced or if it was not shot with a filter over the lens to balance the light (*see opposite and page 228*). With a color negative film, color balance can be adjusted when prints are made.

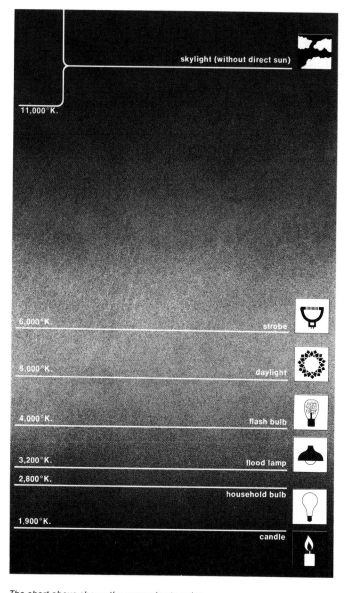

The chart above shows the approximate color temperatures of "white" light sources. The ordinary description of colors as warm or cool doesn't match their actual color temperature. Red is often called a warm color, but the color temperature of reddish light is low on the scale. Blue is called a cool color, but its color temperature is high on the scale.

The pictures opposite illustrate how different ▶ types of color film record different colors when exposed to the same light. The top pictures were all taken in daylight (color temperature 5500K). Photographed with daylight film (left), the colors of the bus look normal. When shot with indoor (tungsten) film designed for 3200K (center), the bus takes on a heavy bluish cast. If a corrective 85B filter is used, however, the colors produced by the indoor film improve significantly (right).

The bottom pictures were all taken indoors in 3200K light. The bride looks normal when photographed with indoor film (left), but daylight film in the same light produces a yellowish cast (center). A corrective 80A filter produces a near-normal color rendition with the daylight film (right).

Since the filter blocks part of the light reaching the film, the exposure must be increased (about ⅔ stop with an 85B filter, 2⅓ stops with an 80A filter). This can create inconveniently long exposures, so it is more efficient to use the correct type of film.

daylight film in daylight

tungsten film in daylight

85B filter

tungsten film in daylight with 85B filter

tungsten film in tungsten light

daylight film in tungsten light

80A filter

daylight film in tungsten light with 80A filter

Filters to Balance Color

color film in fluorescent light

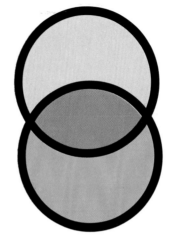

The penny arcade fortune-telling machine (left) was lighted mostly with fluorescent lights. The greenish cast in the picture is due to the concentration of green wavelengths in fluorescent lighting. A combination of pale filters—magenta (which absorbs greens) and blue (which absorbs reds and greens)—alters the light exposing the film so that the color image looks closer to normal (right). An FL (fluorescent) filter combines magenta and blue and improves the color balance for average scenes. It is difficult to give exact filter recommendations for fluorescent light because the color balance varies depending on the type of lamp, the manufacturer, how old the lamp is, and even voltage fluctuations.

color film in fluorescent light with FL filter

What happens if the color balance of light does not match the color balance of your film? Most color films are balanced to match the color temperatures of one of three possible light sources— midday sunlight and two types of incandescent lamp. Any other lighting conditions may give an unusual color balance. Sometimes you may want this imbalance. If not, you can use **filters** to correct to a more standard color balance.

It is not unusual to encounter light conditions that do not match the color balance of any film. For example, the light is reddish late in the day because the low-lying sun is filtered by the earth's atmosphere to a color temperature lower than 5500K. You may want to photograph this scene unfiltered to keep a reddish cast that looks like sunset.

In a picture of a field of snow having sunlit and shadowed areas, the shadows will be illuminated mainly by clear blue skylight of a very high color temperature. Shadowed snow comes out blue when photographed with ordinary daylight film. A pale "skylight" filter, designed to block some of the blue light, would reduce the bluish cast of the shadows as the film records it. Actually, if you look at a snowfield under such conditions, you can often see the bluish cast in the shadows—but ordinarily the brain adapts what the eye sees to what it expects the snow to look like.

A similar problem occurs when a light source does not emit a smooth distribu-

Filters for Color Film

number or designation	color or name	type of film	physical effect	practical use	increase in stops	factor
1A or UV	skylight / ultraviolet	daylight	Absorbs ultraviolet rays.	Eliminates ultraviolet that eye does not see but that film records as blue. Useful for snow, mountain, marine, and aerial scenes, on rainy or overcast days, in open shade.	–	–
81A	yellow	daylight	Absorbs ultraviolet and blue rays.	Stronger than 1A filter. Reduces excessive blue in similar situations. Use with electronic flash if pictures are consistently too blue.	⅓	1.2
		tungsten		Corrects color balance when tungsten film is used with 3400K light sources.	⅓	1.2
82A	light blue	daylight	Absorbs red and yellow rays.	Reduces warm color cast of early morning and late afternoon light.	⅓	1.2
		Type A		Corrects color balance when Type A film is used with 3200K light source.	⅓	1.2
80	blue	daylight	Absorbs red and yellow rays.	Stronger than 82A. Corrects color balance when daylight film is used with tungsten light. Use 80A with 3200K sources and with ordinary tungsten lights. Use 80B with 3400K sources.	2⅓ (A) 2 (tungsten)	5 4
85	amber	Type A or tungsten	Absorbs blue rays.	Corrects color balance when indoor films are used outdoors. Use 85 filter with Type A film, 85B filter with tungsten film.	⅔	1.5
FL	fluorescent	daylight or tungsten	Absorbs blue and green rays.	Approximate correction for excessive blue-green cast of fluorescent lights. FL-D used with daylight film, FL-B with tungsten film.	1	2
CC	color compensating			Used for precise color balancing. Filters come in various densities in each of six colors—red, green, blue, yellow, magenta, cyan (coded R, G, B, Y, M, C). Density indicated by numbers—CC10R, CC20R, etc.	Varies	
	polarizing	any	Absorbs polarized light (light waves traveling in certain planes relative to the filter).	Reduces reflections from nonmetallic surfaces, such as water or glass (see page 106). Penetrates haze by reducing reflections from atmospheric particles. The only filter that darkens a blue sky without affecting color balance overall.	1⅓	2.5
ND	neutral density	any	Absorbs equal quantities of light from all parts of the spectrum.	Increases required exposure so camera can be set to wider aperture or slower shutter speed. Comes in densities from 0.10 (⅓ stop more exposure) to 1.00 (3⅓ stops more exposure).	Varies with density	

tion of colors across the spectrum but gives off concentrations of one or a few colors. Fluorescent lights are examples of this kind of discontinuous spectrum, having, in addition to other colors, large amounts of blues and greens. Although the brain compensates for such uneven distribution, there are no color films that do so.

It is particularly important to balance the light the way you want it when making color slides, because the film in the camera is the final product that will be projected for viewing. With color negative film used for color prints, exact balancing is not so critical because some corrections can be made during the printing process. Printing will be easier, though, with a properly balanced negative.

For the most accurate color rendition, you may need to use a filter in addition to matching the film to the color temperature of the illumination. Some commonly used filters are listed above; more detailed information is supplied by film and filter manufacturers. The color temperature is marked on most electronic flash units and on photographic bulbs. Color temperature meters are available if it is important to balance the light critically.

The examples opposite and on page 227 show the imbalance that occurs when films are not matched to the light. In each case, you can use a corrective filter to adjust the balance of the light so that the image more nearly matches what your eye sees.

Color Casts

Almost every photographer has, at one time or another, found that in a picture a subject has taken on the colors reflected by a nearby strongly colored surface, like a wall or drapery. The eye tends to see almost every scene as if it were illuminated by white light, whereas color film reacts to the true color balance of the light. **Color casts,** or shifts of color, are less noticeable on objects that are strongly colored but are easy to see on more neutral shades, such as skin tones or snow.

A color cast can be a desirable addition, as in the picture on the opposite page, where the bluish light adds an icy coldness to the snow, or on this page, where the photographer added gold tones to the light to enhance the naturally warm colors of the fruit.

But sometimes the color shift can be a problem, as in a portrait shot beneath a tree. People photographed under such seemingly flattering conditions can appear a seasick green because the sunlight that reaches them is filtered and reflected by the green foliage.

Colors can add the impression of heat or cold to a picture. Because they trigger mental associations, golden yellows and reds appear distinctly warm, while blues and yellowish greens seem cool. But the impressions go beyond mere illusions of temperature. Warm colors, especially if they are dark, can make an object seem heavy and dense. Pale, cool colors, on the other hand, give an object a light, less substantial appearance. Warm colors can appear to be farther forward, cool colors farther back. You can use this distance effect to increase the illusion of depth within a picture by placing warm-colored objects against a cool-colored background.

RICHARD STEINBERG: *Fruit*

The photographer wanted to intensify the reds and yellows in the fruit above. To do so he enclosed the fruit in a specially constructed tunnel (diagram at left) lined with gold foil, which strongly reflected yellow and red wavelengths, to suffuse the entire scene with very warm golden light. Light entering at the far end of the tunnel was bounced down on the fruit from the slanting roof. A second light, positioned directly under the glass table supporting the fruit, illuminated the arrangement from below. He could also have used color-compensating (CC) filters over the lens to shift the color balance.

DAVID MUENCH: *Reflection of El Capitan in Merced River,* 1970

Shadowed areas can appear surprisingly blue in a photograph, especially if the subject itself is not strongly colored. In this Yosemite landscape, the rocks and snow are shaded from direct light from the sun and are illuminated only by skylight, light reflected from the blue dome of the sky. Sunlight, direct rays from the sun, is much less blue. Com-pare the skylit snow to the sunlit—and less blue—granite outcropping of El Capitan, visible in the reflection in the water. Here, the contrast between the two tones adds interest to the picture, but for less of a bluish cast, a 1A, UV, or light yellow filter could have been used over the lens.

Color Changes Throughout the Day

EMIL SCHULTHESS and EMIL SPÜHLER: *A Day of Never-setting Sun*, 1950

Colors in your photographs will vary depending on the time of day that you made them. Photographing very early or late in the day can produce strikingly beautiful pictures simply because the light is not its usual "white" color.

In the earliest hours of the day, before sunrise, the world is essentially black and white. The light has a cool, shadowless quality. Colors are muted. They grow in intensity slowly, gradually differentiating themselves. But right up to the moment of sunrise, they remain pearly and flat.

As soon as the sun rises, the light warms up. Because of the great amount of atmosphere that the low-lying sun must penetrate, the light that gets through is much warmer in color than it will be later in the day—that is, more on the red or orange side because the

colder blue hues are filtered out by the air. Shadows, by contrast, may look blue because they lack gold sunlight and also because they reflect blue from the sky.

The higher the sun climbs in the sky, the greater the contrast between colors. At noon, particularly in the summer, this contrast is at its peak. Film for use in daylight is balanced for midday sunlight, so colors appear accurately rendered. Each color stands out in its own true hue. Shadows at noon are more likely to be neutral black.

As the sun goes down, the light begins to warm up again. This occurs so gradually that you must remember to look for it; otherwise the steady increase of red in the low light will do things to your film that you do not expect. Luckily, these things can be beau-

tiful. If the evening is clear and the sun remains visible right down to the horizon, objects will begin to take on an unearthly glow. Shadows lengthen, so surfaces become strongly textured.

After sunset there is a good deal of light left in the sky, often tinted by sunset colors. This light can be used, with longer and longer exposures, almost up to the point of darkness, and it sometimes produces pinkish or even greenish-violet effects that are delicate and lovely. Just as before sunrise, there are no shadows and the contrast between colors lessens.

Finally, just before night, with the tinted glow gone from the sky, colors disappear, and the world once again becomes black and white.

The sun never sinks below the horizon in this time-lapse sequence of photographs taken on a Norwegian island far above the Arctic Circle during the summertime period of the midnight sun. The changing colors of light are clearly visible, however, as the sun rises and sets. Objects seem to be more realistically colored when the sun is high in the sky than when it is close to the horizon; compare the color of the water in the segments on this page with its color in the segments on the opposite page.

Resting in the shadow of his camel, a Sahara caravan guide talks with a driver during an early morning stop in western Libya. With the sun still low in the sky, shadows are very long and colors are warm and golden. ▶

KAZUYOSHI NOMACHI: *Untitled, near Fezzan, Libya, 1975*

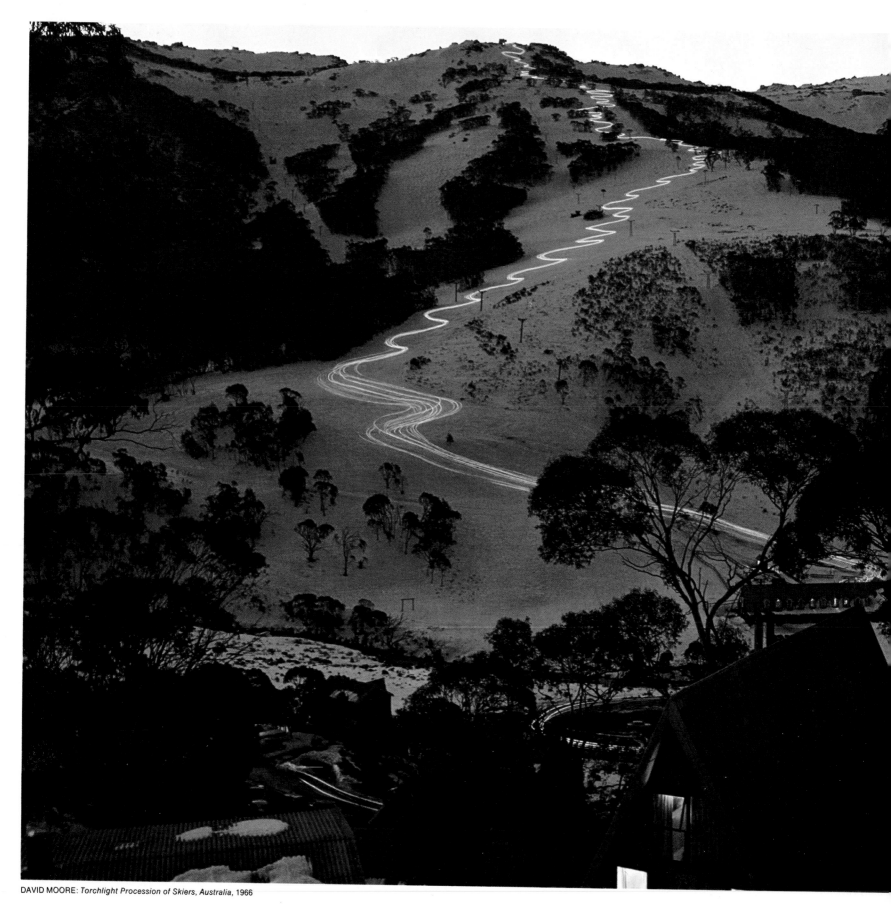

DAVID MOORE: *Torchlight Procession of Skiers, Australia*, 1966

Shifted Colors from Reciprocity Effect

PETER deLORY: *Summer,* 1970

The warm purple tint over the snow (left) and the two-toned sky (above) were produced by the reciprocity effect that causes shifts in color balance during exposures that are longer than about 1 sec. Both pictures were shot in the dim light of *dusk and given lengthy exposures. David Moore exposed the film for the full five minutes it took the skiers to run the trail (the zigzag thread of light that bisects his picture).*

At dusk, at dawn, sometimes indoors, the light may be so dim that exposure times become very long, even with the lens aperture wide open. Very long exposures with color film produce the same **reciprocity effect** that takes place with black-and-white films (*page 124*)— the exposure must be increased even more or the film will be underexposed. Various types of color film react differently to long exposures; check the manufacturer's instructions for recommended exposure increases. Very long exposures are not recommended at all for some color films. In general, however, increase the exposure about one stop for a 1-second exposure, two stops for a 10-second exposure, three stops for a 100-second exposure. Bracket the exposures by making a shot at the calculated exposure plus another at one-half stop more and a third at one stop more. When exposures are very long, underexposure is more likely to be a problem than overexposure.

Reciprocity effect with color films is even more complicated than with black-and-white films. Since color films contain three separate emulsion layers, each layer may be affected differently, and the varied speed losses will change the color balance of the film. The result is color shifts like those shown here. Often the shifts are pleasing, but if you want a more accurate color rendition, use the color filters listed in the film's instruction sheet.

Exposure Latitude: How Much Can Exposures Vary?

You will get the best results with any film if you expose it correctly, but accurate exposure is particularly important with color reversal film because the film in the camera becomes the final transparency or slide. Transparency film has very little **exposure latitude**; that is, it tolerates very little under- or overexposure. With as little as one-half stop underexposure, colors in a slide begin to look dark and murky; there is even less tolerance for overexposure before colors begin to look pale and washed out.

Color negative film has more exposure latitude because a picture can be lightened or darkened when the negatives are printed. You will have a printable negative even with about one stop underexposure or one to two stops overexposure, but best results come from a correctly exposed negative.

In contrasty lighting, such as the sunlit scene at right, color film is not able to record color and details accurately in both very bright highlights and very dark shadows because the range of brightness in the scene is greater than the usable exposure range of the film. If the brightest areas are correctly exposed, the shadows will be too dark. If shadows look good, highlights will be too bright. Try exposing for the most important part of the scene, then bracket additional exposures. Another possibility is to use dark shadows as a part of the composition.

It is easier to get good exposures with color if lighting is flat, with relatively little difference in brightness between the lightest and darkest areas (see opposite page). With such a scene it is less likely that areas will be much too light or much too dark. Sometimes you can use a reflector or a flash unit to add fill light to even out the contrast in a scene (see pages 270–271 and 283).

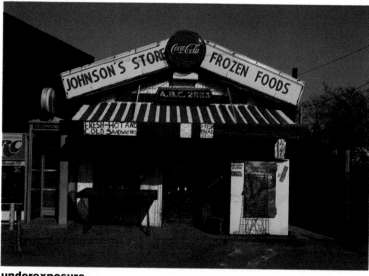

When exposing color transparency film, even a small change in exposure makes a large change in the lightness or darkness of the picture. With about 1½ stops underexposure, shadows are black, and middle tones, such as the awning's stripes, are unnaturally dark. Highlight details, such as the signs on the awning, show clearly.

underexposure

Normal exposure for the overall scene produced bright colors, with details visible in sunlit areas as well as in shadows, except for the darkest areas by the fence and under the awning.

correct exposure

With about 1 stop overexposure, colors are noticeably washed out and too light. The shadow areas, however, now show clearly.

overexposure

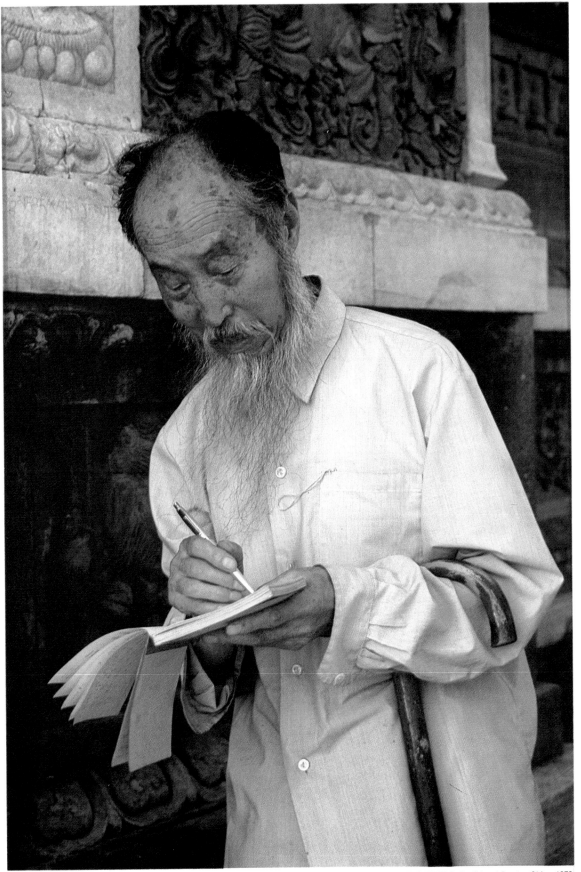

Shooting in soft, diffused light is a bit simpler than working in contrasty light, because the range of tones from light to dark is not so extreme. Diffused light is also kind to the human face, creating soft shadows that are often more complimentary than the hard-edged, dark ones of direct light.

EVE ARNOLD: *Traditional Doctor, China*, 1979

Processing Your Own Color

ERNST HAAS: *Hardangerfjord*, 1959

◀ *The brain judges distance in a landscape in part by the lightness or darkness of objects. The farther a range of hills is, the more that particles of moisture or dust in the atmosphere tend to lighten it and obscure details. In a view of a Norwegian fjord, the darker blues of the nearby coastline make it appear closer, while the paler background recedes. Optically, however, dark objects seem to recede, while lighter ones move toward the viewer. So if you look at the photograph for a while, the blues of the hills and water appear to occupy an interestingly ambiguous space, sometimes near, sometimes far.*

For a spread in Sports Style, *a trade magazine* ▶ *that features fashionable bodywear for athletes and dancers, Kathie McGinty used multiple exposures with electronic flash. McGinty set up three flash units, one on the model and two on the background. She opened the shutter, set off the first flash unit to expose the model, then moved the camera slightly and made a second exposure with the lights on the background. Moving the camera between the exposures made them slightly out of register and gave a feeling of action and motion to the image. McGinty also cropped the image unconventionally. She deliberately cropped into the model's arms and feet to add tension to the image. "I like to do the unexpected,"* she says.

Processing color materials is similar to processing black-and-white materials except that any change in the processing has a greater effect on the final product. Color materials are more sensitive to changes in processing times, temperatures, and other variables; color balance and density shift significantly with even slight variations in processing.

Photographers are more likely to use a commercial lab for **developing color film** than they will for black-and-white film. Many feel that a commercial lab with sophisticated equipment for temperature control produces more consistent results than they could in their own darkrooms. In addition, some films,

such as Kodak Kodachrome, have a complicated processing procedure that is designed for automated commercial equipment.

Nonetheless, some photographers prefer to do their own color film processing. Doing your own film processing may be less expensive than lab work. It may be faster than a lab if you are in a hurry to get your film developed. You may be able to maintain better quality control if you don't have a good lab nearby. Some popular and readily available color negative films that you can develop are Kodak Vericolor III and all Kodacolor VR films. Among the reversal (slide) films that you can process yourself are Agfa Ag-

fachrome, Fuji Film Fujichrome, and Kodak Ektachrome. See the film manufacturer's instructions for the processing chemicals and procedures to use.

The real advantage is in doing your own **color printing** from color negatives or transparencies. Although making color prints is somewhat more exacting than making black-and-white prints, it is not a difficult process to learn and you have the advantage of full control over the final image. Only the most expensive professional printing labs will give you color prints made to your specifications. A much less expensive alternative—and one that produces a print exactly to your taste—is to make your own.

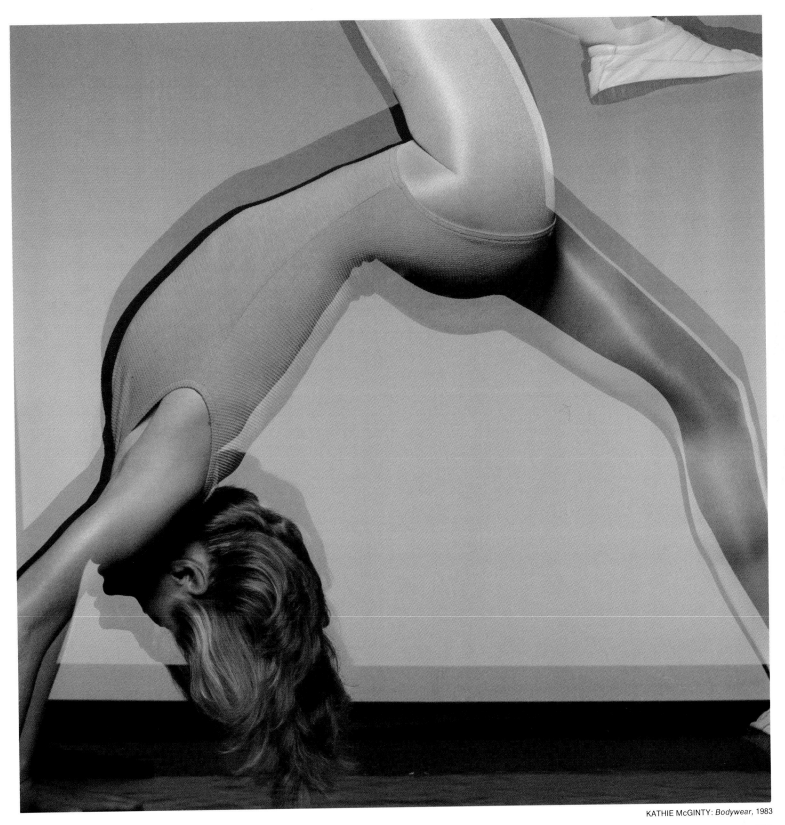

KATHIE McGINTY: *Bodywear*, 1983

Making a Color Print from a Negative
Materials Needed

Once you have assembled the materials needed to make color prints (*see box at right*), the first step is to make test prints to establish a **standard filter pack.** The color balance of color prints is adjusted by inserting colored filters between the enlarger's beam of light and the paper. Paper manufacturers suggest combinations of filters to produce a print of normal color balance from an average negative or transparency. However, these suggestions are only a starting point for your own tests to determine a standard filter pack for your particular combination of enlarger, film, paper, processing chemicals, and technique. Personal testing is essential because so many variables affect the color balance of prints. Once your standard filter pack has been established, only slight changes in filtration will be needed for most normal printing.

You will need a negative (or a transparency, if you are using reversal materials) that is of normal density and color balance. It should be a simple composition and contain a range of familiar colors plus flesh tones or neutral grays. Do not use a sunset or other scene in which almost any color balance would be acceptable. Your aim is to find a filter pack that will be good as a first trial for most negatives.

Consistency is absolutely vital. The temperature of the developer is critical and must be maintained within the limits suggested by the manufacturer. The same pattern of agitation should be used for all tests and final prints. Even the time between exposure and development must be fairly uniform with some processes.

Pages 242–250 show how to produce and evaluate a print from a negative. Pages 252–254 show how to make a print from a positive transparency.

Color Printing: Materials Needed

Color printing paper and processing chemicals. *Two basic types are available. Color prints can be produced from color negatives with negative/positive processes such as Color by Beseler materials, Kodak Ektacolor papers with Ektaprint 2 chemicals, or Kodak Hobby-Pac Print Kit. Color prints can also be made from positive color transparencies by using processes such as Cibachrome materials, Kodak Ektachrome 22 paper with Ektaprint R-3 chemicals, or Kodak Hobby-Pac Color Reversal Print Kit. Not all processing chemistries can be used with all papers; make sure the paper and chemicals are compatible. See the manufacturer's instructions regarding storage of unexposed paper. Most papers should be stored in a refrigerator at 50° F (10° C) or lower. Remove the package from the refrigerator several hours before opening it to bring the paper to room temperature and prevent moisture from condensing.*

Enlarger. *Any enlarger that uses a tungsten or tungsten-halogen lamp may be used. A fluorescent enlarger lamp is not recommended.*

Filtration. *The color balance of the print is adjusted by placing filters of the subtractive primaries—yellow (Y), magenta (M), and cyan (C)—between the enlarger lamp and the paper. The strength of the filtration is indicated by a density number: the higher the number, the stronger the filter. For example, 20M means a magenta filter with a density designated 20; it is 4 times denser than an 05M filter.*

If your enlarger, like the one shown here, has built-in dichroic filters, the strength of each color is adjusted simply by turning knobs or other controls on the enlarger to dial in the desired filtration. Without dial-in filtration, some means must be provided to hold filters in place.

If your enlarger has a drawer for holding filters between the lamp and negative, acetate color printing or CP filters can be used. Filters of the same color can be added to provide a stronger density of a color: 20Y + 20Y gives the same density of yellow as a filter marked 40Y. Any number of filters can be positioned above the negative to create the color balance desired, although the least number that is convenient should be used.

If your enlarger is an older model that does not have a filter drawer, a filter holder can be attached below the lens. In this position, acetate filters cause optical distortions, so the more expensive gelatin color compensating or CC filters must be used. To preserve good optical quality, do not use more than three CC filters below the lens at any one time.

Kodak recommends the following CP or CC filters as a basic kit: 05, 10, 20, 40Y; 05, 10, 20M; 40R (a red filter equivalent to a 40Y + 40M).

Heat-absorbing glass. *The light sources of many enlargers give off enough heat to damage color negatives and filters unless some of the heat is absorbed. To prevent this, a piece of heat-absorbing glass is often placed in the enlarger head if it isn't built in. See enlarger manufacturer's instructions.*

Voltage control. *Electric current varies in voltage from time to time, and a change of only 5 volts will cause a change in the color of the enlarger light—and a visible change in the color of the print being made. So although you can print without it, some type of voltage control is desirable. A voltage stabilizer or regulator automatically maintains a steady output of power if the line voltage fluctuates. A manually adjustable variable transformer is less expensive; you turn a control knob as necessary to maintain uniform voltage. Either type plugs into a wall outlet, then the enlarger plugs into it. Some enlargers have built-in voltage control.*

Analyzers and calculators. *A color analyzer is an electronic device that reads the density and color balance of a negative, compares it to a preprogrammed standard, then recommends exposure and filtration. Good ones are very expensive, and while they make printing easier, you can work without one. Another type of printing aid is a color matrix or subtractive color calculator. Some people find these useful, others do not. Briefly, you use this device to make a test print in which colors are scrambled to an overall tone. You compare this test to a standard tone to determine exposure and filtration.*

Processing drum. *A tube-shaped plastic processing drum is an inexpensive and popular device for color print processing. Each print is processed in small quantities of fresh chemicals, which are discarded after use. This provides economical use of materials as well as consistent processing. Once the drum is loaded and capped, room lights can be turned on so you don't have to work in the dark. See manufacturer's instructions for the correct method of sealing, filling, and draining solutions and for agitating.*

Miscellaneous. *Most of the other materials needed are also commonly used in black-and-white printing: darkroom timer, accurate thermometer, trays, and so on.*

1 | color printing paper
2 | enlarger with heat-absorbing glass
3 | dichroic color head or filters
4 | timer with sweep-second hand
5 | focusing magnifier
6 | printing-paper easel
7 | color negatives
8 | antistatic brush
9 | two masking cards for test prints
10 | notebook for record keeping
11 | processing drum
12 | rubber gloves
13 | photographic thermometer
14 | graduates for premeasuring solutions
15 | print-processing chemicals
16 | temperature control and washing tray
17 | squeegee or photographic sponge

Exposing a Test Print

The following pages show how to make prints from a color negative on Kodak Ektacolor print paper processed in Ektaprint 2 chemicals. Other papers and developers also work well. Read the manufacturer's current directions carefully, because filtration, safelight recommendations, processing, and so on vary considerably with different materials and may change from time to time.

It is not difficult to work with the paper in total darkness, and once the paper is loaded in the drum, room lights can be turned on. If you need some light before then, the recommended safelight for Ektacolor 74 paper is a 7½-watt bulb with a Number 13 amber safelight filter used at least four feet from the paper for no more than three minutes.

1 | clean the negative

Clean dust off the negative and carrier. Place negative (dull, emulsion side toward paper) in carrier and insert in enlarger. Set out a clean, dry processing drum and its cap.

2 | set up the enlarger

Insert the 2B (ultraviolet) filter and heat-absorbing glass, if required. Dial in filtration (or insert CP or CC filters) for the test: 50M (magenta) and 90Y (yellow).

Exposing a Test Print

Five exposures of the same negative are made in the test print shown at right, producing a range of densities from light to dark. See the manufacturer's suggestions for a starting point for filtration. For Ektacolor 74 paper, Kodak recommends a starting filter pack of 50M + 90Y + 2B. (The 2B ultraviolet-absorbing filter is always part of the pack.)

When feasible, it is better to change the aperture while keeping the exposure time the same. This is because extremely long or extremely short exposures could change the color balance and make test results difficult to interpret (the same reciprocity effect that affects film, pages 234–235). In this test each successive strip received one additional full stop of exposure, but the best exposure for a particular negative is often between two of the stops. Exposure times between 5 sec and 30 sec generally do not create noticeable reciprocity effect, so after you get an approximate exposure you can fine-tune by changing the time.

Keep notes of time, aperture, and filtration for each print if you want to save time and materials at your next printing session.

f/4   10 sec

f/5.6 10 sec

f/8   10 sec

f/11   10 sec

f/16   10 sec

3 | adjust the image size

Turn off the room lights. Project the image onto a sheet of paper placed in the easel. Raise or lower the head until the image is the desired size—here 8 × 10 inches.

4 | focus the image

Looking through a focusing magnifier (if you use one), adjust the focus control of the enlarger until the image is sharp. Focus on the edge of an object since a color negative has no easily visible grain.

5 | set the lens aperture

Stop down the lens to f/16. Set the timer for 10 sec. Turn off the enlarger light. Place a sheet of printing paper on the easel, emulsion side up.

6 | make the first test exposure

Hold a masking card over all but one-fifth of the paper and expose the first test wedge. Cover the first wedge with another card. Move the first card to uncover the next one-fifth of the paper.

7 | reset aperture, complete the test

Open the aperture one stop. Reset the timer and expose the next wedge. Continue moving the cards, opening the aperture one stop and exposing until the last one-fifth of the paper is exposed.

8 | load the paper in the processing drum

Insert the paper in the processing drum with the emulsion (exposed) side curled to the center of the drum. Put the cap on the drum and secure it carefully. Turn on the room lights.

Processing

With the exposed print stored in the drum away from light, prepare the **chemicals for processing.** Shown here is processing in Kodak Ektaprint 2 chemicals. Dilute the chemicals as the instructions direct. Color chemicals are stronger than black-and-white chemicals; read instructions and warnings carefully, and protect your hands with rubber gloves. Contamination will cause trouble: don't splash one chemical into another or on the dry side of the darkroom. Kodak recommends mixing Ektaprint 2 Bleach-Fix using separate equipment since even very small quantities of it in other solutions will cause very large variations in the print. Wash tools carefully after use.

Double-check the manufacturer's directions about solution temperatures (particularly for the developer) during processing. With some processes, prints exhibit unpredictable shifts in color and density if the developer varies even slightly from the recommended temperature. If **temperature control** is critical, the best control is obtained from a processing drum that can be agitated while immersed in a constant-temperature water bath. In practice, however, you can deviate somewhat from the exact temperature if you do the same thing every time.

1 | mix and measure out solutions and check temperatures

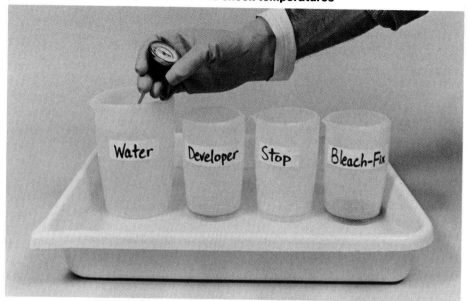

Wearing gloves, mix and measure out the required amounts of solutions. Use the same container each time for a solution to avoid contamination. Bring solutions to the recommended temperature and place them in a water bath at that temperature. Check and keep handy the times for each step.

2 | pour in prewet

Set timer for prewet time. Fill drum with prewet water, start timer, and begin agitation. (Prewet warms up the paper and softens the emulsion so chemicals can penetrate easily.)

3 | agitate the prewet

Solutions are agitated across the surface of the paper by rolling or rotating the drum. Use a consistent pattern of agitation to prevent unwanted variations in prints.

4 | drain the prewet

Ten seconds before the end of the prewet period, pour out the prewet. Become familiar with your drum; some drums take slightly longer to drain or need a tilt or shake to drain thoroughly.

5 | development

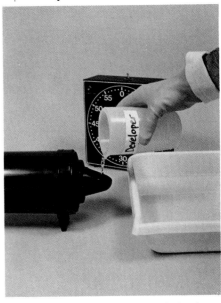

Set timer for development time. Pour in developer, start timer, and agitate as before. Ten seconds before the end of the development period, pour out the developer.

6 | stop bath

Set timer for stop-bath time. Pour in stop bath, start timer, and agitate. Ten seconds before the end of the period, pour out the stop bath.

7 | washing prior to bleach-fix

Set timer for wash time. Fill drum with wash water, start timer, and agitate. Ten seconds before the end of the period, pour out the wash water.

8 | bleach-fix

Set timer for bleach-fix time. Pour in bleach-fix, start timer, and agitate. Ten seconds before the end of the period, pour out bleach-fix. The drum can now be opened.

9 | wash

Remove print carefully from drum and place in a tray of water. Wash by rocking the tray, dumping and refilling with water. Repeat three more times for the recommended wash period.

10 | dry

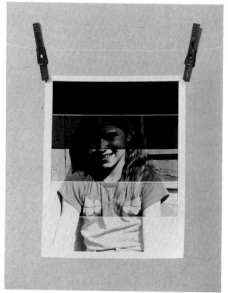

Sponge or squeegee excess water gently from print and hang or place in dust-free place to dry. Warm air, as from a hair dryer, will hasten drying. Do not use a hot drum dryer.

11 | clean up

Wash all equipment that has come in contact with chemicals. Be particularly careful to wash and dry the processing drum thoroughly so that no trace of bleach-fix remains.

1 stop too dark
Give ½ the previous exposure: close enlarger lens 1 stop or multiply exposure time by .5

½ stop too dark
Give ¾ the previous exposure: close enlarger lens ½ stop or multiply exposure time by .75

correct density

½ stop too light
Give 1½ times the previous exposure: open enlarger lens ½ stop or multiply exposure time by 1.5

1 stop too light
Give twice the previous exposure: open enlarger lens 1 stop or multiply exposure time by 2

Judging a color print is similar to judging a black-and-white print in that you have to judge two characteristics separately. In a black-and-white print you judge density first, then contrast. In a color print, you **judge density first** (*shown at left*), then color balance (*see pages 248–249*).

The color balance of a test print will probably be off, so try to disregard it and look only at the density, or darkness, of the print. Look for the exposure that produces the best overall density in midtones such as skin or blue sky. Important shadow areas should be dark but with visible detail, textured highlights should be bright but not burned-out white. Some local control with burning and dodging may be needed (*see page 250*).

The **illumination for judging** a color print affects not only how dark the print looks but also its color balance. Ideally you should evaluate prints using light of the same intensity and color balance under which the print finally will be seen. Since this is seldom practical, some average viewing conditions have been established. Fluorescent tubes, such as Westinghouse Living White bulbs or Deluxe Cool White bulbs, are recommended. You can also combine tungsten and fluorescent light with one 75-watt tungsten bulb used for every two 40-watt Deluxe Cool White fluorescent tubes. You should examine prints carefully, but when judging density, don't view a print very close to a very bright light. Average viewing conditions are likely to be less bright, and the final print may then appear too dark.

Judging Color Balance in a Print Made from a Negative

Almost always, the first print you make from a negative can be improved by some change in the **color balance,** done by changing the filtration of the enlarger light. If your enlarger has a dichroic head, just dial in the filter change. If you are using CP or CC filters, you must replace individual filters in the pack. Decide what color is in excess in the print and how much it is in excess, then change the strength of the appropriate filters accordingly. Ordinarily it is best to evaluate dry prints, since wet prints have a bluish color cast and appear slightly darker than they do after drying.

You can check your print against pictures whose colors are shifted in a known direction, such as the **ring-around test chart** on the opposite page. The chart helps identify basic color shifts, but printing inks seldom exactly match photographic dyes.

A better method for evaluating prints is to look at them through colored **viewing filters** to see which filter improves the color balance. Kodak makes a Color Print Viewing Kit for this purpose.

Find the viewing filter that makes the print look best. Hold the filter away from the print, not directly on top of it, and flick the filter in and out of your line of vision. Look at light midtones in the print such as light grays or flesh tones rather than dark shadows or bright highlights. Follow the directions with the filters but, in general, change the enlarger filtration half the value of the viewing filter. If you lay the filter on top of the print, the color change increases. If the print looks best this way, change the enlarger filtration the same value as the viewing filter.

To correct the color balance of a print made from a negative, **make the opposite color change in the enlarger filtration from the color change you want in the print.** In other words, if you want to remove a color from a print, add that color to the enlarger filtration. Almost always, you should change only the magenta or yellow filters, either subtracting the viewing filter color that corrects the print or adding the complement (the opposite on the color wheel) of the viewing filter color that corrects. See chart and color wheel at right. Kodak's Color Print Viewing Kit also tells you exactly which colors to change.

The cure for a print with too much magenta is to add—not decrease—the magenta in the filter pack; more magenta in the printing light produces a print with less of a magenta cast. A green viewing filter will correct a print that is too magenta, so you add magenta (the complement of green) to the filter pack.

Similarly, excess blue is corrected by lightening the filter that absorbs blue, the yellow filter; the filter pack will then pass more blue light, so the print (reacting in an opposite direction) will show less blue. A yellow viewing filter will correct a too-blue print, so subtract yellow (the complement of blue) from the filter pack.

Color printing is a skill that requires both experience and written information from a book or manufacturer's literature. Once you have made a few prints, not only is written information easier to understand but the whole process of printing becomes easier. Help from someone who knows how to print and who can help you judge your prints is invaluable.

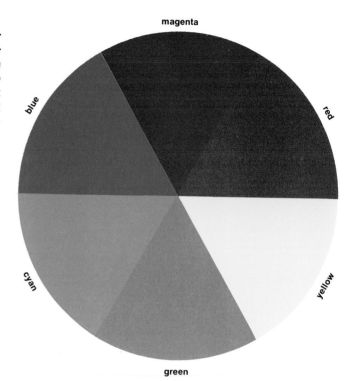

The primary colors of light are shown here arranged in a circle—a color wheel. Each color is composed of equal amounts of adjacent colors (red is composed of equal parts of magenta and yellow). Each color is complementary to the color that is opposite (magenta and green are complementary).

Balancing a Print Made from a Negative

To adjust the color balance of a print made from a negative, change the amount of the subtractive primary colors (magenta, yellow, and cyan) in the enlarger printing light. Usually, changes are made only in magenta and yellow (M and Y).

Print is	Do this	Could also do this
Too magenta	Add M	Subtract C + Y
Too red	Add M + Y	Subtract C
Too yellow	Add Y	Subtract C + M
Too green	Subtract M	Add C + Y
Too cyan	Subtract M + Y	Add C
Too blue	Subtract Y	Add C + M

Print is too blue. Yellow viewing filter corrects. Subtract yellow from filtration.

Print is too magenta. Green viewing filter corrects. Add magenta to filtration.

Print is too red. Cyan viewing filter corrects. Add magenta and yellow to filtration.

−40Y

−20Y

−10Y

+40M

+20M

+10M

+40M +40Y

+20M +20Y

+10M +10Y

Normal color balance

−10M −10Y

−20M −20Y

−40M −40Y

+10Y

+20Y

+40Y

−10M

−20M

−40M

Print is too cyan. Red viewing filter corrects. Subtract magenta and yellow from filtration.

Print is too green. Magenta viewing filter corrects. Subtract magenta from filtration.

Print is too yellow. Blue viewing filter corrects. Add yellow to filtration.

More About Color Balance/Print Finishing

After you change the filtration of a test print, you may then need to make a **final exposure change,** because the filtration affects the strength of the exposing light and thus the density of the print. When feasible, adjust aperture rather than time.

Dichroic filters need minimum exposure adjustment. See the manufacturer's literature or make no adjustment for yellow filter change and 1 percent adjustment for each 01M change. CP or CC filters require exposure adjustment for changes in both filter density and the number of filters. See the manufacturer's literature or Kodak's Complete Darkroom Dataguide, which contains a computing wheel that simplifies calculation of new exposures with Kodak materials. As a rough guide, ignore yellow changes, adjust exposure 20 percent for every 10M change, then adjust 10 percent for changes in the number of filter sheets (including yellow).

Try not to end up with all three subtractive primaries (Y, M, C) in your filter pack. This condition produces **neutral density**—a reduction in the intensity of the light without any accompanying color correction—and may cause an overlong exposure. To remove neutral density without changing color balance, subtract the lowest filter density from all three colors.

70Y	30M	10C	working pack
10Y	10M	10C	subtract
60Y	20M		new pack

Dodging and burning a color print is feasible to some extent, as in black-and-white printing, to darken or lighten an area. For example, you may want to darken the sky or lighten a face or shadow area. If you dodge too much, an area will show loss of detail and color (smoky-looking is one description), but some control is possible.

You can also change color balance locally. To improve shadows that are too blue, which is a common problem, keep a blue filter in motion over that area during part of the exposure. Burning in can cause a change in color balance in the part of the print that receives the extra exposure. If a burned-in white or very light area picks up a color cast, use a filter of that color over the hole in the burning-in card to keep the area neutral. Try a CC30 or CC50 filter of the appropriate color. CP filters should not be used for this purpose.

Like black-and-white prints, color prints may need **spotting** to remove white or light specks caused by dust on the negative. Retouching colors made for photographic prints come in liquid or cake form. Either can be used to spot out small specks. The dry cake colors are useful for tinting large areas. Black spots on a print are more difficult to correct. One way is to apply white opaquing fluid to the spot, then tint to the desired tone with colored pencils.

For **mounting,** dry-mount tissue is usable, but low temperatures are recommended for RC paper, no higher than 210° F (99° C). Since the thermostat settings on dry-mount presses are seldom accurate, use the lowest setting that is effective. Preheat the press, the mount board, and the protective cover sheet placed on top of the print, then insert the print for the minimum time that will fuse the dry-mount tissue to print and mount board.

Color prints fade over time, particularly on exposure to ultraviolet light. Prints will retain their original colors much longer if protected from strong sources of ultraviolet light such as bright daylight.

WHITE LIGHT DATA		
	CC	-10 M
	CC	00 Y
	Ex. Factor	70

The color response of color-printing paper varies slightly from batch to batch. Manufacturers test each batch and list on the label of the box or package the emulsion batch number plus white-light data—the changes in filtration and exposure you should make to get the same results from one batch to the next. Here's how to make the changes:

Filtration. *Subtract the old white-light data from your working filter pack (or from the pack for a given negative), then add in the new data.*

40M	70Y	working pack
00M + 15Y		subtract old white-light data
40M	55Y	
−10M	00Y	add new white-light data
30M	55Y	new working pack

Exposure. *Divide the new exposure factor (ex. factor) by the old ex. factor and multiply by the old exposure time to get the new exposure time.*

$$\frac{new\ ex.\ factor}{old\ ex.\ factor} \times old\ time = new\ time$$

$$\frac{70}{90} \times 10\ sec = 8\ sec$$

Dan McCoy specializes in illustrations of scientific and medical subjects, in this case a photograph for an article on a new diagnostic tool, a nuclear magnetic resonance scanner. The device was not itself very spectacular, a metal doughnut with a table running through the hole, but McCoy managed to convey the high-tech intensity of the procedure as well as to keep the human presence strong. The cross on the patient's forehead is light from the laser used for positioning the scanner. The exaggerated perspective is caused by shooting close to the patient's head with a wide-angle lens. The orange color cast is from orange filters on the photographer's lights.

DAN McCOY: *Patient in an NMR scanner*, 1982

Making a Color Print from a Transparency

1 | processing chemicals
2 | measuring cups or small graduates
3 | printing paper
4 | filters or enlarger with dichroic head
5 | manual
6 | processing drum
7 | timer
8 | half-gallon waste container
9 | mixing graduates
10 | solution storage bottles
11 | washing tray
12 | washing siphon
13 | gloves
14 | thermometer
15 | stirring rod
16 | soft rubber squeegee or photographic sponge

Color prints can be made from transparencies (slides) as well as from negatives. You can make a positive print directly from a positive color transparency with materials like Cibachrome-A II paper processed in P-30 chemicals, Kodak Ektachrome 22 paper processed in Ektaprint R-3 chemicals, or Kodak's Hobby-Pac Color Reversal Print Kit.

Cibachrome-A II paper and P-30 chemistry are shown here. Cibachrome prints are noted for their brilliant, saturated colors, good detail and sharpness, and excellent color dye stability. For best results, print from a fully exposed transparency with saturated colors and low to normal contrast. The print material is inherently somewhat contrasty, so starting with a contrasty transparency often leads to considerable print dodging or burning in or even the need for masking (sandwiching the transparency in register with a black-and-white contact negative made on

film such as Kodak Pan Masking Film 4570). The transparency should be absolutely clean because specks of dust on it will appear as black spots on the print. Clean the transparency carefully before you place it in the enlarger.

Two types of paper are available: a glossy-surface paper on a polyester base dries to a high-gloss finish; a pearl-surface paper on a resin-coated (RC) base dries to a slightly stippled, less glossy finish. The pearl surface is not as likely as the glossy surface to show fingerprints or surface scratches and is suitable for general printing. However, the polyester base of the glossy paper provides better color stability and is the preferred choice to meet museum standards of archival preservation.

See general instructions for color printing on page 240. From time to time, manufacturers change materials and the specifications for their use, so be

sure your printing paper and chemicals are designed to be used together and that you have current instructions.

Begin by preparing the solutions. Be particularly careful with color processing chemicals. Mix chemicals in a well-ventilated area. Wear rubber gloves to prevent contact of the chemicals with your skin. Do not pour Cibachrome chemicals directly down the drain; the bleach is corrosive and must be mixed with the other solutions to neutralize it for disposal. This is done by draining the spent processing solutions into the same plastic container in the order that they are used.

Your first print should be a test to determine exposure and filtration (see manufacturer's instructions). Unlike printing from a negative, greater exposure will make the print lighter, heavier filtration will add more of that filter's color to the print (see page 254).

1 | Clean the transparency carefully and place it in the enlarger's film carrier. Depending on the carrier, you may have to remove a 35mm slide from its mount. Expose your first test print.

2 | Curl the exposed print toward the emulsion side and put it into a dry, clean drum. Seal the drum. You can now turn on the room lights.

3 | Adjust temperatures and measure out solutions —developer, water rinse, bleach, fixer—into individual cups or graduates. Note the times for each processing step. Follow the sequence of steps 4, 5, and 6 for each solution.

4 | For each stage of processing, set the timer and empty the cup of solution into the drum. When using the Cibachrome drum, start timer when drum is laid on its side. Solutions do not contact the print until then.

5 | A consistent agitation pattern is important. Roll the drum smoothly back and forth on a level, even surface or use a motorized base.

6 | At the end of each process time, drain the drum for 15 sec into the same half-gallon plastic waste container. Full drainage of the drum is important. Do not discard the solutions until the end of the processing.

7 | Fill the drum with water and carefully remove the print. Wash the print in rapidly flowing water for 3 min. Handle the print carefully; the surface is soft and delicate while wet.

8 | Squeegee the print to prevent water spots but do so gently to avoid damaging the print. Evaluate the print after drying. It will look somewhat red while it is still damp.

9 | Dry the print in a dust-free place. Hang the print, place on an absorbent surface, or for fast drying, use a hair dryer on the warm setting. Do not use a hot drum dryer.

Judging a Print Made from a Transparency

Evaluating a reversal print—one made from a transparency or slide—is similar in many ways to evaluating a print made from a negative (*see pages 247–249*). View the print when it is dry in light similar to that under which you will view the finished print. Evaluate and adjust density first, because what looks like a problem in filtration may simply be a print that is too dark or too light. Evaluate color balance by examining the print with viewing filters or by comparing the print against ringaround prints (*right*).

The most important difference between reversal printing and negative/positive printing is in the response to changes in exposure or filtration. **Reversal materials respond the same way that slide film does when you expose it in the camera.** If the print is too dark, increase the exposure (don't decrease it as you would in negative/positive printing). Adjust the color balance by making the same change in the filter pack that you want in the print. Adding a color to the filter pack will increase that color in the print; decreasing a color in the pack will decrease it in the print. For example, if a print is too yellow, remove Y from the filtration (*see chart and prints at right*).

The suggested beginning **filter pack** for a print made from a transparency may have yellow and cyan filtration. (This is different from the beginning pack for a print made from a negative, which has yellow and magenta filtration.) If so, try to adjust the balance by changing only the Y and C filtration to avoid the neutral density caused by having all three primary colors in the same pack (*see page 250*).

One thing is the same in both processes: keep notes—on the print, on the negative envelope, or in a notebook.

Print is too magenta. Green viewing filter corrects. Add yellow and cyan to filtration.

Print is too blue. Yellow viewing filter corrects. Add yellow to filtration.

Print is too red. Cyan viewing filter corrects. Add cyan to filtration.

normal color balance

Print is too cyan. Red viewing filter corrects. Subtract cyan from filtration.

Print is too yellow. Blue viewing filter corrects. Subtract yellow from filtration.

Print is too green. Magenta viewing filter corrects. Subtract yellow and cyan from filtration.

Balancing a Print Made from a Slide

	Print is	Do this	Could also do this
To adjust the color balance of a print made from a positive transparency, change the amount of the subtractive primary (yellow, cyan, and magenta) filtration. Make changes first in Y or C filtration.	Too dark	Increase exposure	—
	Too light	Decrease exposure	—
	Too magenta	Add Y + C	Subtract M
	Too red	Add C	Subtract Y + M
	Too yellow	Subtract Y	Add C + M
	Too green	Subtract Y + C	Add M
	Too cyan	Subtract C	Add Y + M
	Too blue	Add Y	Subtract C + M

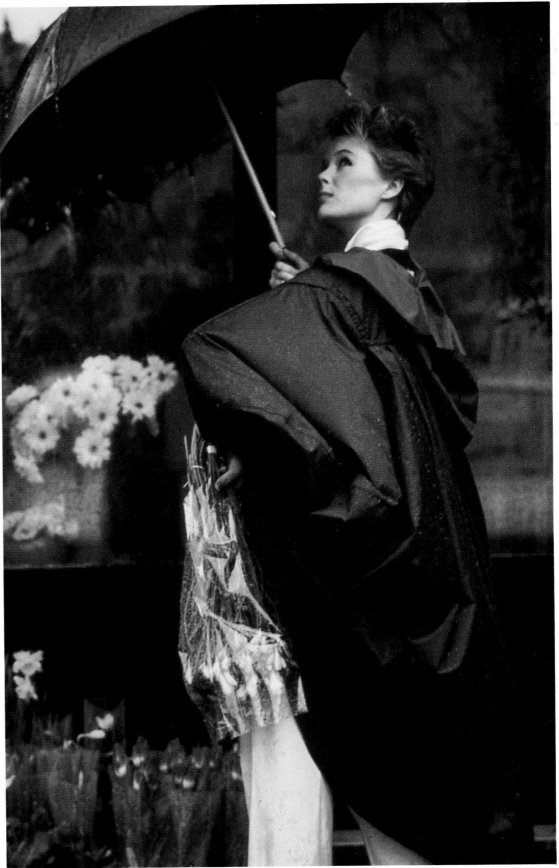

The setting for a fashion photograph can help convey the style of a garment and something about the type of person who might wear it. Andrea Blanch favors a realistic approach to fashion and avoids complicated lighting and artificial settings, which are not as much a part of fashion photography as they once were. For an article on raincoats, the setting was a flower market in Paris. A model holds a bunch of flowers upside down, a gesture the photographer once saw a woman make in real life. The picture was taken on an overcast day with light from a reflector card added to illuminate the model's face, a rain machine to add raindrops, and probably a filter over the lens to reduce the blue cast of light in the shade.

ANDREA BLANCH: *It's Raining,* 1981

Instant Color Film

Instant color pictures are a favorite with photographers because the processing takes care of itself and within seconds a finished print is ready. Although processing instant color film is very simple for the user, the chemistry on which the film is based is extremely complex. It involves a multilayered negative of light-sensitive silver halides and developer dyes sandwiched with printing paper and an alkaline developing agent when the print is pulled from the camera. Integral films such as Polaroid's SX-70 or 600 film and Kodak Instant Color Film are even more complex; the processing takes place within the print itself.

Instant film has its own unique characteristics. Marie Cosindas enhances the rich tones of Polacolor film. Her photographs, like the one on the opposite page, are given long exposure times (as much as 10 seconds) and extended developing times (as much as 90 seconds, instead of the regular 60 seconds). The results of these deviations from standard exposure and development are muted, soft tones that she feels give a sense of quiet and timelessness to the image. (Extended development cannot be used with integral films such as Polaroid SX-70 because the processing takes place automatically.)

In portraits, the long exposures force subjects to hold still longer, involving them more in the photograph. Cosindas's portraits are often reminiscent of photographs made in the 19th century, when exposures were long and sitters often projected a quiet seriousness owing at least in part to staying still for a long time.

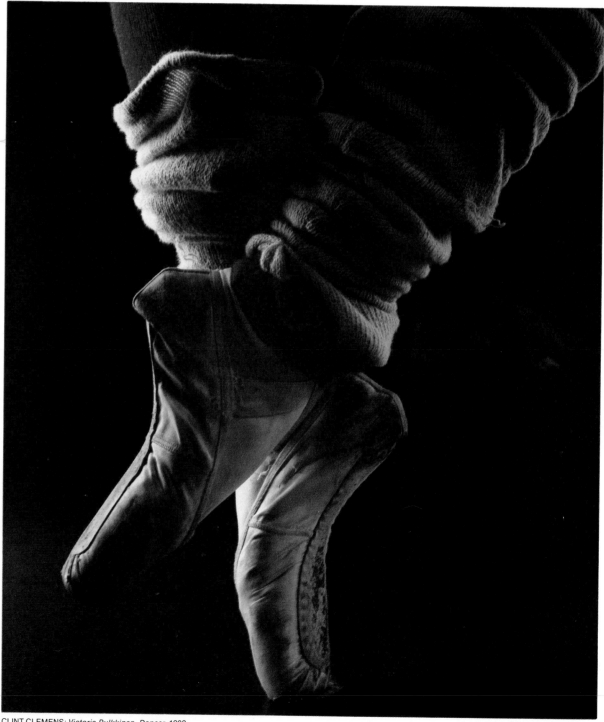

CLINT CLEMENS: *Victoria Pulkkinen, Dancer, 1982*

MARIE COSINDAS: *Sailors, Key West*, 1966

◀ *For a close-up of a dancer, Clint Clemens hung his 8 × 10 view camera upside down from a camera stand in order to get the camera close to the floor, then shot using Polaroid Polacolor ER 8 × 10 film. Photographing an object in motion—like a dancer's feet—can be difficult with a view camera because at the moment of exposure, you are not looking through the lens or even through a viewfinder. The instant feedback from the Polaroid let Clemens shoot until he got the results he wanted. Clemens leaves nothing to chance: to get the colors he wanted in the dancer's tights and leg warmers, he purchased them new, but to get them to look well-worn, which he also wanted, he pulled threads loose until the fabric looked properly "distressed."*

Marie Cosindas uses longer-than-normal exposure and development times to produce rich, muted colors in her Polaroid photographs. Her portraits often project an atmosphere of quiet that is caused in part by the subject having to hold still during a long exposure.

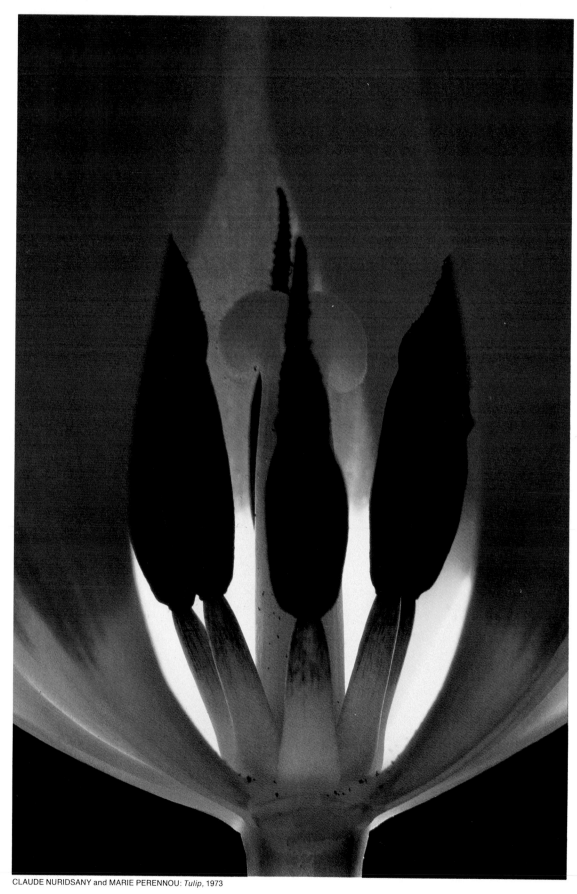

CLAUDE NURIDSANY and MARIE PERENNOU: *Tulip*, 1973

To produce this back-lighted close-up of a tulip, the photographers removed a petal to open a clear view of the pistils and stamen in the center of the flower. They placed a flash unit behind the flower and arranged reflectors above and below it. The back petals of the tulip diffused and softened the light from the flash; the reflectors bounced some of the light onto the front and center of the flower. The flower seems to glow from within, an effect enhanced by its warm, flamelike tones. The close-up was shot half life size on the original transparency, reproduced here about 3× life size.

11
Lighting

Y. R. OKAMOTO: *Arnold Newman Photographing President Lyndon B. Johnson*, 1963

▲ *When Arnold Newman was asked to make a portrait of President Lyndon B. Johnson in the Oval Room at the White House, Newman was given 90 minutes to arrange his equipment, but only 15 minutes for the actual shooting. He covered the windows with cloths to block unwanted light, mounted two view cameras—a 4 × 5 and an 8 × 10—and arranged his lights and reflectors, using an assistant as a stand-in. Here, Newman is coaxing the President into the poses and facial expressions he wants, as a Secret Service man watches in the background.*

The lighting setup looks complicated, but its intention is simple—to illuminate the subject in a way that resembles ordinary daytime lighting. This type of lighting looks natural and realistic because it is the kind people see most often. It consists of one main source of light coming from above (usually cast by the sun, here cast by the large umbrella reflector) plus additional fill light to illuminate shadow areas (in nature, light from the entire dome of the sky or from other reflective surfaces; here, cast by the smaller light sources).

Photography is dependent on light, even for its name—*photo-graphy:* light-writing. The physical process is activated by light striking the light-sensitive emulsion of film or paper. The informational or emotional process—what people learn or feel when they look at a photograph—is activated in part by the quality of light the photographer recorded. Harsh or gentle, ominous or peaceful, the variations are limited only by the photographer's ability to capture them. Light can even be the main subject of the photograph, more interesting than the objects in the picture themselves.

All light has certain fundamental qualities, whether it comes directly from the sun, already exists in a room, or is brought into the room by the photographer. The light source used, whether it be sun, photoflood, or flash, is not as important as what that light is doing to the subject, since any type of light can be used to create identical qualities. This chapter shows how to understand the effects of lighting on a subject, and how to use lighting to get the results you want.

Direct Light

How does light shape and reveal a subject? Here and on the following pages are three kinds of light: direct light, directional-diffused light, and fully diffused light. The kind of light, the subject, and its surroundings as well as the exposure and development chosen by the photographer all affect the final image.

Direct light creates hard-edged, dark shadows. The rays of light are parallel (or nearly so), striking the subject all from one direction. The smaller the light (relative to the size of the subject) or the farther the light is from the subject, the sharper and darker the shadows will be. Very sharp shadows are created by a point source, a single point of light.

A spotlight is one source of direct light. A stage spotlight, which could have been used for the photograph on this page, is small and rather far away and often has a built-in lens to focus the light even more directly. The shadows here are empty of detail: there were no reflective areas near the subject to bounce light into the shadows to add fill light (pages 270–271).

The sun on a clear day is another source of direct light. Although the sun is large in actual size, it is so far away that it occupies only a small area of the sky and casts sharp, dark shadows. It does not cast direct light when its rays are scattered in many directions by clouds or other atmospheric matter: then its light is directional-diffused or even fully diffused.

GJON MILI: *Avon Long as Sportin' Life,* 1942

DANNY LYON: *Sparky and Cowboy (Gary Rogues),* 1965

Fully diffused light scatters onto the subject from many directions. It shows very little or no directionality. In the photograph on this page, light is coming from above, as can be seen from the brightly lighted foreheads, noses, and cheekbones, but light is also bouncing in from both sides and probably from below. Shadow edges are indistinct and subjects seem surrounded by light.

Sources of diffused light are broad compared to the size of the subject—a heavily overcast sky, for example, where the sun's rays are completely scattered and the entire sky becomes the source of light. Fully diffused light indoors would require a very large, diffused light source close to the subject plus reflectors or fill lights to further open the shadows. Tenting (*page 277*) is one way of fully diffusing light.

Directional-Diffused Light

Directional-diffused light is partially direct with some diffused or scattered rays. It appears to come from a definite direction and creates distinct shadows, but with edges that are softer than those of direct light (*photograph this page*). The shadow edges change smoothly from light to medium-dark to dark, and the shadows tend to have more visible detail.

Sources of directional-diffused light are relatively broad. Indoors, windows or doorways are sources when sunlight is bouncing in from outdoors rather than shining directly into the room. Floodlights used relatively close to the subject are also sources; their light is even more diffused if directed first at a reflector and bounced onto the subject (like the umbrella light on page 259) or if partially scattered by a diffusion screen placed in front of the light. Outdoors, the usually direct light from the sun is broadened on a slightly hazy day, when the sun's rays are partially scattered and the surrounding sky becomes a more important part of the light source. Bright sunlight can also produce directional-diffused light when it shines on a reflective surface such as concrete and then bounces onto a subject shaded from direct rays by a tree or building.

In the photograph on this page, the light is probably coming from one or more large windows. The shadows show full details because the white sheets and nightgowns bounce the light back to open up the shadows. Notice the brightness of the left cheek of the child in the background, caused by the light bounced up by the pillow.

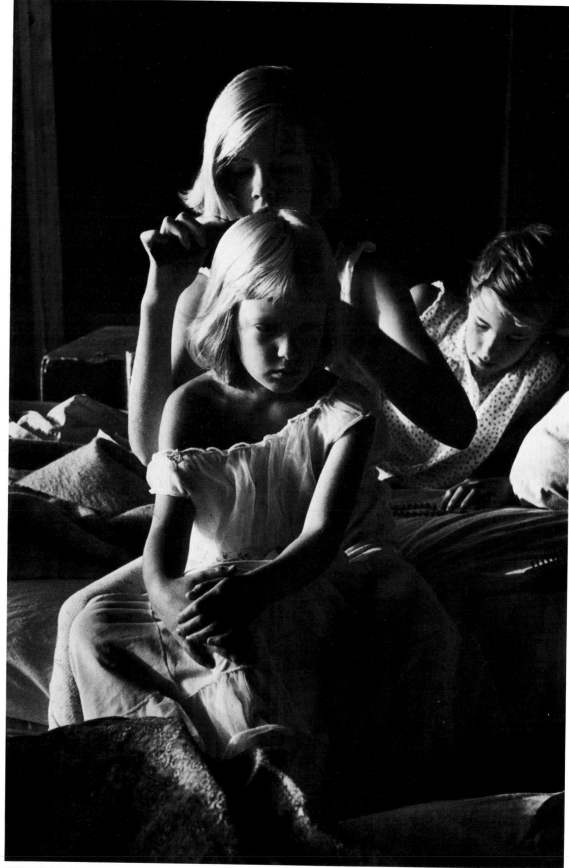

WAYNE MILLER: *Morning Repose, Orinda, California,* 1957

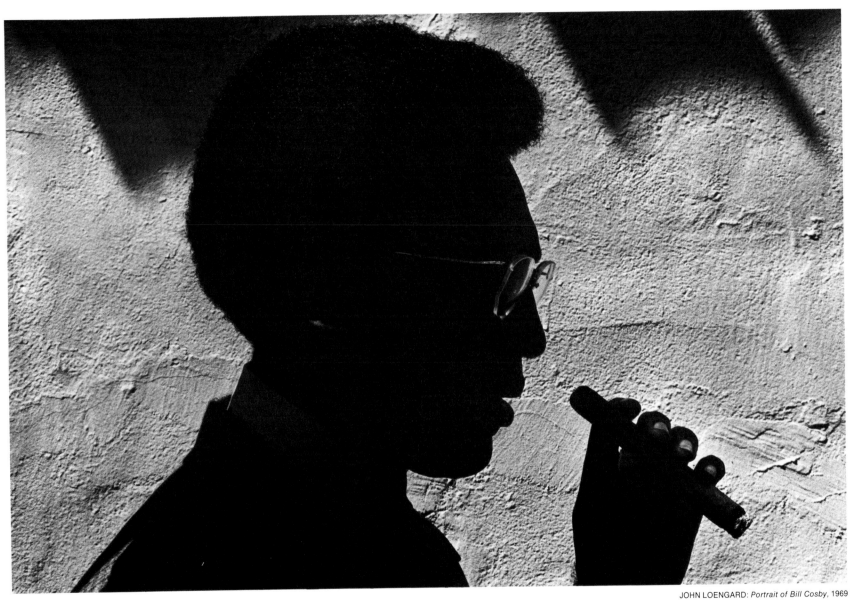

JOHN LOENGARD: *Portrait of Bill Cosby,* 1969

In a **silhouette,** the subject is in deep shadow against a brightly lighted background. A silhouette is created if the subject is underexposed because of a great difference in brightness between the subject and the background. This requires a combination of the position of the light and an exposure decision.

In the photograph above, light was shining on the wall, but not on the part of the subject visible from camera position. The wall was actually a brilliant, glaring white, but exposing it as a middle-gray tone caused the subject to be grossly underexposed. Four stops' more exposure would have produced a

normal rendering of the person against an almost white background. This is the same effect that underexposes the subject if a bright background such as the sky is included when a subject is metered (*page 119*).

Light as You Find It—Outdoors

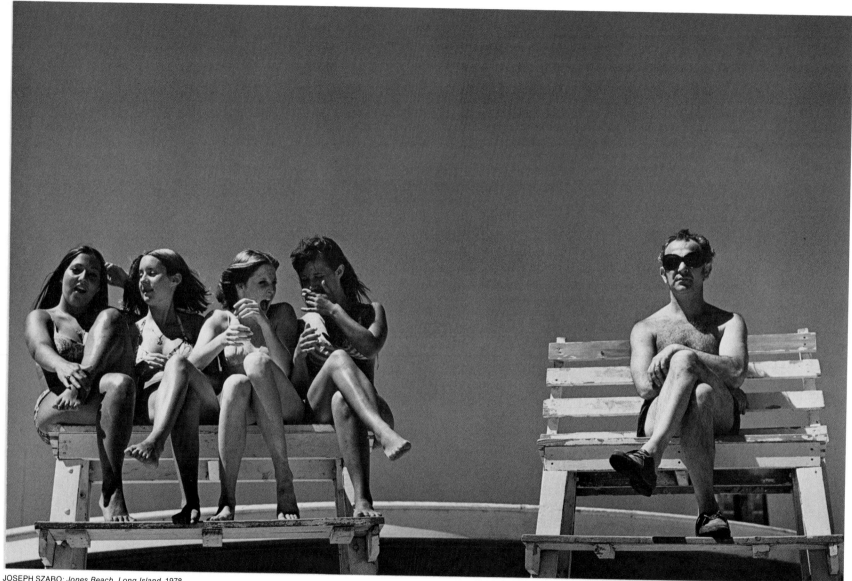

JOSEPH SZABO: *Jones Beach, Long Island,* 1978

What kind of light will you find when you photograph outdoors? It may be any of the lighting situations shown on the preceding pages, so it is important to stop for a moment to look at the light and see how it affects the photograph.

A clear, sunny day creates bright highlights and dark, hard-edged shadows (*above*). In this group scene, the shadows on any single person's face are not very important. But what if you were making a portrait in this kind of light of just one person? You might want to lighten the shadows by adding fill light or by taking the person out of the sun and into the shade where the light is not so contrasty. On a sunny day, take a look at the direction the light is coming from. You might want to move the subject or move around it yourself so the light better reveals the

LOU BERNSTEIN: *Coney Island,* 1943

subject's shape or texture as seen by the camera.

On an overcast day or at dusk, the light will be diffused and soft, as in the photograph above. This is a revealing light that illuminates all parts of the scene and shows every step in the sand and wavy wrinkle in the blanket. It is a beautiful light for portraits, gently modeling the planes of the face.

The light changes as the time of day changes. The sun gets higher and then lower in the sky, affecting the direction in which shadows fall. If the day is sunny, many photographers prefer to work in the early morning or late afternoon; when the sun is close to the horizon, it casts long shadows and rakes across the surface of objects, increasing the sense of texture and volume.

Light as You Find It—Indoors

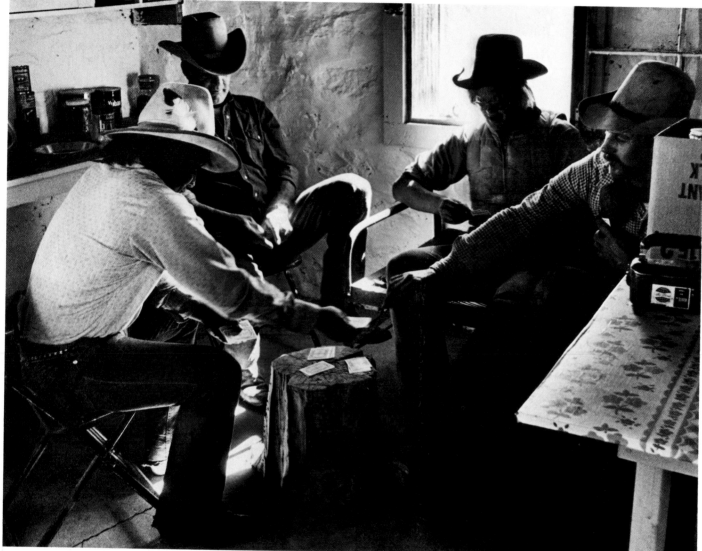

SUZI JONES: *Cowboys, Paradise Valley, Nevada,* 1978

Light indoors can be contrasty or flat, depending on the source of light. Near a lighting fixture or window, especially if there are not many in the room, the light is directional and contrasty, with bright areas fading off quickly into shadow. In the photograph above, the contrast between light and dark was so strong that the film showed no detail in the brightest and darkest areas. But if there are many light fixtures, as in the photograph opposite, the light can be diffused and flat, illuminating all parts of the scene evenly.

When shooting indoors, it is important to meter carefully and expose for the most important parts of the picture. The eye adapts easily to variations in light; it can glance at a light area then quickly see detail in a nearby dark area. But there will often be a greater range of contrast indoors than film can record.

ELLIOTT ERWITT: *Slot Machines, Las Vegas, Nevada,* 1957

The Main Light: The Most Important Source

Front lighting. *With the light placed as near the lens axis as possible (here just to the left of the camera), only thin shadows are visible from camera position. This axis lighting seems to flatten out the volume of the subject and minimize textures.*

Under lighting. *When the light is aimed upward, the subject's face assumes unnatural shadows and a faintly evil look. In special circumstances this kind of lighting can be put to use to give the picture an aura of mystery.*

High side lighting. *A main light aimed at about 45° to the subject has long been the classic angle for portrait lighting, one that seems most natural for most people. It models the face into a three-dimensional form.*

Making a photograph by natural or available light is relatively easy. You begin with the light that is already there and observe what it is doing to the subject. But where do you begin when making a photograph by artificial light? Since the most natural-looking light imitates that from the sun—one **main light** source casting one dominant set of shadows—the place to begin is by positioning the main light. This light, also called the **key light,** should create the only visible shadows, or at least the most important ones, if a natural effect is desired. Two or three equally bright lights producing crisscrossing shadows create a feeling of artificiality and confusion.

The position of the main light affects the appearance of texture and volume (*see pictures above*). Flat frontal lighting (*first photograph*) decreases both texture and volume, while lighting that grazes across surface features as seen from camera position increases it. Since lighting conveys emotional information as well as factual data, the pictures also show how the mood of a photograph can be influenced merely by changing the position of one light. If photographs never lie, some of those above at least bend the truth about the subject's personality.

Top lighting. *A light almost directly above the subject creates deep shadows in the eye sockets and under the nose and chin. This effect is often seen in pictures made outdoors at noon when the sun is overhead.*

Side lighting. *Sometimes called "hatchet" lighting because it appears to split the subject in half, this type of lighting can be useful in emphasizing rugged features or in revealing the texture of skin or fabrics.*

Side-rear lighting. *A light to the side and slightly behind the subject yields an even more dramatic effect. If the light were directly behind it would bring out the shape or silhouette of the subject and turn the hair into a halo.*

Lighting can convey an emotional tone. Since natural light usually comes from overhead, this is the most common location for the main source of artificial light. Lighting from a very low angle or from below suggests mystery, drama, or even menace just because it seems unnatural. The grisly demon in a horror movie is typically lighted from below.

Other types of lighting have come to be associated with "glamour" poses. One example is butterfly lighting, which is named for the symmetrical shadow underneath the nose similar to, though not as long as, the one in the photograph in top lighting above. The main light is placed high and in front of the subject to produce sculptured facial shadows (*see page 273, far right*).

Most photographs made with artificial light employ more than one light source. Almost always a fill light is used to lighten shadows, and often two more lights are added: an accent light to produce bright highlights and a background light to create tonal separation between the subject and the background. Pages 272–273 show standard lighting setups using these lights.

The Fill Light: Modifying Shadows

Fill light adds light to shadow areas, which is useful with most artificial lighting and some scenes in daylight to reduce harsh contrasts and bring out details that would otherwise be lost. The human eye looking at a scene automatically adjusts for differences in brightness—as it glances to a shadowed area the pupil opens up to admit more light. But since photographic film records only the existing levels of light, shadows that appear reasonably bright to the eye may appear on the film as black areas that are empty of detail.

There are several ways to tell if shadows are so dark they need fill light. One way is to squint while looking at the scene; shadow areas will appear darker and thus more noticeable. Viewing the scene through the camera's lens with the aperture stopped down also helps. But a more accurate way is to measure the light with an exposure meter. If large shadow areas measure three or more stops darker than midtones, they will be very dark or even black in the final print.

Color transparencies show the need for fill light more than prints do. Color transparencies have very little exposure latitude, so as little as two stops difference between highlights and shadows can make shadows look very dark. Also, the film in the camera is the final product, so corrections can't be made later during printing.

The difference between the lit side of a subject and the shadow side is sometimes described as a ratio. A 2:1 ratio means the lit side is twice as light as the shadow side: there will be a one-stop difference between the readings each side will give on a reflected light meter.

A 2:1 ratio will render shadows as visible, but very light. A 4:1 ratio (a two-stop difference) will render shadows darker, but still showing texture and detail. Portraits are conventionally made with the shadowed side of the face between one and one-half and two stops darker than the bright side of the face, approximately a 3:1 to 4:1 ratio.

A **reflector** is a simple, effective, and inexpensive way to add fill light. A reflector bounces the main light into areas where it is needed (*pictures opposite*). A simple reflector, or flat, can be made from a piece of stiff cardboard, about 16 × 20 inches, with a soft matte white finish on one side. The other side can be covered with aluminum foil that has first been crumpled and then partially smoothed flat. The white side will give a soft, diffused, even light suitable for lightening shadows in portraits, still lifes, and other subjects. The foil side reflects a more brilliant, harder light.

A floodlight or flash can also be used for fill lighting. A light source used as a fill is generally placed close to the lens so that any secondary shadows will not be visible. The fill is usually not intended to eliminate the shadow altogether, so it is normally of less intensity than the main light. A floodlight could have lower wattage than the main light, be placed farther away from the subject, or have a translucent diffusing screen placed in front of it. See page 283 for how to use a flash for fill light.

A black reflector is useful at times. It is a sort of antifill that absorbs light and prevents it from reaching the subject. If you want to darken a shadow, a black reflector will remove fill light by absorbing light from the main light.

MARY ELLEN MARK: *Turkish Schoolgirl,* 1965

A light-colored wall, snow or sand on the ground, white papers on a desk, or other objects can act as natural reflectors, bouncing light into shadow areas. A single window can be a very contrasty source of light, causing those parts of the subject facing away from the window to appear very dark, but here the light-colored wall bounced some of the window light onto the darker side of the girl's face and dress, considerably decreasing the contrast between light and dark.

No reflector. *A single floodlight is positioned at about 45° above and to the left of the sculptured head (see drawing above). The sidelighting on the statue brings out its rounded contours, but leaves one side of the face darkly shadowed.*

White reflector. *A flat piece of white matte cardboard has been placed to the right of the head, held in a clamp stand, and angled so that the light bounces back into the shadow areas on the cheek and chin to add fill light.*

Standard Portrait Lighting

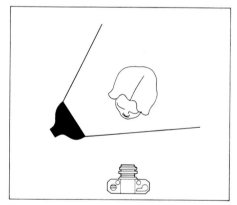

Short lighting *places the main light on the side of the face away from the camera. Here a 500-watt photoflood is placed at a 45° angle at a distance of about 4 ft. The main light is positioned high, with the catchlight, the reflection of the light source in the eyes, at 11 or 1 o'clock.*

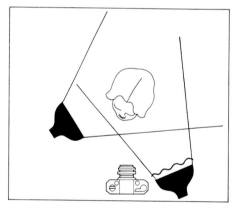

The fill light, *a diffused 500-watt photoflood, is close to the camera lens on the opposite side from the main light. Since it is farther away than the main light, it lightens but does not eliminate the shadows from the main light. Catchlights from the fill are usually spotted out in the final print.*

The accent or back light *(usually a spotlight) is placed high behind the subject, shining toward the camera but not into the lens. It rakes across the hair to emphasize texture and bring out sheen. Sometimes a second accent light places an edge highlight on hair or clothing.*

Conventional **portrait lighting** is realistic but flattering. If you have ever gone to a portrait studio to have your picture made, the photographer probably arranged the lights somewhat as in the diagrams above. The goal of the commercial portrait photographer is usually to create a rather idealized image, and these lighting setups do just that. They model most faces in a pleasing manner and can be used to improve some features—for example, using broad lighting to widen a thin face. Obviously, a good portrait does not need to be lighted in a standardized manner (none of the pictures on pages 260–263 are conventionally lighted), but it is useful to know how to do so. First, you will sometimes want to make a conventional portrait with unobtrusive lighting. Second, if you want to produce an unconventional portrait, knowing the rules will give you a better idea of how to break them.

Broad lighting *places the main light on the side of the face toward the camera; again the main light is high so the catchlight is at 11 or 1 o'clock. The main light in this position may make the side of the head, often the ear, too bright. A "barn door" on the light (see drawing) will shade the ear.*

The background light *helps separate the subject from the background. Here it is a small photoflood on a short stand hidden behind the subject. A larger photoflood or spot could be used, placed to one side. The secondary catchlight reflection from the fill has been spotted out of the eyes.*

Butterfly lighting *is conventionally used as a glamour lighting. The main light is placed directly in front of the face, positioned high enough to create a symmetrical shadow under the nose but not so high that the upper lip or the eye sockets are excessively shadowed.*

A typical studio portrait setup uses a moderately long camera lens so that the subject can be placed about 6 feet from the camera; this avoids the distortion that would be caused by having the camera too close to the subject. The subject's head is often positioned at a slight angle to the camera—turned just enough to hide one ear. The first four photographs above show short or narrow lighting where the main light is on the side of the face away from the camera. This is the most common lighting, used with average oval faces as well as to thin down a too-round face.

The fifth photograph shows a broad lighting setup where the side of the face turned toward the camera is illuminated by the main light. This type of lighting tends to widen the features, so it is used mainly with thin or narrow faces. The last setup shows butterfly lighting; the main light is placed high—directly in front of the face.

Lighting Translucent Objects

Try lighting translucent or partially transparent objects from behind—glassware, ice, thin fabrics, leaves and flowers, for example. The light can seem to shine from within, giving the object a depth and luminance that could not be achieved with flat frontal lighting (*see flower, page 258*). If you illuminate the background (as in the lighting setup below) instead of shining the light directly on the object, the lighting will be soft and diffused. Glassware is almost always lighted from behind since frontal illumination usually causes distracting reflections.

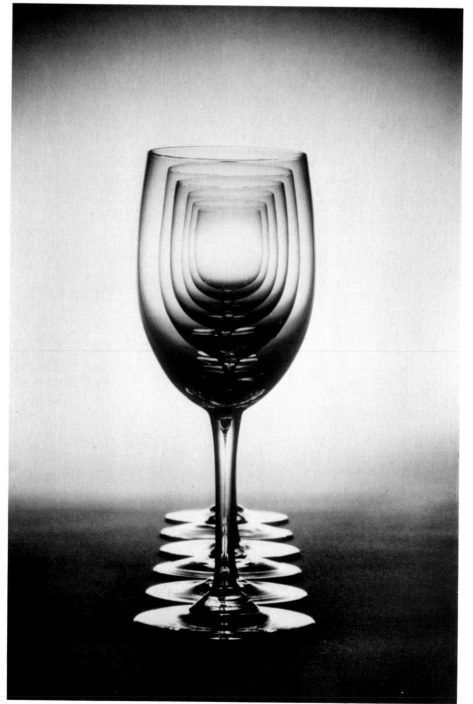

A row of crystal glasses (right) is softly lighted from the back by two large spotlights whose joined beams bounce off a sheet of seamless white paper, as shown above. The shadow that surrounds the bases of the glassware provides contrast with the brilliance cast by the reflected light and lends an air of cool elegance to the photograph.

ERICH HARTMANN: *Crystal Glassware*

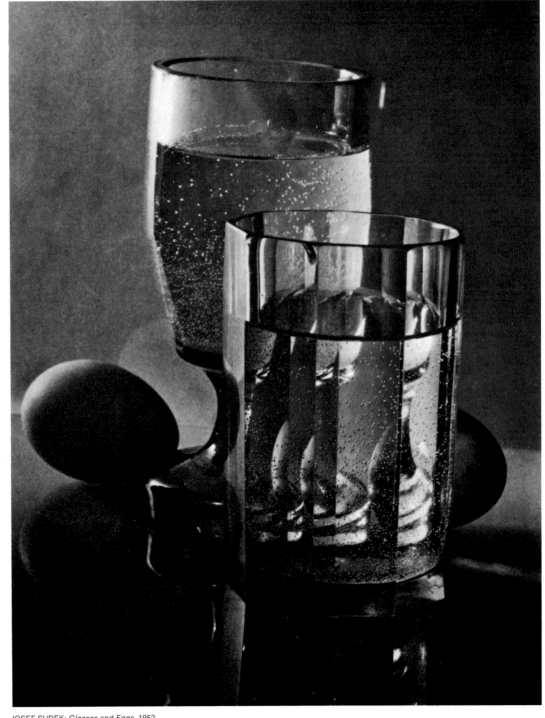

Josef Sudek sought to photograph the poetic and extraordinary qualities in ordinary objects. Here, a quiet still life of two glasses of water and two eggs is more complex than it looks at first glance. Shapes reflect, refract, and multiply themselves. Light glows on and within the objects. Sudek once said, "I like to tell stories about the life of inanimate objects, to relate something mysterious."

JOSEF SUDEK: *Glasses and Eggs,* 1952

275

Lighting Textured Objects

Lighting for a textured object depends on whether you want to emphasize texture. Every ripple of paint shows in the photograph at right because the light is raking across the object at a low angle to the surface, creating shadows that underline every bump and ripple. The same principle can be put to work with any textured object, such as rocks, textured fabrics, or facial wrinkles. Simply aim a source of direct light so it skims across the surface, choose a time of day when the sun is at a low angle in relation to the object, or arrange the object so light strikes it from the desired direction.

Shadows must be seen if the texture is to be prominent, which is why side or back lighting is used when a pronounced texture is desired; the shadows cast will be visible from camera position. A light pointed at an object from the same direction as the lens, called **axis light,** may also produce shadows, but they will be just barely visible from camera position, if at all. Axis light tends to produce the least sense of texture (*see first photograph, page 268, and diagrams at right*). If you want to minimize textures in a portrait because your subject is self-conscious about facial wrinkles, place the main light close to the lens.

side lighting

back lighting

axis lighting

Texture is emphasized in a photograph when light skims across the surface at a low angle and produces shadows that are visible from camera position. For most objects this requires side or back lighting. Axis lighting, which comes from the camera direction, produces the least texture.

SEBASTIAN MILITO: *Doorknob,* 1970

Lighting Reflective Objects

FIL HUNTER: *Cornet*, 1982

The cornet (left) was so shiny that it reflected images of the camera and lights that the photographer needed to shoot it. To solve the problem, Fil Hunter isolated the horn inside a light tent (see drawing above). The horn and its background are lit evenly and diffusely with two spotlights shining through the thin material of the tent, which itself makes a pleasing and simple pattern of reflections in the horn's shiny surfaces. The camera, looking in through the opening in the tent from the shadows outside, stays out of the picture, as do other potentially distracting reflections.

Photographing objects with glossy surfaces can be like photographing a mirror. Highly polished materials such as metal, ceramic, or plastic can reflect every detail of their surroundings, a distracting trait when the surroundings include such irrelevant items as lights, photographer, and camera. Sometimes reflections work well in a photograph, making interesting patterns, but usually it is necessary to eliminate at least some of them.

Reflections can be controlled. To some extent this can be done by moving the equipment or the object around until reflections are no longer distracting. If the reflections must be reduced still further, two methods are available. You can use matte spray, a special dulling agent available in art supply stores. Use it sparingly or it will produce a flat, lifeless image. Another solution is to **tent** the object, that is, surround it with plain surfaces like large sheets of paper that are then lighted and whose reflections in the object are photographed (*diagram at left*). You can also hang strips of paper just outside the picture area to place reflections where you want them. When checking a shiny object for reflections, through-the-lens viewing is best. Even a slight change in position can change the pattern of reflections.

Lighting with Flash

Flash units provide a convenient means of increasing the light, indoors or out. **Electronic flash,** also called **strobe,** has mostly replaced the earlier flashbulb, except with some amateur cameras and for a few specialty uses. The light of an electronic flash unit comes from a tube filled with xenon or other inert gas, which glows brightly for an instant when subjected to a surge of electricity. A unit can be fired many thousands of times before the tube burns out, unlike a flashbulb, which fires only once. In either case, the flash has to be synchronized with the camera's shutter so that it fires exactly when the shutter is fully open. Types of flash equipment and accessories are described on pages 280–281.

Some electronic flash units control exposure automatically by regulating the length of the flash. After the flash is triggered, light striking the subject is reflected back to a light-sensitive cell, or sensor, mounted on the flash unit. When enough light for correct exposure has been reflected back to the sensor, it cuts off the flash. The duration of the flash in an automatic unit may vary from as long as $\frac{1}{400}$ second to as short as $\frac{1}{50,000}$ second. See page 281 for how to use automatic flash.

Manually controlled electronic flash units put out a consistently bright flash for a fixed length of time—usually about $\frac{1}{1000}$ second. Exposure is controlled by the photographer adjusting the size of the lens aperture based on the distance from flash to subject; the greater the distance, the weaker the illumination that reaches the subject and the wider the aperture that is needed. See pages 282–283 for how and when to use flash manually.

A camera-mounted flash unit is convenient to carry and use. The light from the flash illuminates whatever is directly in front of the lens. But flash on camera (or any single light that is positioned very close to the lens axis) creates a nearly shadowless light; the result is a flatness of modeling and lack of texture that may not be desirable for every subject. There is nothing necessarily wrong with this type of lighting—Weegee was a master of its use (*see photograph, opposite*)—but there are other positions for the flash (*see pages 284–285*).

The burst of light from electronic flash is very brief. Even $\frac{1}{1000}$ second, which is a relatively long flash duration, will show most moving subjects sharply, a great advantage in many situations (*see photograph, this page*). The disadvantage is that the flash is so brief that you can't see how the light affects the subject—for example, where the shadows will fall. Some flash units avoid this problem by the addition of a **modeling light,** a small tungsten light positioned close to or even built into the flash unit and used as an aid in positioning the flash. Even without a modeling light, however, you will eventually be able to predict the effects of various flash positions.

HARRY BENSON: *Beatles' Pillow Fight,* 1964

To photograph the Beatles in a hotel room during a 1964 concert tour, photojournalist Harry Benson used bounce flash, a softer and more natural-looking light than direct flash. It is the photographer's use of flash and not flash lighting itself that creates a harsh or soft effect.

Photojournalists like flash for several reasons. Flash stops motion; the burst of light from a flash is so brief—usually faster than the fastest shutter speed on a camera—that it shows most moving subjects sharply and also prevents camera motion from blurring a picture. The light is portable and predictable; unlike existing lighting, which may be too dim or otherwise unsuitable, a flash delivers a measured and repeatable quantity of light anywhere the photographer takes it.

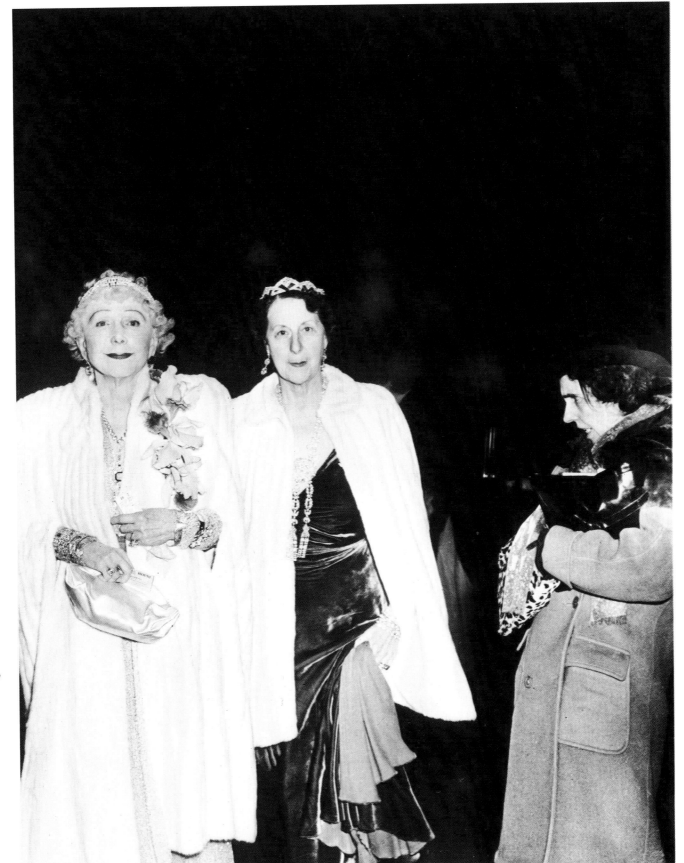

Weegee (Arthur Fellig) specialized in street scenes in New York City—here, a close encounter between denizens of two different worlds. He almost always used direct flash on camera, a harsh, two-dimensional lighting that reveals every detail with a head-on and merciless burst of light—a perfect illumination for his subject matter.

The picture also shows that light rapidly gets dimmer as the distance from the light source to the subject increases. This is why the three people in the foreground are adequately exposed while the background is almost black; by the time the light from the flash reached the background, it was too dim to illuminate it.

WEEGEE: *The Critic*, 1943

Flash Equipment

Electronic Flash

Electronic flash or strobe *is a tube containing gas that glows brightly when electrified. It is reusable and can be fired thousands of times, drawing power from either batteries or AC current.*

An automatic flash *has a light-sensitive cell and electronic circuitry that determines the duration of the flash by measuring the light reflected back from the subject.*

A dedicated (or designated) flash *is always an automatic flash and is designed to be used with a particular camera. The flash automatically sets the camera's shutter to the correct speed for flash and activates a signal in the viewfinder when the flash is ready to fire. A dedicated flash can also be used as an ordinary flash with other cameras.*

A hot-shoe flash *has a mounting foot that slips into the hot-shoe bracket on top of a camera. The hot shoe provides an electrical connection that fires the flash when the camera shutter is released. Some hot-shoe units, like the one shown here, have a head that tilts so the flash can be used on the camera but still provide indirect bounce light.*

In the early days of flash photography, taking pictures was something of a gamble. Flash powder, an early source of artificial light, was a dangerously explosive mixture that could easily burn or blind the photographer. Not until the 1930s did flash photography become simple and safe with the mass production of flashbulbs. Today's flash units provide a measured quantity of light in a convenient and easy-to-use form.

To **synchronize** flash and shutter so that the flash is lit when the shutter is open, an electrical connection is needed between them. If a camera has a socket in which a flash is inserted directly, the connection is made within the socket. Some cameras have a **hot shoe,** a bracket on top of the camera that both attaches a suitable flash unit and has a built-in electrical connection to the shutter. Other cameras have a synchronization socket (a PC terminal) to which one end of an electrical wire, called a PC cord or **synch cord,** is connected; the other end of the cord attaches to the flash. Consult the manufacturer's instructions for the way to synchronize your flash and camera.

Electronic flash is synchronized to fire when the shutter is fully open because the flash reaches its peak brilliance almost instantly and has a very brief duration. A camera with a leaf shutter (for example, any rangefinder camera) can be used with electronic flash at any shutter speed when the camera is set for X synch. A camera with a focal-plane shutter (any single-lens reflex camera) is used with electronic flash only at relatively slow shutter speeds because the shutter is fully open at only 1/60 second (sometimes 1/125 second) or slower.

Synchronization with flashbulbs depends on the type of bulb. Flashbulbs have a slight delay between ignition and the peak of usable light. The most common bulbs, Class M, have a medium peak delay. A camera with a leaf-type shutter can be used with an M bulb at any shutter speed when the camera is set for M synch; however, the full light from the bulb will not be used if the shutter speed is faster than the usable duration of the flash (about 1/60 second). A focal-plane shutter can be set to X synch and used with Class M bulbs at slow shutter speeds (up to about 1/30 second). Class FP (focal-plane) bulbs have a flash of long duration and uniform brightness to provide even illumination for focal-plane shutters at all shutter speeds. Class S (slow peak) bulbs give the maximum light output and are used either at very slow shutter speeds (about 1/15 second) or are fired after the shutter is manually opened.

A handle-mount flash *puts out more light than a typical hot-shoe unit. Its "potato masher" handle serves as a grip and can hold batteries to power the unit.*

Flashbulbs

flash bulb and reflector   flash cube

A flashbulb *consumes its filaments when flashed and can be used only once. Bulbs are often used in reflectors that have a polished finish.*

A flash cube or flash bar *contains several bulbs that fire one at a time. The bulbs are built into a single unit with a reflector behind each bulb and a plastic shield in front.*

Studio flash units *are powerful devices that fire one or more flash heads when triggered either by a cord connection or by a flash slave eye, a sensor that fires a unit when it detects a pulse of light from a primary unit that is synchronized with the camera.*

Using Automatic Flash

Labels (top to bottom):
- aperture scale
- distance scale
- film speed scale
- mode selector
- power switch
- hot-shoe connection

Using an automatic flash on camera is very simple, but models vary in operation, so check the manufacturer's instruction book before shooting.

1 | *Set the camera shutter-speed dial to the correct speed for flash operation. Attach the flash to the camera's hot-shoe bracket.*

2 | *Set the flash mode selector (if there is one) for automatic operation.*

3 | *Set the flash calculator dial to the film speed you are using.*

4 | *On the calculator dial find the correct lens aperture for flash operation (some flash units offer a choice of apertures). Set the lens aperture accordingly.*

5 | *Focus the camera. The calculator dial will show the range of distances (for example, 3–20 ft) within which the flash will automatically produce a correct exposure for an average subject. Turn the flash on; shoot after the flash signals that it is charged and ready to fire. Some units have a signal light that confirms if the subject was adequately exposed.*

An **automatic flash** controls the exposure for you. You have to do little more than attach the unit, make a few adjustments, and shoot (*see the box at left*). Within the working range of distances, the flash adjusts itself automatically to produce the correct exposure for most subjects. You can spend more time with the subject and less with your equipment because you don't have to reset the lens aperture every time the distance changes from flash to subject.

When doesn't automatic flash work well? Mostly in the same scenes where you have to be careful with any exposure metering. If the subject does not fill enough of the center of the frame and is against a much lighter background, such as a white wall, the subject may be underexposed and too dark. If the subject is against a much darker background, such as outdoors at night, it may be overexposed and too light. The flash sensor, like the sensor in an exposure meter, reads the brightness of the scene overall and computes a correct overall exposure—but one that may be wrong for just the part of the scene that is of interest to you. See page 286 for troubleshooting automatic flash exposures and pages 282–283 for how to set flash exposures manually.

TERRY EILER: *Foxhounds at a Field Trial, Carroll County, Virginia, 1978*

Automatic flash works well as long as the main subject fills the central part of the frame. Adjust the exposure or use the flash on manual if the subject is relatively small against a much darker or lighter background (see page 286).

Controlling Flash Exposure Manually

With **manual flash exposure** you adjust the lightness or darkness of the picture by widening or closing the lens aperture. Even if you have an automatic flash, you may want manual operation when the background is much lighter or much darker than the subject, with multiple flash setups, off-camera flash, or bounce flash, or simply to give you greater control of the lighting.

The farther away an object is from a light source, the less light it receives. To find the correct aperture, measure the distance from your flash to your subject and divide it into the **guide number** (the manufacturer's rating for the flash when used with a given film speed). The result will be the lens f-stop to use (*see diagram, below*).

Guide numbers are only guides. If you consistently underexpose flash shots, use a lower guide number; if you consistently overexpose, use a higher number. If the room where you are photographing is very small, with white walls and ceilings, close down the aperture one stop. If the room is very large or you are using the flash outdoors at night, open up the aperture one stop. When firing a diffused or reflectorless flash, open up about one stop since only part of the light will reach the subject.

The distance to the subject with bounce flash is the distance the light travels. This is measured from the flash to the reflecting surface to the subject, not straight from flash to subject. You must also open the lens a bit more to allow for light absorbed by the reflect-

ing surface. A white, painted wall or ceiling might need an extra half-stop exposure, white curtains or an acoustic tile ceiling a full extra stop, and a darker surface even more. An umbrella reflector designed for photographic use, such as the one shown on page 259, may not need any additional exposure. Bracket your exposures to be safe.

A **flash meter** is often used by studio photographers or other professionals. It is similar to an ordinary exposure meter but is designed to read the brief, intense burst of light from flash, which most ordinary meters cannot. A flash meter simplifies exposure calculations in situations such as multiple light setups, with bounce flash, or if cumulative firings are used to build an exposure.

Flash manufacturers measure the power of a unit and assign it a guide number, a rating for the flash when used with a given film speed. To set your own exposure, divide the distance from flash to subject into the guide number for your film. Often manufacturers list two guide numbers for each film speed: one if you measure the flash-to-subject distance in feet and the other if you measure in meters.

The farther a subject is from the flash, the less light it will receive and the wider the aperture needed to keep exposure constant. The level of light drops rapidly as the distance increases between light and subject; at twice a given distance from a light source, an object receives only one-fourth the light. This is the inverse square law: intensity of illumination is inversely proportional to the square of the distance from light to subject.

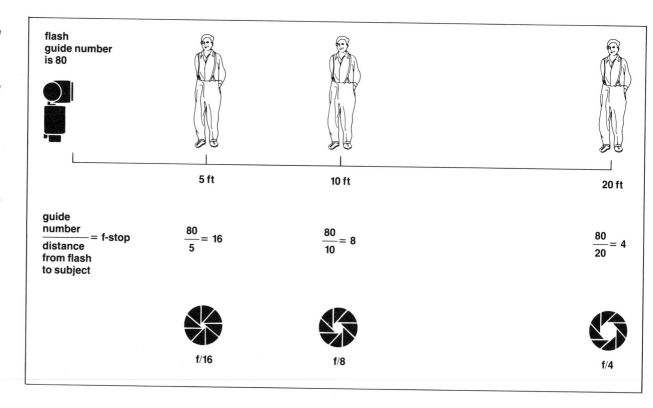

flash
guide number
is 80

5 ft   10 ft   20 ft

$$\frac{\text{guide number}}{\text{distance from flash to subject}} = \text{f-stop}$$

$$\frac{80}{5} = 16 \qquad \frac{80}{10} = 8 \qquad \frac{80}{20} = 4$$

f/16   f/8   f/4

Flash can be a fill light outdoors. A bright, sunny day is a pleasant time to photograph, but it isn't always the most flattering light for portraits. Facing someone directly into the sun will light the face overall but often causes the person to squint. Turning someone away from the sun can put too much of the face in dark shadow. Flash used on the camera as an addition to the basic exposure will open up dark shadows so that they show printable detail (see photographs at right). It is better not to overpower the sunlight with the flash but to add just enough fill so that the shadows are still somewhat darker than the highlights—for portraits, about one or two stops darker.

sunlit subject without fill

sunlit subject with flash fill

A photograph made in direct sun may have too-dark shadows (top, left). You can use flash as a fill light to decrease the contrast between shadows and highlights (bottom, left). Setting the exposure takes a little juggling. Here is one way:

1 | Set your camera shutter speed to the correct speed to synchronize with flash. Let's assume it is 1/60 sec. If your camera synchronizes at another speed, use that speed throughout.

2 | Meter the scene as if you were not going to use flash. Find the f-stop that correctly combines with 1/60 sec. Set your lens to that f-stop.

3 | Locate the f-stop from step 2 on the flash calculator dial and find the distance that is opposite it. Position the flash that distance from the subject. In this position the light from the flash will equal the sunlight.

4 | A better effect is to cut the flash exposure to a half or a quarter of the sunlight exposure. To do this with manual operation, drape a layer or two of white handkerchief over the flash head or set the flash to half or quarter power. With automatic operation, adjust lens or flash settings for one or two stops less than normal exposure (different units have different ways of doing this; see manufacturer's instructions).

— aperture scale

distance scale

film speed scale

If your flash has a calculator dial, it will do the arithmetic of manual exposure calculation for you.

1 | Set your film speed into the calculator dial.

2 | Find the distance from flash to subject. You can estimate the distance or read it off the distance scale on the lens after you focus on the subject. (The distance for bounce flash is measured from flash to reflecting surface to subject.)

3 | Set your lens to the aperture that is opposite that distance on the calculator dial. Set your shutter speed to the one that will synchronize your camera with flash.

Six Ways to Use Flash

Using a flash unit mounted on top of the camera is an easy way to light a scene. An adequately exposed picture is almost guaranteed if you follow the simple instructions that come with the unit. The trouble is that this type of lighting is relatively uninteresting: the subject looks two-dimensional with texture and volume flattened by the frontal lighting. The fault lies not with the flash but with its position so close to the camera.

You can get more varied and natural-looking results with the light in other positions, as demonstrated at right. Basically these techniques are the same as those used with photofloods: they make the lighting more nearly resemble natural illumination. Since almost all natural lighting—whether supplied by the sun, a window, a household lamp, or a ceiling fixture—comes from above the subject, the most natural-looking pictures will result from a flash held above the level of the lens and slightly to one side or bounced in such a way that light comes from above. But while the main light should be the most important light, natural lighting, indoors or outdoors, rarely strikes a subject exclusively from one direction; covering the flash with a diffusing screen, bouncing some of its light off walls, and adding a second or third flash will create softer shadows, more interesting textures, and more lifelike depth.

Flash duration is too short to see the effect of different positions while shooting. You have to point the flash carefully so that the light doesn't illuminate only part of the subject or create odd shadows or distracting reflections (*see page 286*).

Direct flash on camera. *This is the quickest and simplest method, allowing the photographer to move around and shoot quickly. But the light tends to be flat, producing few of the shadows that add volume and texture. (See the Weegee photograph, page 279.)*

Diffused flash on camera. *For a softer effect, the harshness and intensity of the flash can be reduced by placing a diffusing screen in front of the unit or by simply draping a handkerchief over it. This is a particularly useful way of preventing glaring white highlights in close-ups.*

Direct flash off camera. *When using a single light source, this is one way to get more interesting shadows and a three-dimensional feeling. The flash here is connected to the camera by a long synch cord and held about 1½ ft above the camera and slightly to the right.*

Multiple flash. *This gives good dimensionality and separates the subject from the background. The main light was placed to the right; a second flash lighted the background; a unit on the camera provided fill light for facial shadows. One flash was connected to the camera by a synch cord; the others were triggered by slave eyes.*

Flash bounced from side. *For soft, natural-looking lighting, with good modeling of features, the flash unit can be pointed so that its light does not reach the subject directly but is reflected from a white or light-colored wall or from an umbrella reflector like the one shown on page 259.*

Flash bounced from above. *In a room with a relatively low ceiling, the flash can be pointed upward and bounced off the ceiling. This type of flash lighting is easy if you are using a unit with a head that swivels upward. The light is soft and natural-looking.*

Lighting with Flash: continued

What Went Wrong?

Troubleshooting Flash Problems

unwanted reflection—shot head-on

Until you have used flash often, it is difficult to tell exactly what effect its light will have. Shadows and reflections are nonexistent until the flash goes off, and even then they disappear too fast to be seen. The film records them, though, sometimes with the results shown here. See also Troubleshooting Camera and Lens Problems (page 83), Negative Problems (page 151), and Print Problems (page 181).

Unwanted reflections

Cause: Shooting at a shiny surface like glass that is parallel to the camera. Light from the flash was reflected directly back into the lens (top photograph).

Prevention: When photographing scenes that include reflective shiny objects such as windows, mirrors, paneled walls, or metal surfaces, move the camera and/or the flash to one side so that you shoot or illuminate the scene at an angle to the reflecting surface (see second photograph). Eyeglasses can also reflect the light—once in a great while to advantage (see photograph opposite).

Red eye—a person's or animal's eyes appear red in a color picture.

Cause: Light from the flash reflecting from the blood-rich retina inside the eye.

Prevention: Have the subject look away from the camera or move the flash away from the camera.

Unwanted shadows

Cause: Flash positioned off camera at an angle that caused shadows you didn't predict (see third photograph).

Prevention: Sighting along a line from flash to subject will help predict how shadows will be cast. A small tungsten light positioned close to the flash will also help; large studio flashes have such modeling lights built into the flash for just this purpose.

Only part of frame exposed

Cause: Shooting at too fast a shutter speed with a camera that has a focal-plane shutter. The flash fired before the shutter was fully open (bottom photograph).

Prevention: Set your shutter to the correct speed for flash synchronization. Most single-lens reflex cameras have focal-plane shutters that synchronize at 1/60 sec (a few synchronize as fast as 1/125 sec). Check manufacturer's instructions.

Moving subject partly blurred

Cause: In addition to the flash-lit image, strong existing light in the scene recorded an image that showed the subject in motion. The part of the subject lit by the flash is sharp, other parts lit mainly by the existing light are blurred.

Prevention: Dim the existing light or shoot when the subject isn't moving so much. If your camera has a leaf shutter (rangefinder cameras and view cameras do), shoot at a faster shutter speed.

Subject too light

Cause: Overexposure—too much light reached the film.

Prevention: If this happens once in a while, you may have set the film speed too low on the flash calculator dial, opened the lens to too wide an aperture, or overestimated the distance from flash to subject. If your flash pictures are usually overexposed, your flash is putting out more light than you (or the manufacturer) think it is. If your flash has a calculator dial, increase the film speed ratings that you set into it. Every doubling of the rated film speed cuts the exposure by a factor of two, a decrease of one stop. For example, if your film speed is ISO/ASA 100 and you set 200 into the calculator dial, your pictures will get one stop less exposure. If you are using a guide number and calculating exposure manually, multiply the guide number by 1.4 for every stop you want the exposure decreased.

Subject too dark

Cause: Underexposure—too little light reached the film.

Prevention: Occasional underexposure is often due to setting the film speed too high on the flash calculator dial, setting the lens to too small an aperture, or underestimating the distance from flash to subject. If your flash pictures are usually underexposed, your flash is putting out too little light. The cure is to cut the film speed rating in half or divide the guide number by 1.4 for every stop you want exposure increased.

Part of scene exposed correctly, part too light or too dark

Cause: Parts of the scene are at different distances from the flash. Parts that are farther away are darker than those that are close because the farther that light travels from the flash, the dimmer it becomes (see page 282).

Prevention: Try to group important parts of the scene at about the same distance from the flash.

no reflection—shot at an angle

unwanted shadows

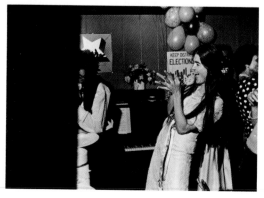

only part of frame exposed

286   *11/Lighting*

NORMAN SEEFF: *Frank Zappa,* 1976

Reflections in someone's eyeglasses are usually unwanted in a portrait—but not always. Norman Seeff specializes in photographing rock performers such as Frank Zappa, whose eyes here light up with double images of the umbrella reflector Seeff used to bounce the light onto him.

Using Lighting

RUTH BERNHARD: *Lifesavers*, 1930

Using light can also mean using shadows. Side lighting can add interest to a subject because it creates shadows that are visible from camera position. Part of the charm of Ruth Bernhard's picture is that she created such an unexpectedly complex pattern out of such a commonplace item —and that she hid two half-Lifesavers among the whole ones, too.

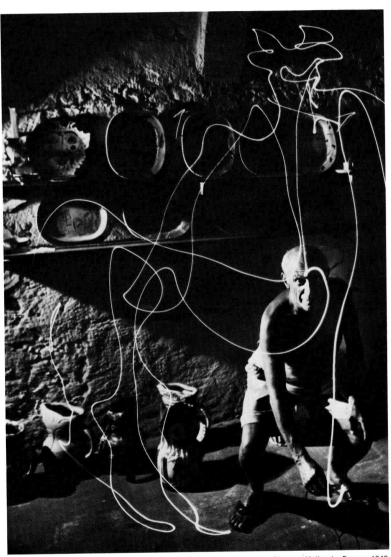

GJON MILI: *Centaur by Picasso, Vallauris, France,* 1949

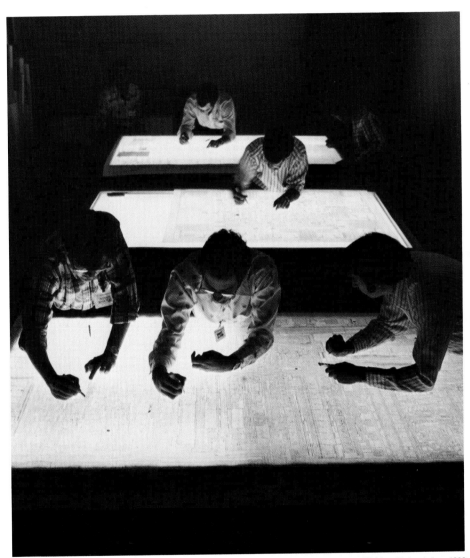

ARCHIE LIEBERMAN: *Motorola Design Engineers, Semiconductor Products Division, Motorola Inc.,* 1982

The fanciful centaur drawn by Pablo Picasso exists only on film (above). The artist traced it in total darkness with a flashlight bulb while Gjon Mili kept his camera shutter open. Just before the drawing was complete, Mili triggered a flash, placed to the left. The flash caught Picasso at the end of the downstroke that completed his drawing.

For a corporate report for Motorola, Inc., Archie Lieberman wanted to convey a high-tech image of the company. At one of Motorola's plants, Lieberman found a group of design engineers working at light tables. He chose the location in part because of the dramatic lighting he saw there. He used only the light existing in the room, bracketing his exposures so he could select the best one later—one shot at the exposure he thought might be best, a second with one stop less exposure, and a third with one stop more.

PHOTOGRAPHER UNKNOWN: *William Henry Jackson with his 20 × 24-inch camera photographing Zuni Pueblo near Laguna, New Mexico*, c. 1877

In the early days of photography, a practical method of enlarging an image had not yet been devised. So if you wanted a big print, you made a big negative. Opposite, William Henry Jackson's 20 × 24-inch view camera was a standard size used for making scenic views. Jackson had to transport not only the view camera but as many 20 × 24-inch glass plates as he needed to make all the photographs on a trip. (For more about early travel photography, see pages 362–363.)

12

View Camera

In today's world of small, hand-held cameras that are fast working and convenient to use, why would a photographer use a bulky, heavy, slow-working **view camera**—a camera that has few or no automatic features, that must almost always be used with a tripod, that shows you an image that is upside down and backward and so dim that you need to put a dark cloth over the camera and your head to see it? The answer is that the view camera does some jobs so well that it is worth the trouble of using it.

A view camera's **movements** give you an extraordinary amount of control over the image. The camera's back (film plane) and front (lens board) can be independently moved in a number of directions: up, down, or sideways, tilted forward or back, swiveled to either side. These movements can eliminate or increase distortion, control the extent of the depth of field, alter perspective, and change the area of the scene recorded on the negative.

The **large film size** that can be used is also an advantage. The most common size is 4 × 5 inches; 5 × 7, 8 × 10 inches, and sometimes larger sizes are also used. (Comparable European sizes range from 9 × 12 cm to 18 × 24 cm and larger.) While modern small-camera films (1 × 1½ inches is the size of 35mm film) can make excellent enlargements, the greatest image clarity and detail and the least grain are produced by a contact print or a moderate enlargement from a large-size negative.

A view camera is the most satisfactory camera to use when control of the image is vital, as in architectural or product photography. Some photographers use a view camera in all but the fastest-moving situations because they feel that its benefits—the control gained, plus the detail a large-size negative records—more than compensate for any disadvantages.

Inside the Modern View Camera

The ability of a view camera to change and control an image is due to its **movements.** Unlike most cameras, which are permanently aligned so that lens and film are exactly parallel, a view camera can be deliberately unaligned. The movements and their effects, explained on the following pages, are easier to understand if you have a view camera at hand so you can demonstrate the effects for yourself.

Rise, fall, and shift (also called slide) move the entire front or back of the camera in a flat plane. Rise moves the front or back up, fall moves the front or back down, shift moves the front or back to the left or right.

Tilt and swing move the front or back of the camera at an angle. Tilt moves the front or back around a horizontal axis; it tips either one forward or backward. Swing is a movement around a vertical axis; it twists one side of the front or back to the left or right.

To make full use of a view camera's movements, you must use it with a lens of adequate **covering power;** that is, a lens that produces a large image circle. As shown below, a lens projects a circular image that decreases in sharpness and brightness at the edges. If a camera has a rigid body, the image circle needs to be just large enough to cover the size of the film being used. But a view camera lens must produce an image circle larger than the film size so that there is plenty of room within the image circle for various camera movements. If the movements are so great that the film comes too close to the edge of the image circle, the photograph will be vignetted—out of focus and dark at the edges. Covering power increases—the usable image circle gets larger—as the lens is stopped down.

parts		movements	
A	lens	**1**	back-rise
B	aperture scale	**2**	back-fall
C	shutter-speed scale	**3**	front-rise
D	lens board	**4**	front-fall
E	lens-board-adjustment knob	**5**	back-shift left
F	front standard	**6**	back-shift right
G	front-standard-adjustment knob	**7**	front-shift left
H	shutter-release cable	**8**	front-shift right
J	bellows	**9**	back-tilt backward
K	tripod mount	**10**	back-tilt forward
L	ground-glass viewing screen	**11**	front-tilt backward
M	back-adjustment knob	**12**	front-tilt forward
N	back	**13**	back-swing left
O	back standard	**14**	back-swing right
P	back-standard-adjustment knob	**15**	front-swing left
Q	dark slide	**16**	front-swing right
R	film holder	**17**	front focusing
S	film sheet	**18**	back focusing

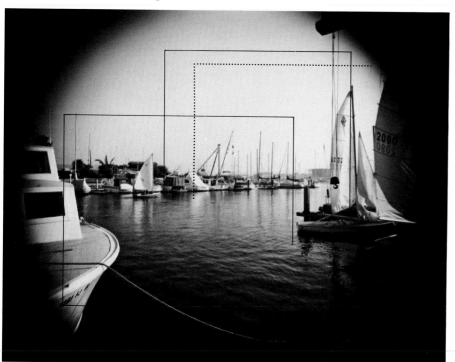

This simplified cutaway of a view camera makes ▶ clear its basic relationship to all cameras: it is a box with a lens at one end and a sheet of film at the other. Unlike other cameras, however, the box is not rigid. The front face, to which the lens is fastened, can be moved independently—up or down, forward or back—by loosening a pair of knobs (E). A second pair of knobs (M) permits similar movements of the back. Knobs (as in G and P) permit front or back to be shifted, swung or focused. The camera-back (N) can be rotated to take a picture in either a horizontal or a vertical format. In addition, different sizes of film can be used by substituting film holders and camera-backs that are designed for those sizes. The front end of the camera will accept different lenses. Extra bellows can be inserted for extreme extensions in close-up work; or if the focal length of the lens is so short that the regular bellows cannot be squeezed tight enough, a bag bellows can be used (shown on page 302).

◀ A lens with good covering power (producing a large image circle) is needed for view camera use. Camera movements such as rise, fall, or shift move the position of the film within the image circle (as shown at left), so the lens should produce an image that is larger than the actual size of the film. The corners of the viewing screen should be checked before exposure to make sure the camera movements have not placed the film outside the image circle, vignetting the picture (dotted lines).

View Camera Movements
Rise and Fall

controls zeroed

back-rise or front-fall

back-fall or front-rise

The diagrams above show how rise or fall of the camera's front or back changes the position of the image on the negative. In the top diagram, the object being photographed appears in the center of the ground-glass viewing screen. It is inverted (upside down and reversed left to right). In the center diagram, the object has been moved to the bottom of the viewing screen (the top of the picture when viewed right side up); this is accomplished by either raising the back or lowering the lens. To move the object to the top of the viewing screen (the bottom of the actual picture), lower the back or raise the lens (bottom diagram).

It is easier to understand the effect each movement can have on a photograph if you first look at a picture where no movement has been set into any part of the camera. This has been done with the first cube at right. Camera position was centered on the cube. All controls were set at zero. Focus was on the top front edge.

The result is an image that falls in the center of the picture frame. The cube's top front edge, being closest to the camera, is the largest. It is also the sharpest, since it lies along the focal plane. The two visible surfaces of the cube fall away in size and sharpness at an equal rate. If you compare this reference cube to the photographs of it that follow, you can see the changes in its shape, sharpness and position that take place as a result of camera movements.

Rise, an upward movement, and **fall, a downward movement,** of the camera's front or back, change the placement of the image on the film by changing the position of film and lens relative to each other. Moving the back moves the film to include various parts of the image circle. Moving the front moves the image circle so that a different part of it falls on the film.

Rise or fall of the back changes the location of the image but does not affect its shape. The effect is not unlike cropping a photograph during printing—the amount of the object shown or its position within the frame may change but not the shape of the object itself. Front movement changes the point of view and to some extent the shape. In these pictures, the change in shape is too slight to be seen in the cube, but the difference in point of view is visible in the change of relationship between the cube and the small post.

Rise and fall are up or down movements. Rise or fall of the front or back changes the position of the image in the frame. Rise or fall of the front also affects the position of foreground and background objects relative to each other.

For the sake of simplicity, the pictures and text at right relate not to the inverted (upside down and backwards) image seen on the ground-glass viewing screen, but to the photograph as you would see it after it was printed. The diagrams at left show the image as you would see it while you were focusing and adjusting the camera.

reference cube

The reference cube was shot with all camera adjustments set at zero position, looking down from an angle of 45°. This puts the cube in the center of the film and produces a symmetrical figure.

back-rise

back-fall

front-rise

front-fall

Raising the back of the camera moves the cube higher on the film without changing its shape. Nor does this movement affect the position or shape of the small post that has been centered exactly in front of the cube, with its top in line with the cube's front edge—as comparison with the photograph of the reference cube shows.

Lowering the back of the camera lowers the position of the cube on the film. Other than that, as before, there is no change in the shape of the cube or in its relationship with the post. This happens because the film, though raised or lowered, still gets the same image from the lens, which has not moved relative to the original alignment of cube and post.

Raising the lens lowers the image of the cube on the film. In this its effect is the same as back-fall. However, lens movement causes a change that does not occur with back movement: it affects the relationship between cube and post because the lens is now looking at them from a slightly different position. Compare the apparent height of the post here with its height in the two pictures at left.

A drop in the lens raises the image on the film. Lens movement also affects the space relationship between cube and post. Now the post top appears to have moved above the front edge of the cube, whereas in the previous picture it dropped below the edge.

Shift

controls zeroed

back-shift left or front-shift right

back-shift right or front-shift left

In the diagrams above, the position of the cube on the negative is moved by shifting the camera's front or its back to the side. In the top diagram, the controls are zeroed and the image is in the center of the viewing screen. In the center diagram, the object has been moved to the right side of the viewing screen (left side of the actual photograph) by moving the camera-back to the left or the lens to the right. To move the object to the other side of the picture, move the back to the right or the lens to the left (bottom diagram).

Shift, a sideways movement of either the front or the back of the camera, is the same as rise and fall except the movement takes place from side to side. If you were to lay the camera on its side and raise or drop the back, you would produce the same effect as back-shift.

The reason that rise and fall are the same as shift is that neither changes the angle between the planes of film, lens, and subject. Raise, lower, or shift the back of the camera, and the film is still squarely facing the lens; the only difference is that a different part of the film is now directly behind the lens.

Since shift is simply a sideways version of rise and fall, the results are similar. Back movement to the left moves the subject to the left; back movement to the right moves it to the right. Left or right lens movements have just the opposite results. Image shape does not change with back-shift, but it does change slightly with front-shift.

Again in common with rise and fall, shift of the lens affects the spatial relationship of objects because the lens views them from a different point. The examples at right illustrate these movements, with the reference cube included for comparison.

Remember that the cubes are shown here right side up as they would appear in the final prints. On the ground glass the image is inverted as shown in the diagrams at left.

Shift is an up or down movement. ▶
Shift of the front or back changes the position of the image in the frame. Shift of the front also affects the position of foreground and background objects relative to each other.

reference cube

Shift, like rise and fall, has no perceptible effect on the shape of an object. Compare the reference cube with the four cubes to the right of it. While the cubes move back and forth on the film, they continue to look very much the same.

back-shift left

back-shift right

front-shift left

front-shift right

A camera equipped with a back that can move the film from side to side, as well as up and down, can place an object wherever desired on a sheet of film. Here a shift of the camera-back to the left moves the cube to the left on the film.

A rightward movement of the camera-back moves the image to the right. Comparison of this picture with the previous one reveals that there has been no change in the shape of either the cube or the post in front of it. Their spatial relationship has remained unchanged also, despite the movement of the image on the film.

Moving the lens to the left moves the image on the film to the right. It also changes the relationship of post to cube. Since the lens actually moves to left or right, it views the two objects from a slightly different position, and so one object appears to have moved slightly with respect to the other. Check the position of the post against the vertical lines on the cube in this picture and the next to confirm this change.

A rightward movement of the lens, as above, (1) moves the image to the left and (2) changes the relationships in space between objects. To summarize: if you want to move the image on the film but otherwise change nothing, raise, lower, or shift the back. If you want to move the image and also change the spatial relationship of objects, raise, lower, or shift the lens.

Tilt

controls zeroed

back-tilt of camera-back

forward-tilt of camera-back

The diagrams above show how the shape of objects can be changed by tilting the camera-back and thus changing the angle between it and the lens. In the top diagram, two objects of identical size, placed the same distance from the camera, are being photographed. When the camera controls are zeroed, the objects appear the same size on the viewing screen. In the center diagram, the camera-back has been tilted back. Now when the image leaves the lens, it has to travel farther to reach the top of the viewing screen than it does to reach the bottom. As the light rays travel, they spread apart, increasing the size of the object on the top of the viewing screen (the bottom of the actual photograph). To increase the size of an object on the bottom of the viewing screen, tilt the camera-back forward (bottom diagram).

The preceding pages show that rise, fall, and shift have little or no effect on the shape of an object being photographed because they do not change the angular relationship of the planes of film, lens, and object. But what happens with **tilt, a forward or backward movement** of either the camera-front or camera-back? That depends on whether you tilt the front or back of the camera.

Tilting the back of the camera changes the shape of the object considerably and changes the focus somewhat. Tilting the front of the camera changes the focus significantly without changing the shape of the object.

To understand why this happens, look again at the reference cube. In that picture the bottom of the film sheet was the same distance from the lens as the top of the film sheet. As a result, light rays coming from the lens to the top and the bottom of the film traveled the same distance, and the top back edge and the bottom front edge of the cube are the same size in the photograph. But change those distances by tilting the camera-back, and the sizes change. The rule is: the farther the image travels inside the camera, the larger it gets. Since images appear upside down on film, tilting the top of the camera-back to the rear will make the bottom of the cube bigger in the photograph (*diagrams, left*).

A tilt of the camera-front does not change distances inside the camera and thus does not affect image size or shape, but it does affect focus by altering the lens's focal plane. Tilting the lens will bring the focal plane more nearly into parallel with one cube face or the other and thereby will improve the focus on that face and worsen it on the other.

Tilt is a forward or backward movement. Tilt of the back mostly affects the shape of an object, and so helps to control convergence. Tilt of the front mostly affects the plane of focus, and so helps to control depth of field. ▶

Checking the reference cube again, note that the 45° angle of view has produced an image that falls off in both size and sharpness at an equal rate on both the top and the front faces. As a result the two faces are exactly the same size and shape. Note also that the vertical lines on the front face are not parallel, but converge (come closer together) toward the bottom.

back-tilt of the camera-back

When the back of the camera is tilted so that the top of the film is farther away from the lens than in the reference shot, this movement enlarges the bottom of the cube and tends to square up its front face, bringing its lines more nearly into parallel. At the same time, this tilt has moved the bottom of the film closer to the lens than it was in the reference shot, shrinking the top back edge of the cube so that it converges more than before.

forward-tilt of the camera-back

If the back of the camera is tilted the other way, so that the top of the film is forward and the bottom is moved away from the lens, the top of the cube tends to square up and the front bottom converges more. Squaring up one face of the cube results in increasing light loss and increasing fuzziness toward the far edge of the squared face. In this case the back edge of the top face is affected. In the picture at left the bottom edge of the front face is affected.

back-tilt of the camera-front

When the lens is tilted, there is no change in the distance from lens to film; thus there is no change in the shape of the cube. However, there is a distinct change in focus. Here the lens has been tipped backward. This brings its focal plane more nearly parallel to the front face of the cube, pulling all of it into sharp focus. The top of the cube, however, is now more blurred than in the reference shot.

forward-tilt of the camera-front

If the lens is tilted forward, the top of the cube becomes sharp and the front more blurred. The focus control that lens-tilt gives can be put to good use when combined with back-tilt. Look again at the two back-tilt shots at the left; their squared—and blurry—sides could have been made much sharper by tilting the lens to improve their overall focus.

Swing

controls zeroed

left-swing of camera-back

right-swing of camera-back

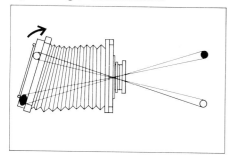

Swinging the camera-back changes the shape of objects by changing the angle between the camera-back and the lens. This top view of a camera shows why. As with back-tilt, if part of an image has to travel farther to reach the camera-back, it will increase in size. In the top diagram, both objects are the same size and the camera's controls are zeroed. In the center diagram, the image on the left side of the viewing screen (the right side of the actual photograph) has been increased in size by swinging the camera-back to the left. To change the size of the image on the right side of the viewing screen, swing the camera-back to the right (bottom diagram).

Swing, a sideways movement of either the front or the back of the camera has different effects depending on whether the front or back is swung.

Swinging the back of the camera, like tilting the back, moves one part of the film closer to the lens while moving another part farther away. This produces changes of shape in the image plus some change in focus (*diagrams, left*).

Swinging the front of the camera swivels the lens to the left or right and as a result skews the focal plane of the lens to one side or the other. The general effect is to create a sharply defined zone of focus that travels at an angle across an object. A close look at the two right-hand cubes on the opposite page reveals this. There is a narrow diagonal path of sharp focus traveling across the top of each cube and running down one side of the front.

The practical applications of the four camera movements are virtually endless. For example, assume that the reference cube is a house with a large garden in front of it. Raising the back of the camera (*page 295, first picture*) will raise the image on the film and show more of the garden. Or assume that you wish to increase the apparent height of the house. Tilting the back of the camera toward the front (*second picture, page 299*) is one way to produce that effect. The following pages show how swings, tilts, rises, and shifts can be applied in real situations to solve specific photographic problems.

Swing is a sideways movement. ▶
Swing of the back mostly affects the shape of an object, and so helps to control convergence. Swing of the front mostly affects the plane of focus, and so helps to control depth of field.

Comparing the reference cube to the pictures at right shows the distortions in shape that can be made by changing the angle of film to lens. Compare the cube with the first two pictures on its right. If you didn't understand the process by which such changes can be made, it would be hard to know that these swing shots —or the two back-tilt shots on the previous page—are all of the same object, taken from the same spot with the same camera and lens.

left-swing of the camera-back

This movement of the camera-back swings the left side of the film away from the lens and the right side closer to it, making the left side of the cube smaller and the right side larger. (Remember, the image is inverted on the ground glass.) This effect is the same as tilt, but sideways instead of up and down.

right-swing of the camera-back

Here the right side of the film is swung away from the lens and the left side closer to it. The results are the opposite of those in the previous picture. In both of them it can be seen that there is a falling off of sharpness on the "enlarged" edges of the cube. This can be corrected by swinging the lens or by closing the aperture a few stops to increase depth of field.

left-swing of the camera-front

Since it is the lens that is being swung, and not the film, there is no change in the cube's shape. However, the position of the focal plane has been radically altered. In the reference shot it was parallel to the near edge of the cube, and that edge was sharp from one end to the other. Here the focus is skewed. Its plane cuts through the cube, on a course diagonally across the top and down the left side of the cube's face.

right-swing of the camera-front

Here is the same phenomenon as in the previous picture, except that the plane of sharp focus cuts the cube along its right side instead of its left. This selectivity of focus, particularly when tilt and swing of the lens are combined, can move the focal plane around very precisely to sharpen certain objects and throw others out of focus. For a good example of this, see page 303.

Controlling the Plane of Focus

The photograph above is partly out of focus because the camera-back (line aa') and lens plane (line bb') are parallel to each other but not to the subject plane (line cc').

Tilting the front of the camera forward so that the lens plane is more nearly parallel to the subject plane brings the entire page into sharp focus. The diagrams show a loose bag bellows on the camera instead of a regular accordion bellows.

Controlling the plane of focus—the part of a scene that is most sharply focused—is easy with a view camera. Not only can you see on the ground-glass viewing screen exactly where the plane of focus is, but you can adjust its position by tilting or swinging the front of the camera and so the lens.

With a camera that does not have swings and tilts, the lens plane (the front of the camera) is always parallel to the film plane (the back of the camera), and the plane of focus is parallel to both. You increase the depth of field (the area near the plane of focus that will also be sharp) by stopping down the lens aperture.

The disadvantage of using a camera without swings and tilts becomes evident when photographing something that is not parallel to the camera, like the rare book above. You must angle the camera down at the book. If you focus on the part of the book close to the camera, the top of the book is blurred and vice versa. A compromise focus on the middle of the page might not give enough depth of field even if you stopped the lens all the way down.

A view camera can get around this problem. The plane of the subject that is most nearly parallel to the plane of the lens will be the sharpest in the pic-

With the camera's back and front in zero position, a close-up shot of some spilled beans requires that the lens be stopped down for both the foreground beans and those in the jar to be perfectly sharp. This also brings the other jars into focus—which the photographer did not want.

A simple swing of the camera-front to the right brings the lens plane parallel to the receding pile of beans—all the way from the right foreground back through the tipped-over jar. Now the photographer can focus on the beans and open up the lens to its maximum of f/5.6, which throws the other jars out of focus and directs attention to the beans.

ture. As shown above, you can increase the sharpness of the book page by tilting the camera-front forward so that the lens is more nearly parallel to the page. If the page is still not completely sharp, stopping down the lens aperture will increase the depth of field so that more of the page will be sharp.

Furthermore, if you adjust a view camera so that the planes of film, lens, and subject all meet at a common point,

the subject plane will be completely sharp, even if the plane of the subject is not parallel to the plane of the lens and if the lens is opened to its widest aperture. This phenomenon (named the Scheimpflug rule, after its discoverer) is diagrammed on the opposite page. Fortunately, you don't have to calculate the hypothetical meeting point of the planes (you will be able to see on the ground glass when the image is sharp),

but it does explain why a plane can be sharp even if it is not parallel to the lens.

If you want only part of the picture to be sharp, this too is adjustable with a view camera. By swinging or tilting the camera-front, the plane of focus can be angled across the picture, as in the photographs above of the spilled beans.

Controlling Perspective

A view camera is often used in architectural photography for **controlling perspective.** It is almost impossible to photograph a building without distortion unless a view camera is used. You don't *have* to correct the distortion, but a view camera provides the means if you want to do so.

Suppose you wanted to photograph the building at right with just one side or face showing. If you leveled the camera and pointed it straight at the building, you would show only the bottom of the building (*first photograph, right*). Tilting up the camera shows the entire building but introduces a distortion in perspective (*second photograph*): the vertical lines seem to come together or **converge.** This happens because the top of the building is farther away and so appears smaller than the bottom of the building. When you look up at any building, your eyes also see the same converging lines, but the brain compensates for the convergence and it usually passes unnoticed. In a photograph, however, it is immediately noticeable. The view camera cure for the distortion is shown in the third photograph. The camera is adjusted to remain parallel to the building (eliminating the distortion), while still showing the building from bottom to top.

Another problem arises if you want to photograph a building with two sides showing. In the fourth photograph, the vertical lines appear correct but the horizontal lines converge. They make the near top corner of the building seem to jut up unnaturally sharp and high in a so-called **ship's-prow effect.** Swinging the back more nearly parallel to one of the sides (usually the wider one) reduces the horizontal convergence and with it the ship's prow (*last photograph*).

Photographer Philip Trager uses a view camera for his architectural work, such as the photograph on page 310. Here he demonstrates its usefulness. Standing at street level and shooting straight at a building produces too much street and too little building. Sometimes it is possible to move back far enough to show the entire building while keeping the camera level, but this adds even more foreground and usually something gets in the way.

Tilting the whole camera up shows the entire building but distorts its shape. Since the top is farther from the camera than the bottom, it appears smaller; the vertical lines of the building seem to be coming closer together, or converging, near the top. This convergence gives the illusion that the building is falling backward—an effect particularly noticeable when only one side of the building is visible.

To straighten up the converging vertical lines, keep the camera-back parallel to the face of the building. To keep all parts of the building in focus, make sure the lens is parallel to the camera-back. One way to do this is to level the camera and then use the rising-front or falling-back movements or both. Another solution is to point the camera upward toward the top of the building, then use the tilting movements—first to tilt the back to a vertical position (which squares the shape of the building), then to tilt the lens so it is parallel to the camera-back (which brings the face of the building into focus). You may need to finish by raising the camera-front somewhat.

In this view showing two sides of a building, the camera has been adjusted as in the preceding picture. The vertical lines of the building do not converge, but the horizontal lines of the building's sides do, since they are still at an angle to the camera. This produces an exaggeratedly sharp angle, called the ship's-prow effect, at the top left front corner of the building.

Two more movements are added, as shown in this top view of the camera. The ship's-prow effect is lessened by swinging the camera-back so it is parallel to one side of the building. Here the back is parallel to the wider side. The lens is also swung so it is parallel to the camera-back, which keeps the entire side of the building in focus. It is important to check the edges of the image for vignetting when camera movements are used.

Dealing with Distortion

Every attempt to project a three-dimensional object onto a two-dimensional surface results in a **distortion** of one kind or another. Yet cleaning up distortion in one part of a photograph will usually produce a different kind of distortion in another part. The book and orange in the two still lifes at right are examples of this. In the first picture, shot from above with all camera adjustments at zero, the book shows two kinds of distortion. Since its bottom is farther away from the camera than the top, the bottom looks smaller. Also the book seems to be leaning slightly to the left. These effects would have been less pronounced if the camera had been farther away from the book—the farther away an object is from a lens, the smaller are the differences in distance from the lens to various parts of the object. It is these differences that cause distortions in scale.

Can distortion be corrected? It can with a view camera, using a combination of tilt, swing, and fall. Back-tilt of the camera-back straightens the book's left edge. A left-swing of the camera-back squares up the face of the book. Since these changes enlarged the image somewhat, back-fall was added to show all of the book.

Is the result a less distorted picture? That depends. The book is certainly squared up nicely, as if it were being looked at head on, but the spine, oddly enough, is still visible. Furthermore, the round orange of the first picture has now become somewhat melon-shaped. All pictures contain distortions; what you must do is manipulate them to suit your own taste.

With camera settings at zero, a downward view of a book makes the upper part seem larger than the lower part—just as the top front edge of the first cube on page 298 was larger than the bottom edge. The book also appears to be tipping to the left. The orange, on the other hand, a sphere seen straight on in the center of the picture, appears normal.

The book is straightened by back-tilt and left-swing of the back, but this forces the orange out of shape. These back movements also affected the focus; it was necessary to back-tilt the lens and swing it to the left to bring the lens—and so the plane of focus—into better line with the book's face.

Because a view camera is so adjustable, its use requires the photographer to make many decisions. A beginner can easily get an I-don't-know-what-to-do-next feeling. So here are some suggestions.

1. Set up the camera and zero the controls. Set the camera on a sturdy tripod, attach a cable release to the shutter mechanism, point the camera toward the scene, zero the controls, and level the camera (*below left*). Open the shutter for viewing and open the diaphragm. You will almost always need to use a focusing cloth to see the image clearly (*center*).

2. Roughly frame and focus. Adjust the back for a horizontal or vertical format and roughly frame the image on the ground glass. Roughly focus by adjusting the distance between the camera-front and camera-back. The closer you are to the subject, the more you will need to increase the distance between front and back.

3. Make more precise adjustments. To change the shape or perspective of the objects in the scene, tilt or swing the camera-back. You may also want to move the position of the image on the film by adjusting the tripod or using the rising, falling, or shifting movements. Now check the focus (*right*). If necessary, adjust the plane of focus by tilting or swinging the lens. You can preview the depth of field by stopping down the lens diaphragm.

4. Make final adjustments. When the image is the way you want it, tighten all the controls. Check the corners of the viewing screen for possible vignetting. You may need to decrease some of the camera movements (especially lens movements) to eliminate vignetting.

5. Make an exposure. Close the shutter, adjust the aperture and shutter speed, and cock the shutter. Now insert a loaded film holder until it reaches the stop flange that positions it. Remove the holder's dark slide to uncover the sheet of film facing the lens, make sure the camera is steady and release the shutter. Replace the dark slide so the all-black side faces out. Your exposure is now complete.

leveling camera

Zero the controls and level the camera before making any other adjustments. Zeroing is important because even a slight tilt or swing of the lens, for example, can distinctly change the focus. Vertical leveling is important if you want the camera to be parallel to a vertical plane such as a building face. Horizontal leveling (above) is vital; without it the picture may seem off balance even if there are no horizontal lines in the scene.

using focusing cloth

The view camera's ground glass shows a relatively dim image. A focusing cloth that covers the camera-back and your head makes the image much more visible by keeping out stray light. You may not need the cloth if the subject is brightly lighted in an otherwise darkened room, but in most cases it is a necessity. Some photographers like a two-layer cloth—black on one side and white on the other—to reflect heat outdoors and to double as a fill-light reflector.

checking focus

A hand-held magnifier, sometimes called a loupe, is useful for checking the focus on the ground glass. Check the depth of field by examining the focus with the lens stopped down. The image will be dim but can usually be judged if you let your eyes become accustomed to the lower level of illumination. Using a focusing cloth helps. Examine the ground glass carefully for vignetting if camera movements (especially lens movements) are used.

Loading and Processing Sheet Film

Using **sheet film** is easy once you have practiced the procedures a few times, but do pay attention to some important details. Film is loaded in total darkness into sheet-film holders that accept two sheets of film, one on each side. Each sheet is protected by a light-tight dark slide that is removed after the holder is inserted in the camera for exposure. The film must be loaded with the emulsion side out; film loaded with the backing side out will not produce a usable image. The emulsion side is identified by a **notching code;** when the film is in a vertical position, the notches are in the upper right-hand (or lower left-hand) corner when the emulsion side of the film faces you. After exposure but before you remove the holder from the camera, insert the holder's slide with the all-black side facing out; this is the only way to tell that the film has been exposed and to avoid an unintentional double exposure. Some points on loading film holders are given in the pictures and captions on this page.

Developing sheet film follows the same basic procedure as developing roll film, except three tanks or trays are used—for developer, stop bath, and fixer. Some photographers add a fourth step, a water presoak before development. The film is agitated and transferred from one solution to the next in total darkness; it is not feasible to do this with just one tank as is possible with roll film. Fill tanks with enough solution to more than cover the film in the hanger. Fill trays deep enough for the number of sheets to be developed— one inch is probably a minimum.

Check the instructions carefully for the proper development time. The time will depend on whether you use intermittent agitation in a tank or constant agitation in a tray.

dusting holders

It is a good idea to dust the film holders each time before loading them. This is much less trouble than trying to etch off a dark spot on your print caused by a speck of dust on the unexposed film. A soft, wide paintbrush (used only for this purpose) or an antistatic brush works well. Dust both sides of the dark slide, under the film guides, and around the bottom flap.

checking notching code

Sheet film has a notching code—different for each type of film—so you can identify it and determine the emulsion side. The notches are always located so the emulsion side is facing you when the film is in a vertical position and the notches are in the upper right-hand corner. Load the film with the holder in your left hand and the film in your right with your index finger resting on the notches. (If you are left-handed you may want to load with the holder in your right hand and the film in your left.)

checking film insertion

The film is inserted in the bottom (flap) end of the holder underneath narrow metal guides. If you rest your fingers lightly on top of the guides you can feel even in the dark if the film is loading properly. Also make sure that the film is inserted all the way past the raised ridge at the flap end. When the film is in, hold the flap shut with one hand while you push the dark slide in with the other.

unexposed/exposed film

The dark slide has two different sides—one all black, the other with a shiny band at the top—so you can tell if the film in the holder is unexposed or exposed. When you load unexposed film, insert the slide with the shiny side out. After exposure, reinsert the slide with the all-black side facing out. The shiny band also has a series of raised dots or a notch so you can identify it in the dark.

loading hangers

Tank development using film hangers is a convenient way to develop a number of sheets of film at one time. The hanger is loaded in the dark. First spring back its top channel. Then slip the film down into the side channels until it fits into the bottom channel. Spring back the top channel, locking the film in place. Stack loaded hangers upright against the wall until all the film is ready for processing.

tank development

Hold the stack of loaded hangers in both hands with your forefingers under the protruding ends. Don't squeeze too many hangers into the tank; allow at least ½ inch of space between hangers. To start development, lower the stack into the developer. Tap the hangers sharply against the top of the tank to dislodge any air bubbles from the film (this is not necessary if the film has been presoaked in water before development). Make sure the hangers are separated.

tank agitation

Agitation for tank development takes place for about 8 sec, once for each minute of development time. Lift the entire stack of hangers, completely out of the developer. Tip it almost 90° to one side to drain the developer from the film. Replace it in the developer. Immediately lift the stack again and tilt almost 90° to drain to the opposite side. Replace in solution. Make sure the hangers are separated. Always remove and replace hangers slowly.

tray development

Tray development is easy if you have just a few sheets of film to process. Fan the sheets so that they can be grasped quickly one at a time. Hold the film in one hand. With the other hand take a sheet and completely immerse it, emulsion side up, in the developer. Repeat until all sheets are immersed. (A water presoak before development is useful to prevent the sheets from sticking to each other.) Touch the film as little as possible—especially the emulsion side—to avoid scratches.

tray agitation

All the film should be emulsion side up toward one corner of the tray. Slip out the bottom sheet of film and place it on top of the pile. Gently push it under the solution. Continue shuffling the pile of film a sheet at a time until the end of the development period. If you are developing only a single sheet of film, agitate by gently rocking the tray back and forth, then side to side.

washing and drying

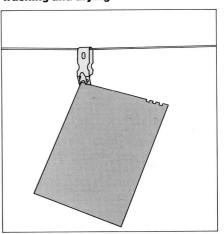

Film in hangers can be washed and then hung up to dry right in the hangers or it can be dried on a line as shown above. Separate the film enough so that the sheets do not accidentally stick together. A few loose sheets of film at a time can be washed in a tray, but the water flow must be regulated carefully to avoid excessive swirling that could cause scratching.

Using a View Camera

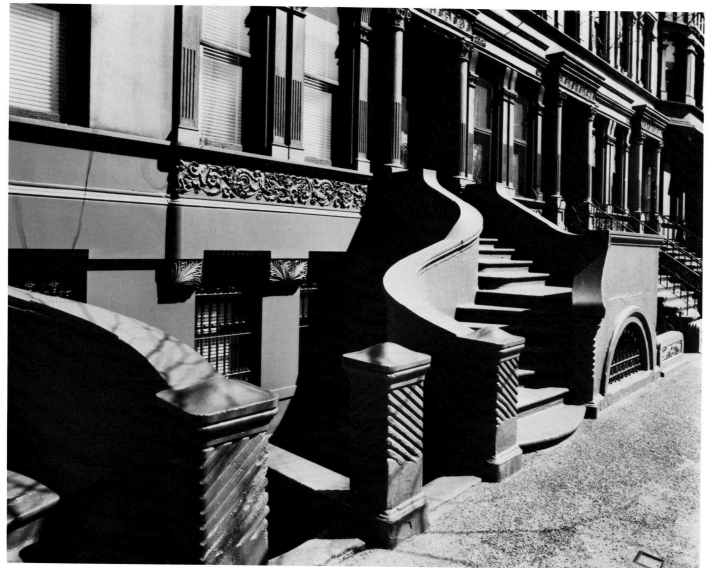

PHILIP TRAGER: *New York*, 1979

Above and opposite, two photographs that demonstrate why many photographers like to use a view camera. The front and back of the camera are adjustable, which gives extensive control over the perspective and sharpness of an image. For example, in the photograph above, Phil Trager raised the front instead of tilting up the camera, which gave the height he wanted to show but prevented convergence of vertical lines; then he swung the camera-back to the left to avoid excessive convergence of horizontal lines; and swung the camera-front to the left to align the plane of focus with the front of the buildings so that the entire row of buildings was sharp.

Michael A. Smith used an 8 × 10 view camera for ▶ the photograph opposite. The large film size that a view camera accepts can record subtle details of texture and tonality that a small-format negative cannot, details that are even more evident in an original print than in a book reproduction.

MICHAEL A. SMITH: *Canyon de Chelly, Arizona*, 1975

ANSEL ADAMS: *Moonrise, Hernandez, New Mexico*, 1941

312

13
Zone System

Have you ever looked at a scene and known just how you wanted the final print to appear? Sooner or later every photographer does. Sometimes the image turns out just the way you expected, but as often as not for the beginning photographer, the negative you end up with makes it impossible to produce the print you had in mind. When you expose and develop a negative, you build into it certain shadow and highlight values that can only be partially changed during printing. In other words, the negative sets limits on the kind of print you can make.

The **Zone System** is a method conceived by Ansel Adams (*photograph opposite*) and Fred Archer for controlling the black-and-white photographic process. It applies the principles of **sensitometry** (the measurement of the effects of light on light-sensitive materials), and it organizes into one coherent procedure the many decisions that go into exposing, developing, and printing a negative. Briefly, it works this way. You make exposure meter readings of the luminances (the brightnesses) of important elements in the scene. You decide what print values (shades of gray) you want these elements to have in the final print. Then you expose and develop the film to produce a negative that can, in fact, produce the print you had visualized.

Luminances in a scene can be pegged to precise values through the systematic application of an old photographic rule of thumb: **expose for the shadows and develop for the highlights.** Exposure largely controls density and detail in thin areas of the negative (which produce dark or shadow areas in the print), whereas exposure *plus* development affect negative density and detail in the dense areas (which produce light areas in the print). In effect, development controls contrast in a negative, and you can increase contrast by increasing development or decrease it by decreasing development. Pages 318–319 explain this further.

The Zone System allows you to visualize how the tones in any scene will look in a print and to choose either a literal recording or a departure from reality. Even if you continue to use ordinary exposure and development techniques, understanding the Zone System will help you apply them more confidently. This chapter is only a brief introduction to show the usefulness of the Zone System. Other books that tell how to put it into full use are listed in the Bibliography.

◀ *Ansel Adams is the acknowledged master of the grand landscape. His great vistas are mythic images that reinforce our romantic ideals of nature. Adams was a superb technician who controlled his medium completely to amplify and bring to life the tonalities in an image. No book reproduction can convey the range of tones in the original print, from the glowing brilliance of the clouds and crosses to the subtle detail in the dark shadows. The photograph is everything that we imagine such a scene might look like in reality and for many of us will forever serve as a substitute.*

The Zone System Scales

To control the value (lightness or darkness) of an area, you must first find a way to name and describe how light or how dark the area is. The Zone System has four scales to use for this purpose (*right*).

Subject values. The steps on this scale describe the amounts of light reflected or emitted by various objects in a scene. Subject values or luminances can be measured by a reflected-light meter: a low or dark subject value produces a low meter reading; a high or bright subject value produces a high meter reading.

Negative-density values. Divisions of this scale describe the amounts of silver in various parts of the negative after it has been developed. Clear or thin areas of a negative have little or no silver; dense areas have a great deal of silver. These values can be measured by a densitometer, a device that gauges the amount of light stopped or passed by different portions of the negative.

Print values. These steps describe the amounts of silver in various parts of a print. The darkest areas of a print have the most silver, the lightest areas the least. These values can be measured by a reflection densitometer if desired but are ordinarily simply evaluated by eye in terms of how light or dark they appear.

Zones. This scale is crucial because it links the values on the other three scales. It provides fixed descriptions of values to which subject values, negative-density values, and print values can be compared. Each zone is one stop away from the next (it has received either twice or half the negative exposure).

Familiarizing yourself with the divisions of the zone scale (*opposite page*) is particularly important because it gives you a means of visualizing the final print: the zones aid you in examining subject values, in deciding how you want them to appear as print values, and in then planning how to expose and develop a negative that will produce the desired print.

The zone scale on the opposite page has 11 steps and is based on Ansel Adams's description of zones in his book *The Negative*. Some commonly photographed surfaces are listed in the zones where they are often placed if a realistic representation is desired; average light-toned skin in sunlight, for example, appears realistically rendered in Zone VI.

Zone 0 (zero) relates to the deepest black print value that photographic printing paper can produce, resulting from a clear area (a low negative-density value) on the corresponding part of the negative, which in turn was caused by a dark area (a low subject value) in the corresponding part of the scene that was photographed.

Zone X relates to the lightest possible print value—the pure white of the paper base, a dense area of the negative (a high negative-density value) and a bright area in the scene (a high subject value).

Zone V corresponds to a middle gray, the tone of a standard-gray test card of 18 percent reflectance. A reflected-light exposure meter measures the brightnesses of all the objects in its field of view and then gives an exposure recommendation that would render the average of those brightnesses in Zone V middle gray.

There are, of course, more than 11 shades of gray in a print—Zone VII, for example, represents all tones between Zones VI and VIII—but the 11 zones provide a convenient method of visualizing and identifying tones in the subject, the negative, and the print.

subject values (luminances)

low meter reading — high meter reading

negative-density values

little or no silver — dense silver

print values

maximum black silver — white paper base

zones

0 I II III IV V VI VII VIII IX X

The Zone System has four scales that describe the lightness or darkness of an area at the various stages in making a photograph: metering the scene (subject values); the developed negative (negative-density values); the print (print values); and visualizing in your mind how light or dark you want an area to be in the final print (zones). The divisions of all the scales are labeled with roman numerals to avoid confusion with f-stops or other settings.

In Ansel Adams's original version of the Zone System, he divided these scales into ten segments (0–IX). Later he revised the scales, dividing them into eleven segments (0–X). The material here reflects Adams's last published version of the system.

Zone X. *Five (or more) stops more exposure than Zone V middle gray. Maximum white of the paper base. Whites without texture: glaring white surfaces, light sources.*

Zone IX. *Four stops more exposure than Zone V middle gray. Near white. Slight tonality, but no visible texture: snow in flat sunlight, the lightest wood at right.*

Zone VIII. *Three stops more exposure than Zone V middle gray. Very light gray. High values with delicate texture: very bright cement, textured snow, highlights on light-toned skin.*

Zone VII. *Two stops more exposure than Zone V middle gray. Light gray. High values with full texture and detail: very light surfaces with full sense of texture, sand or snow with acute side lighting.*

Zone VI. *One stop more exposure than Zone V middle gray. Medium-light gray. Lighted side of average light-toned skin in sunlight, light stone or weathered wood, shadows on snow in a scene that includes both shaded and sunlit snow.*

Zone V. *Middle gray. The tone that a reflected-light meter assumes it is reading and for which it gives exposure recommendations. 18 percent reflectance neutral-gray test card, clear north sky, dark skin.*

Zone IV. *One stop less exposure than Zone V middle gray. Medium-dark gray. Dark stone, average dark foliage, shadows in landscapes, shadows on skin in sunlit portrait.*

Zone III. *Two stops less exposure than Zone V middle gray. Dark gray. Shadow areas with full texture and detail: very dark soil, very dark fabrics with full texture, the dark boards at right.*

Zone II. *Three stops less exposure than Zone V middle gray. Gray-black. Darkest area in which some suggestion of texture will appear in the print.*

Zone I. *Four stops less exposure than Zone V middle gray. A near black with slight tonality but no visible texture.*

Zone 0. *Five (or more) stops less exposure than Zone V middle gray. Maximum black that photographic paper can produce. The opening to a dark interior space, the open windows at right.*

Using the Zone Scale While Metering

When you are standing in front of a subject and visualizing how it might look as a black-and-white print, you have to take into account that ordinary photographic materials given normal exposure, development, and printing cannot record with realistic texture and detail the entire range of luminances (subject brightnesses) in many scenes. For example, a scene in bright sunlight can generally be rendered with texture and detail in either dark shadows or bright highlights but not both. Usually, you have to choose those areas in which you want the most detail in the print and then expose the negative accordingly.

You can accurately visualize the black-and-white tones in the final print by using the zone scale described on the preceding pages plus a reflected-light exposure meter, either hand-held or built into a camera. (An incident-light meter cannot be used because it measures the light falling on the scene and you will need to measure the luminances of individual areas.)

When you meter different areas, you can determine where each lies on the zone scale for any given exposure. Then, by adjusting the negative development if necessary (*pages 318–319 tell how*), you can produce the print value (shade of gray) that you want each area to have in the final print. Metering must be done carefully to get consistent results. Try to read areas of more or less uniform tone; the results from an area of mixed light and dark tones will be more difficult to predict. A spot meter is useful for reading small areas or those that are at a distance.

The meter does not know what area is being read or how you want it rendered in the print. It assumes it is reading a uniform middle-gray subject tone (such as a neutral-gray test card of 18 percent reflectance) and gives exposure recommendations accordingly. The meter

measures the total amount of light that strikes its light-sensitive cell from an area, then, taking into account the film speed, it calculates f-stop and shutter speed combinations that will produce sufficient negative density to reproduce the area as middle gray in a print.

If you choose one of the f-stop and shutter-speed combinations recommended by the meter, you will have placed the metered area in Zone V and it will reproduce as middle gray in the print (print Value V). By altering the negative exposure you can **place** any one area in any zone you wish. One stop difference in exposure will produce one zone difference in tone. For example, one stop less than the recommended exposure places a metered area in Zone IV; one stop more places it in Zone VI.

Once one tone is placed in any zone, all other luminances in the scene **fall** in zones relative to the first one depending on whether they are lighter or darker and by how much. Suppose a medium-bright area gives a meter reading of 7 (*see meter and illustration, near right*). Basing the exposure on this value (by setting 7 opposite the arrow on the meter's calculator dial) places this area in Zone V. Metering other areas shows that an important dark wood area reads two stops lower (5) and falls in Zone III, while a bright wood area reads three stops higher (10) and falls in Zone VIII.

A different exposure could have been chosen, causing all of the zones to shift equally lighter or darker (*illustrations, far right*). For instance, by giving one stop more exposure you could have lightened the tones of the dark wood, placing them in Zone IV instead of III, but many of the bright values in the lightest wood would then fall in the undetailed white Zone IX. The Zone System allows you to visualize your options in advance.

Each position on an exposure meter gauge measures a luminance (subject value) one stop or one zone from the next position. Metering a medium-bright area gives a reading of 7. Setting 7 opposite the arrow on the calculator dial places this area in Zone V. A brighter area meters 10, so it will fall three zones lighter, in Zone VIII. A dark area meters at 5 and falls in Zone III. The first area metered will appear in the print as middle-gray print Value V, the bright wood as very light gray print Value VIII, and the dark wood as dark-gray print Value III (with standard negative development and printing).

Using Exposure Settings to Count Zones

What do you do if you can't read the difference in subject values (and so, the difference in zones) directly off the meter dial, as you can with the meter above? If you are using a meter built into a camera, the viewfinder often displays the exposure setting—the aperture and shutter-speed combination—for a given reading. You can find the various zones if you count the number of stops between exposure settings for different areas.

Suppose that metering the scene at right suggests exposures of f/5.6 at 1/60 sec for one area and f/16 at 1/60 sec for a brighter area. In this example, f/16 gives three stops less exposure than f/5.6 (f/5.6 to f/8 is one stop less; f/8 to f/11, two stops; f/11 to f/16, three stops). Placing the first area in Zone V will cause the other to fall three zones higher in Zone VIII.

one stop more negative exposure than photograph, left

One stop difference in negative exposure creates one zone difference in all areas (if other factors remain the same). The negative exposure for the top print was one stop less than that given to the photograph at left. The negative exposure for the bottom print was one stop more than that for the photograph at left. All the values changed one zone with one stop difference in negative exposure.

How Development Controls Contrast

You can, with careful metering and exposure choice, place any one subject value in any zone you desire. You can also predict in which zones the other subject values will fall. But exposure is still only half the story in producing a negative. Development can also be used to adjust certain values and, as a result, to control the overall contrast of the negative. You may want to decrease contrast if the subject has a greater range of values than the paper can print. Or if the subject has only a narrow range of values, you may want to increase contrast so that the print doesn't look flat and dull.

The most common way to adjust contrast is to change the contrast grade of the paper—print a high-contrast negative on a low-contrast paper and vice versa. But another way is to change the development time of the negative. In general, increasing the negative's development time increases its overall contrast range, while decreasing the development time decreases contrast. There are advantages to adjusting the negative's contrast. A negative that prints with a minimum of dodging and burning on a normal-contrast grade of paper is easier to print than, for example, a contrasty negative with dense highlight values that require considerable burning in even on a low-contrast grade of paper. And some scenes are so contrasty that the negative does not print well even on the lowest-contrast grade of paper.

A film's response to changes in development time is strong in the areas of greatest exposure (high, bright values) and weak in areas of little exposure (low, shadow values). This happens because the developer quickly reduces to silver the relatively few silver halide crystals that were struck by light in the slightly exposed shadow areas. Development of shadow areas is completed long before all the crystals in the greatly exposed highlight areas are converted to silver. The longer a negative is developed (up to a limit), the greater the silver density that develops in high values, while the shadow densities remain about the same. And the greater the difference between high-value and low-value densities, the greater the contrast.

Development control of high values can be quite precise. If an area is placed in Zone VIII during exposure, it will produce a negative-density Value VIII if the film is given normal development. That same area could be developed to a negative-density Value VII with less development or to a negative-density Value IX with more development.

The process by which subject values increase to higher values on the negative through increased development time is termed Normal-Plus development, or **expansion,** since the contrast range of the negative is increased or expanded. The reverse process, in which subject values (and contrast) are reduced by decreasing the development

time, is called Normal-Minus development, or **contraction.**

In Zone System terms, **N** stands for normal development. With normal development, values remain where they were placed or fell during exposure; an area falling in Zone VII would appear as a negative-density Value VII and (given normal printing) as print Value VII.

N + 1 (normal-plus-one) indicates expanded development; a Zone VII value would be increased one zone to Zone VIII (*diagram, opposite*). **N + 2** indicates a greater expansion; a Zone VII value would be increased two zones. **N – 1** (normal-minus-one) indicates contracted development; a Zone VII value moves one zone down to Zone VI, **N – 2** is a greater contraction.

Although the upper values shift considerably with changes in development time, the lower values change little or not at all. Middle values change somewhat, although not as much as the upper ones. Therefore, the low density values in a negative (dark or shadow areas in the original scene) are the result of the amount of exposure, while high density values are the product of both exposure and development. Changing the development time is simple with sheet film, since each exposure can be given individual development. With roll film, changing the contrast grade of the paper is often more practical.

The length of time a negative is ▶ *developed has an important effect on the contrast. The three versions of this scene received identical negative exposures and identical printing: only the development time was changed. Center, normal development was given to the negative.*

Top, more development time expanded the contrast by increasing the density of the high values in the negative. As a result, high values, such as the sidewalk, are lighter in the print. Bottom, less development time decreased the contrast by decreasing the density of high values, which now appear darker in the print. Low shadow values were set during exposure and remained the same with any development.

expansion (increased development)

normal development

contraction (decreased development)

Expansions   Contractions

If a negative is given normal development, the densities of various areas in the negative will correspond to the relative luminances of those areas in the original scene. But if the development time is increased (N + 1 or N + 2 in the chart above), the differences between densities will be expanded, especially in the upper zones, V to IX,

and the contrast of the negative will be increased. If development time is decreased (N − 1 or N − 2), the differences between densities will be decreased, especially in the upper zones, so negative contrast overall will be decreased. See page 324 for how much to increase or decrease development.

A Full-Scale Print

Often (although not always) photographers want to make a **full-scale print** with normal contrast; that is, with a full range of values from black through many shades of gray to white and with considerable texture and detail showing in important areas.

If that is your goal, then the darkest area in which you want at least a minimum sense of detail should be no darker than Zone II; for full texture and detail, the area should be no darker than Zone III. The lightest area for minimum detail should be no lighter than Zone VIII; for full texture and detail, it should be no lighter than Zone VII. Areas lighter or darker than this will be at the edge of the printing paper's ability to render detail.

Begin by placing the most important shadow area. It is worse to underexpose a negative than to overexpose one because dark values are affected only by exposure, and no darkroom wizardry can add details to an important shadow area if inadequate exposure was given to the film. If you used the Zone System to calculate the exposure for the scene at right, you could place the dark wood boards in the windows in Zone III by metering them, then giving two stops less exposure than the meter calls for (remember that meters calculate exposures for Zone V; *see page 316*). Suppose the boards read 5 on the meter gauge. Placing 5 opposite the arrow on the calculator dial (the Zone V position) would place the boards in Zone V. Since you want the boards in Zone III, place 5 two stops from the calculator arrow toward underexposure, as shown at right.

Then see where the important light areas fall. Light values are affected by both exposure and development. Some small, very bright areas might read 10 on the meter dial and fall in Zone VIII, while larger bright areas might read 9

and fall in Zone VII. Is this the way you want the print to look? If so, developing the film normally would produce a negative that, when printed on a normal-contrast grade of paper, would show the dark boards as dark but with good detail, the brightest areas just showing texture, and the larger bright areas light but with full detail.

Suppose the scene was more contrasty and the dark boards metered 5, large bright areas metered 10, and the brightest boards metered 11. If you placed the dark boards in Zone III, the brightest areas would fall in near white Zone IX, while much of the scene would fall in very light gray Zone VIII. Giving N − 1 (contracted) development would reduce the brightest areas to Value VIII and other bright areas to a fully textured Value VII, while the Value III dark boards would not change. The contrast would have been decreased by reducing the development time. The negative would print well on a normal-contrast grade of paper with the important areas rendered as you visualized them.

Another way to decrease the contrast would be to plan to use a low-contrast grade of paper during printing. The advantage of analyzing the exposure in Zone System terms is that you know in advance what the range of contrast is in the scene in terms of the print's ability to show detail.

In a photograph that is a portrait, the face is often the first area a viewer notices, so it is important to meter skin tones carefully and see that they will have the desired rendering—either by placing them in the zone where you want them or seeing that they fall there, or by developing them to that value. Normal values for the sunlit side of a face are V for dark skin, VI for medium-light skin, and VII for very light skin. The shaded side of a face in sunlight usually appears normally rendered as Value IV.

Opposite is a full-scale print of normal contrast. The tones range from black through many shades of gray to white, and full texture is visible in both the darkest and lightest areas in which texture is important. Some readings that you might have registered for the scene are shown on the meter above. Dark board areas metered at about 5. They were placed in Zone III (the darkest value that can show full texture) by positioning the meter arrow (which indicates Zone V) two stops higher on the calculator dial. Large bright areas metered 9 and fell in Zone VII (light but with full texture). Smaller brighter areas metered 10 and fell in Zone VIII (very light gray). A spread of four or five zones between the darkest textured shadow and the lightest textured white will produce a full-scale, rich print on a normal-contrast grade of paper.

X

IX

VIII

VII

VI

V

IV

III

II

I

0

321

Using the Zone System

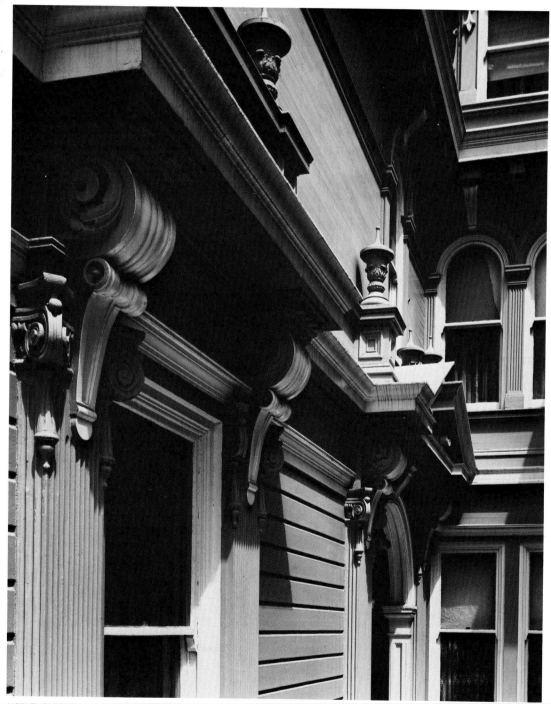

MORLEY BAER: *Window Cornice Detail, San Francisco,* c. 1966

Using the Zone System makes it possible to plan the exposure and development that will produce the tonal range you want in a negative and print. Morley Baer made the photograph at left for a book on Victorian houses in San Francisco. Baer says that he often has to expand contrast when shooting in the slightly hazy sunlight that is common in San Francisco.

He metered the shadow just under the window cornice, an area that he wanted to be dark but still showing detail, and placed that area in Zone III. Then he metered the lightest area in which he wanted to retain good detail; it fell only in Zone VI, which would have made the scene too flat. To correct this, Baer increased the development time to give the scene a one-zone expansion. Another option that he sometimes takes is to plan to print the scene on a more contrasty grade of paper.

Chris Rainier's photograph taken from inside a ▶ cave looking out demonstrates the extreme contrast control that the Zone System makes it possible to plan exactly. Rainier wanted the shadows on the top and left side of the central rock to print as Print Value III, dark but with texture. He wanted the highlights on the bright rock surfaces to be almost Print Value VIII, very light, but still showing texture. When he metered the two areas, and placed the shadows in Zone III, the highlights fell in Zone XIII and would have been completely white if he had exposed and developed the negative normally.

Instead, he planned for a five-zone contracted development. He used a highly diluted developer that gives results similar to the low-contrast development procedures described on page 149. The resulting negative printed on a normal contrast paper; it required no dodging and just a slight amount of burning in to intensify the black tones in a few parts of the print. Personal testing is essential for best use of the Zone System. Ansel Adams's books give full details (see Bibliography).

322

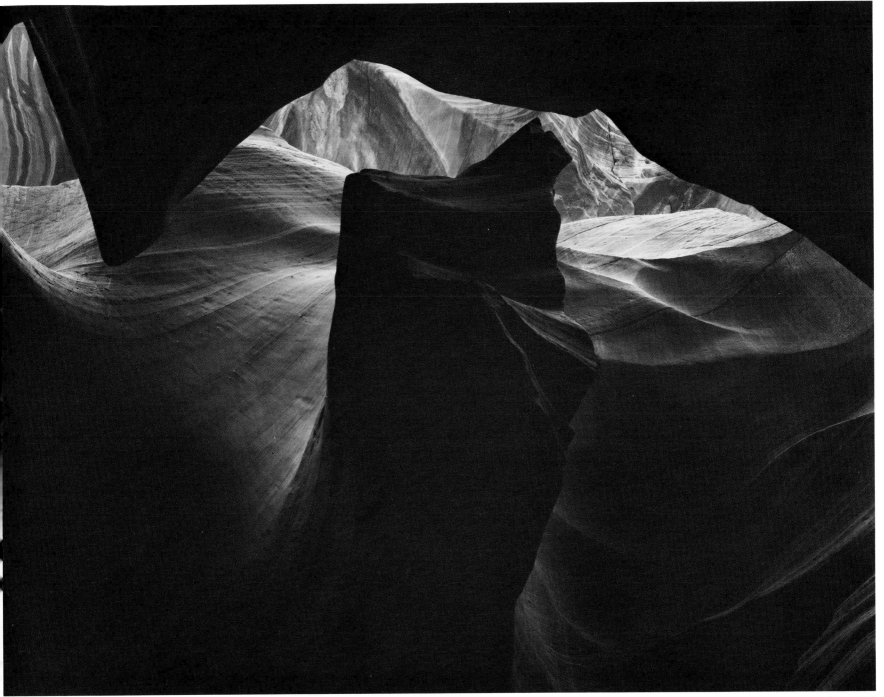

CHRIS RAINIER: *Cave, Southwest Desert, Arizona,* 1982

Putting It All Together

The Zone System procedure has three basic steps.

Step 1: Meter the most important area in the scene and **place** it in the zone where you want it rendered. Often this is the darkest area in which you want full texture (usually Zone III). Placing a value determines your exposure.

Step 2: Meter other areas (especially the lightest area in which you want full texture) to see in which zones they **fall** in relation to the area you have placed.

Step 3: Visualize the final print and make exposure and development choices. If you want the negative-density values to correspond to the relative luminances of various areas in the scene, develop the negative normally. Change the development time if you want to change the densities of the upper values while leaving the lower values about the same. Increasing the time increases the negative densities of the high values (which will make those areas lighter in the print) and also increases the contrast. Decreasing the development time decreases the negative densities of the high values (they will be darker in the print) and decreases the contrast.

You could also plan to print on a contrast grade of paper higher or lower than normal to control densities and contrast. A change of one contrast grade in printing paper causes approximately a one-zone shift in the high values (when low values are matched in tone).

Testing is the best way to determine normal development time and to establish the changes in development needed to move a value from one zone to another. The tests, covered in detail in the books listed in the Bibliography, establish five standard elements for the individual photographer: actual film speed, normal development time, expanded development times, contracted development times, and standard printing time.

Personal testing is recommended since cameras, meters, films, enlargers, papers, developers, and personal techniques all differ and affect the results. However, here are some rough guidelines for expanded and contracted development that you can use without testing and that will be helpful for approximate control of contrast. First, use the manufacturer's stated film speed rating to calculate the exposure. For normal development, use one of the manufacturer's suggested time and temperature combinations.

For N + 1 expanded development, increase the development time by half. If the recommended development time is 8 minutes for a given film-developer-temperature combination, then the high values can be shifted up one zone each by a 12-minute development. For N + 2 expansion, double the development time; for N + 3, triple it.

For N − 1 contracted development, which will shift the high values downward one zone each, develop for three-quarters of the normal time. For N − 2 contraction, develop for two-thirds of the normal time.

Changing the development time is easy with view camera photography, where sheets of film can be processed individually. But it can also be valuable with **roll film** even though a whole roll of exposures is processed at one time. Sometimes a single image or situation is so important that it deserves special development; the other images on the roll will probably still be printable, possibly on a different grade of paper. Or an entire roll may be shot under one set of conditions and so can be exposed and processed accordingly.

With roll film, Zone System metering and control of negative contrast is often combined with changes in printing-paper contrast. The primary objective is to give enough exposure to dark areas to produce printable densities in the negative while at the same time keeping bright areas from becoming too dense to be printable. For example, if you are shooting on the street on a generally sunny day and trial metering indicates about one stop too much contrast (that is, with shadows placed in Zone III, the high values in which you want full detail fall in Zone VIII or IX), contracted development for the entire roll will be useful. Most of the frames shot will print on a normal-contrast grade of paper; those shot under more contrasty conditions will print on a low-contrast grade; those shot in the shade (now low in contrast because of contracted development) will print on a high-contrast grade.

With **color materials,** the Zone System provides a way to place a specific value and check where other values will fall. With color negatives, place the most important shadow value, just as you would with a black-and-white negative; overly bright highlights can usually be burned in later during printing. Correct exposure is vital with color transparencies because the film in the camera is the final viewing product. High values in a transparency lose texture and detail more easily than shadows do, so meter and place the most important light area rather than shadows. If you want a light area to retain texture, place it no higher than Zone VII. Changing development time to control contrast is not recommended for most color materials.

The advantage in using the Zone System is that you have better control over the final image. Many photographers are satisfied with their technique without using the Zone System. But if you feel you want to add more precision to your photography, the Zone System gives you a method to do so.

Although best known for his photographs of large landscapes, Ansel Adams did many other types of photographs including portraits and architectural and commercial work. He said, "I have tried to visualize all my pictures before taking them. I think all photographers do that but it takes a long time to be in total command of the technique. . . . [Some photographers] don't understand the way that the lens 'sees' and the film 'sees.' . . . You just have to 'look' at the world like this or you are lost."

ANSEL ADAMS: *Foujita, Artist*, 1933

CECIL BEATON: *Eileen Dunne*, 1940

14
Seeing Photographs

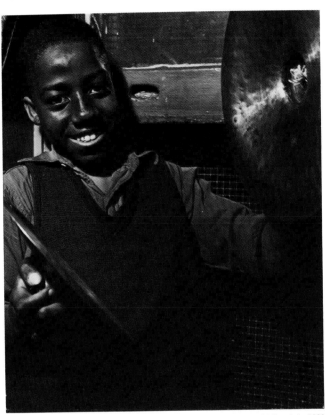

JACK MANNING: *Boy with Cymbals*, 1938

Opposite and above are two photographs that differ in composition but are equally effective. Above, a member of a band at a settlement house was photographed as part of the Harlem Document project organized by the Photo League in the 1930s. Part of the picture's dynamic appeal is that the subject is off center, which often makes a more interesting composition than positioning the same subject dead center in the frame. Also, instead of just staring at the camera, the child is doing something, which adds life and interest to a portrait.

◄ *Opposite, a young English victim of World War II recuperates in a hospital from shrapnel wounds suffered during a German bombing. The child is doing nothing but clutching her doll and staring at the camera—but there is an enormous difference between a revealing look and a blank one. And in this case, the symmetrical positioning in the center of the frame adds to the impact by reinforcing the direct confrontation with the child.*

How do you learn to make better pictures? Once you know the technical basics, where do you go from there? Every time you make an exposure you make choices, either deliberately or accidentally. Do you show the whole scene or just a detail? Do you make everything sharp from foreground to background or have only part of the scene in focus? Do you use a fast shutter speed to freeze motion sharply or a slow shutter speed to blur it? These are only some of your choices, and you can't expect to get immediate control over all of them. Photography is an exciting and sometimes frustrating medium just because there are so many ways to deal with a subject.

So your first step is to *see* your options, to see the potential photographs in front of your camera. Before you make an exposure, try to visualize the way the scene will look as a print. Looking through the viewfinder or at the ground glass helps. The scene is then at least reduced to a smaller size and confined within the edges of the picture format, just as it will be in the print. As you look through the viewfinder, pretend you are looking at a print, but remember that you can still change it. You can eliminate a distracting background by making sure it will be out of focus, by changing your position to a better angle, and so on.

When you look at a photograph—one of your own or someone else's—try to see how the picture communicates its visual content. Photography transforms the passing moment of a three-dimensional event into a frozen instant reduced in size on a flat piece of paper, often in black and white instead of color. The event is abstracted, and even if you were there and can remember how it "really" was, the image in front of you is the tangible remaining object. This concentration on the actual image will help you visualize scenes as photographs when you are shooting.

Edward Weston said, "Good composition is only the strongest way of seeing the subject. It cannot be taught because, like all creative effort, it is a matter of personal growth." It cannot be taught, but it *can* be learned by looking at photographs, responding to them, asking questions, looking at a scene, trying something, seeing how it looks—and trying again.

327

Basic Choices: Content

Do you want **the whole scene or a detail?** One of the first choices you have to make is how much of a scene to show. Whether the subject is a person, a building, or a tree, beginners often are reluctant to show anything less than the whole thing. If you look at snapshot albums, you will see that people often photograph a subject in its entirety—Grandpa is shown from head to toe even if that makes his head so small that you can't see his face clearly. In many cases, however, it was a particular aspect of the subject that attracted the photographer's attention in the first place, perhaps the expression on the face of the person, the peeling paint on the building, or a bent branch of the tree.

Get closer to your subject. "If your pictures aren't good enough, you aren't close enough," said Robert Capa, a war photographer known for the intensity and immediacy of his images. This simple piece of advice can help most beginning photographers improve their work. Getting closer eliminates distracting objects and simplifies the contents of a picture. It reduces the confusion of busy backgrounds, focuses attention on the main subject, and lets you see expressions on people's faces. (*See photographs, right.*)

What is your photograph about? Instead of shooting right away, stop a moment to decide which part of a scene you really want to show. You might want to take one picture of the whole scene, then try a few details. Let the content determine the size of important objects. Is your picture about the look of an entire neighborhood, about what it's like to walk by a single house in the neighborhood, or about the detail on the gate in front of a house? Sometimes you won't want to move closer, as in photographing a prairie landscape where the spacious expanse of land and sky is important or in making an environmental portrait where the setting reveals something about the person.

Before you bring the camera to your eye, try to visualize what you want the photograph to look like. Then move around a bit as you look through the viewfinder. Examine the edges of the image frame. Do they enclose or cut into the subject the way you want? (More about the frame on pages 330–331 and 344–345.) In time, these decisions come more intuitively, but it can be useful at first to work through them deliberately.

What do you want the subject of your photograph to be? Above, the photographer wanted to show the family members but stood so far back that the picture seems more like one of the back yard. Below, by moving closer, the photographer turned the same scene into an appealing family portrait.

A detail of a scene can tell as much as and sometimes more than an overall shot. Right, part of the life of a working cowboy, a buckaroo, from Paradise Valley, Nevada. Below, the end of a cattle drive to the 96 Ranch's Hartscrabble camp in Paradise Valley.

RICHARD E. AHLBORN: *Boots, Paradise Valley, Nevada,* 1978

CARL FLEISCHHAUER: *Herding Cattle, Paradise Valley, Nevada,* 1978

Basic Choices: Framing the Subject

The **frame** (the edges of a picture) isolates part of a larger scene. Photography is different from other visual arts in the way in which a picture is composed. A painter starts with a blank canvas and places shapes within it. A photographer generally uses the frame of the viewfinder or ground glass to select a portion of the surrounding visual possibilities.

Choices have to be made, consciously or not, about how you crop into a scene and how the edges of the frame relate to the portion of the scene that is shown.

You can leave considerable space between the frame and a particular shape, bring the frame very close so it almost touches the shape, or use the frame to cut into the shape. You can position an edge of an object or a line within an object so that it is parallel to one edge of the frame or position it at an angle to the frame. Such choices are important because the viewer, who can't see the surroundings that were left out of the picture, *will* see how the frame meets the shapes in the print. There is no need to be too analytical about this. Try looking at the edges of the viewfinder image as well as at the center of the picture and then move the frame around until the image you see through the viewfinder seems right to you. You can also cut a small rectangle in an 8 × 10-inch piece of black cardboard and look through the opening at a scene. Such a frame is easier to move around and see through than a camera and can help you visualize your choices.

Judicious cropping, as in the photo-graph of the young boy at right, can strengthen a picture, but awkward cropping can be distracting. Ordinarily it is best not to cut off the foot of someone in motion or the hand of someone gesturing, but the deliberate use of such unconventional cropping can be effective (*see photograph, page 239*). Some pictures depend on the completion of a gesture or motion and are difficult or impossible to crop successfully; try cropping off parts of the dancers, opposite, for example.

Portrait photographers recommend that you do not crop a person at a joint, such as a wrist or knee, because that part of the body will look unnaturally amputated or will seem to protrude into the picture without connection. Try cropping about half an inch off the bottom of the portrait on page 268 and notice how the hand and pipe will seem to float away from the man. It can also seem awkward if the top of a head or an elbow or a toe just touches the edge of the frame. Generally, it is better to crop in slightly or to leave a space.

Should your picture be **horizontal or vertical?** Unless you have a reason for doing otherwise, hold the camera horizontally for a horizontal subject, vertically for a vertical one. Otherwise, you are likely to create empty space that adds nothing to the picture. A horizontal format shows width side to side (*see page 340*), while a vertical format shows height or depth near to far (*see page 333*). Even if your film format is square, you may later want to crop the picture to a rectangular format.

JOE WRINN: *Boy in School*, 1977

Cropping with a purpose can add impact to a picture. Above, cropping the adult to a directing arm plus shooting from the child's height lets the viewer enter this scene from the child's point of view.

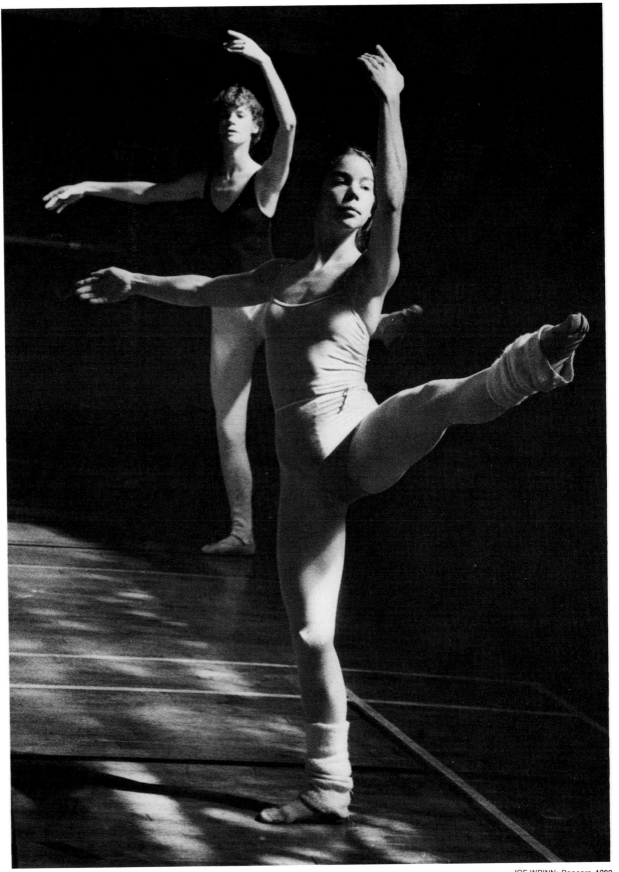

How does the frame of a photograph (its edges) enclose a subject? How much space, if any, is needed around a subject? You may overlook framing when you are shooting, but it will be immediately evident in the final picture. Right, try cropping slightly into a foot or hand of the female dancer. Try to find any way to crop this picture that improves it.

JOE WRINN: *Dancers,* 1980

Basic Choices: Backgrounds

The **background** is part of the picture. Although some photographs are made to show an overall view or a texture or pattern, and so have no single subject, most photographs have a particular object or group of objects as a center of interest. When we look at a scene we tend to focus our attention on whatever is of interest to us and ignore the rest, but the lens includes everything within its angle of view. What do you do when your subject happens to be in front of a less interesting or even distracting background?

If background objects don't add anything to a picture except visual clutter, do what you can to eliminate them or at least to minimize their importance. Usually it is easiest to change your position so that you see the subject against a simpler background (*see right*). Sometimes you can move the subject instead.

Even a busy background will call less attention to itself if it is blurred and indistinct rather than sharply focused. Set your lens to a wide aperture if you want to make the background out of focus while keeping the subject sharp. This works best if the background is relatively far away and you are focused on a subject that is relatively close to the camera. (See pages 74–75 for more about controlling the depth of field, the area that is sharp in a photograph.) The viewfinder of a single-lens reflex camera shows you the scene at the lens's widest aperture; if you examine the scene through the viewfinder you will get an idea of what the background will look like at that aperture. Some lenses have a preview button that stops down the lens so you can see depth of field at any aperture.

Use the background when it contributes something. Even though many photographs could be improved by shooting closer to the subject, don't always zero in on a subject or you may cut out a setting that makes a picture come alive. An environmental portrait like the one on page 3 uses the background to tell you something about the subject. Backgrounds can give scale to a subject, or vice versa. And some backgrounds are what the picture is all about (*see opposite page*).

What's in the background? In a photograph, objects that are far apart in depth can appear to be close together if they are in the same line of sight. Check the background before you take a picture, or you may end up with a distracting background that was easy to overlook while you were shooting but that will be hard to ignore in a print. Top, a classic example: a person with a tree (or telephone pole or lamp or other unrelated object) growing out of her head. Below, choosing another angle and moving in slightly closer produced a less distracting background.

Some backgrounds make it worthwhile to set yourself up and wait
until someone walks in front of
them. Above, a Paris policeman
crosses the entrance to an aban-
doned night spot, L'Enfer (Hell).

ROBERT DOISNEAU: *Cabaret L'Enfer, Boulevard de Clichy, Paris*, 1952

Basic Design: Spot/Line

What good is design? Most photographs are not constructed but are taken in a pre-existing environment from which the photographer, often working quickly, must select the best views possible. Nevertheless, it is still important for photographers to understand design concepts such as the spot, the line, emphasis, and balance because certain elements of design are very powerful in their ability to control and direct a viewer's attention.

Knowing, for example, that a single small object—a spot—against a contrasting background attracts attention will help you predict where attention will go in a photograph. For example, see the photograph on page 392. Even if you want to work fast and intuitively rather than with slow precision, some basic knowledge about design will help you fine-tune and speed up your responses to a scene, and it will make you better able to evaluate your own and other people's work.

A single element of design seldom occurs in isolation. Although one can talk about the effect of a spot, for example, other design elements are almost always present, moderating each other's effect. Attention might be drawn by a spot and then attracted away by a pattern of lines elsewhere in the print. The simpler the subject, the more important any single element becomes, but one element rarely totally dominates any composition. The human element may attract the most attention of all; people will search out human presence in a photograph despite every obstacle of insistent design.

Any small shape, not necessarily a round one, can act as a **spot.** The word *spotlight* is a clue to the effect of a single spot against a neutral or contrasting background: it draws attention to itself and away from the surrounding area.

This can be good if the spot itself is the subject or if in some way it adds interest to the subject. But a single spot can also be a distraction. For instance, a small bright object in a dark area can drag attention away from the subject; even a tiny, dark dust speck can attract attention if it is in a blank sky area.

The eye tends to connect two or more spots like a connect-the-numbers drawing. If there are only two spots, the eye continues to shift back and forth between them, sometimes a confusing effect if the eye has no place on which to settle attention. If there are three or more spots, suitably arranged, the brain will make shapes—a triangle, a square, and so on—out of them.

A **line** is a shape that is longer than it is wide. It may be actual or implied, as when the eye connects a series of spots or follows the direction of a person's gaze. Lines give direction by moving the eye across the picture. They help create shapes when the eye completes a shape formed by a series of lines. In a photograph, lines are perceived in relation to the edges of the film format, which are very strong implied lines. This relationship is impossible to ignore, even when the lines are not near the edges of the print.

According to some theories, lines have psychological overtones: horizontal (calm, stability); vertical (stature, strength); diagonal (activity, motion); zigzag (rapid motion); curved (gracefulness, slowness). Horizontal objects, for example, tend to be stable, so we may come to associate horizontality with stability. In a similar way, yellows and reds conventionally have overtones of warmth by way of their associations with fire. However, such associations vary from person to person and are as much dependent on the subject as on any inherent quality in a line.

RUSSELL LEE: *Willamette River, Oregon.* 1941

There is no way for the logs to move except downstream, and there is no way for the eye to move except down the lines formed by the logs. Notice how the brighter logs at the bottom of the frame get more attention than the darker ones at the top, and how the light patch of ground at top left also attracts the eye.

RUSSELL LEE: *Hidalgo County, Texas,* 1939

The eye tends to connect two or more spots into a line or shape, and above, the spots formed by the dark hardware against the light cabinets are an insistent element. Russell Lee often used direct flash on camera, especially in his work, as here, for the Farm Security Administration (see page 370). Lee liked direct flash because it rendered details sharply and was easy to use. It also produces minimal shadows and so tends to flatten out the objects in a scene into their graphic elements. The scene above has a harsh, clean brightness that is appealing in its austerity and to which the direct flash contributed.

Basic Design: Shape/Pattern

A **shape** is any defined area. In life, a shape can be two-dimensional, like a pattern on a wall, which has height and width; or three-dimensional, like a building, which has height, width, and depth. In a photograph, a shape is always two-dimensional, but tonal changes across an object can give the illusion of depth. Notice in the illustration at right how flat the large leaf, with its almost uniform gray tone, looks compared with the light and dark ridges of the smaller leaf. You can flatten out the shape of an object entirely by reducing it to one tone, as in a silhouette. The contour or edge shape of the object then becomes dominant, especially if the object is photographed against a contrasting background (*see page 263*).

A single object standing alone draws attention to its shape, while two or more objects, such as the leaves at right, invite comparison of their shapes, including the shape of the space between them. The eye tends to complete a strong shape that has been cropped by the edge of the film format; such cropping can draw attention repeatedly to the edge or even out of the picture area. Try cropping just into the left edge of the large leaf to see this effect.

Objects that are close together can be seen as a single shape. Objects of equal importance that are separated can cause the eye to shift back and forth between them, as between two spots. Bringing objects closer together can make them into a single unit; for example, the women on the opposite page. Portrait studio photographers try to enhance the feeling of a family as a group by posing the members close together, often with some physical contact, such as placing one person's hand on another's shoulder. Notice how The Critic (*page 279*) is separated from the society women by space as well as by social standing.

Groupings can be visual as well as actual. Aligning objects one behind the other, intentionally or not, can make a visual grouping that may be easy to overlook when photographing a fast-moving scene but which will be readily apparent in a photograph.

The repetition of spots, lines, or shapes in a **pattern** can add interest and unite the elements in a scene, as do the lines in the photograph on page 334. A viewer quickly notices variations in a pattern or the contrast between two patterns, in the same way that contrast between colors or between light and dark attracts the eye.

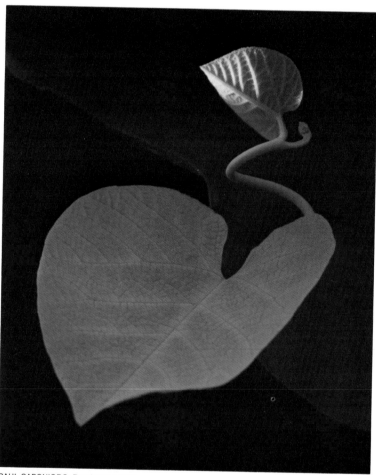

PAUL CAPONIGRO: *Two Leaves*, 1963

What route does your eye follow when it looks at the photograph above? One path might be up the right edge of the larger leaf, up the curved stem, around the smaller leaf to its bright tip, then down again to make the same journey. Take a small scrap of white paper and put it over the bottom tip of the larger leaf. Does your eye follow the same path as before, or does it jump back and forth between what are now two bright spots?

A group of Black Muslim women form a solid band behind one of their leaders. Gordon Parks photographed relatively closer to the woman in front than to the others, which made her appear larger; being closer to her also reduced the depth of field so that when Parks focused on her, only she was sharp. The individual identities of the other women have been submerged by their being out of focus and by the repeated shapes of their headdresses forming a pattern. The picture clearly identifies the leader and makes a visual statement about the solidarity of her followers.

GORDON PARKS: *Muslim Women*, 1962

337

Basic Design: Emphasis/Balance

Emphasis on an element will direct attention to it. If too many parts of a photograph demand equal attention, a viewer won't be sure what to look at first. How do you emphasize some part of a photograph or play down another so that the viewer knows what is important and what isn't?

Contrast attracts attention. The eye quickly notices differences such as sharp versus unsharp, light versus dark, large versus small. If you want to emphasize a subject, try to show it in a setting against which it stands out. Viewers tend to look at the sharpest part of a picture first, so you can call attention to a subject by focusing it sharply while leaving other objects out of focus (*see pages 340–341*). The contrast of light and dark also adds emphasis; a small object can dominate a much larger background if it is of a contrasting tone or color (*see pages 342–343*).

Camera angle can emphasize a subject. If unnecessary clutter draws attention away from your subject, get closer. Shooting closer to an object will make it bigger while eliminating much of the surroundings. Sometimes shooting from a slightly higher or lower angle will remove unnecessary elements from the camera's angle of view.

Use surrounding parts of the scene to reinforce emphasis. Objects that are of secondary interest, such as fences, roads, or edges, can form sight lines directed to the subject (*right, top*). The point at which two lines (real or implied) intersect attracts notice, as does the direction in which people are looking. You may be able to find something in the foreground to frame the main subject and concentrate attention on it (*see*

opposite page). A dark object may be easier than a light one to use as a frame because lighter areas tend to attract the eye first, but this is not always the case.

People know when a picture is in **balance** even if they can't explain why. A picture that is balanced does not call attention to that fact, but an unbalanced one can feel uncomfortably off center or top-heavy. Visually, dark is heavier than light, large is heavier than small, an object at the edge has more weight than at the center (like a weight on a seesaw), and a picture needs more apparent weight at the bottom to avoid a top-heavy feeling. Except in the simplest cases, however, it is difficult to analyze exactly the weights and tensions that balance a picture, nor do you need to do so. A viewer intuitively weighs complexities of tone, size, position, and other elements, and you can do the same as you look through the viewfinder. Ask yourself if the viewfinder image feels balanced or if something isn't quite right that you would like to change. Move around a bit as you continue to look through the viewfinder. Even a slight change can make a big difference in a scene.

A centered, symmetrical arrangement, the same on one side as it is on the other, will certainly feel balanced and possibly satisfyingly stable, but it also may be boring. Some tension in a picture can be an asset. Perfect balance, total harmony, and exact symmetry make little demand on the viewer and consequently can fail to arouse interest. Try some off-center, asymmetrical arrangements; they risk feeling unbalanced but may succeed in adding impact (*right, bottom*).

ROY CLARK: *Troublesome Creek, Kentucky,* 1965

A man crosses a footbridge over Troublesome Creek in Kentucky. Lines formed by the sides and planks of the bridge focus attention on the man, as does his placement near the center of the picture. The quiet scene gets added interest from the man's dark form against the lighter boards of the bridge, his foot just raised in midstep, and the house in front of him as his visible destination.

R. O. BRANDENBERGER: *Skier, Idaho,* 1966

An off-center, asymmetrical composition can have a dynamic balance that is absent from a centered, symmetrical one. Take some sheets of white paper and lay them over the top, bottom, and right side of the photo above so that the skier is centered in the frame. The picture is still interesting but lacks the headlong rush that it has when the long slope of the hill and the trees far below are visible.

DENNIS STOCK: *James Dean in Light and Shadow*, 1955

To emphasize your main subject, you can use a foreground object as a frame. A portrait of the actor James Dean, made in the year of his death, uses the dark shadows of a stairwell to frame him in a diamond-shaped patch of light. Dean's image was full of contradictions—tough and sensitive, boyish and manly, polite and wild—and the photograph echoes this in its split between light and dark, face only half visible, head shown both straight on and profiled in the shadow cast on the wall.

More Choices: Using Contrasts of Sharpness

In ordinary life, if your eyes are reasonably good, you seldom have to consider whether things are sharp or not. The human eye, like a camera lens, must refocus for objects at different distances, but the eye scans and refocuses so quickly that you rarely are aware of the process. The sharpness of a photograph or of its various parts, however, is immediately noticeable.

People tend to look at the sharpest part of a photograph before they look at parts that are less sharp. If a photograph is sharp overall, the viewer is more likely to see all parts of it as having equal value (see below). You can emphasize some part of a subject by making it sharper than the rest of the picture (see page 73).

Depth of field affects sharpness from near to far. If you focus on an object and set your lens to a wide aperture, you will decrease the depth of field (the acceptably sharp area) so that the background and foreground are more likely to be unsharp. Or you can use a small aperture to have the picture sharper overall.

Motion can be photographed either sharp or blurred. In life, moving objects appear sharp unless they are moving extremely fast, such as a hummingbird's wings. In a photograph, you can use a fast shutter speed to freeze the motion of a moving object. Or you can use a slow shutter speed to deliberately blur the motion—just enough to indicate movement or so much that the

subject's shape is altered (see opposite page, left). Although the sharpest part is usually emphasized because the viewer tends to look there first, occasionally, blurred motion attracts attention because it transmits information about how fast and in what manner the subject is moving.

If you change to a faster shutter speed to show motion sharp, you have to open to a larger aperture to keep the exposure the same. Since a larger aperture gives less depth of field, you may have to decide whether the sharpness of a moving object is more important than the sharpness of depth of field. It may be impossible to have both. (To review the relation of shutter speed and aperture, see pages 50–51.)

U.S. DEPARTMENT OF AGRICULTURE: *Family and Food,* 1981

Pictures that convey data are often sharp overall. The United States Department of Agriculture photographed (left to right) Cynthia, John, Clint, and

Valerie Schnekloth of Eldridge, Iowa, surrounded by the two and a half tons of food an average American family of four consumes in a year.

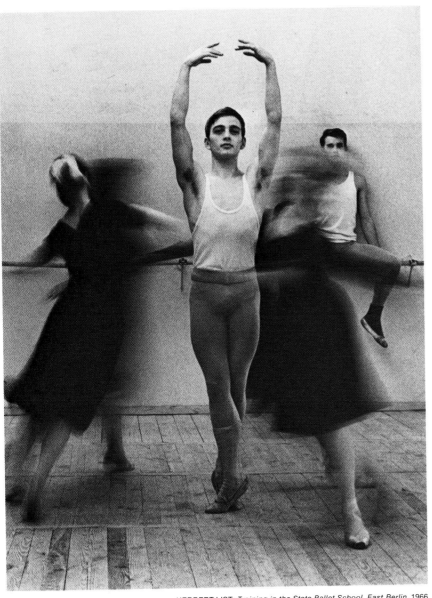

HERBERT LIST: *Training in the State Ballet School, East Berlin,* 1966

In his photograph of dancers, Herbert List used a relatively slow shutter speed. The contrast between the blur of the moving dancers and the sharpness of those that are not moving makes the blurred areas look even more in motion than if all the dancers had been blurred. Photographs such as this give an impression of time and movement that belies the term "still" photograph.

U.S. DEPARTMENT OF AGRICULTURE: *Hydraulic Engineer,* 1964

A hydraulic engineer watches the flow of water through a plastic model. Photographing a moving subject at a very fast shutter speed or lighting the subject with flash (which has a very short duration) can show a moving subject more sharply than we normally see it. Here, the crispness of the moving water compared to the slightly out-of-focus engineer in the background includes the man in the scene but concentrates attention on the water. The presence of the man is also subordinated by having only part of his face visible.

More Choices: Using Contrasts of Light and Dark

Contrast between light and dark draws a viewer's eye. A farmer's hands against a dark background, the outline of a leafless tree against a bright sky, a rim of light on someone's hair, a neon sign on a dark street—light not only illuminates a subject enough to record it on film but by itself can be the subject of a photograph.

Contrast sets off one part of a scene from another. Would you put a black ebony carving against a dark background or a light one? The dark background might make a picture that would be interesting for its somber tones. The light one would make a setting against which the carving would stand out prominently, just as a dark background contrasts with and sets off light tones (*photograph, this page*).

Contrast between two objects may be more apparent in color than in black and white. A red flower against green leaves is distinctly visible to the eye but may merge disappointingly into the foliage in a black-and-white print. The brightness of the flower is very similar to that of the leaves even though the colors are different. If you squint as you look at a scene, you can get a better idea of what the tones will look like in black and white and whether you should change your angle or move the subject to position it against a better background. (See also information on filters, pages 104–105.)

Light along the edge of an object can make its shape stand out. If you chose to work with a dark background for an ebony statue, you could use edge lighting to make sure the statue didn't merge into the shadows behind it. Studio photographers often position a light so that it spills just over the edge of a subject from the back, making a bright outline that is effective against a darker background (*see illustration, opposite*). Outdoors, the sun can create a similar effect if it illuminates the back or side of an object rather than the front.

Shadows or highlights can be shown as separate shapes. The contrast range of many scenes it too great for photographic materials to record realistically both dark shadows and bright highlights in one picture. This can be a problem, but it also gives you the option of deliberately using detailless shadows or highlights as independent forms (*see page 288*).

You can adjust contrast somewhat during film processing and printing. Once film has been processed, the relative lightness or darkness of an area is fixed on the negative, but you can still change tones to some extent during printing by such techniques as changing the contrast grade of the paper or printing filter, burning in (adding exposure to darken part of a print), and dodging (holding back exposure to lighten an area). Contrast control with black-and-white prints is relatively easy; color prints allow less manipulation.

DAVID F. WARREN: *Hands, South Carolina*, 1974

Use a contrasting background if you want to set off one part of a scene from another. Above, the dark background makes the gesture and work-worn texture of a farmer's hands prominent.

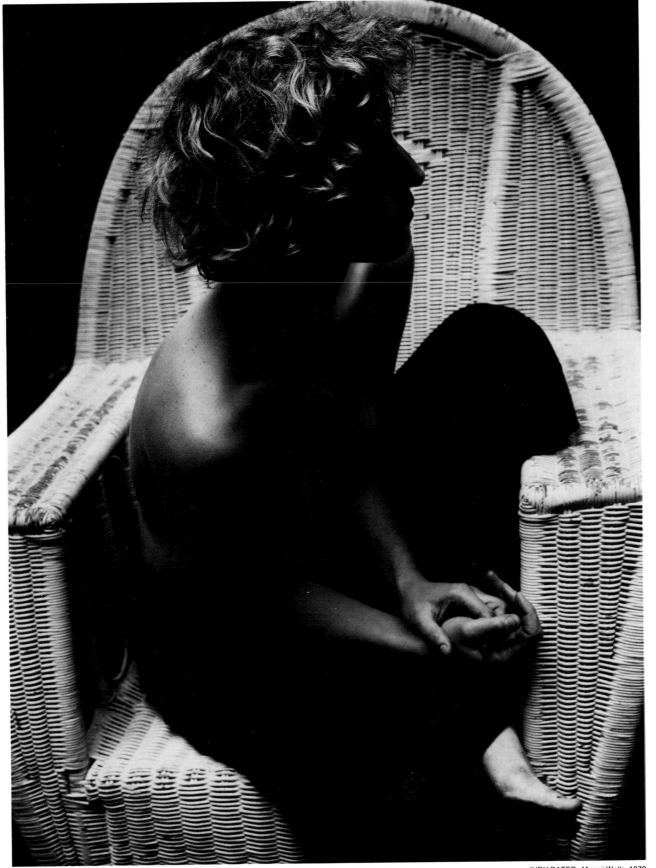

Film may show shadows as darker than they seemed during shooting. Our eyes make adjustments for differences in light level, but film can record details in only a fixed range of brightnesses. So a photograph may record shapes of light and dark that in life we find easy to overlook. Right, a portrait that is more than just a silhouette of someone's profile against a lighter background. The portrait is expressive and informative, even though—and partly because—the face is hidden.

JUDY DATER: *Maggi Wells*, 1970

More Choices in Framing

Placement of the subject within the frame can strengthen an image. If you look at a scene through a camera's viewfinder as you move the camera around, you will probably see several choices for positioning the subject within the frame of the film format: dead center or off to one side, high or low, at one angle or another. Placement can draw attention to or away from a part of a scene. It can add stability or create momentum and tension. Some situations move too fast to allow any but the most intuitive shooting, but often you will have time to see what the effect will be with the subject in one part of the frame rather than another.

The most effective composition arises naturally from the subject itself. There are traditional formulas for positioning the center of interest (*see box, right*), but don't try to apply them rigidly. The goal of all the suggestions in this chapter is not to provide a set of rules but to help you become more flexible as you develop your own style. The subject may also have something to say if you can hear it. Minor White, who was a teacher as well as a photographer, used to tell his students to let the subject generate its own composition.

The **horizon line**—the dividing line between land and sky—is a strong visual element. It can be easy, without much thought, to position the horizon line across the center of a landscape, dividing a scene into halves. Some photographers divide a landscape this way as a stylistic device, but unless handled skillfully, this can divide a picture into two areas of equal and competing interest that won't let the eye settle on either one. One suggestion for placement is to divide the image in thirds horizontally, then position the horizon in either the upper or lower third (*photograph, this page*). You can also try putting the hori-

zon very near the top or the bottom of the frame.

Stop for a moment to consider what you want to emphasize. A horizon line toward the bottom of the frame emphasizes the sky. A horizon toward the top lets you see more of the land but still includes the strong contrast of sky. Omitting the horizon altogether leaves the eye free to concentrate on details of the land. Even if no horizon line is visible, a photograph can feel misaligned if the camera is tilted to one side. Unless you want to tilt a picture for a purpose, always level the camera from side to side. (More about tilting on page 399.)

Motion should usually lead into, rather than immediately out of, the image area. Allow enough space in front of a moving subject so it does not seem uncomfortably crowded by the edge of the frame. The amount of space depends on the scene and your own intention. In a photograph, the direction in which a person (or even a statue) looks is an implied movement and requires space because a viewer tends to follow that direction to see what the person is looking at. Although it is usually best to allow adequate space, you can deliberately create tension to add interest to some scenes by framing a subject so that it looks or moves directly out of the picture area.

A subtler tension may be added simply by movement of a subject from right to left. Westerners read from left to right; therefore, a subject with strong left-to-right movement may seem slightly more natural or comfortable to a Westerner than a subject with strong right-to-left motion. You can see if you get this effect by looking at the photograph of the skier on page 338 and then looking at it in a mirror to reverse the subject's direction.

Compositional Formulas

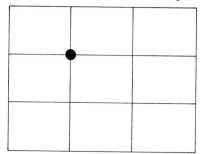

In the 19th century, rules of photographic composition were proposed based on techniques used by certain painters of the period. The rule of thirds, for example, was (and still is for some photographers) a popular compositional device. Draw imaginary lines dividing the picture area into thirds horizontally, then vertically. According to this formula, important subject areas should fall on the intersections of the lines or along the lines. A person's face, for example, might be located on the upper left (theoretically the strongest) intersection, a horizon line on either the upper or lower horizontal line, and so on.

Try such formulas out for yourself. Experimenting with them will make you more aware of your options when you look at a scene, but don't expect a compositional cure-all for every picture. Look at photographs that work well, such as the one opposite or on page 65, to see if they fit a particular rule. If they don't, what makes them successful images?

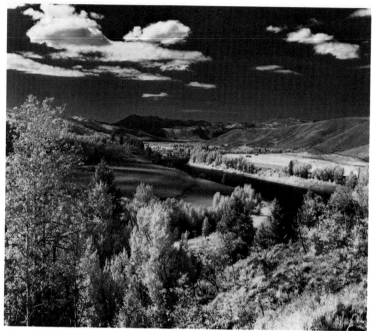

ROBERT BRANSTEAD: *Along the Snake River, Wyoming*, 1971

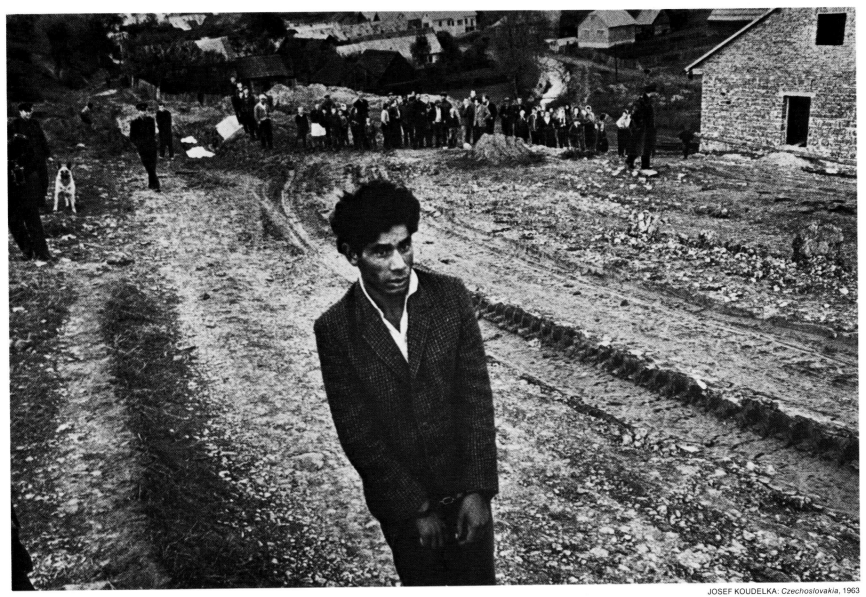

JOSEF KOUDELKA: *Czechoslovakia*, 1963

◄ The conventional placement for a horizon line in a landscape is more or less in the upper (or lower) third of the picture. (The unusual lightness of the grass and trees is due to the use of infrared film. See pages 100–101.)

The most extraordinary photographs merge composition with content on a level that rules do not explain. Above, one of many photographs made by Josef Koudelka showing Gypsies of Eastern Europe. The man, having been found guilty of murder, is on the way to the execution ground.

John Szarkowski wrote about this photograph, "The handcuffs have compressed his silhouette to the shape of a simple wooden coffin. The track of a truck tire in the earth, like a rope from his neck, leads him forward. Within the tilted frame his body falls backward, as in recognition of the terror."

More Choices: Perspective and Point of View

Perspective creates an illusion of three dimensions in a two-dimensional photograph. The relative distance of objects from the lens and from each other is the most direct control of perspective. The brain judges depth in a scene mostly by comparing the size of objects in the foreground with that of objects in the background; the bigger the apparent difference in the size of similar objects, the greater the distance between them seems to be. Move some object (or some part of it) very close to the lens, and it will look much bigger and therefore much closer than the rest of the scene. Parallel lines that appear to converge (to meet in the distance) are a strong indicator of depth (*see photograph, page 101*). The convergence is caused by the nearer part of the lines appearing bigger than the farther part.

Other factors affect perspective to a lesser degree. A sharply focused object may appear closer than out-of-focus ones. Side lighting enhances the impression of volume and depth, while front lighting or a silhouette reduces it. The lower half of a picture appears to be (and generally is) closer than the upper half. Overlapping objects also indicate which is closer. Warm colors (reds and oranges) often appear to come forward, while cool colors (blues and greens) appear to recede. In general, light-toned objects often appear to be closer than dark ones, with an important exception: atmospheric haze makes objects that are farther away lighter in tone than those that are closer, and a viewer recognizes this effect as an indication of distance in a landscape. Another factor is less consciously perceived by many people but still influences their impression of depth: objects appear to rise gradually relative to a viewer's position as they approach the horizon (*see landscape, this page*).

Photographs of landscapes often fail because the photographer was unable to convey an impression of depth. This is why people have to resort to words when they show you their vacation snapshots: they have to tell you how wonderful the scenery was because their pictures make even the Grand Canyon look flat and boring. To extend the impression of depth, especially in landscapes but also in any scene, try some or all of the following. Position some object in the foreground; if similar objects (or others of a known size) are farther away, the viewer will make the size comparisons that indicate depth. This technique can also add interest to an otherwise bland scene. Position the horizon line in the upper part of the picture. Introduce lines (particularly converging ones), such as a road or a fence, that appear to lead from foreground to background.

An eye-level **point of view** is unobtrusive in a photograph, but shooting from higher or lower than eye level is more noticeable. Photographing an object by looking up at it can give it an imposing air as it looms above the viewer. Vertical lines, as in a building, appear to converge when the camera is pointed up, increasing the feeling of height. Looking straight down on a subject produces the opposite effect: objects are flattened out. See photographs, opposite.

A moderate change in camera angle up or down can give a slight shift to the point of view, making a subject appear somewhat bigger or somewhat smaller without unduly attracting the viewer's attention. When you approach a scene, don't always shoot at eye level or in the first position from which you saw the subject. Look for interesting angles, the best background, or other elements that could add interest.

MARION POST WOLCOTT: *Fields of Shucked Corn, West Virginia,* 1940

One of the standard recommendations for landscape photography is, ''Put something in the foreground to give the scene depth.'' The reason that this device is used so often is that it does give a feeling of depth. Our perception of depth is mostly due to size comparisons between near and far objects, and in the photograph above, it is easy to compare the size of the fence rails in the foreground with those at the end of the field.

It is your handling of whatever you put in the foreground that can rescue a well-used device of this sort from being a cliché. So many photographers have sighted along a fence or randomly included a branch of a tree across the top of a scene that it can be hard to see past the device itself. Here, the device gains interest because the line of the fence also draws the eye from the foreground deeper into the scene, and then down the rows of corn even farther away.

DAVID MOORE: *Sisters of Charity, Washington, D.C.*, 1956

Looking straight down on a subject can appear to flatten space and reduce a subject to its graphic elements. Above, David Moore looked down from an airport mezzanine at a group of nuns. Their white coifs stand out in flowerlike shapes against their black robes.

DOROTHEA LANGE: *Lettuce Cutters, Salinas Valley, California*, 1935

Dorothea Lange, like Marion Post Wolcott, made many photographs for the Farm Security Administration to document the plight caused by the Depression of the 1930s. Lange's photographs often had an almost epic quality. Above, seemingly impassive as statues, members of a gang of migrant laborers bend to a crop of lettuce. Shooting from a low point of view can create an intimacy with a subject as the photograph—and so the viewer—joins the scene instead of impassively observing it from above. See also the Lange photograph on page 371.

PHOTOGRAPHER UNKNOWN: *Daguerreotype of couple holding a daguerreotype,* c. 1850

15

History of Photography

Of all the many inventions of the 19th century—the electric lamp, the safety pin, dynamite, and the automobile are just a few—the invention of photography probably created the most astonishment and delight. Today most people take photographs for granted, but early viewers were awed and amazed by the objective records the camera made: "We distinguish the smallest details; we count the paving-stones; we see the dampness caused by the rain; we read the inscription on a shop sign. . . ."

Photography gradually took over what previously had been one of the main functions of art—the recording of factual visual information, such as the shape of an object, its size, and its relation to other objects. Instead of having a portrait painted, people had "Sun Drawn Miniatures" made. Instead of forming romantic notions of battles and faraway places from paintings, people began to see firsthand visual reports. Photographs recorded images that the unaided eye could not see and social miseries that the eye did not *want* to see. And photography began to function as an art in its own right.

This chapter touches on only a few of the categories into which the history of photography can be divided. Other categories, equally interesting, and many photographers have been omitted only because of limitations of space. Other chapters, however, show additional work.

◀ In the 19th century, photographs of people who were dead or unable to be present were often included in family photographs. It is tempting to try to interpret the relationships among the people shown opposite. The man holds the daguerreotype carefully, his fingers loose and relaxed; he even touches his head to the frame. The woman makes a minimum of contact with the photograph with her right hand and clenches her left hand into a fist. She stares directly into the lens, the corners of her mouth pulled down, unlike the man, who softly gazes into space as if recalling a dear memory. The photograph is revealing, but still unexplained.

The Invention of Photography

A solar eclipse, 1544, first published illustration of a camera obscura

A tabletop camera obscura

"The wish to capture evanescent reflections is not only impossible, as has been shown by thorough German investigation, but the mere desire alone, the will to do so, is blasphemy. God created man in His own image, and no man-made machine may fix the image of God." Thus thundered a German publication, *Leipziger Stadtanzeiger,* in 1839 in response to the first public announcement of the invention of a successful photographic process. The *Stadtanzeiger* held that if such wise men of the past as Archimedes and Moses "knew nothing of mirror pictures made permanent, then one can straightway call the Frenchman Daguerre, who boasts of such unheard of things, the fool of fools." Such a supreme disbelief is surprising, since most of the basic optical and chemical principles that make photography possible had long been established.

The **camera obscura** was the forerunner of the modern camera. Since at least the time of Aristotle, it had been known that rays of light passing through a pinhole would form an image

(*page 58*). The 10th-century Arabian scholar Alhazen described the effect in detail and told how to view an eclipse of the sun in a camera obscura (literally, "dark chamber"), a darkened room with a pinhole opening to the outside.

By the time of the Renaissance, a lens had been fitted into the hole to improve the image, and the camera obscura was becoming smaller and more portable; it shrank from a fixed room to a small hut, to a kind of sedan chair, to a small tent, and finally to a small box that could easily be carried about (*above*). In the 16th century, Giovanni Battista della Porta suggested in his book *Natural Magic* that artists use a camera obscura. "If you cannot paint, you can by this arrangement draw [the outline of the images] with a pencil. You will have then only to lay on the colours. This is done by reflecting the image . . . on to a drawing-board with paper." The suggestion was taken up with enthusiasm because the realistic portrayal of objects and their correct positioning to create an illusion of depth were important goals of artists in the Western

world at that time. The camera obscura became such a useful aid that by the 18th century an art expert was writing, "The best modern painters among the Italians have availed themselves greatly of this contrivance; nor is it possible that they should have otherwise represented things so much to the life."

As yet, however, there was no way to fix the camera obscura image permanently. The darkening of certain silver compounds by exposure to light had been observed as early as the 17th century, but the unsolved and difficult problem was how to halt this reaction so that the image would not darken completely. At the beginning of the 19th century, Thomas Wedgwood, son of the famous British potter, was the first to attempt to record the images created by a lens in a camera obscura. He was unsuccessful with the camera image, but he did make negative silhouettes of leaves and insect wings by placing them on white paper or white leather sensitized with silver nitrate and exposing them to the sun. The paper darkened where it was exposed to light

Long before the invention of photography, many artists used a camera obscura as an aid in drawing. An image that the artist could trace was formed as rays of light passed through a pinhole opening or a lens. The tabletop model shown works exactly like a modern reflex camera; the rays are reflected by a mirror onto a ground-glass viewing screen.

Niépce produced the world's first photographic image—a view of the courtyard buildings on his estate (right) in about 1826. It was made on a sheet of pewter covered with bitumen of Judea, a kind of asphalt that hardened when exposed to light. The unexposed, still soft bitumen was then dissolved, leaving a permanent image. The exposure time was so long (8 hr) that the sun moved across the sky and illuminated both sides of the courtyard.

JOSEPH NICÉPHORE NIÉPCE: *View from His Window at Gras,* c. 1826

but not where it was shielded by the object placed on top. Wedgwood tried many ways to make these silhouettes permanent, but nothing worked. When light struck the images, they began to darken like the rest of the coating.

Although Wedgwood had been working along the right lines with his investigations of silver compounds, silver played no part at all in the first permanent picture that can be called a true photograph. This was made no later than 1826 by Joseph Nicéphore Niépce, a gentleman inventor living in central France. Niépce had become interested in the new process of lithography, which at that time required that drawings first be copied by hand in reverse onto a printing plate. Niépce decided to devise an automatic method of transferring drawings and soon extended that idea to an attempt to take views directly from nature using the camera obscura. Niépce first experimented with silver chloride, but by the early 1820s he had turned his attention to bitumen of Judea, a kind of asphalt that hardened when exposed to light.

Niépce dissolved the bitumen in lavender oil, a solvent used in varnishes, then coated a sheet of pewter with the mixture. He placed the sheet in a camera obscura aimed through an open window at his courtyard and exposed it for eight hours. The light forming the image on the plate hardened the bitumen in bright areas and left it soft and soluble in dark areas. Niépce then washed the plate with lavender oil. This removed the still-soft bitumen that had not been struck by light. Niépce had succeeded where Wedgwood had failed; he had found a way to remove the unexposed and still light-sensitive material so that the image remained permanent.

The result (*above*), which Niépce called a **heliograph** (from the Greek *helios,* "sun," and *graphos,* "drawing"), was crude, but it spurred him to continue his experiments. Meanwhile news of his work reached another Frenchman, Louis Jacques Mandé Daguerre. Daguerre had developed a popular attraction, the Diorama, a spectacle in which famous scenes, such as panora-

mas of the Swiss Alps, were re-created with illusionary effects through the use of huge translucent paintings and special lighting. Daguerre used the camera obscura in sketching scenes for the Diorama and had also become interested in trying to preserve its images. He wrote Niépce suggesting an exchange of information and eventually became his partner in 1829.

The mid-19th century was ripe for an invention like photography. In Western countries a rising middle class with money to spend wanted pictures, especially family portraits, which until then only the rich had been able to afford. In addition, people were interested in faraway places; they traveled to them when they could and bought travel books and pictures when they couldn't. Niépce did not live to see the impact that photography was to have. He died in 1833, several years before Daguerre perfected a process that he considered different enough from Niépce's to be announced to the world as the daguerreotype.

Daguerreotype: "Designs on Silver Bright"

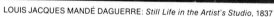
LOUIS JACQUES MANDÉ DAGUERRE: *Still Life in the Artist's Studio*, 1837

PLATT D. BABBITT: *Group at Niagara Falls*, c. 1855

The response to the **daguerreotype** was sensational. After experimenting for many years, both with Niépce and alone, Daguerre was finally satisfied with his daguerreotype process, and it was announced before the French Academy of Sciences on January 7, 1839. A French newspaper rhapsodized: "What fineness in the strokes! What knowledge of chiaroscuro! What delicacy! What exquisite finish!... How admirably are the foreshortenings given: this is Nature itself!" A British scientist was more specific: "The perfection and fidelity of the pictures are such that on examining them by microscopic power, details are discovered which are not perceivable to the naked eye in the original objects: a crack in plaster, a withered leaf lying on a projecting cornice, or an accumulation of dust in a hollow moulding of a distant building, are faithfully copied in these wonderful pictures." A daguerreotype viewed close up is still exciting to see. Several are reproduced here, but no printing process conveys the luminous tonal range and detail of an original.

The daguerreotype was made on a highly polished surface of silver that was plated on a copper sheet. It was sensitized by being placed, silver side down, over a container of iodine crystals inside a box. Rising vapor from the iodine reacted with the silver, producing the light-sensitive compound silver iodide. During exposure in the camera, the plate recorded a latent image: a chemical change had taken place, but no evidence of it was visible. To develop the image the plate was placed, silver side down, in another box containing a dish of heated mercury at the bottom. Vapor from the mercury reacted with the exposed areas of the plate. Wherever light had struck the plate, mercury formed a frostlike amalgam, or alloy, with the silver. This amalgam made up the bright areas of the image. Where no light had struck, no amalgam was formed; the unchanged silver iodide was dissolved in sodium thiosulfate fixer, leaving the bare metal plate, which looked black, to form the dark areas of the picture.

Almost immediately after the process was announced, daguerreotype studios were opened to provide "Sun Drawn Miniatures" to a very willing public. By 1853 an estimated three million per year were being produced in the United States alone—mostly portraits but also scenic views.

The daguerreotype was very popular in its time, but it was a technological dead end. There were complaints about the difficulty of viewing, for the image could be seen clearly only from certain angles. The mercury vapor used in the process was highly poisonous and probably shortened the life of more than one daguerreotypist. But the most serious drawback was that each plate was unique; there was no way of producing copies except by rephotographing the original. What was needed was a negative-positive process where any number of positive images could be made from a single negative. Just such a process had already been invented.

The earliest known daguerreotype (far left) is by the inventor of the process, Louis Daguerre. The exposure was probably several minutes long—much less than the 8 hr required by Niépce's heliograph. The enthusiastic reception of Daguerre's process extended to poetry: "Light is that silent artist / Which without the aid of man / Designs on silver bright / Daguerre's immortal plan." Niagara Falls (near left) was already a world-famous tourist attraction when Platt Babbitt made this daguerreotype about 1855.

It was in America that the daguerreotype reached the height of its popularity. Millions of Americans, famous (right) and obscure, had their portraits made. Although the exposure time was reduced to less than a minute, it was still long enough to demand a quiet dignity on the part of the subject. This portrait, taken by an itinerant daguerreotypist, is the only known photograph of the 19th-century poet Emily Dickinson. Just like her poems, it seems direct on the surface but elusive on more intimate levels. Dickinson later described herself as "small, like the wren; and my hair is bold, like the chestnut burr; and my eyes, like the sherry in the glass that the guest leaves."

PHOTOGRAPHER UNKNOWN: *Emily Dickinson at Seventeen*, c. 1847

Calotype: Pictures on Paper

Talbot's photographic establishment, c. 1844

On January 25, 1839, less than three weeks after the announcement of Daguerre's process to the French Academy, an English amateur scientist, William Henry Fox Talbot, appeared before the Royal Institution of Great Britain to announce that he too had invented a way to fix the image of the camera obscura. Talbot was a disappointed man when he gave his hastily prepared report; he admitted later that Daguerre's prior announcement "frustrated the hope with which I had pursued, during nearly five years, this long and complicated series of experiments —the hope, namely, of being the first to announce to the world the existence of the New Art—which has since been named Photography."

Talbot's first experiments had been similar to Wedgwood's; he had made negative silhouettes by placing objects on paper sensitized with silver chloride and exposing them to light. Then he experimented with images formed by a camera obscura. The light-sensitive coating used in his early experiments was exposed long enough for the image to become visible during the exposure.

In June 1840 Talbot announced a technique that not only shortened the exposure time considerably but also became the basis of modern photographic chemistry: the sensitized paper was exposed only long enough to produce a latent image, which then was chemically developed. Talbot reported that nothing could be seen on the paper after exposure, but "the picture existed there, although invisible; and by a chemical process . . . it was made to appear in all its perfection." To make the latent negative image visible, Talbot used silver iodide (the light-sensitive element of the daguerreotype) treated with gallo nitrate of silver. He called his invention a **calotype** (after the Greek *kalos,* "beautiful," and *typos,* "impression").

Talbot realized the value of having photographs on paper rather than on metal: his images were easily reproducible. He placed the fully developed paper negative in contact with another sheet of sensitized paper and exposed both to light, a procedure now known as contact printing. The dark areas of the negative blocked the light from the other sheet of paper, while the clear areas allowed light through. The result was a positive image on paper resembling the natural tones of the original scene.

Because of its reproducibility, the calotype had a major advantage over the one-of-a-kind daguerreotype. It never became widely popular, however, primarily because the calotype image seemed inferior to many viewers. The fibers in the paper produced a soft, slightly textured photograph that has been compared to a charcoal drawing. The calotype is beautiful in its own way, but viewers comparing it to a daguerreotype were disappointed in its lack of sharp detail.

Some of the activities at Talbot's establishment in Reading, near London, are shown in this early calotype taken in two parts and pieced together. At left, an assistant copies a painting. In the center, possibly Talbot himself prepares a camera to take a portrait. At right, the technician at the racks makes contact prints and another assistant photographs a statue. At far right, the kneeling man holds a target for the maker of this photograph to focus on. The prints for the first book to be illustrated with photographs, The Pencil of Nature, were made at Reading. In a "Notice to the Reader," Talbot gave his assurance that "The plates of the present work are impressed by the agency of light alone, without any aid whatever from the artist's pencil. They are the sun pictures themselves, and not, as some persons have imagined, engravings in imitation."

Miss Murray

William Leighton Leitch

In a brief but productive collaboration between 1843 and 1847, landscape painter David Octavius Hill and photographer Robert Adamson made elegant use of the soft texture characteristic of the calotype's paper negative, basing their compositions on broad masses of light and shade. Their photographs of mid-19th-century Scotland include masterfully composed portraits that almost always display character and naturalness, despite the fact that their subjects were braced to prevent movement during long exposures.

Bonaly Tower

John Brown, M.D.

DAVID OCTAVIUS HILL and ROBERT ADAMSON: 1843–1847

Collodion Wet-Plate: Sharp and Reproducible

A photographer in the field, c. 1865

The collodion wet-plate process had many advantages, but convenience was not among them. The glass plates on which the emulsion was spread had to be coated, exposed, and developed before the emulsion dried, which required transporting an entire darkroom to wherever the photograph was to be made. A photographer described a typical load that an amateur might use: "I reached the railway station with a cab-load consisting of the following items: A 9" × 11" brass-bound camera weighing 21 lbs. A water-tight glass bath in a wooden case holding over 90 ozs. of solution [nitrate of silver] and weighing 12 lbs. A plate box with a dozen 9" × 11" plates weighing almost as many pounds. A box 24" × 18" × 12" into which were packed lenses, chemicals, and all the hundred-and-one articles necessary for a hard day's work, and weighing something like 28 lbs. [A tripod] over 5 ft in length. It weighed about 5 lbs. Lastly, there was the tent, that made a most convenient darkroom, about 40" × 40" and 6½ ft high, with ample table accommodation; the whole packed into a leather case and weighed over 40 lbs . . . a load of about 120 lbs."

The **collodion wet-plate** process combined so many advantages that despite its drawbacks virtually all photographers used it from its introduction in 1851 until the development of the gelatin dry plate about 30 years later. It had the best feature of the daguerreotype—sharpness—and the best of the calotype—reproducibility. And it was more light sensitive than either of them, with exposures as short as five seconds.

For some time, workers had been looking for a substance that would bind a light-sensitive emulsion to a glass plate. Glass was better than paper or metal as a support for emulsion because it was textureless, uniformly transparent, and chemically inert. A cousin of Niépce, Abel Niepce de Saint-Victor, found that egg white could be used, but since his albumen glass plates required very long exposures the search for a better substance continued. Even the slime exuded by snails was tried. One suggested material was the newly invented collodion (nitrocel-lulose dissolved in ether and alcohol), which is sticky when wet and dries into a tough, transparent skin. Frederick Scott Archer, an English sculptor who had been making calotypes of his sitters to use as studies, discovered that the collodion was an excellent basis for an emulsion. But the plate had to be exposed and processed while it was still wet.

Coating a plate required skill—nimble fingers, flexible wrists, and practiced timing. A mixture of collodion and potassium iodide was poured onto the middle of the plate. The photographer held the glass by the edges and tilted it back and forth and from side to side until the surface was evenly covered. The excess collodion was poured back into its container. Then the plate was sensitized by being dipped in a bath of silver nitrate. It was exposed for a latent image while still damp, developed in pyrogallic acid or iron sulfate, fixed, washed, and dried. All this had to be done right where the photograph was taken, which meant that to take a picture the photographer had to lug a complete darkroom along (*above*).

Collodion could be used to form either a negative or a positive image. Coated on glass, it produced a negative from which a positive could be printed onto albumen-coated paper (*opposite, top*). If the glass was backed with a dark material like black velvet, paper, or paint, the image was transformed into a positive **ambrotype** image (*opposite, bottom*), a kind of imitation daguerreotype. Coated on dark enameled metal it also formed a positive image—the durable, cheap **tintype** popular in America for portraits to be placed in albums, on campaign buttons, and even on tombs.

By the 1860s the world had millions of photographic images; 25 years earlier there had been none. Photographers were everywhere—taking portraits, going to war, exploring distant places and bringing home pictures to prove they had been there.

A popular home entertainment during the 1850s and 1860s was looking at stereographic photographs like the one at right. If two photographs are taken side by side and then viewed through a stereoscope (a device that presents only one photograph to each eye), the impression is of a three-dimensional image. The stereo cards were inexpensive enough for almost everyone to own, and millions were sold. Rather like television today, stereographs brought the world into every person's home. "Oh, infinite volumes of poems that I treasure in this small library of glass and pasteboard!" exclaimed Oliver Wendell Holmes of his collection of stereographs. With it, he wrote, "I stroll through Rhenish vineyards, I sit under Roman arches, I walk the streets of once-buried cities, I look into the chasms of Alpine glaciers, and on the rush of wasteful cataracts. I pass, in a moment, from the banks of the Charles to the ford of the Jordan."

TIMOTHY H. O'SULLIVAN: *Ruins of Canyon de Chelly,* 1875

An ambrotype (right) is a collodion-on-glass negative backed with a dark material such as black cloth or varnish. Half of the plate shown here has not been backed and looks like an ordinary negative. The dark backing behind the other half causes a positive image to appear.

Early Portraits

People wanted **portraits.** Even when exposure times were long and having one's portrait meant sitting in bright sunlight for several minutes with eyes watering, trying not to blink or move, people flocked to portrait studios to have their likenesses drawn by "the sacred radiance of the Sun." Images of almost every famous person who had not died before 1839 have come down to us in portraits by photographers such as Nadar and Julia Margaret Cameron (*right*). Ordinary people were photographed as well—in Plumbe's National Daguerrian Gallery, where hand-tinted "Patent Premium Coloured Likenesses" were made, and in cut-rate shops where double-lens cameras took them "two at a pop." Small portraits called **cartes-de-visite** were immensely popular in the 1860s (*opposite*). For pioneers moving West in America, the pictures were a link to the family and friends they had left behind. Two books went West with the pioneers—a Bible and a photograph album.

After seeing some daguerreotype portraits, the poet Elizabeth Barrett wrote to a friend in 1843, "several of these wonderful portraits . . . like engravings—only exquisite and delicate beyond the work of graver—have I seen lately—longing to have such a memorial of every Being dear to me in the world. It is not merely the likeness which is precious in such cases—but the association and the sense of nearness involved in the thing . . . the fact of the *very shadow of the person* lying there fixed for ever! . . . I would rather have such a memorial of one I dearly loved, than the noblest artist's work ever produced. I do not say so in respect (or disrespect) to Art, but for Love's sake. Will you understand?— even if you will not agree?" The couple on the opening page of this chapter would have understood.

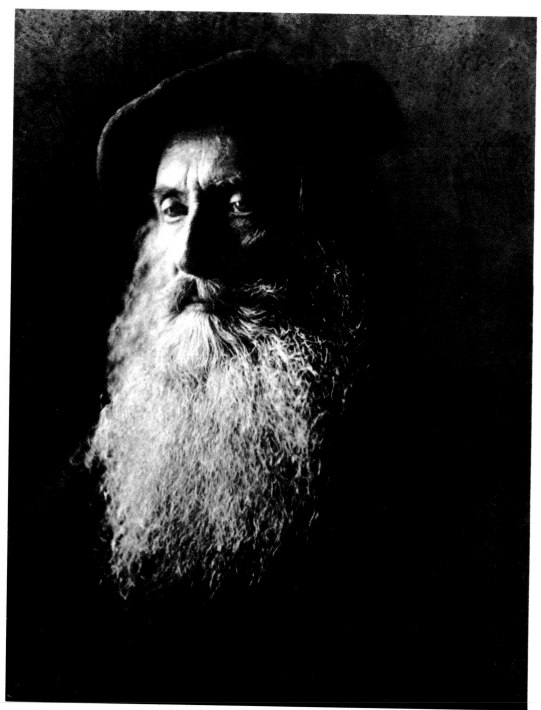

JULIA MARGARET CAMERON: *Sir Henry Taylor,* c. 1865

André Adolphe Disdéri, popularizer of the carte-de-visite

Cartes-de-visite were taken with a camera that exposed only one section of the photographic plate at a time. Thus the customer could strike several different poses for the price of one. At left is shown a print before it is cut into separate pictures. People collected cartes-de-visite in albums, inserting pictures of themselves, friends, relatives, and famous people like Queen Victoria. One album cover advised: ''Yes, this is my Album, but learn ere you look; / that all are expected to add to my book. / You are welcome to quiz it, the penalty is, / that you add your own Portrait for others to quiz.'' André Adolphe Disdéri, who popularized these multiple portraits, is shown above on a carte-de-visite. Carte portraits became a fad when Napoleon III stopped on the way to war to pose for cartes-de-visite at Disdéri's studio.

Images of War

ROGER FENTON: *Cavalry Camp, Balaklava,* 1855

Roger Fenton took many picturesque views of the Crimean War
such as the one at left. The Charge
of the Light Brigade, a military blun-
der that needlessly took the lives of
hundreds of soldiers, occurred during this war. The famous charge
was immortalized in Tennyson's
equally famous poem. Like Fenton's
views, the poem deals only with the
palatable aspects of war:

Half a league, half a league.
Half a league onward,
All in the valley of Death
Rode the six hundred.
"Forward, the Light Brigade!
Charge for the guns!" he said:
Into the valley of Death
Rode the six hundred.

When can their glory fade?
O the wild charge they made!
All the world wonder'd.
Honour the charge they made!
Honour the Light Brigade.
Noble six hundred!

Photographs of war made such scenes more immediate for those at home. Until the invention of photography, wars often seemed remote and rather exciting. People learned details of war only from delayed news accounts or even later from returning soldiers or from paintings or poems. The British campaigns in the Crimean War of the 1850s were the first to be extensively photographed. It was a disastrous war for Great Britain. The ill-fated Charge of the Light Brigade was only one of the catastrophes; official bungling, dis-ease, starvation, and exposure took

more British lives than did the enemy. However, Roger Fenton, the official photographer, generally showed views of the war (*above*) as idealized as Ten-nyson's poem about the Charge.

Not until the American Civil War did many photographs appear that showed a less romantic side of war (*opposite*). Mathew B. Brady, a successful portrait photographer, conceived the idea of sending teams to photograph the war. Photographing during a battle was haz-ardous. The collodion process required up to several seconds' exposure and the glass plates had to be processed on

the spot, which made the photogra-pher's darkroom-wagon a target for enemy gunners. Although Brady had hoped to sell his photographs, they often showed what people wanted only to forget. Brady took only a few, if any, photographs himself, and some of his men (Alexander Gardner and Timothy H. O'Sullivan among them) broke with him and set up their own operation. But it was Brady's idea and personal invest-ment that launched an invaluable docu-mentation of American history.

TIMOTHY H. O'SULLIVAN: *A Harvest of Death, Gettysburg,* July 1863

Another view of war was shown by Civil War photographers such as Brady, Gardner, and O'Sullivan (above). Oliver Wendell Holmes had been on the battlefield at Antietam searching for his wounded son and later saw the photographs Brady made there: "*Let him who wishes to know what war is look at this series of illustrations. . . .*

It was so nearly like visiting the battlefield to look over these views, that all the emotions excited by the actual sight of the stained and sordid scene, strewed with rags and wrecks, came back to us, and we buried them in the recesses of our cabinet as we would have buried the mutilated remains of the dead they too vividly represented."

Early Travel Photography

MAXIME Du CAMP: *The Sphinx and Pyramids, Egypt,* 1851

Expeditions to take photographs of faraway places were begun almost as soon as the invention of photography was announced. In addition to all the materials, chemicals, and knowledge needed to coat, expose, and process their photographs in remote places, expeditionary photographers also had to have considerable fortitude. Timothy H. O'Sullivan, whose darkroom on a boat appears opposite, described an area called the Humboldt Sink: "It was a pretty location to work in, and viewing there was as pleasant work as could be desired; the only drawback was an unlimited number of the most voracious and particularly poisonous mosquitoes that we met with during our entire trip. Add to this . . . frequent attacks of that most enervating of all fevers, known as the 'mountain ail,' and you will see why we did not work up more of that country."

In the mid-19th century, the world seemed full of unexplored wonders. Steamships and railroads were making it possible for more people to travel, but distant lands still seemed exotic and mysterious and people were hungry for photographs of them. There had always been drawings portraying unfamiliar places, but they were an artist's personal vision. The camera seemed an extension of one's own vision; **travel photographs** were accepted as real, faithful images created by a mechanical process.

The Near East was of special interest. Not only was it exotic, but its association with biblical places and ancient cultures made it even more fascinating. Within a few months of the announcement of Daguerre's process in 1839, a photographic team was in Egypt. "We keep daguerreotyping away like lions," they reported, "and from Cairo hope to send home an interesting batch." Since there was no way of reproducing the daguerreotypes directly, they had to be traced and reproduced as copperplate engravings. With the invention of the calotype and later the collodion processes, actual pictures from the Near East taken by photographers such as Maxime Du Camp (*above*) and Francis Frith were soon available.

One of the most spectacular regions of all, the western United States, was not much photographed until the late 1860s. Explorers and artists had been in the Rocky Mountain area long before this time, but the tales they told of the region and the sketches they made were often thought to be exaggerations. After the Civil War, when several government expeditions set out to explore and map the West, photographers accompanied them, not always to the delight of the other members of the expeditions. "The camera in its strong box was a heavy load to carry up the rocks," says a description of a Grand Canyon trip in 1871, "but it was nothing to the chemical and plate-holder box, which in turn was featherweight compared to the imitation hand organ which served for a darkroom." Civil War photographers O'Sullivan (*opposite*) and Gardner both went West with government expeditions. William Henry Jackson's photographs of Yellowstone helped convince Congress to set the area aside as a National Park, as did the photographs of Yosemite made by Carleton Eugene Watkins.

TIMOTHY H. O'SULLIVAN: *Black Canyon, Colorado River*, 1871

Gelatin Emulsion/Roll-Film Base: Photography for Everyone

Until the 1880s, few photographs were made by the general public. Almost everyone had been photographed at one time or another, certainly everyone had seen photographs, and probably many people had thought of taking pictures themselves. But the technical skill and the large quantity of equipment needed for the collodion wet-plate process restricted photography to the professionals and the most dedicated amateurs. Even they complained of the inconvenience of the process and made many attempts to improve it.

By the 1880s, the perfection of two techniques not only made possible a fast, dry plate but also eliminated the need for the clumsy, fragile glass plate itself. The first development was a new **gelatin emulsion** in which the light-sensitive silver salts could be suspended. It was based on gelatin—a jellylike substance processed from cattle bones and hides. It retained its speed when dry and could be applied on the other invention—rolls of film. **Roll film** revolutionized photography by making it simple enough for anyone to enjoy.

Much of the credit for popularizing photography goes to one man, George Eastman, who began as a bank clerk in Rochester, New York, and built his Eastman Kodak Company into one of the country's foremost industrial enterprises. Almost from the day Eastman bought his first wet-plate camera in 1877, he searched for a simpler way to take pictures. "It seemed," he said, "that one ought to be able to carry less than a pack-horse load."

Many people had experimented with roll film, but no one was able to produce it commercially until Eastman invented the equipment to mass-produce film. The result was Eastman's American Film, a roll of paper coated with a thin gelatin emulsion. The emulsion had to be stripped from the opaque paper backing to provide a negative that light could shine through for making prints. Most photographers had trouble with this operation, as the negative often stretched when removed from the paper, so the film was usually sent back to the company for processing.

The new film created a great stir among photographers, but it had little immediate meaning for the general public since the heavy, expensive view camera was still necessary for taking pictures. But roll film made possible a new kind of camera—inexpensive, light, and simple to operate—that made everyone a potential photographer. Eastman introduced the Kodak camera in 1888. It came loaded with enough film for 100 pictures. When the roll was used up, the owner returned the camera with the exposed film still in it to the Eastman company in Rochester. Soon the developed and printed photographs and the camera, reloaded with film, were sent back to the owner.

The roll-film Kodak became an international sensation almost overnight. With the invention by Hannibal Goodwin of a truly modern roll film (a transparent, flexible plastic, coated with a thin emulsion and sturdy enough to be used without a paper support), a new photographic era, of simple, light cameras and easy-to-handle roll film, had begun. The Eastman Kodak Company knew very early who would be the main users of its products, and they directed their advertising accordingly: "A collection of these pictures may be made to furnish a pictorial history of life as it is lived by the owner, that will grow more valuable every day that passes."

PHOTOGRAPHER UNKNOWN: *Ruth at Thebes*, c. 1890

Striking a casual pose that was to be repeated in countless tourist snapshots, a camera-carrying girl traveling in Egypt arranged herself by a stone head of Ramses II as a companion immortalized the scene in the round frame that early Kodak cameras produced (above). The photographer is unknown, but the handwritten note in the album from which this picture came indicates that the girl's name was Ruth. Compared to the photograph of the sphinx and pyramids on page 362, this snapshot of a traveler in a middy blouse and wearing a Kodak brings the mysteries of unknown lands down to human size and suddenly makes them seem much less mysterious.

George Eastman, who put the Kodak box camera on the market and thereby put photography into everybody's hands, stands aboard the S.S. Gallia in the act of using his invention (left). Roll film made the camera small enough to carry easily. Fast gelatin emulsions permitted ¹/₂₅-sec exposures so subjects did not have to strain to hold still. The Kodak slogan was, aptly, "You press the button, we do the rest."

FRED CHURCH: *George Eastman with a Kodak*, 1890

Time and Motion in Early Photographs

LOUIS JACQUES MANDÉ DAGUERRE: *Boulevard du Temple, Paris*, 1839

EDWARD ANTHONY: *Broadway*, 1859

Today, photographers using modern high-speed films consider a one-second exposure relatively long. But photographers using earlier processes had to work with much slower emulsions, and an exposure of several seconds was considered quite short. People or objects that moved during the exposure were blurred or, if the exposure was long enough, disappeared completely; busy streets sometimes looked deserted (*above left*) because most people had not stayed still long enough to register an image.

Stereographic photographs (*half of a pair of images is shown above right*) were the first to show action as it was taking place, with people in midstride or horses and carts in motion. This was possible because the short-focal-length lens of the stereo camera produced a bright, sharp image at wide apertures and thus could be used with very brief exposure times. "How infinitely superior to those 'cities of the dead' with which we have hitherto been compelled

to content ourselves," commented one viewer.

These "instantaneous" photographs recorded such a short moment of time that they revealed aspects of motion that the unaided eye was not able to see. Some of the arrested motions were so different from the conventional artistic representations that the photographs looked wrong. A galloping horse, for example, had often been drawn with all four feet off the ground —the front legs extended forward and hind legs extended back. Eadweard Muybridge was a pioneer in **motion studies.** When his photographs of a galloping horse, published in 1878, showed that all four feet were off the ground only when they were bunched under the horse's belly, some people thought that Muybridge had altered the photographs. Using the new, fast gelatin emulsion and specifically constructed multi-lens cameras, Muybridge compiled many studies of different animals and humans in action (*right*).

The busy streets of a Parisian boulevard (*above, left*) appear depopulated because of the long exposure this daguerreotype required. Only a person getting a shoeshine near the corner of the sidewalk stood still long enough to be recorded; all the other people, horses, and carriages had blurred so much that no image of them appeared on the plate. By contrast, the relatively fast collodion process combined with the fast lens of a stereo camera froze the action on another busy street (*above, one of a pair of stereo views*).

The pictures at right were part of Eadweard ▶ Muybridge's project *Animal Locomotion, which analyzed the movements of humans and many animals. This sequence was made with three cameras, each with 12 lenses and shutters synchronized to work together so that each stage of the movement was recorded simultaneously from three sides.*

EADWEARD MUYBRIDGE: *Motion Study*, c. 1885

The Photograph as Document

To early viewers, the most wonderful aspect of photography was its ability to show an immense amount of literal and exact detail. "This is the Daguerreotype! . . . There is not an object . . . which was not in the original [scene]; and it is impossible that one should have been omitted. Think of that!" Faith in the camera as a literal recorder gave rise to a belief, still persisting today, that the camera does not lie; and it provides photographs themselves with the great psychological strength of appearing to tell the truth.

Photographs can be **documents** on many levels. Most snapshots record a particular scene or event simply to help the participants remember it later. A news photograph implies that this is exactly what you would have seen if you had been there yourself. On another level, a photograph can record reality and at the same time communicate the photographer's comment on that reality. Lewis Hine said of his work: "I wanted to show the things that had to be corrected. I wanted to show the things that had to be appreciated." His statement describes the use of photography as an instrument of social change, and a style that has come to be known as documentary (*see pages 370–371*).

Eugène Atget considered his photo-

graphs to be documents, but his work, done in the early part of this century, went beyond simple records. A sign on his door read "Documents pour Artistes," and according to a friend, Atget's ambition was "to create a collection of all that which both in Paris and its surroundings was artistic and picturesque. An immense subject." Atget made thousands of photographs of the streets, cafés, shops (*opposite*), monuments, parks, and people of the Paris he loved. His pictures won him little notice during his lifetime; he barely managed to eke out a living by selling them to artists, architects, and others who wanted visual records of the city. Many photographers can record the external appearance of a place, but Atget did more than that. He conveyed the atmosphere and mood of Paris.

August Sander chose to document a people—the citizens of pre–World War II Germany. His pictures were not meant to reveal personal character but to show the classes making up German society of that period. He photographed laborers (*right*), soldiers, businesspeople, provincial families, and other types, all formally posed. The portraits are so utterly factual and unsentimental as to be chilling at times; the individual disappears and only the type remains.

AUGUST SANDER: *Laborer,* 1927

August Sander's photographs are documents of social types rather than portraits of individuals. This photograph of a Cologne laborer with a load of bricks was one of hundreds of studies Sander made of the types he saw in pre–World War II Germany. Holding his pose as if standing still for a portrait painter, the subject displays his trade with dignity and without becoming a stereotype. The man has paused between taking up his burden and laying it down, but there is no indication of time or even place. In fact, the background is deliberately absent; Sander eliminated it from the negative.

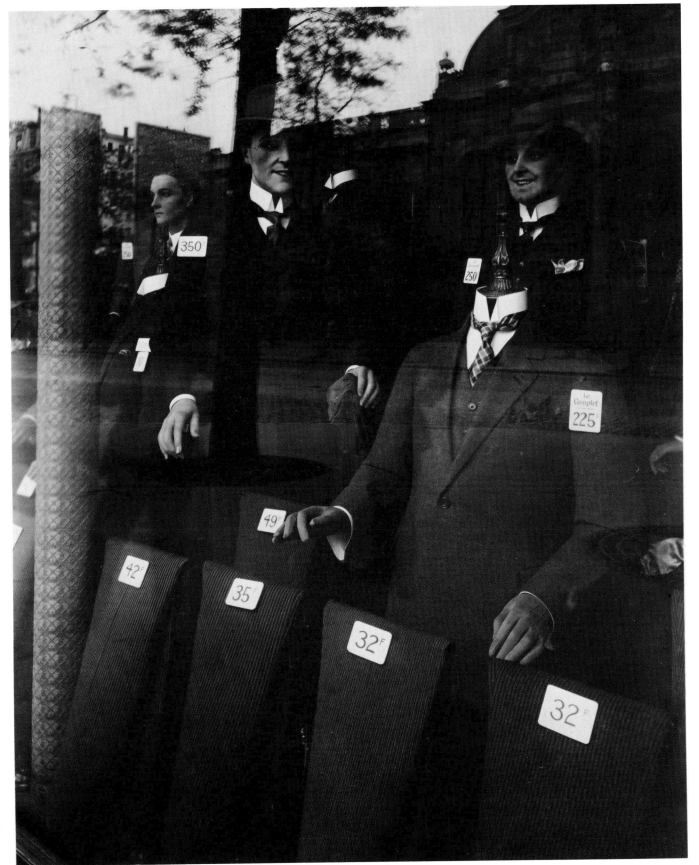

Eugène Atget artfully revealed the essence of Paris while seeming merely to document its external appearance. Here the shop window display and the dummies merge so that the photograph seems to show a ghostly view of Paris populated only by a group of urbane and smartly dressed mannequins.

EUGÈNE ATGET: *Men's Fashions*, 1925

Photography and Social Change

Photography has been called the mirror with a memory; in addition to merely reflecting the world, it can also mirror it with a purpose. Jacob Riis, a Danish-born newspaper reporter of the late 19th century, was one of the first to use photography for **social change.** Riis had been writing about the grinding brutality of life in New York City's slums and began to take pictures to show, as he said, what "no mere description could, the misery and vice that he had noticed in his ten years of experience . . . and suggest the direction in which good might be done."

Lewis W. Hine was a trained sociologist with a passionate social awareness, especially of the abuses of child labor (*right*). This evil was widespread in the early 20th century, and Hine documented it to provide evidence for reformers. With sarcastic fury he wrote of " 'opportunities' for the child and the family to . . . relieve the over-burdened manufacturer, help him pay his rent, supply his equipment, take care of his rush and slack seasons, and help him to keep down his wage scale."

The photographers of the **Farm Security Administration** recorded the Depression of the 1930s, when the nation's entire economic structure was in deep trouble and farm families were in particular need. Assistant Secretary of Agriculture Rexford G. Tugwell realized that the government's program of aid to farmers was expensive and controversial. To prove both the extent of the problem and the effectiveness of the cure, he appointed Roy Stryker to supervise photographic coverage of the program. Stryker recruited a remarkable band of talent, including Dorothea Lange (*see opposite*), Walker Evans, Russell Lee, Marion Post Wolcott, Arthur Rothstein, and Ben Shahn. Their work produced a classic collection of documentary photographs.

LEWIS W. HINE: *Victim of a Mill Accident,* c. 1910

Between 1908 and 1921, Lewis Hine made 5,000 pictures for the National Child Labor Committee documenting the abuses of child labor. This one-armed boy, a casualty of a mill accident, posed for Hine in about 1910. "We don't have many accidents," one foreman said at the time. "Once in a while a finger is mashed or a foot, but it doesn't amount to anything."

In showing the plight of "one third of a nation" during the Depression of the 1930s, the documentary photographers of the Farm Security Administration produced a monumental collection of images. Dorothea Lange had a unique ability to photograph people at the moment that their expressions and gestures revealed their lives and feelings.

Lange's captions for her FSA pictures often supplied verbatim what her subject had told her. For the photograph at right, "The worst thing we did was when we sold the car, but we had to sell it to eat, and now we can't get away from here. . . . You can't get no relief here until you've lived here a year. This county's a hard county. They won't help bury you here. If you die, you're dead, that's all."

DOROTHEA LANGE: *Woman of the High Plains, Texas Panhandle*, 1938

Photography as Art in the 19th Century

Almost from the moment of its birth, photography began staking out claims in areas that had long been reserved for painting. Portraits, still lifes, landscapes, nudes, and even allegories became photographic subject matter. Some artists bristled at the idea of **photography as an art form.** In 1862 a group of French artists formally protested that photography was a soulless, mechanical process, "never resulting in works which could . . . ever be compared with those works which are the fruits of intelligence and the study of art."

Photographers resented such assertions, but they in turn simply regarded photography as another kind of painting. The oldest known daguerreotype (*page 352*), taken by Daguerre himself in 1837, reveals this clearly. It is a still life self-consciously composed in the style of neoclassical painting.

Many photographers adapted styles of painting to the photographic print. From the 1850s through the 1870s there was a rage for illustrative photographs similar to a storytelling style of painting popular at the time. Julia Margaret Cameron, in addition to producing elegant and powerful portraits (*page 358*), indulged in romantic costume scenes such as illustrations for Tennyson's *The Idylls of the King.* Oscar G. Rejlander pieced together 30 negatives to produce an allegorical pseudopainting entitled *The Two Ways of Life*—one way led to dissolution and despair, the other to good works and contentment.

At the time, the most famous and commercially the most successful of those intending to elevate photography to an art was Henry Peach Robinson. Robinson turned out many illustrative and allegorical **composite photographs.** These were carefully plotted in advance and combined several negatives to form the final print (*photograph and drawing, right*). Robinson became

HENRY PEACH ROBINSON: *Fading Away*, 1858

Inspired by romantic literature, the British photographer Henry Peach Robinson perfected a composite photographic technique that allowed him to produce imaginary scenes. Fading Away (above) was staged by posing models separately and piecing together the images. Robinson usually planned such compositions in considerable detail: at right, a half-finished composite for another print shows a cutout photograph of a reclining woman superimposed on a preliminary pencil sketch.

HENRY PEACH ROBINSON: *Preliminary sketch with photograph inserted*, c. 1860

PETER HENRY EMERSON: *Gathering Water Lilies*, 1885

Peter Henry Emerson rejected the methods of the High Art photographers and insisted that photography should not imitate art but should strive for a naturalistic effect that was not artificially contrived. He illustrated his theories with his own photographs of peasants on the East Anglian marshes in England.

the leader of a so-called High Art movement in 19th-century photography, which advocated beauty and artistic effect no matter how it was obtained. In his *Pictorial Effect in Photography,* Robinson advised: "Any dodge, trick and conjuration of any kind is open to the photographer's use. . . . It is his imperative duty to avoid the mean, the bare and the ugly, and to aim to elevate his subject, to avoid awkward forms and to correct the unpicturesque."

By the 1880s a new movement was coming to the fore led by Peter Henry Emerson, the first to campaign against the stand that "art" photographers had taken. He felt that true photographic art was possible only through exploiting the camera's unique ability to capture reality in a direct way (*left*). He scorned the still-popular pictorial school, and its practices of composite printing, costumed models, painted backdrops, and sentimental views of daily life.

Emerson laid down his own rules for what he called **naturalistic photography:** simplicity of equipment; no "faking" by means of lighting, posing, costumes, or props; free composition without reliance on classical rules; and no retouching ("the process by which a good, bad or indifferent photograph is converted into a bad drawing or painting"). He also promoted what he believed was a scientific focusing technique that imitated the way the eye perceives a scene: sharply focused on the main subject, but with the foreground and especially the background slightly out of focus.

Although Emerson later became convinced that photography was not an art at all but only "a handmaiden to science and art," his earlier ideas had already influenced a new generation of photographers who no longer felt the need to imitate painting but began to explore photography as an art in its own right.

Pictorial Photography and the Photo-Secession

Is photography an art? Photographers were still concerned with this question at the turn of the century, and the **pictorialists,** or art photographers, wanted to separate their photographs from those taken for some other purpose—ordinary snapshots, for example. The *American Amateur Photographer* suggested: "If we had in America a dignified 'Photographic Salon,' with a competent jury, in which the only prizes should be the distinction of being admitted to the walls of the 'Salon,' we believe that our art would be greatly advanced. 'Art for art's sake' should be the inspiring word for every camera lover." The pictorial movement was international. Exhibitions and salons where photographs were judged on their aesthetic and artistic merits were organized by the Vienna Camera Club, the Linked Ring Brotherhood in England, the Photo-Club de Paris, the American Photo-Secession, and others.

Many pictorialists believed the artistic merits increased if the photograph looked like some other kind of art—charcoal drawing, mezzotint, or anything other than photography—and they patterned their work quite frankly on painting, especially the work of the French Impressionists, for whom mood and a sense of atmosphere and light were important. The pictorialists favored mist-covered landscapes and soft cityscapes; light was diffused, line was softened, and details were suppressed (*right*).

To achieve these effects, pictorialists often used printing techniques to which handwork was added—for example, gum-bichromate printing, where the image was transferred onto a thick, soft, often tinted coating that could easily be altered as the photographer wished. One critic was delighted: "The results no longer have anything in common with what used to be known as

GERTRUDE KÄSEBIER: *Blessed Art Thou Among Women*, c. 1898

Works by pictorialist photographers at the turn of the century often resembled impressionist paintings, with light and atmosphere more important than sharp details. Gertrude Käsebier created many scenes that depicted the relationships between women and children, including some of their more complex and contradictory aspects.

ALFRED STIEGLITZ: *The Steerage*, 1907

Although Alfred Stieglitz championed pictorialist works that resembled paintings, his own photographs (except for a brief early period) did not include handwork or other alterations of the direct camera image. Above, the patterns made by the people and machinery compelled him to make this photograph. "I saw a picture of shapes and underlying that the feeling I had about life."

photography. For that reason, one could proudly say that these photographers have broken with the tradition of the artificial reproduction of nature. They have freed themselves from photography. They have sought the ideal in the works of artists. They have done away with photographic sharpness, the clear and disturbing representation of details, so that they can achieve simple, broad effects." Not everybody agreed. This did not fit at all into Peter Henry Emerson's ideas of naturalistic photography: "If pure photography is not good enough or 'high' enough . . . by all means let him become an artist and leave us alone and not try and foist 'fakes' upon us."

In America, one person, Alfred Stieglitz, was the leader and catalyst for pictorialists, and his influence on photography as an art form is hard to overestimate. For more than 60 years he photographed (*left*), organized shows, and published influential and avant-garde work by photographers and other artists. In his galleries—the Little Galleries of the Photo-Secession (later known simply by its address, 291), the Intimate Gallery, and An American Place—he showed not only what he considered the best photographic works but also, for the first time in the United States, the works of Cézanne, Matisse, Picasso, and other modern artists. In his magazine *Camera Work,* he published photographic criticism and works whose only requirement was that they be worthy of the word *art*. Not only did he eventually force museum curators and art critics to grant photography a place beside the other arts, but by influence, example, and sheer force of personality he twice set the style for American photography: first toward the early pictorial impressionistic ideal and later toward sharply realistic, "straight" photography (see pages 376–377).

The Direct and Unmanipulated Image

PAUL STRAND: *The White Fence, Port Kent, New York*, 1916

Paul Strand's straight approach to photography as an art form combined an objective view of the world with personal meaning. "Look at the things around you, the immediate world around you. If you are alive it will mean something to you, and if you care enough about photography, and if you know how to use it, you will want to photograph that meaningness."

While many pictorialists were making photographs that looked very much like paintings, a few were seeking ways to use characteristics unique to the photographic process itself. They wanted to return to the direct and unmanipulated photographs that characterized so much of 19th-century imagery. In 1917 Stieglitz devoted the last issue of *Camera Work* to Paul Strand, whose photographs he saw as representing a powerful new approach to photography as an art form. Strand believed that "objectivity is of the very essence of photography. . . . The fullest realization of this is accomplished without tricks of process or manipulation, through the use of straight photographic methods."

Stieglitz's own photographs were direct and unmanipulated. He felt that many of them were visual metaphors, accurate representations of objects in front of his camera and at the same time external counterparts or "equivalents" of his inner feelings. Since 1950, Minor White (*pages 89, 101*) carried on and expanded Stieglitz's concept of the equivalent. For White, the goal of the serious photographer was "to get from the tangible to the intangible" so that a straight photograph of real objects functions as a metaphor for the photographer's or the viewer's state of mind.

Straight photography, which dominated photography as an art form from the 1930s to the 1950s, is exemplified by Edward Weston. He used the simplest technique and a bare minimum of equipment: generally, an 8 × 10 view camera with lens stopped down to the smallest aperture for sharpness in all parts of the picture and contact-printed negatives that were seldom cropped. "My way of working—I start with no preconceived idea—discovery excites me to focus—then rediscovery through the lens—final form of presentation seen on ground glass, the finished print previsioned complete in every detail of texture, movement, proportion, *before exposure*—the shutter's release automatically and finally fixes my conception, allowing no after manipulation—the ultimate end, the print, is but a duplication of all that I saw and felt through my camera." Weston's photographs were both objective and personal. "Clouds, torsos, shells, peppers [*opposite, far right*], trees, rocks, smokestacks are but interdependent, interrelated parts of a whole, which is life." Many other photographers, such as Ansel Adams (*pages 312, 325*), Imogen Cunningham (*page 95*), and Paul Caponigro (*page 126*), have used the straight approach.

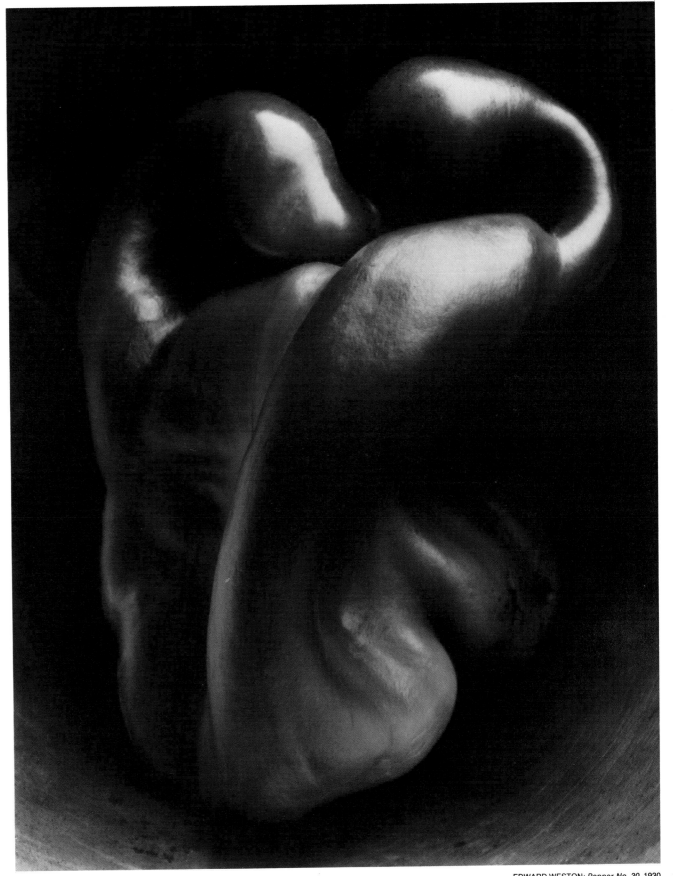

Edward Weston wrote about this photograph: "It is classic, completely satisfying—a pepper—but more than a pepper: abstract, in that it is completely outside subject matter."

EDWARD WESTON: *Pepper No. 30,* 1930

377

The Quest for a New Vision

MAN RAY: *Solarization*, 1929

The beginning of the 20th century was a period of great revolution in many areas, including science, technology, mathematics, politics, and also the arts. Movements like Fauvism, Expressionism, Cubism, Dada, and Surrealism were permanently changing the meaning of the word *art*. The Futurist art movement proposed "to sweep from the field of art all motifs and subjects that have already been exploited . . . to destroy the cult of the past . . . to despise utterly every form of imitation . . . to extol every form of originality." At the center of radical art, design, and think-

ing was the Berlin Bauhaus, a school to which the Hungarian artist László Moholy-Nagy came in 1922. He attempted to find new ways of seeing the world and experimented with radical uses of photographic materials in an attempt to replace 19th-century pictorialist conventions with a "new vision" compatible with modern life. Moholy explored many ways of expanding photographic vision, through photograms, photomontage (*opposite, far right*), the Sabattier effect (often called solarization), unusual angles (*opposite, near right*), optical distortions, and multiple expo-

sures. He felt that "properly used, they help to create a more complex and imaginary language of photography."

Another artist exploring new art forms was Man Ray, an American expatriate in Paris. He was drawn to Dada, a philosophy that commented on the absurdities of modern existence by introducing even greater absurdities. "I like contradictions," he said. "We have never obtained the infinite variety and contradictions that exist in nature." Like Moholy, Man Ray used many techniques, including solarizations (*this page*) and photograms (*page 204*).

LÁSZLÓ MOHOLY-NAGY: *From the Radio Tower*, 1928

Photographers such as László Moholy-Nagy and Man Ray used many techniques in their explorations of real, unreal, and abstract imagery. The dark lines along the woman's hand (opposite) as well as other altered tones are due to solarization, exposing the image to light during development. In the photograph above, the extreme angle of the camera pointing straight down onto a snow-covered courtyard merged the walkways, trees, and building into a single abstract design. The photomontage (right) combines pieces of several photographs. Moholy defined photomontage as "a tumultuous collision of whimsical detail from which hidden meanings flash," a definition that fits this ambiguous picture.

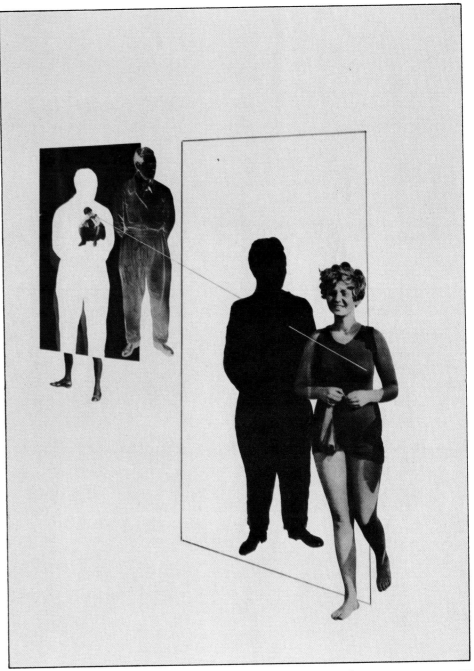

LÁSZLÓ MOHOLY-NAGY: *Jealousy*, 1927

Photography as Art in the 1950s and Beyond

A tremendous growth has taken place in the acceptance of photography as an art form, a change that started in the 1950s. Since then, photography has become a part of the college and art school curriculum; art museums have devoted considerable attention to photography; art galleries opened to sell only photographs, while photography entered other galleries that previously had sold only paintings or other traditional arts; and magazines such as *Artforum* and *Art in America* began to regularly publish photographs and essays about the medium.

American work of the 1950s was often described in terms of regional styles. Chicago was identified with the often abstract work of Aaron Siskind (*right*) and Harry Callahan. The West Coast was linked to the so-called straight photographers, such as Ansel Adams (*pages 312 and 325*) and Minor White (*pages 89 and 101*). New York was thought of as the center for social documentation, such as by photographers in the politically active Photo League (*265 and 327*). Meanwhile, tied to no region, Robert Frank, a Swiss, was traveling across the United States photographing his own view of life in the 1950s (*opposite*).

As an increasing number of colleges and art schools in the 1960s offered photography courses, often in the art departments of the schools, a cross-fertilization of ideas took place between photographers and artists working in traditional art media. Some painters and other artists integrated photographs in their work or sometimes switched to photography altogether. Some photographers combined their images with painting, printmaking, or other media. Older photographic processes were revived, such as cyanotyping (*page 216*) and platinum printing (*pages 184-185*).

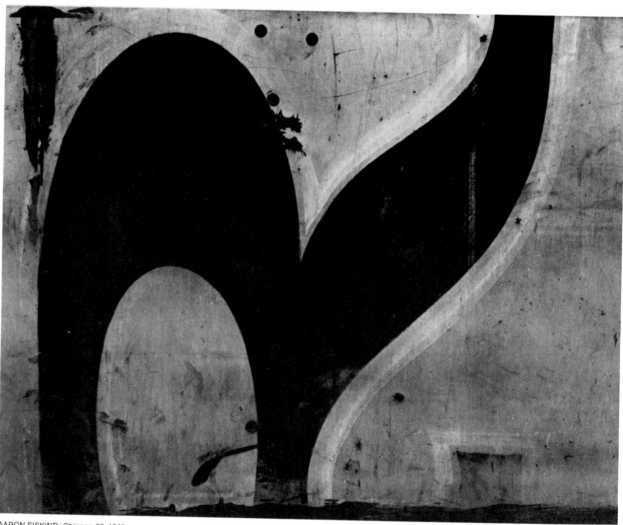

AARON SISKIND: *Chicago 30*, 1949

Minor White used to say that in the 1950s photographers functioning as artists were so few that they used to clump together for warmth. Today, photography continues to develop in many directions, but the long battle over whether photography was an art, a battle that had been waged almost from the invention of the medium, seems finally to have been resolved. The winners were those who said it was.

Aaron Siskind was active as a documentary photographer during the 1930s, but as he later recalled, "For some reason or other there was in me the desire to see the world clean and fresh and alive, as primitive things are clean and fresh and alive. The so-called documentary picture left me wanting something." His best-known work consists of surfaces abstracted from their normal context (above), such as peeled and chipped paint or posters on walls. The subject of the photograph is the shapes, tonality, and other elements that appear in it, not the particular wall itself.

ROBERT FRANK: *Bar, New York City,* 1955

When Robert Frank's work was published in 1959, it was attacked by critics for its ironic view of America, but it was to exert a great influence on both the subject matter and style of photography as an art form. Like Frank's photographs, the works of Diane Arbus (page 400), Garry Winogrand (page 399), Lee Friedlander, and others were personal observations of some of the peculiar and occasionally grotesque aspects of American society. Above, a glimpse inside a New York bar is an unsettling comment on the emptiness of modern society. Jack Kerouac wrote in his introduction to Frank's book, The Americans, *"After seeing these pictures you end up finally not knowing any more whether a jukebox is sadder than a coffin."*

Photojournalism

Today we take **photojournalism** for granted, and whatever the news event —from a prizefight to a war—we expect to see pictures of it. But news and pictures were not always partners. Drawings and cartoons appeared only occasionally in the drab 18th-century press. The *Pennsylvania Gazette* in the 1750s printed a woodcut of a snake chopped into many pieces over the caption "Join, or die." That was scarcely spot news, but it touched on one of the major concerns of the time: the necessity for unity in the American colonies. The 19th century saw the growth of illustrated newspapers such as the *Illustrated London News* and, in America, *Harper's Weekly* and *Frank Leslie's Illustrated Newspaper*. Because the various tones of gray needed to reproduce a photograph could not be printed simultaneously with ordinary type, photographs had to be converted into drawings and then into woodcuts before they could appear as news pictures. The photograph merely furnished material for the artist.

The perfection in the 1880s of the **halftone** process (*diagram, right*) permitted photographs and type to be printed together, and photographs became an expected addition to news stories. "These are no fancy sketches," the *Illustrated American* promised, "they are the actual life of the place reproduced upon paper." The **photo essay**— a sequence of photographs plus brief textual material—came of age in the 1930s. It was pioneered by Stefan Lorant in European picture magazines and later in America by a score of publications such as *Life* and *Look* (pages 384–385). Today, although the heyday of the picture magazine has passed, due in part to competition from television, photographs remain a major source of our information about the world.

Early cameras were relatively bulky, and the slowness of available films meant that using a camera indoors required a blinding burst of flashpowder. Not until the 1920s did photographers get a small camera able to take pictures easily in dim light. The first of these cameras, the Ermanox, to be followed soon by the Leica, had a lens so fast— f/2—that unobtrusive, candid shooting became practical. Erich Salomon (below) was one of the pioneers of such shooting, with a special talent for dressing in formal clothes and crashing diplomatic gatherings, where his camera let him record those in power while they were preoccupied with other matters, such as at the 1931 meeting (right) of German and Italian statesmen. In tribute to Salomon, the French foreign minister, Aristide Briand, is said to have remarked, "There are just three things necessary for a League of Nations conference: a few foreign secretaries, a table and a Salomon."

ERICH SALOMON: *Visit of German Statesmen to Rome*, 1931

PETER HUNTER: *Erich Salomon*, 1929

The halftone process converts the continuous shades of gray in a photograph into distinct units of black and white that can be printed with ink on paper. First, the original (above left) is rephotographed through a "screen"—a plate of clear plastic crosscut with a grid pattern. The grid breaks the continuous tones of the picture into dots (above right). This scheme of dots is then transferred chemically onto a printing plate.

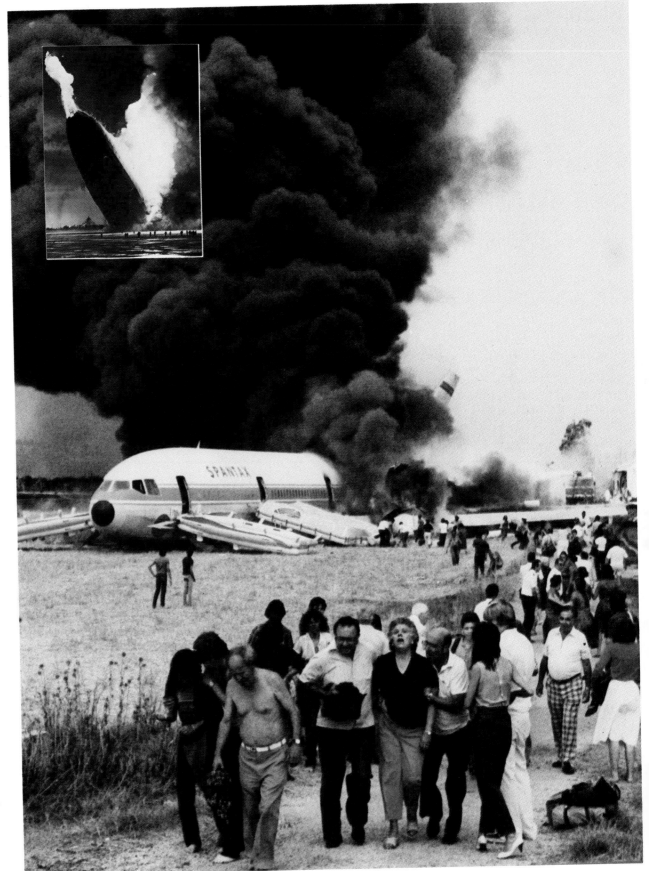

The Disaster Photo—one of the staples of news photography: the stunned survivors in the foreground, the crashed plane or burning house or flood waters in the background. Many news photographs show us the world in standardized ways or patterns, but the best reveal the particulars, the uniqueness of a scene.

The disaster photo at right is a classic of its kind. A black cloud of smoke billows from the big jet crashed in the background. The plane lies in the stubble of a field, looking as out of place and helpless as a beached whale. The picture combines the intensity of the moment with strong graphic composition as the survivors, some grieving, others in shock, move along a path curving to the foreground. One can imagine the photograph as a still from a disaster movie, set up to evoke emotion plus have pictorial appeal.

Inset: An equally powerful photograph of the 1937 crash of the dirigible Hindenburg. The tiny figures near the aircraft give some idea of its size, 800 feet long. The press had turned out to record what was supposed to be a routine landing, though still enough of a novelty in air travel to be covered. Instead they were witness to an astounding catastrophe as the huge craft burst into flames and exploded.

WERNER VOIGHT: *Spantax Crash, Malaga, Spain,* September 13, 1982
(*Inset*) MURRAY BECKER: *Hindenburg Crash, Lakehurst, New Jersey,* May 6, 1937

Spanish Village CONTINUED

A CHRISTENING

While his godfather holds him over a font, the priest Don Manuel dries the head of newborn Bautista-munoz Jose-nio Moreno after his baptism at village church.

THE THREAD MAKER

A peasant woman moistens the fibers of locally grown flax as she pries them in a long strand which is spun tight by the spindle (right), then wrapped around it.

GUARDIA CIVIL

These stern men, enforcers of national law, are Franco's rural police. They patrol countryside, are feared by people in villages, which also have local police.

VILLAGE SCHOOL

Girls are taught in separate classes from the boys. Four rooms and four lay teachers handle all pupils, as many as 300 in winter, between the ages of 6 and 11.

◀ FAMILY DINNER

The Curiels eat thick bean and potato soup from common pot on dirt floor of their kitchen. The father, mother and four children all share the one bedroom.

CONTINUED ON NEXT PAGE

126   127

W. EUGENE SMITH: From *Spanish Village*, 1951

The photo essay—pictures plus supporting text— was the mainstay of mass-circulation picture magazines such as Life and Look. Above and opposite are four pages from Spanish Village, photo- *graphed for Life by W. Eugene Smith, whose picture essays are unsurpassed in their power and photographic beauty.*

Spanish Village CONTINUED

HIS WIFE, DAUGHTER, GRANDDAUGHTER AND FRIENDS
HAVE THEIR LAST EARTHLY VISIT WITH A VILLAGER

128

129

"I try to do work that affects people," Smith said. "I try to lead them with my photographs so that they can draw their own conclusions." Smith was intensely committed to his work. "I never made any picture, good or bad, without paying for it in emotional turmoil."

History of Color Photography

Daguerre himself knew that only one thing was needed to make his wonderful invention complete—color. "There is nothing else to be desired," he wrote, "but the presentation of these children of light to the astonished eye in the full splendour of their colors." He and Niépce both experimented with various means of recording color without significant success. In 1850 an American minister and daguerreotypist, Levi L. Hill, made some color daguerreotypes, apparently by accident. Unfortunately, he was not able to reproduce the circumstances that had caused his materials to produce colors.

After several other false starts, one of the first successes was demonstrated in 1861 by the British physicist James Clerk Maxwell. To illustrate a lecture on color vision, he devised a way to recreate the colors of a tartan ribbon. He had three negatives of the ribbon made, each through a different color filter—red, green, and blue. Positive black-and-white transparencies were made and projected through filters like those on the camera. When the three images were superimposed, they produced an image of the ribbon in its original colors.

Maxwell had demonstrated additive color mixing, in which colors are produced by adding together varying amounts of light of the three primary colors, red, green, and blue. In 1869, an even more significant theory was made public. Louis Ducos du Hauron and Charles Cros, two Frenchmen working independently of each other, announced almost simultaneously their researches in subtractive color mixing. In subtractive mixing, the basis of present-day color photography, colors are created by combining cyan, magenta, and yellow dyes (the complements of red, green, and blue). The dyes subtract colors from the "white" light that contains all colors. (More about additive and subtractive theory on pages 222–223.) There were many variations of Ducos du Hauron's basic subtractive process in which three separately dyed images were superimposed to form a full-color image. They include his own three-color carbon process (*right, top*), the carbro process (*opposite*), and modern dye transfer printing.

The first commercially practical color was an additive process. In 1907, two French brothers, Antoine and Louis Lumière, marketed their Autochrome process. A glass plate was covered with tiny grains of potato starch dyed red-orange, green, and violet, in a layer only one starch grain thick. Then, a light-sensitive emulsion was added. Light struck the emulsion after passing through the colored grains. The emulsion behind each grain was exposed only by light from the scene that was the same color as that grain. The result after development was a full-color transparency (*right, bottom*).

The greatest advance in making color photography practical was perfected by Leopold Mannes and Leopold Godowsky, two musicians and amateur photographic researchers who eventually joined forces with Eastman Kodak research scientists. Their collaboration led to the introduction in 1935 of Kodachrome, a subtractive process in which a single sheet of film is coated with three layers of emulsion, each sensitive to one primary color (red, green, and blue). A single exposure produces a color image (*see pages 224–225*).

Today it is difficult to imagine photography without color. The amateur market is huge, and the ubiquitous snapshot is now always in color. Commercial and publishing markets use color extensively. Even photography as an art form, which has been in black and white for most of its history, has recently been turning to color.

LOUIS DUCOS du HAURON: *View of Angoulême, France,* 1877. Three-color carbon print

ARNOLD GENTHE: *Helen Cooke Wilson in a California Poppy Field,* c. 1908. Autochrome

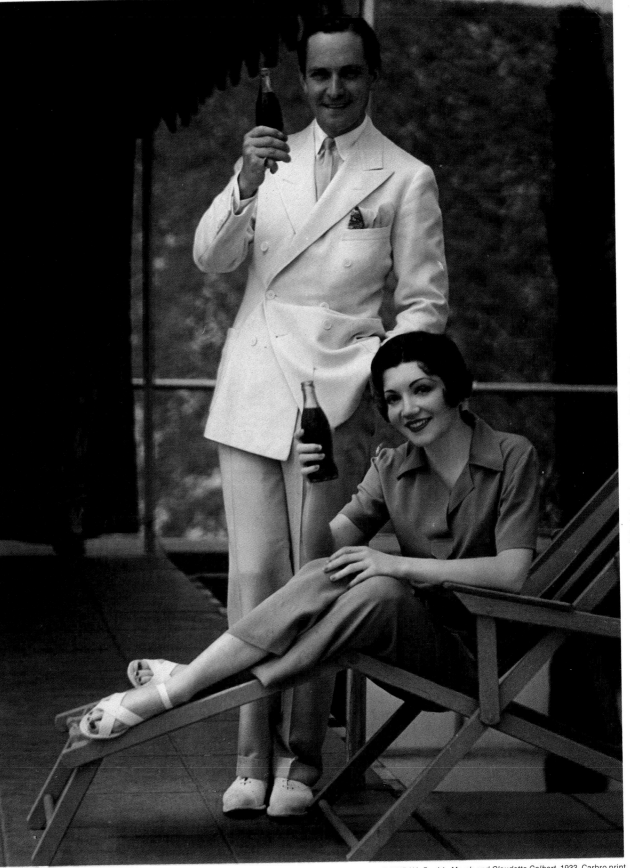

◄ Louis Ducos du Hauron's three-color carbon process required three separate black-and-white negatives, one for each of the primary colors red, green, and blue. Each image was dyed the color of its primary and then superimposed to form a full-color image.

◄ The Autochrome process was popular at the turn of the century with pictorialists who liked its graininess and subdued colors. The dots of color that composed the image blended at a normal viewing distance into a full range of colors, not unlike the effect that pointillist painters created with individual dots of paint.

The carbro process preceded the ▶ development of Kodachrome and other modern color films. Like Ducos du Hauron's three-color carbon print (opposite, top), carbros required three black-and-white negatives made with three different color filters. A cumbersome "one-shot" camera was used. Light passed through a lens into the camera to an arrangement of mirrors that split the light so that all three negatives were made simultaneously. To make a print, the negatives were converted into three layers of dyed gelatin that were mounted in register on a white backing. Here, two famous movie stars pose for a soft-drink advertisement made by Nickolas Muray, one of the earliest and best of color advertising photographers.

NICKOLAS MURAY: *Fredric March and Claudette Colbert*, 1933. Carbro print

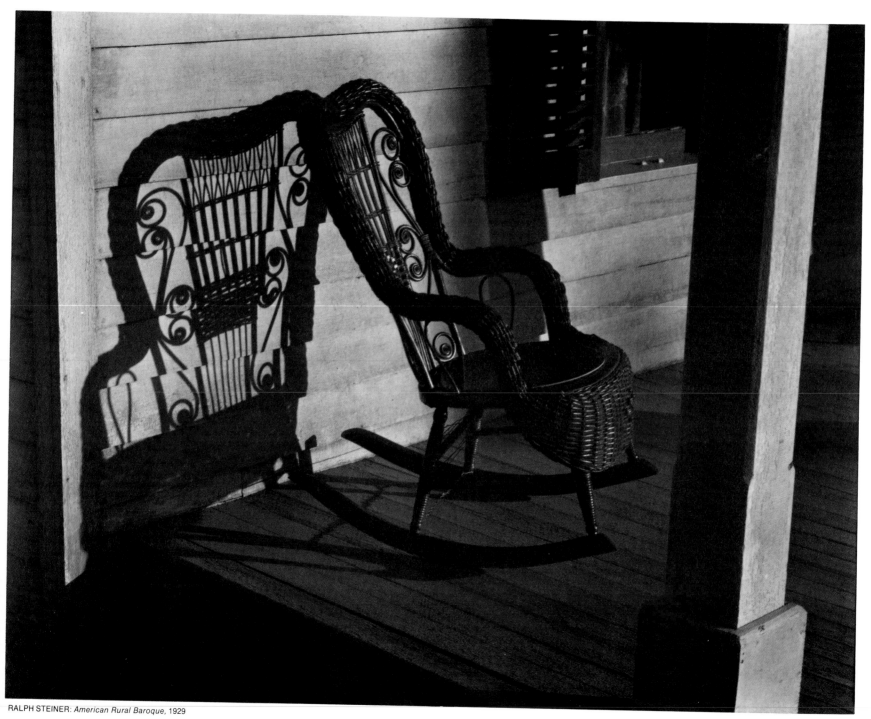

RALPH STEINER: *American Rural Baroque*, 1929

16
Portfolio

This chapter is a sampler of photographs. Its purpose, like the selection of all the pictures in this book, is to show the broad potential of photography. Whatever your goal in photography is, looking at the best of other people's work is an excellent way to improve your own pictures.

The understanding of a particular photograph, like the understanding of a piece of music, a poem, or a painting, is enhanced when you consider *how* the work means in addition to *what* it means. For example, the appreciation of music is intensified if you know something about its craft, such as harmony, counterpoint, rhythm, and the other elements of musical composition. Photographs, like music, have elements of composition such as structural, tonal, or color relationships, point of view, illusionistic space, and other visual characteristics (*see pages 326–347*). Photographers use these pictorial elements to suggest a feeling or mood or to state an idea.

Photographers also work from a variety of philosophical attitudes. Some are picture-*makers:* they build their photographs like tableaux and control or sometimes even physically make every part of their picture. Others are picture-*takers:* they prefer to select or frame their images from the flux of the world around them. Some alter the photographic image or photographic materials and may use nonphotographic media such as drawing, painting, or printmaking. Others believe that a direct and unmanipulated photograph is the most inherently aesthetic object.

Knowledge about the photographer, technique, or situation will help you as a viewer to respond more intelligently to a photograph, but ultimately you have to trust your own response to the picture itself. And any photograph—from a snapshot to a work of art—if examined openly and without prejudice, can help you to see with a more sophisticated eye.

◀ *Ralph Steiner has often photographed ordinary objects, such as a chair on a porch (opposite), bedsheets hanging on a laundry line, or clouds, at just that moment when the light on the subject briefly transforms it. Here, a homey wicker chair is paired with its flattened, abstracted, and cubist shadow. They make an unlikely but charming couple that will disappear with the changing light.*

GREGORY HEISLER: *Low Riders, Santa Ana, California,* 1979

Gregory Heisler combined electronic flash and available light to make this glossy portrait of two people and their 1947 Fleetline Chevrolet. The picture was made in dim light at dusk. While the car slowly backed up, Heisler set off two battery-powered flash units, then left the shutter open for 2 sec more. The image is sharp where the car and riders were lit by the flash; the image is streaked and blurred where available light provided the illumination, as on the front fender and in the reflections in the chrome strips.

BILL SHROUT: *Cars Crushed for Recycling, Flowood, Mississippi*

The inevitable end of all industrial products, even the glossiest, is documented above. In 1972 the Environmental Protection Agency (EPA) hired photographers to illustrate environmental problems and to show what the EPA was doing about them, in much the same way that the Farm Security Administration hired photographers to document government activity during the Depression of the 1930s.

Notice how pictures can be affected by other images nearby: placing these two opposite each other adds a wry comment to the Heisler picture by showing the car's possible fate.

JOEL MEYEROWITZ: *Bay/Sky, Provincetown, 1977*

BRADFORD WASHBURN: *After the Storm, Switzerland,* 1960

◀ Opposite, a sensuous, glowing palette of colors transforms an almost empty, flat beach scene into a romantic vista of glowing light. The particular place is not as important as the play of light and color across its surfaces. "Color makes everything more interesting," says Joel Meyerowitz. "Color suggests more things to look at. Color suggests that the light itself is a subject."

Although the landscape above is as imposing as can be found anywhere, the way in which the photographer has chosen to show the scene creates at least as much interest as the mountain itself. The sweep of line across the top of the mountain is echoed by the clouds above it. The same line is traced in the path of the tiny figures, who give almost the only clue to the scene's immense scale.

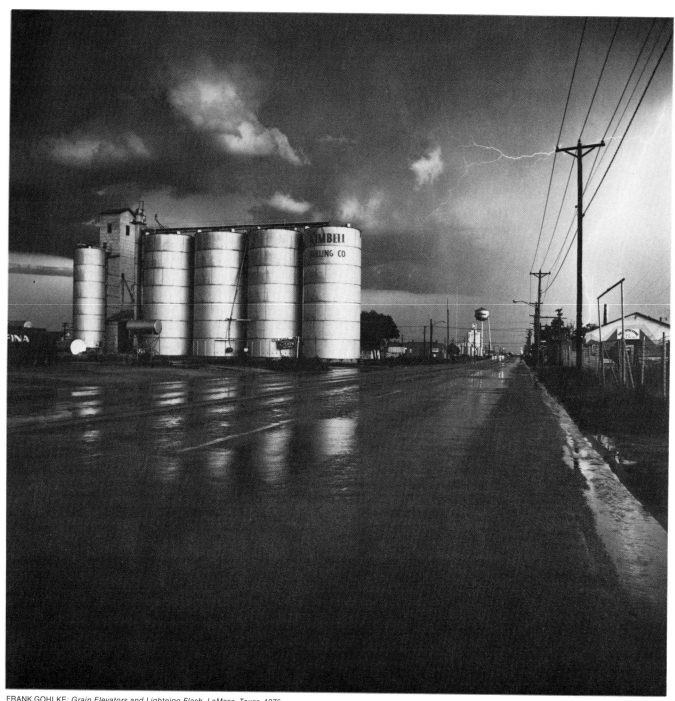

FRANK GOHLKE: *Grain Elevators and Lightning Flash, LaMesa, Texas, 1975*

Pictorial beauty exists in places where it may not be evident at first. It is relatively easy to appreciate a photograph of a colorful seascape or a sweeping vista of mountains and clouds (pages 392–393), but grain elevators, railroad yards, and other seemingly ordinary scenes can also be poetic and majestic.

Frank Gohlke's photographs are carefully composed scenes of epic scale that are rich in detail and tonality, such as the grain elevators, left, or the desolated area around Mount St. Helens after its eruption.

BERENICE ABBOTT: *Jersey Railroad Yard,* 1932

Berenice Abbott says she fell in love with New York and could have worked all her life photographing it. Here, the skyline of the city stands like a distant mountain range behind the New Jersey railroad yards that are just west of the city across the Hudson River. Abbott skillfully orchestrated a complex scene in which no single element dominates. As you look at the print, try to notice the path your eye follows. It may slide up and down the shiny rails, then jump from one white spot to another, to return to the rails.

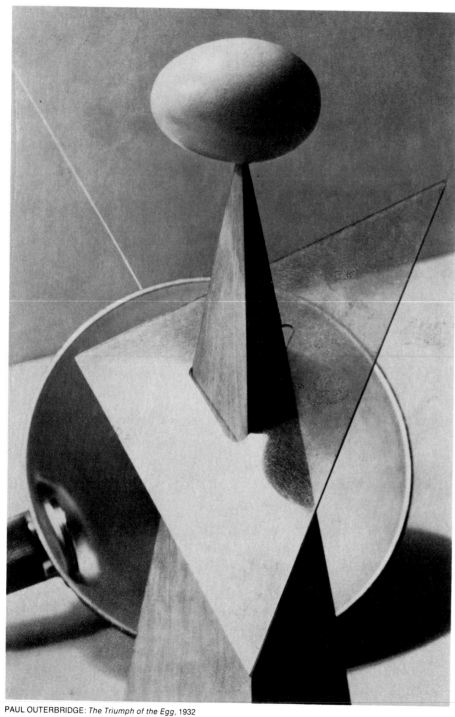

PAUL OUTERBRIDGE: *The Triumph of the Egg*, 1932

Paul Outerbridge was a successful commercial photographer who as early as 1921 made extraordinary graphic designs from ordinary objects, as here, a pyramid, an artist's triangle, the circle of a flash reflector, and an egg perched improbably over all. The egg is an amusing addition, but the objects themselves are not as important as the arrangement of their shapes.

The objects in Jan Groover's still life are common
house plants and kitchen utensils, but the subject
of the photograph is its compositional elements—
the shapes, colors, scale, and placement of the
objects and their relationship to the rectangle of
the picture format. See also work by Barbara Kasten (pages 10–11).

JAN GROOVER: *Untitled.* 1978

WILLIAM WEGMAN: *Fey Ray*, 1979

William Wegman is an artist whose work includes drawings, videotapes, and photographs. Wegman was blessed by ownership of a large weimaraner named Man Ray who liked nothing better than dressing up and having his picture taken. Together Wegman and Man Ray transformed the dog into such diverse creatures as an elephant (complete with plastic tusks and a stuffed sock for a trunk), a garden (covered with flowers), and a lovely lady, Fey Ray (left).

As a bit of whimsy, photography critic Owen Edwards once formulated a Dog/No Dog Criterion for photographic criticism in which pictures with dogs in them are the only ones worth thinking about. Man Ray would have agreed without a moment's pause.

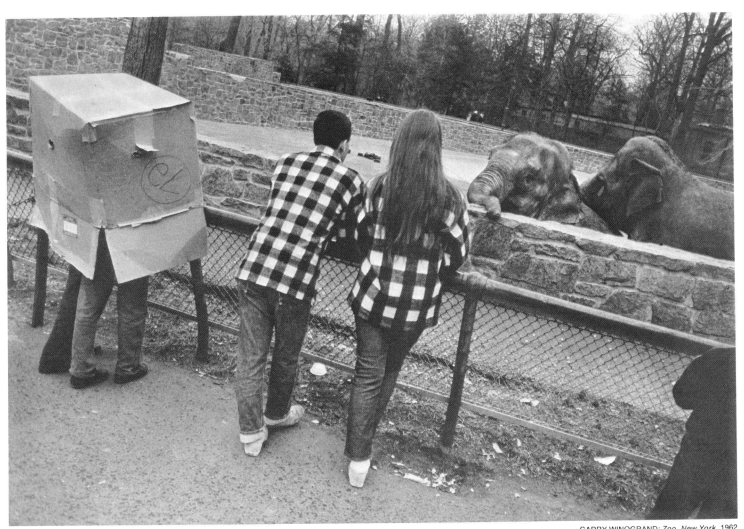

GARRY WINOGRAND: *Zoo, New York, 1962*

Many of Garry Winogrand's pictures involve unusual confrontations. This one depicts a three-way face-off between humans and animals at the Bronx Zoo, with all three couples apparently equally intrigued by the event. Winogrand exploited the camera's ability to collect facts. He said, "Photography is about finding out what can happen in the frame. When you put four edges around some facts, you change those facts. The frame creates a world and photography is about [that] world." When asked why his images were tilted, he replied, "What tilt? There's only a tilt if you believe that the horizon line must be parallel to the horizontal edge. That's arbitrary."

DIANE ARBUS: *A Tattooed Man at a Carnival, Maryland,* 1970

Diane Arbus photographed anybody and everybody who drew her attention because they were different: twins and triplets, giants and midgets, carnival performers and transvestites as well as so-called ordinary people engaged in such rituals as beauty contests and masked balls. She recorded all of them with a riveting concentration, as if she were an anthropologist studying the behavior of a newly found and rather exotic tribe. Often she photographed people head-on so that they fully confronted the camera and the photographer to present their unique selves, as in the photograph at left.

Cindy Sherman photographs herself but doesn't make self-portraits. She uses herself as a model—costumed, made up, posed, and emoting in roles from popular culture such as dreamy teenager, tough female, and woman in crisis. Sherman's goal is to tell a story but to leave the story as ambiguous as possible so that viewers can add whatever details they want. "These are pictures of emotions personified, entirely of themselves with their own presence. . . . I'm trying to make other people recognize something of themselves rather than me."

CINDY SHERMAN: *Untitled*, 1982

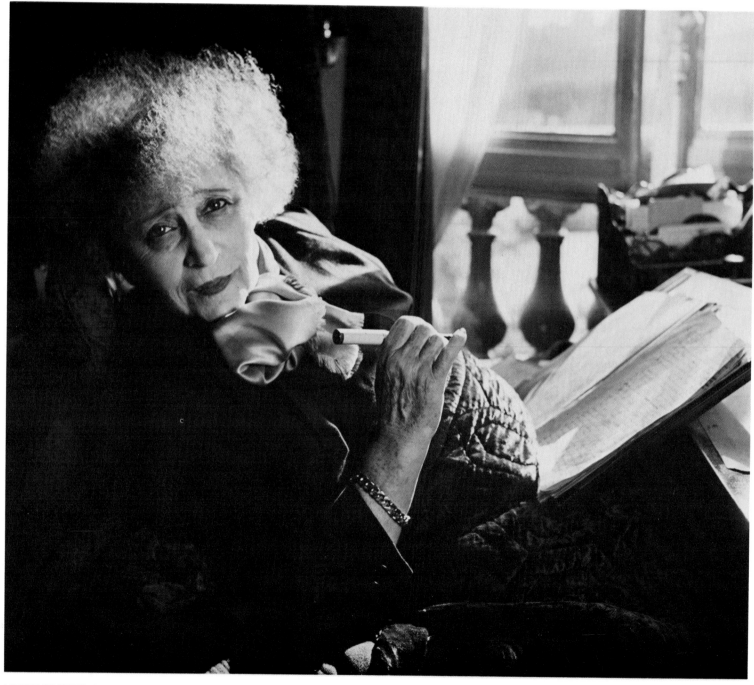

LOUISE DAHL-WOLFE: *Colette, Paris*, 1951

Environmental portraits, those that show people in their ordinary surroundings, seem to reveal information about character. It feels as if we know more about the women here because they are shown in their own surroundings. The photographer, however, is usually in control of which objects are included in the frame of the photograph and so can shape the impression that the viewer has of a subject.

Louise Dahl-Wolfe is best known for her fashion photography, which appeared frequently in Harper's Bazaar from 1936 to 1958. She was an innovator in bringing a naturalness and intimacy to fashion photography that replaced the rather artificially polished glamour of the preceding era. She also made many portraits, like this one of the French writer Colette late in her life working propped up in bed. Although Colette seems to have paused in the midst of writing a sentence to look at the camera for just a moment, Dahl-Wolfe was a perfectionist in her work and would not simply have walked into the room and snapped the shutter.

Yousuf Karsh's portraits include presidents, popes, and most of the century's greatest musicians, writers, and artists, including the painter Georgia O'Keeffe (right). This portrait is typical of Karsh's work, conveying very strongly the sitter's public image, that is, what we expect that particular person to look like. Karsh generally photographs people in their own environments but imposes on his portraits his distinctive style: carefully posed and lighted setups, rich black tones, often with face and hands highlighted.

YOUSUF KARSH: *Georgia O'Keeffe*, 1956

Serial imagery, sequences, and photo essays release the photographer from the confinement of the single picture. They can show variations of a single photograph or theme, show the same scene from different angles or at different times, bring together different images to make a particular statement, or, as above, tell a story.

Ruth Orkin had just gotten her first 35mm camera in 1946, put the first roll of film into it, and gone outside her apartment to look for something to photograph when she came upon a boy giving his friends a synopsis of Kitty, *a costume movie starring Paulette Goddard. The story goes, in part, "Da pitchah starts where da king is tellin' off Kitty's boyfriend. Da king is puttin' on da dog for Kitty. Den dis crazy guy—he goes to grab her. Annuder woman chases her up da stairs and yells 'Ya won't get away wid dis!' Den da udder woman screams an' falls down da stairs. Wait . . . I'll go back a little furder, I skipped some."*

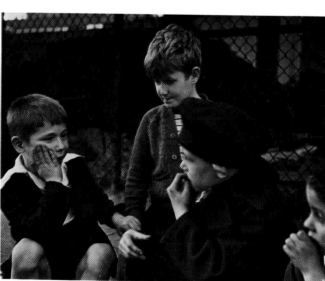

RUTH ORKIN: *Jimmy the Storyteller, New York City, 1947*

Robert Cumming often photo- ▶
graphs imaginary scenes that he disguises as factual documents. On first glance, the series opposite seems to be a high-speed photographic analysis of a projectile in motion. But the floodlights are a clue that the exposure was long, as are the flying fragments that don't move from one frame to the next (they were strung up on wires). Cumming's factual document is, in fact, an elaborately staged and drily humorous fiction that asks the viewer to question the honesty of its own medium.

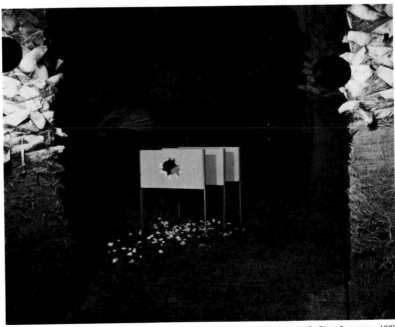

ROBERT CUMMING: *Blast Sequence*, 1973

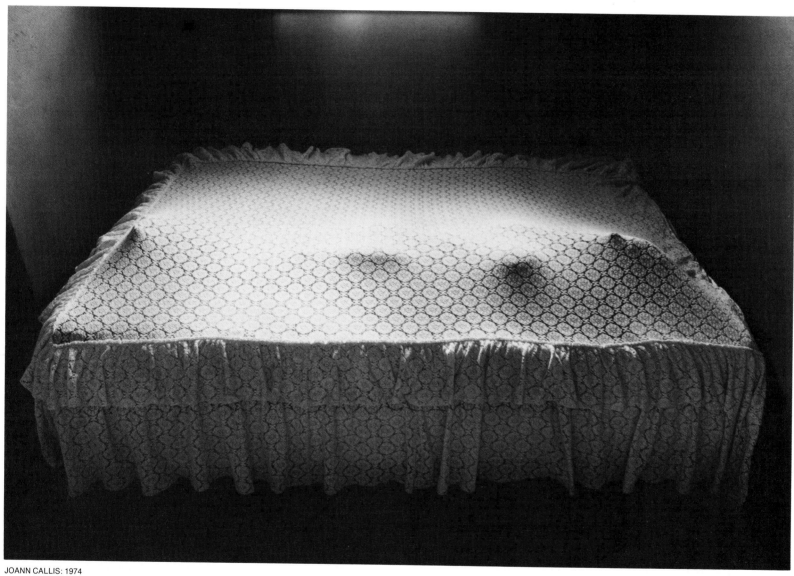

JOANN CALLIS: 1974

JoAnn Callis has used her own dreams or fanta-
sies as the basis for some of her photographs,
selecting the appropriate models, costumes,
props, and settings in order to materialize her
imaginings as a photograph. The figure above,
surrounded by darkness, can be seen as a fantasy
or dream image or as symbolic of the unconscious
mind itself, the hidden or buried self whose shape
is barely perceptible to the conscious mind.

SYLVIA PLACHY: *Night Mare,* 1980

Sylvia Plachy is a photojournalist whose newspaper, New York's Village Voice, has encouraged her to develop her personal vision. Her work often combines reportage with symbolic or interpretive elements. Above, a racehorse struggles to keep its head above water in an exercise pool. The picture is a document of an ordinary racetrack activity but takes on frightening proportions, even more so with its title.

Plachy says she takes pictures in a sort of trance. "I look for the hum. I see this hum all the time—even when I don't have a camera. But I have to be very quick to catch it. It's there for a second and then it's gone."

Morley Baer from the book *Here Today.* 323: Chris Rainier. 325: Photograph by Ansel Adams. Courtesy of the Ansel Adams Publishing Rights Trust. All rights reserved.

CHAPTER 14 326: Cecil Beaton, courtesy of Sotheby's London. 327: Jack Manning, from "Harlem Document." 328: Linda Bartlett. 329: Richard E. Ahlborn, American Folklife Center— Carl Fleischhauer, American Folklife Center. 330, 331: Joe Wrinn. 332: John Senzer. 333: Robert Doisneau. 334, 335: Russell Lee, courtesy Library of Congress. 336: Paul Caponigro. 337: Gordon Parks. 338: Roy Clark, U.S. Dept. of Agriculture— R. O. Brandenberger, U.S. Dept. of Agriculture. 339: Dennis Stock / Magnum. 340: U.S. Department of Agriculture. 341: Herbert List / Herbert List Estate, Max Scheler—U.S. Department of Agriculture. 342: David F. Warren, U.S. Department of Agriculture. 343: Judy Dater. 344: Robert Branstead, U.S. Dept. of Agriculture. 345: Josef Koudelka / Magnum. 346: Marion Post Wolcott, courtesy Library of Congress. 347: David Moore; Dorothea Lange, © The City of Oakland, The Oakland Museum, Calif.

CHAPTER 15 348: One-quarter plate daguerreotype, 3¼ × 4¼". Collection, The Museum of Modern Art, New York. Gift of Virginia Cuthbert Elliott. 350: Gernsheim Collection, Harry Ransom Humanities Research Center, University of Texas at Austin; International Museum of Photography at George Eastman House. 351: Gernsheim Collection, Harry Ransom Humanities Research Center, University of Texas at Austin. 352: Collections de la Société Française de Photographie; International Museum of Photography at George Eastman House. 353: By permission of the Trustees of Amherst College.

354: Courtesy Lee Boltin Picture Library. 355: G. R. Rinhart Collection. 356: Gernsheim Collection, Harry Ransom Humanities Research Center, University of Texas at Austin. 357: T. H. O'Sullivan, courtesy Library of Congress—Division of Photographic History, Smithsonian Institution. 358: Crown Copyright Victoria and Albert Museum. 359: Bibliothèque Nationale, Eddy Van der Veen. 360: Gernsheim Collection, Harry Ransom Humanities Research Center, University of Texas at Austin. 361: Courtesy Library of Congress. 362: Courtesy Arnold Crane Collection, Chicago, Illinois. 363: Courtesy Library of Congress. 364, 365: International Museum of Photography at George Eastman House. 366: Bayerische Nationalmuseum: International Museum of Photography at George Eastman House. 367: International Museum of Photography at George Eastman House. 368: Copyright the Estate of August Sander. Courtesy of the Sander Gallery, New York. 369: From portfolio published by Berenice Abbott. Gelatin-silver print, 9¹⁄₁₆ x 6¾". Collection, The Museum of Modern Art, New York. Gift of Edward Steichen. 370: International Museum of Photography at George Eastman House. 371: Dorothea Lange, © The City of Oakland, The Oakland Museum, Calif. 372: From the Collection of The Royal Photographic Society —Gernsheim Collection, Harry Ransom Humanities Research Center, University of Texas at Austin. 373: Gernsheim Collection, Harry Ransom Humanities Research Center, University of Texas at Austin. 374: Gertrude Käsebier, platinum print on Japanese tissue, 9⅜ x 5½", Collection, The Museum of Modern Art, New York. Gift of Mrs. Hermine M. Turner. 375: Photogravure (artist's proof) from *Camera Work*, No. 36, 1911. Size of print, 7¾ x 6½". Collection, The Museum of Modern Art, New York. Gift of Alfred Stieglitz. 376:

From *Camera Work,* No. 49–50, June 1917. Gravure, 6¹¹⁄₁₆ x 8¹¹⁄₁₆". Collection, The Museum of Modern Art, New York. Given anonymously. Ga. 377: Edward Weston. © 1981. Arizona Board of Regents, Center for Creative Photography. 378: Copyright 1984 Juliet Man Ray. Reproduced courtesy of the International Museum of Photography at George Eastman House. 379: Reproduced courtesy of Hattula Moholy-Nagy and the International Museum of Photography at George Eastman House. 380: Aaron Siskind. 381: Robert Frank, collection of the Museum of Fine Art, Houston Texas. 382: Peter Hunter / Magnum; Erich Salomon, courtesy Bildarchiv Preussischer Kulturbesitz, Berlin, West Germany. 383: Werner Voight / SIPA, Special Features; Murray Becker, Associated Press / Wide World. 384–385: W. Eugene Smith, courtesy *Life* Picture Service, *Life* Magazine, © 1951 Time Inc. 386: Louis Ducos Du Hauron, International Museum of Photography at George Eastman House—Arnold Genthe, courtesy Library of Congress. 387: Nickolas Muray, International Museum of Photography at George Eastman House.

CHAPTER 16 388: Ralph Steiner. 390: Gregory Heisler. 391: Bill Shrout. 392: Joel Meyerowitz. 393: Bradford Washburn. 394: Copyright Frank Gohlke, courtesy Daniel Wolfe, Inc., New York. 395: Courtesy Berenice Abbott / Parasol Dress, Ltd. 396: Paul Outerbridge, courtesy G. Ray Hawkins Gallery, Los Angeles, Calif. 397: Jan Groover. 398: William Wegman. 399: Garry Winogrand. 400: © 1970 The Estate of Diane Arbus. 401: Cindy Sherman, photo courtesy Metro Pictures, New York. 402: Louise Dahl-Wolfe. 403: © Karsh, Ottawa. 404: © 1947, 1975 Ruth Orkin. 405: Robert Cumming. 406: Joann Callis. 407: Sylvia Plachy.

Glossary

aberration An optical defect in a lens causing it to form an image that is not sharp or that is distorted. *See astigmatism, barrel distortion, chromatic aberration, coma, field curvature, pincushion distortion, spherical aberration.*

acid A substance with a pH below 7. Since an acid neutralizes an alkali, a stop bath is usually an acidic solution that stops the action of the alkaline developer.

additive color A way to produce colors of light by mixing light of the three additive primary colors —red, green, and blue. Each primary color contains about one-third of the wavelengths in the visible spectrum. Varying proportions of the additive primaries can be combined to create light of all other colors, including white, which is a mixture of all wavelengths.

agitate To move a solution over the surface of film or paper during the development process so that fresh liquid comes into contact with the surface.

albumen Egg white. Used in early photographic emulsions as a coating for glass plates (1850s) and, more commonly, for printing paper (1850–c. 1900).

alkali A substance with a pH above 7. Developers are usually alkaline solutions.

ambrotype A collodion wet-plate process in which the emulsion was coated on a glass plate. The negative image produced was visible as a positive image when the glass was backed with a dark material.

angle of view The amount of a scene covered by a lens or viewfinder or read by a light meter.

aperture The size of the lens opening through which light passes. The relative aperture is measured as the focal length of the lens divided by the diameter of the aperture; this is expressed as an f-number: f/8, f/11, and so on.

aperture-priority A mode of automatic exposure in which the photographer selects the aperture and the camera sets the shutter speed that will produce the correct exposure.

archival processing Processing designed to protect a print or negative as much as possible from premature deterioration caused by chemical reactions.

artificial light Light from an electric lamp, a flash bulb, or electronic flash. Often describes lights that the photographer has set up to illuminate a scene.

ASA A numerical rating that describes the sensitivity of a film to light. The ASA rating doubles as the sensitivity of the film doubles.

astigmatism A lens aberration or defect that is caused by the inability of a simple lens to focus oblique rays uniformly.

automatic exposure A mode of camera operation in which the camera adjusts the shutter speed, the aperture, or both to produce the correct exposure.

automatic flash An electronic flash unit with a light-sensitive cell and electronic circuitry that measures the light reflected back from the subject and terminates the flash when the exposure is correct.

available light A general term implying relatively dim light that already exists where a photograph is to be made.

axis lighting Light pointed at the subject from a position close to the lens.

B *See bulb.*

back lighting Light that comes from behind the subject toward the camera.

brightness Strictly speaking, a subjective impression of the lightness of an object. The correct term for the measurable quantity of light reflected or produced by an object is *luminance*. *See luminance.*

barrel distortion A lens aberration or defect that causes straight lines to bow outward, away from the center of the image.

bellows A flexible, light-tight and usually accordion-folded part of a view camera that connects the lens board in front to the viewing screen in back. Also used on a smaller camera when the lens must be positioned farther than normal from the film.

bleed mount To mount a print so that there is no border between the edges of the print and the edges of the mounting surface.

blocked up Describes a portion of an overexposed or overdeveloped negative so dense with silver that texture and detail in the subject are unclear.

blotters Sheets of absorbent paper made expressly for photographic use. Wet prints dry when placed between blotters.

bounce light Light that does not travel directly from its source to the subject but is first reflected off another surface.

bracket To make several exposures, some greater and some less than the exposure that is calculated to be correct. Bracketing allows for error and permits selection of the best exposure after development.

broad lighting Portrait lighting in which the main source of light illuminates the side of the face turned most toward the camera.

built-in meter A reflected-light exposure meter built into a camera so that light readings can be made directly from camera position.

bulb A shutter setting marked *B* at which the shutter remains open as long as the shutter release is held down.

burn in To darken a specific area of a print by giving it additional printing exposure.

butterfly lighting Portrait lighting in which the main source of light is placed high and directly in front of the face.

cable release A long coiled wire with a plunger at one end and a socket at the other that attaches to a camera's shutter release. Pressing the plunger releases the shutter without touching (and possibly moving) the camera.

calotype The first successful negative/positive photographic process; it produced an image on paper. Invented by Talbot; also called Talbotype.

camera A picture-taking device usually consisting of a light-tight box, a film holder, a shutter to admit a measured quantity of light, and a lens to focus the image.

camera obscura Latin for "dark chamber": a darkened room with a small opening through which rays of light could enter and form an image of the scene outside. Eventually, a lens was added at the opening to improve the image, and the room was replaced by a small, portable box.

carrier A frame that holds a negative flat in an enlarger.

carte-de-visite A small portrait, about the size of a visiting card, popular during the 1860s. People often collected them in albums.

cartridge *See cassette.*

cassette A light-tight metal or plastic container that permits a roll of 35mm film to be loaded into a camera in the light. Also called a cartridge.

catchlight A reflection of a light source in a subject's eye.

changing bag A light-tight bag into which a photographer can insert his or her hands to handle film when a darkroom is not available.

characteristic curve A diagram of the response to light of a photographic material, showing how increasing exposure affects silver density during development. Also called the D log E curve, since density is plotted against the logarithm of the exposure.

chromagenic film Film in which the final image is composed of chemical dyes rather than silver.

chromatic aberration A lens defect that bends rays of different colors at different angles and therefore focuses them on different planes.

chrome A color transparency.

circle of confusion The tiny circle of light formed by a lens as it projects the image of a single point of a subject. The smaller the diameters of all the circles of confusion in an image, the sharper the image will be.

close-up A larger-than-normal image that is formed on a negative by focusing the subject closer than normal to the lens with the use of supplementary lenses, extension tubes, or bellows.

cold-light enlarger A diffusion enlarger that uses a fluorescent tube instead of a tungsten bulb as the light source.

collodion A transparent, syrupy solution of pyroxylin (a nitrocellulose) dissolved in ether and alcohol. Used as the basis for the emulsion in the wet-plate process.

color balance 1) The ability of a film to reproduce accurately the colors of a scene. Color films are balanced for use with specific light sources. 2) The reproduction of colors in a color print, alterable during printing.

color cast A slight trace of one color in all the colors in an image.

color-compensating filters Gelatin filters used to adjust the color balance in color printing. More expensive than acetate color printing filters, they can be used below the enlarger lens if the enlarger has no other place for filters. Abbreviated CC filters.

color-printing filters Acetate filters used to adjust the color balance in color printing. They must be used with an enlarger that can hold filters between the enlarger lamp and the negative. Abbreviated CP filters.

color temperature A numerical description of the color of light. It is the temperature in degrees Kelvin (K) to which a perfect black-body radiator (an object that does not reflect any light falling on it) would have to be heated to produce a given color.

color temperature meter A device for estimating the color temperature of a light source. Usually used to determine the filtration needed to match the color balance of the light source with that of standard types of color film.

coma A lens aberration or defect that causes rays that pass obliquely through the lens to be focused at different points on the film plane.

complementary colors 1) Any two colors of light that when combined include all the wavelengths of light and thus produce white light (*see additive color*). 2) Any two dye colors that when combined absorb all wavelengths of light and thus produce black (*see subtractive color*). A colored filter absorbs light of its complementary color and passes light of its own color.

condenser enlarger An enlarger that illuminates the negative with light that has been concentrated and directed by condenser lenses placed between the light source and the negative.

contact printing The process of placing a negative in contact with sensitized material, usually paper, and then passing light through the negative onto the material. The resulting image is the same size as the negative.

contamination Traces of chemicals that are present where they don't belong, causing loss of chemical activity, staining, or other problems.

continuous tone Describes an image containing a range of tones from black through many intermediate shades of gray to white.

contrast The difference in darkness or density between one tone and another.

contrast grade The contrast that a printing paper produces. Systems of grading contrast are not uniform, but in general grades 0 and 1 have low or soft contrast; grades 2 and 3 have normal or medium contrast; grades 4, 5, and 6 have high or hard contrast.

contrasty Describes a scene, negative, or print with very great differences in brightness between light and dark areas. Opposite: *flat.*

convergence The phenomenon in which lines that are parallel in a subject, such as the vertical lines of a building, appear nonparallel in an image.

cool Refers to bluish colors that, by association with common objects (water, ice, and so on), give an impression of coolness.

coupled rangefinder *See rangefinder.*

covering power The area of the focal plane over which a lens projects an image that is acceptably sharp and uniformly illuminated.

crop To trim the edges of an image, often to improve the composition. Cropping can be done by moving the camera position while viewing a scene, by adjusting the enlarger or easel during printing, or by trimming the finished print with a paper cutter.

curvilinear distortion *See barrel distortion, pincushion distortion.*

cut film *See sheet film.*

daguerreotype The first practical photographic process, invented by Daguerre and described by him in 1839. The process produced a positive image formed by mercury vapor on a metal plate coated with silver iodide.

darkroom A room where photographs are developed and printed, sufficiently dark to handle light-sensitive materials without causing unwanted exposure.

dark slide *See slide (2).*

daylight film Color film that is balanced to produce accurate color renditions when the light source illuminating the photographed scene has a color temperature of about 5500K, such as in midday sunlight or with electronic flash or a blue flashbulb.

dedicated flash An electronic flash unit that, when used with certain cameras, will automatically set the correct shutter speed for use with flash and will trigger a light in the viewfinder when the flash is charged and ready to fire. Also called designated flash.

dense Describes a negative or an area of a negative in which a large amount of silver has been deposited. A dense negative transmits relatively little light. Opposite: *thin.*

densitometer An instrument that measures the darkness or density of a negative or print.

density The relative amount of silver present in various areas of film or paper after exposure or development. Therefore, the darkness of a photographic print or the light-stopping ability of a negative or transparency.

depth of field The area between the nearest and farthest points from the camera that are acceptably sharp in the focused image.

depth of focus The small range of error within which an acceptably sharp image is produced when a lens is focused.

designated flash *See dedicated flash.*

developer A chemical solution that changes the invisible, latent image produced during exposure into a visible one.

development 1) The entire process by which exposed film or paper is treated with various chemicals to make an image that is visible and permanent. 2) Specifically, the step in which film or paper is immersed in developer.

diaphragm The mechanism controlling the brightness of light that passes through a lens. An iris diaphragm has overlapping metal leaves whose central opening can be adjusted to a larger or smaller size. *See aperture.*

dichroic head An enlarger head that contains yellow, magenta, and cyan filters that can be moved in calibrated stages into or out of the light beam to change the color balance of the enlarging light.

diffuse Scattered, not all coming from the same direction. For example, the light on a cloudy day.

diffusion enlarger An enlarger that illuminates the negative by scattering light from many angles evenly over the surface of the negative.

DIN A numerical rating used in Europe to describe the sensitivity of film to light. The DIN rating increases by 3 as the sensitivity of the film doubles.

diopter An optician's term to describe the power of a lens. In photography, it mainly indicates the magnifying power and focal length of a supplementary close-up lens.

distortion 1) A lens aberration that causes straight lines at the edge of an image to appear curved. 2) The changes in perspective that take place when a lens is used very close to (wide-angle effect) or very far from (telephoto effect) a subject.

dodge To lighten an area of a print by shading it during part of the printing exposure.

dropout An image with black and white areas only and no intermediate gray tones. Usually made by using high-contrast lith film.

dry down To become very slightly darker and less

contrasty, as most photographic printing papers do while they dry after processing.

dry mount To attach a print to another surface, usually cardboard, by placing a sheet of dry-mount tissue between the print and the mounting surface. This sandwich is placed in a heated mounting press to melt an adhesive in the tissue.

easel A holder to keep sensitized material, normally paper, flat and in position on the baseboard of an enlarger during projection printing. It may have adjustable borders to frame the image to various sizes.

electromagnetic spectrum The forms of radiant energy arranged by size of wavelength ranging from thousand-millionths of a millimeter (gamma rays) to several miles (radio waves). The visible spectrum is the part that the human eye sees as light: wavelengths of 400 to 700 nanometers (billionths of a meter), producing the sensation of the colors violet, blue, green, yellow, and red.

electronic flash A tube containing gas that produces a brief, brilliant flash of light when electrified. Unlike a flashbulb, an electronic flash unit is reusable. Also called a strobe.

emulsion A light-sensitive coating applied to photographic films or papers. It consists of silver halide crystals and other chemicals suspended in gelatin.

enlargement An image, usually a print, that is larger than the negative. Made by projecting an enlarged image of the negative onto sensitized paper.

enlarger An optical instrument ordinarily used to project an image of a negative onto sensitized paper. More accurately called a projection printer because it can project an image that is either larger or smaller than the negative.

etch To remove a small, dark imperfection in a print or negative by scraping away part of the emulsion.

exposure 1) The act of letting light fall on a light-sensitive material. 2) The amount of light reaching the light-sensitive material; specifically, the intensity of light multiplied by the length of time it falls on the material.

exposure meter An instrument that measures the amount of light falling on a subject (incident-light meter) or emitted or reflected by a subject (reflected-light meter), allowing aperture and shutter speed settings to be computed. Commonly called a light meter.

extension tubes Metal rings that can be attached between a camera body and lens for close-up work. They extend the lens farther than normal from the film plane so that the lens can focus closer than normal to an object.

factor A number that tells how many times exposure must be increased to compensate for loss of light (for example, due to use of a filter).

Farmer's reducer A solution of potassium ferricyanide and sodium thiosulfate that is used to decrease the amount of silver in a developed image.

fast Describes 1) a film or paper that is very sensitive to light; 2) a lens that opens to a very wide aperture; 3) a short shutter speed. Opposite: *slow.*

ferrotype To give a glossy printing paper a very high sheen by drying the print with its emulsion pressed against a smooth metal plate, usually the hot metal drum or plate of a heat dryer.

fiber-base paper Formerly the standard type of paper available; now being replaced to a certain extent by resin-coated papers. Printed instructions for washing, drying, and so forth refer to fiber-base papers unless resin-coated papers are specifically mentioned.

field curvature A lens aberration or defect that causes the image to be formed along a curve instead of on a flat plane.

fill light A source of illumination that lightens shadows cast by the main light and thereby reduces the contrast in a photograph.

film The material used in a camera to record a photographic image. Generally it is a light-sensitive emulsion coated on a flexible acetate or plastic base.

film holder A light-tight container to hold the sheet film used in a view camera.

film plane See *focal plane.*

film speed The relative sensitivity to light of a film. There are several rating systems: ISO/ASA (the most common in the United States and Great Britain), DIN (common in Europe), and others. Film speed ratings increase as the sensitivity of the film increases.

filter 1) A piece of colored glass, plastic, or other material that selectively absorbs some of the wavelengths of light passing through it. 2) To use such a filter to modify the wavelengths of light reaching a light-sensitive material.

filter factor See *factor.*

fisheye lens A lens with an extremely wide angle of view (as much as 180°) and considerable barrel distortion (straight lines at the edges of a scene appear to curve around the center of the image).

fixer A chemical solution (sodium thiosulfate or ammonium thiosulfate) that makes a photographic image insensitive to light. It dissolves unexposed silver halide crystals while leaving the developed silver image. Also called hypo.

flare Unwanted light that reflects and scatters inside a lens or camera. When it reaches the film, it causes a loss of contrast in the image.

flash 1) A light source, such as a flashbulb or strobe, that emits a very brief, bright burst of light. 2) To blacken an area in a print by exposing it to white light, such as from a penlight flashlight.

flash bar or **flash cube** A lighting device containing several very small flashbulbs and producing several separate flashes before the unit is discarded.

flashbulb A bulb containing a mass of aluminum wire, oxygen, and an explosive primer. When the primer is electrically fired, it ignites the wire, which emits a brief burst of brilliant light. A flashbulb is used once and then discarded.

flash meter An exposure meter that measures the brightness of flash lighting to determine the correct exposure for a particular setup.

flat 1) A scene, negative, or print with very little difference in brightness between light and dark areas. Opposite: *contrasty.* 2) See *reflector.*

floodlight An electric light designed to produce a broad, relatively diffused beam of light.

f-number A number that equals the focal length of a lens divided by the diameter of the aperture at a given stop. Theoretically, all lenses at the same f-number produce images of equal brightness.

focal length The distance from the lens to the focal plane when the lens is focused on infinity. The longer the focal length, the greater the magnification of the image.

focal plane The plane or surface on which a focused lens forms a sharp image. Also called the film plane.

focal-plane shutter A camera mechanism that admits light to expose film by moving a slit or opening in a roller blind just in front of the film (focal) plane.

focal point The point on a focused image where the rays of light intersect after reflecting from a single point on a subject.

focus 1) The position at which rays of light from a lens converge to form a sharp image. 2) To adjust the distance between lens and image to make the image as sharp as possible.

focusing cloth A dark cloth used in focusing a view camera. The cloth fits over the camera back and the photographer's head to keep out light and to make the ground-glass image more visible.

fog An overall density in the photographic image caused by unintentional exposure to light or unwanted chemical activity.

frame 1) The edges of an image. 2) A single image in a roll of film.

f-stop See *f-number, stop.*

full-scale Describes a print having a wide range of tonal values from deep, rich black through many shades of gray to brilliant white.

gelatin A substance produced from animal skins and bones, it is the basis for modern photographic emulsions. It holds light-sensitive silver halide crystals in suspension.

glossy Describes a printing paper with a great deal of surface sheen. Opposite: *matte.*

graded-contrast paper A printing paper that produces a single level of contrast. To produce less or more contrast, a change has to be made to another grade of paper. *See variable-contrast paper.*

graininess In an enlarged image, a speckled or mottled effect caused by clumps of silver in the negative.

gray card A card that reflects a known percentage of the light falling on it. Often has a gray side reflecting 18 percent and a white side reflectng 90 percent of the light. Used to take accurate exposure meter readings (meters base their exposures on a gray tone of 18 percent reflectance) or to provide a known gray tone in color work.

ground glass 1) A piece of glass roughened on one side so that an image focused on it can be seen on the other side. 2) The viewing screen in a reflex or view camera.

guide number A number used to calculate the f-setting (aperture) that correctly exposes a film of a given sensitivity (ASA rating) when the film is used with a specific flash unit at various distances from flash to subject. To find the f-setting, divide the guide number by the distance (usually in feet).

gum-bichromate process An early photographic process revived by contemporary photographers. The emulsion is a sensitized gum solution containing color pigments. The surface can be altered by hand during the printing process.

halftone An image that can be reproduced on the same printing press with ordinary type. The tones of gray in the photograph are screened to a pattern of dots (close together in dark areas, farther apart in light areas) that give the illusion of continuous tone.

hanger A frame for holding sheet film during processing in a tank.

hard 1) Describes a scene, negative, or print of high contrast. Opposite: *soft or low contrast.* 2) Describes a printing paper emulsion of high contrast such as grades 5 and 6.

heliography An early photographic process, invented by Niépce, employing a polished pewter plate coated with bitumen of Judea, a substance that hardens on exposure to light.

highlight A very bright area in a scene, print, or transparency; a very dense, dark area in a negative. Also called a high value.

hot shoe A bracket on the top of the camera that attaches a flash unit and provides an electrical connection to synchronize the camera shutter with the firing of the flash.

hyperfocal distance The distance to the nearest plane of the depth of field (the nearest object in focus) when the lens is focused on infinity. Also the distance to the plane of sharpest focus when infinity is at the farthest plane of the depth of field. Focusing on the hyperfocal distance extends the depth of field from half the hyperfocal distance to infinity.

hypo A common name for any fixer; taken from the abbreviation for sodium hyposulfite, the previous name for sodium thiosulfate (the active ingredient in most fixers).

hypo clearing agent or **hypo neutralizing agent** *See washing aid.*

illuminance The strength of light falling on a given area of a surface. Measurable by an incident-light (illuminance) meter.

illuminance meter *See incident-light meter.*

incandescent light Light emitted when a substance is heated by electricity: for example, the tungsten filament in an ordinary light bulb.

incident-light meter An exposure meter that measures the amount of light incident to (falling on) a subject.

indoor film *See Type A film, tungsten film.*

infinity The farthest position (marked ∞) on the distance scale of a lens. It includes all objects at the infinity distance (about 50 feet) from the lens or farther. When the infinity distance is within the depth of field, all objects at that distance or farther will be sharp.

infrared The band of invisible rays just beyond red, which people perceive somewhat as heat. Some photographic materials are sensitized to record infrared.

instant film A film such as Polaroid SX-70 or Kodak Instant Color Film that contains the chemicals needed to automatically develop an image after exposure without the need for darkroom development.

intensification A process increasing the darkness of an already developed image. Used to improve negatives that have too little silver density to make a good print.

interchangeable lens A lens that can be removed from the camera and replaced with another lens, usually of a different focal length.

inverse square law A law of physics stating that the intensity of illumination is inversely proportional to the square of the distance between light and subject. This means that if the distance between light and subject is doubled, the illumination will drop to one quarter of the original. The exposure must be increased accordingly for consistent results.

ISO A film speed rating similar to an ASA rating.

Kelvin temperature *See color temperature.*
key light *See main light.*

latent image An image formed by the changes to the silver halide grains in photographic emulsion upon exposure to light. The image is not visible until chemical development takes place.

latitude The amount of over- or underexposure possible without a significant loss in the quality of an image.

leaf shutter A camera mechanism that admits light to expose film by opening and shutting a circle of overlapping metal leaves.

lens A piece or several pieces of optical glass shaped to focus an image of a subject.

lens shade A shield that fits around a lens to prevent unwanted light from hitting the front of the lens and causing flare. Also called a lens hood.

light meter *See exposure meter.*

light-tight Absolutely dark. Protected by material, overlapping panels, or some other system of baffles through which light cannot pass.

line print An image resembling a pen-and-ink drawing, with black lines on a white background (or white lines on a black background). It is made with high-contrast lith film. Also called tone line print.

lith film A type of film made primarily for use in graphic arts and printing. It produces an image with very high contrast.

local reduction *See reduction (3).*

long lens A lens whose focal length is longer than the diagonal measurement of the film with which it is used. The angle of view with such a lens / film size combination is narrower at a given distance than the angle that the human eye sees.

luminance The light reflected or produced by a given area of a subject in a specific direction. Measurable by a reflected-light (luminance) meter.

luminance meter *See reflected-light meter.*

macro lens A lens designed for taking close-up pictures. Sometimes called a micro lens.

macrophotograph *See photomacrograph.*

main light The principal source of light in a photograph, casting the dominant shadows and defining the texture and volume of the subject. Often refers to a studio setup. Also called key light.

manual exposure A nonautomatic mode of camera operation in which the photographer sets both the shutter speed and the aperture.

manual flash A nonautomatic mode of flash operation in which the photographer controls the exposure by adjusting the size of the aperture.

mat A cardboard rectangle with an opening cut in it that is placed over a print to frame it. Also called an overmat.

mat knife A short knife blade (usually replaceable) set in a large, easy-to-hold handle. Used for cutting cardboard mounts for prints.

matte Describes a printing paper with a relatively dull, nonreflective surface. Opposite: *glossy.*

micro lens *See macro lens.*

middle gray A standard average gray tone of 18 percent reflectance. *See gray card.*

midtone An area of medium brightness, neither a very dark shadow nor a very bright highlight. A medium gray tone in a print.

modeling light A small tungsten light built into

some flash units. It helps the photographer judge the effect of various light positions because the duration of flash light is too brief to be judged directly.

mottle   A mealy gray area of uneven development in a print or negative. Caused by too little agitation or too short a time in the developer.

narrow lighting   *See short lighting.*

negative   1) Any image with tones that are the reverse of those in the subject. Opposite: positive. 2) The film in the camera during exposure and subsequently developed to produce a negative image.

negative film   Film that produces a negative image on exposure and development.

nonsilver process   A printing process that does not depend on the sensitivity of silver to form an image. For example, the cyanotype process, in which the light-sensitive emulsion consists of a mixture of iron salts.

normal lens   A lens whose focal length is about the same as the diagonal measurement of the film with which it is used. The angle of view with this lens / film size combination is roughly the same at a given distance as the angle that the human eye sees clearly.

notching code   Notches cut in the margin of sheet film so that the type of film and its emulsion side can be identified in the dark.

one-shot developer   A developer used once and then discarded.

opaque   Describes 1) any substance or surface that will not allow light to pass; 2) a paint used to block out portions of a negative so that they will not allow light to pass during printing.

open up   To increase the size of a lens aperture. Opposite: *stop down.*

orthochromatic   Film that is sensitive to blue and green but not to red wavelengths of the visible spectrum. Abbreviated ortho.

overdevelop   To give more than the normal amount of development.

overexpose   To give too much exposure to film or paper. The resulting silver density is too great for best results.

oxidation   Loss of chemical activity due to contact with oxygen in the air.

pan   1) To follow the motion of a moving object with the camera. This will cause the object to look sharp and the background blurred. 2) *See panchromatic.*

panchromatic   Film that is sensitive to all (or almost all) wavelengths of the visible spectrum. Abbreviated pan.

parallax   The difference in point of view that occurs when the lens (or other device) through which the eye views a scene is separate from the lens that exposes the film.

PC connector   *See synch cord.*

PC terminal   The socket on a camera or flash unit into which a PC connector (synch cord) is inserted.

perspective   The apparent size and depth of objects within an image.

photoflood   An incandescent lamp that produces a very bright light but has a relatively short life.

photogram   An image formed by placing material directly onto a sheet of sensitized film or printing paper and then exposing the sheet to light.

photomacrograph   A close-up photograph that is life size or larger. Also called macrophotograph.

photomicrograph   A photograph that is taken through a compound microscope.

photomontage   A composite image made by cutting out and assembling parts of several photographs.

pincushion distortion   A lens aberration or defect that causes straight lines to bow inward toward the center of the image.

pinhole   1) A small clear spot on a negative usually caused by dust on the film during exposure or development or by a small air bubble that keeps developer from the film during development. 2) The tiny opening in a pinhole camera that produces a blurred but recognizable image.

plane of critical focus   The part of a scene that is most sharply focused.

plate   In early photographic processes, the sheet of glass or metal on which emulsion was coated.

platinum print   A print in which the final image is formed in platinum rather than silver.

polarizing filter   A filter that reduces reflections from nonmetallic surfaces such as glass or water by blocking light waves that are vibrating at selected angles to the filter.

positive   Any image with tones corresponding to those of the subject. Opposite: *negative.*

posterization   An image with a flat, posterlike quality. High-contrast lith film is used to separate the continuous gray tones of a negative into a few distinct shades of gray.

presoak   To soak film briefly in water prior to immersing it in developer.

primary colors   Basic colors from which all other colors can be mixed. *See subtractive, additive.*

print   1) A photographic image, usually a positive one on paper. 2) To produce such an image from a negative by contact or projection printing.

printing frame   A holder designed to keep sensitized material, usually paper, in full contact with a negative during contact printing.

programmed automatic   A mode of automatic exposure in which the camera sets both the shutter speed and the aperture that will produce the correct exposure.

projection printing   The process of projecting an image of a negative onto sensitized material, usually paper. The image may be projected to any size, usually larger than the negative.

projector   An optical instrument for forming the enlarged image of a transparency or a motion picture on a screen.

proof   A test print made for the purpose of evaluating density, contrast, color balance, subject composition, and the like.

push   To expose film at a higher film speed rating than normal, then to compensate in part for the resulting underexposure by giving greater development than normal. This permits shooting at a dimmer light level, a faster shutter speed, or a smaller aperture than would otherwise be possible.

rangefinder   1) A device on a camera that measures the distance from camera to subject and shows when the subject is in focus. 2) A camera equipped with a rangefinder focusing device.

RC paper   *See resin-coated paper.*

rear nodal points   The point in a lens from which lens focal length (distance from lens to image plane) is measured. Undeviated rays of light cross the lens axis and each other at this point.

reciprocity law   The theoretical relationship between length of exposure and intensity of light, stating that an increase in one will be balanced by a decrease in the other. For example, doubling the light intensity should be balanced exactly by halving the exposure time. In fact, the law does not hold true for very long or very short exposures. This reciprocity failure or reciprocity effect causes underexposure unless the exposure is increased. It also causes color shifts in color materials.

reducing agent   The active ingredient in a developer. It changes exposed silver halide crystals into dark metallic silver. Also called the developing agent.

reduction   1) A print that is smaller than the size of the negative. 2) The part of development in which exposed silver halide crystals forming an invisible latent image are converted to visible metallic silver. 3) A process that decreases the amount of dark silver in a developed image. Negatives are usually reduced to decrease density. Prints are reduced locally (only in certain parts) to brighten highlights. Opposite: *intensification.*

reel   A metal or plastic reel with spiral grooves into which roll film is loaded for development.

reflected-light meter   An exposure meter that measures the amount of light reflected or emitted by a subject. Sometimes called a luminance meter.

reflector   1) A reflective surface, such as a piece of white cardboard, that can be positioned to redirect light, especially into shadow areas. Also called a flat. 2) A reflective surface, often bowl-shaped, that is placed behind a lamp to direct more light from the lamp toward the subject.

reflex camera   A camera with a built-in mirror that reflects the scene being photographed onto a ground-glass viewing screen. *See single-lens reflex, twin-lens reflex.*

relative aperture   *See aperture.*

replenisher   A substance added to some types of developers after use to replace exhausted chemicals so that the developer can be used again.

resin-coated paper   Printing paper with a water-resistant coating that absorbs less moisture than uncoated paper, consequently reducing some processing times. Abbreviated RC.

reticulation   A crinkling of the gelatin emulsion on film that can be caused by extreme temperature changes during processing.

reversal   A process for making a positive image directly from film exposed in the camera; also for making a negative image directly from a negative or a positive image from a positive transparency.

reversal film   Film that produces a positive image (a transparency) on exposure and development.

roll film   Film that comes in a roll, protected from light by a length of paper wound around the film. Loosely applies to any film packaged in a roll rather than in flat sheets.

Sabattier effect   A partial reversal of tones that occurs when film or paper is reexposed to light during development. Commonly called solarization.

safelight   A light used in the darkroom during printing to provide general illumination without giving unwanted exposure.

sharp   Describes an image or part of an image that shows crisp, precise texture and detail. Opposite: *blurred or soft.*

sheet film   Film that is cut into individual flat pieces. Also called cut film.

short lens   A lens whose focal length is shorter than the diagonal measurement of the film with which it is used. The angle of view with this lens / film combination is greater at a given distance than the angle seen by the human eye. Also called a wide-angle or wide-field lens.

short lighting   A portrait lighting setup in which the main source of light illuminates the side of the face partially turned away from the camera. Also called narrow lighting.

shutter   A mechanism that opens and closes to admit light into a camera for a measured length of time.

shutter-priority   A mode of automatic exposure in which the photographer selects the shutter speed and the camera sets the aperture that will produce the correct exposure.

silhouette   A scene or photograph in which the background is much more brightly lit than the subject.

silver halide   The light-sensitive part of common photographic emulsions; the compounds silver chloride, silver bromide, and silver iodide.

single-lens reflex   A camera in which the image formed by the taking lens is reflected by a mirror onto a ground-glass screen for viewing. The mirror swings out of the way just before exposure to let the image reach the film. Abbreviated SLR.

slide   1) A transparency (often a positive image in color) mounted between glass or in a frame of cardboard or other material so that it may be inserted into a projector. 2) A protective cover that is removed from a sheet film holder when film in the holder is to be exposed. Also called dark slide.

slow   *See fast.*

sodium thiosulfate   The active ingredient in most fixers.

soft   1) Describes an image that is blurred or out of focus. Opposite: sharp. 2) Describes a scene, negative, or print of low contrast. Opposite: *hard or high contrast.* 3) Describes a printing paper emulsion of low contrast, such as grade 0 or 1.

solarization   A reversal of image tones that occurs when film is massively overexposed. *See Sabattier effect.*

speed   1) The relative sensitivity to light of film or paper. 2) The relative ability of a lens to admit more light by opening to a wider aperture.

spherical aberration   A lens defect that causes rays that strike at the edges of the lens to be bent more than rays that strike at the center.

spot   To remove small imperfections in a print caused by dust specks, small scratches, or the like. Specifically, to paint a dye over small white blemishes.

spotlight   An electric light that contains a small, bright lamp, a reflector, and often a lens to concentrate the light. Designed to produce a narrow beam of bright light.

spot meter   A reflected-light exposure meter with a very small angle of view, used to measure the brightness of a small portion of a subject.

stereograph   A pair of photographs taken side by side and seen separately by each eye in viewing them through a stereoscope. The resulting image looks three-dimensional.

stock solution   A concentrated chemical solution that must be diluted before use.

stop   1) A diaphragm setting on a lens at one of its apertures. 2) A change in exposure by a factor of two. One stop more exposure doubles the light reaching film or paper. One stop less halves the exposure. Either the aperture or the exposure time can be changed. 3) *See stop down.*

stop bath   An acid solution used between the developer and the fixer to stop the action of the developer and to preserve the effectiveness of the fixer. Generally a dilute solution of acetic acid; plain water is sometimes used as a stop bath for film development.

stop down   To decrease the size of a lens aperture. Opposite: *open up.*

strobe   *See electronic flash.*

subtractive color   A way to produce colors by mixing dyes that contain varying proportions of the three subtractive primary colors—cyan, magenta, and yellow. Each dye subtracts its color from white light, leaving a balance of colored light. Dyes that absorb all wavelengths of light produce black.

supplementary lens   A lens that can be added to a camera lens for close-up work. It magnifies the image and permits focusing closer than normal to an object.

synch cord   An electrical cord connecting a flash unit with a camera so that the two can be synchronized. Pronounced "sink." *See synchronize.*

synchronize   To cause a flash unit to fire at the same time as the camera shutter is open.

synchro-sun   A way to use flash lighting as fill light in a photograph made in direct sunlight. The flash lightens the shadows, decreasing the contrast in the scene.

T   *See time.*

tacking iron   A small, electrically heated tool used to melt the adhesive in dry-mount tissue, attaching it partially to the back of the print and to the mounting surface. This keeps the print in place during the mounting procedure.

taking lens   The lens on a camera through which light passes to expose the film.

tank   A container for developer or other processing chemicals into which film is placed for development.

telephoto effect   A change in perspective caused by using a long focal length lens very far from all parts of a scene. Objects appear closer together than they really are.

telephoto lens   Loosely, any lens of very long focal length. Specifically, one constructed so that its effective focal length is longer than its actual size.

tenting   A way to light a highly reflective object. The object is surrounded with large sheets of paper or translucent material lighted so that the object reflects them and not the lamps, camera, and other items in the studio.

thin   Describes a negative or an area of a negative where relatively little silver has been deposited. A thin negative transmits a large amount of light. Opposite: *dense.*

time   A shutter setting marked *T* at which the shutter remains open until reclosed by the photographer.

tintype   An old collodion wet-plate process in which the emulsion was coated onto a dark metal plate. It produced a positive image.

tone   1) To change the color of a print by immersing it in a chemical solution. 2) The lightness or darkness of a particular area. A highlight is a light tone, a shadow is a dark tone.

transparency   An image set on a transparent base, such as film or glass, and viewed by transmitted light. *See slide (1).*

tripod A three-legged support for a camera. Usually the height is adjustable and the top or head is movable.

tungsten film Color film balanced to produce accurate color renditions when the light source that illuminates the scene has a color temperature of about 3200K, as do many tungsten lamps. Sometimes called Type B film. *See Type A film.*

tungsten light Light such as that from an ordinary light bulb containing a thin tungsten wire that becomes incandescent (emits light) when an electric current is passed along it. Also called incandescent light.

twin-lens reflex A camera in which two lenses are mounted above one another. The bottom (taking) lens forms an image on the exposed film. The top (viewing) lens forms an image that reflects upward onto a ground-glass viewing screen. Abbreviated TLR.

Type A film Color film balanced to produce accurate color renditions when the light source that illuminates the scene has a color temperature of about 3400K, as does a photoflood. *See tungsten film.*

Type B film *See tungsten film.*

ultraviolet The part of the spectrum just beyond violet. Ultraviolet light is invisible to the human eye but strongly affects photographic materials.

underdevelop To give less development than normal.

underexpose To give too little exposure to film or paper. The resulting silver density is less than necessary for best results.

value The relative lightness or darkness of an area. Low values are dark; high values are light.

variable-contrast paper A printing paper in which varying grades of print contrast can be obtained by changing the color of the enlarging light source, as by the use of filters. *See graded-contrast paper.*

view camera A camera in which the taking lens forms an image directly on a ground-glass viewing screen. A film holder is inserted in front of the viewing screen before exposure. The front and back of the camera can be set at various angles to change focus and perspective.

viewfinder A device on a camera through which the subject is seen and framed.

viewing lens The lens on a camera through which the eye views the subject.

viewing screen In a reflex or view camera, the ground-glass surface on which the image is seen and focused.

vignette To underexpose the edges of an image. Sometimes done intentionally but more often caused accidentally by a lens that forms an image covering the film or paper only partially.

warm Reddish colors that by association with common objects (fire, sun, and so on) give an impression of warmth.

washing aid A chemical solution used between fixing and washing film or paper. It shortens the washing time by converting residues from the fixer into forms more easily dissolved by water. Also called hypo neutralizing (or clearing) agent.

wet-plate process A photographic process in which a glass or metal plate was coated with a collodion mixture, then sensitized with silver nitrate, exposed, and developed while the collodion was still wet. It was popular from the 1850s until the introduction of the gelatin dry plate in the 1880s.

wetting agent A chemical solution used after washing film. By reducing the surface tension of the water remaining on the film, it speeds drying and prevents water spots.

white light A mixture of all wavelengths of the visible spectrum. The human eye sees the mixture as light that is colorless or white.

wide-angle distortion A change in perspective caused by using a wide-angle lens very close to a subject. Objects appear stretched out or farther apart than they really are.

wide-angle lens *See short lens.*

working solution A chemical solution diluted to the correct strength for use.

zone focus To preset the focus of a lens so that some future action will take place within the limits of the depth of field.

Zone System A way to plan negative exposure and development to achieve precise control of the darkness of various areas in a print.

zoom lens A lens adjustable to a range of focal lengths.

Bibliography

This bibliography is only a sampling of the literature of photography, which is so extensive that it requires two volumes of its own: *Photographic Literature* and *Photographic Literature 1960–1970,* edited by Albert Boni (Dobbs Ferry, NY: Morgan & Morgan, 1962 and 1972). The Boni bibliographies list more than 32,000 works under 2900 headings and include works on photographic techniques, theory, chemistry, physics, history, biography, aesthetics, and many other subjects.

A useful listing of information is available from the Eastman Kodak Co. (Rochester, NY 14650). Their *Index to Kodak Information* lists the more than 800 books and pamphlets that they publish for a variety of photographic interests ranging from *Good Color Pictures—Quick and Easy* to *Photography Under Arctic Conditions.*

Technical Information: Basic

This book is a basic introductory text in photography, and you will find that other basic textbooks generally cover the same topics. However, you may want to consult one or more additional beginner's texts because authors explain material in individual ways and may emphasize different points. The following books are of about the same level of difficulty as this one.

Blaker, Alfred A. *Photography: Art and Technique.* San Francisco, W. H. Freeman, 1980.

Craven, George M. *Object and Image: An Introduction to Photography.* Englewood Cliffs, NJ: Prentice-Hall, 1975. Explores various styles—reportorial, symbolistic, and so on.

Davis, Phil. *Photography,* 4th ed. Dubuque, IA: William C. Brown, 1982. Covers technical material more extensively than the others.

Horenstein, Henry. *Black and White Photography: A Basic Manual,* 2nd ed. Boston: Little, Brown, 1983.

———. *Beyond Basic Photography.* Boston: Little, Brown, 1977.

Swedlund, Charles. *Photography,* 2nd ed. New York: Holt, Rinehart and Winston, 1981.

Vestal, David. *The Craft of Photography.* New York: Harper & Row, 1974.

Technical Information: Advanced or Specialized

The following books will be useful when you are familiar with the basic material in this text.

Adams, Ansel. *The New Ansel Adams Photography Series,* with Robert Baker. *The Camera,* 1980; *The Negative,* 1981; *The Print,* 1983; *Polaroid Land Photography,* 1978. Boston: New York Graphic Society. Also, from the earlier *Basic Photo Series: Natural-Light Photography,* 1971; *Artificial-Light Photography,* 1968. Boston: New York Graphic Society. Stresses full technical control of the photographic process as an aid to creative expression.

Carroll, John S. *Photographic Lab Handbook,* 5th ed. New York: Amphoto, 1979.

Clerc, L. P. *Photography: Theory and Practice.* Garden City, NY: Amphoto, 1973. A detailed technical reference.

Crawford, William. *The Keepers of Light. A History and Working Guide to Early Photographic Processes.* Dobbs Ferry, NY: Morgan & Morgan, 1979. The history of early photographic media such as the ambrotype, cyanotype, platinum print, gum bichromate print, and others, plus clear directions on how to make these prints yourself.

Eastman Kodak Co. *Printing Color Negatives.* Rochester, NY: Eastman Kodak Co., 1978. Useful information on how to make color prints in general using Kodak materials in particular.

Eaton, George T. *Photographic Chemistry.* Dobbs Ferry, NY: Morgan & Morgan, 1965. Understandable without formal training in chemistry or physics.

The Focal Encyclopedia of Photography. New York: McGraw-Hill, 1971. Alphabetical arrangement of general technical information plus some historical material.

Gassan, Arnold. *Handbook for Contemporary Photography.* Athens, OH: Handbook Co., 1974. A general, advanced workbook with information on nonsilver processes.

Herwig, Ellis. *The Handbook of Color Photography.* New York: Amphoto, 1982.

Keefe, Lawrence E., Jr., and Dennis Inch. *The Life of a Photograph. Archival Processing, Matting, Framing and Storage.* Boston: Focal Press, 1984.

Kobre, Kenneth. *Photojournalism: The Professionals' Approach.* Somerville, MA: Curtin & London, 1980. A comprehensive and readable overview of equipment, techniques, and approaches used by photojournalists.

Langford, Michael J. *Advanced Photography,* 4th ed. Stoneham, MA: Focal Press, 1980.

Larmore, Lewis. *Introduction to Photographic Principles.* New York: Dover Publications, 1965. An inexpensive paperback covering basic chemical and physical theory.

Morgan, Douglas O., David Vestal, and William L. Broecker, eds. *Leica Manual.* Dobbs Ferry, NY: Morgan & Morgan, 1973. Useful information about a specific camera and 35mm photography in general. Other manufacturers also publish comprehensive manuals.

Nadler, Bob. *The Color Printing Manual.* New York: Amphoto, 1978.

Neblette, C. B. *Photography: Its Materials and Processes.* New York: Van Nostrand Reinhold, 1962. A complete, general reference to photographic technology.

Picker, Fred. *The Zone VI Workshop: The Fine Print in Black and White Photography.* Garden City, NY: Amphoto, 1974. Introduction to Zone System exposure plus the author's personal printing techniques.

Pittaro, Ernest M., ed. *Photo-Lab-Index.* Dobbs Ferry, NY: Morgan & Morgan, updated yearly. An extensive looseleaf storehouse of information provided by manufacturers of photographic products. Contains full descriptions of their materials and recommended procedures for their use.

Sealfon, Peggy. *The Magic of Instant Photography.* Boston: CBI Publishing, 1983.

Stone, Jim, ed. *Darkroom Dynamics: A Guide to Creative Darkroom Techniques.* Somerville, MA: Curtin & London, Inc., 1979. Illustrated instructions on how to expand your imagery with multiple printing, toning, hand coloring, high contrast, and other techniques.

Stroebel, Leslie. *View Camera Technique,* 3rd ed. New York: Hastings House Publishers, 1976.

Todd, Hollis N., and Richard D. Zakia. *Photographic Sensitometry: The Study of Tone Reproduction.* Dobbs Ferry, NY: Morgan & Morgan, 1969. Measuring, analyzing, and applying data on the effects of light on photographic materials.

White, Minor. *Zone System Manual.* Dobbs Ferry, NY: Morgan & Morgan, 1972. How to use the Zone System as a creative tool.

History, Criticism, Collections

Barrow, Thomas F., Shelley Armitage, and William E. Tydeman, eds. *Reading Into Photography: Selected Essays, 1959–1980.* Albuquerque: University of New Mexico Press, 1982.

Berger, John. *About Looking.* New York: Pantheon, 1980.

Booth, Pat, ed. *Master Photographers: The World's Great Photographers on Their Art and Technique.* New York: Clarkson N. Potter, 1983.

Browne, Turner, and Elaine Partnow. *Macmillan Biographical Encyclopedia of Photographic Artists and Innovators.* New York: Macmillan, 1983. Several thousand biographies; a *Who's Who* of photography.

Buckland, Gail. *Reality Recorded: Early Documentary Photography.* Boston: New York Graphic Society, 1974.

Coleman, A. D. *Light Readings: A Photography Critic's Writings 1968–1978.* New York: Oxford University Press, 1979.

Coe, Brian. *Cameras, from Daguerreotypes to Instant Pictures.* New York: Crown, 1978. A well-illustrated and complete history of the camera.

Earle, Edward W., ed. *Points of View: The Stereograph in America—A Cultural History.* Rochester, NY: Visual Studies Workshop Press, 1979.

Eauclaire, Sally. *The New Color Photography.* New York: Abbeville Press, 1981. An attempt at a critical vocabulary for color photographs.

Edey, Maitland. *Great Photographic Essays from Life.* Boston: New York Graphic Society, 1978. Twenty-two photographic essays including work by Abbott, Adams, Bourke-White, Cartier-Bresson, and others.

The Family of Man. New York: The Museum of Modern Art, 1955. Edward Steichen organized this show, which was probably the most publicized and widely seen photographic exhibition ever mounted.

Gernsheim, Helmut, and Alison Gernsheim. *The History of Photography 1685–1914*. New York: McGraw-Hill, 1969. A detailed history "from the camera obscura to the beginning of the modern era." Considerable information on European, particularly British, photography.

Green, Jonathan, ed. *Camera Work: A Critical Anthology*. Millerton, NY: Aperture, 1973. Extensive selections from *Camera Work*, "the photographic quarterly published by Alfred Stieglitz, illustrating the evolution of the avant garde in American art and photography from 1903–1917."

Hill, Paul and Thomas Cooper. *Dialogue with Photography*. New York: Farrar, Straus and Giroux, 1979. Interviews with 21 major figures in photography, including Beaton, Cartier-Bresson, Cunningham, Doisneau, Kértèsz, Man Ray, Newhall, W. E. Smith, Strand, and M. White.

Hodgson, Pat. *Early War Photographs*. Boston: New York Graphic Society, 1974. The first 50 years of war photography including coverage of the Crimean War and the American Civil War.

Hurley, F. Jack. *Portrait of a Decade: Roy Stryker and the Development of Documentary Photography in the Thirties*. Baton Rouge: Louisiana State University Press, 1972.

Jammes, André, and Eugenia P. Janis. *The Art of French Calotype*. Princeton, NJ: Princeton University Press, 1983. A scholarly work on Second Empire photography, elegantly produced.

Life Library of Photography, rev. ed. New York: Time-Life Books, 1981–1983. Seventeen volumes plus yearbooks (1973–1981), all profusely illustrated. The books generally contain historical material and technical information and discuss current trends.

The Literature of Photography Series. New York: Arno Press, 1973. Sixty-two long out-of-print technical manuals, historical accounts, and aesthetic treatises, including, for example, the 1858 *American Hand Book of the Daguerreotype*, which gives "the most approved and convenient methods for preparing the chemicals and combinations used in the art." Other publishers that have reprinted early photographic books include Morgan & Morgan (Dobbs Ferry, NY) and Dover Publications (New York).

Lyons, Nathan, ed. *Photographers on Photography: A Critical Anthology*. Englewood Cliffs, NJ: Prentice-Hall, 1966. Twenty-three well-known photographers (1880s to 1960s) discuss their own work and photography in general.

McQuaid, James, ed. *An Index to American Photographic Collections*. Boston: G. K. Hall, 1982. A comprehensive list of public collections: photographers (19,000) by institution (450) and vice versa.

Maddow, Ben. *Faces: A Narrative History of the Portrait in Photography*. Boston: New York

Graphic Society, 1977. Massive and comprehensive.

Mitchell, Margaretta K. *Recollections: Ten Women of Photography*. New York: The Viking Press, 1979. Pictures and recollections by Abbott, Bernhard, Dahl-Wolfe, and others.

Naef, Weston J., and James N. Wood. *Era of Exploration: The Rise of Landscape Photography in the American West, 1860–1885*. New York: The Metropolitan Museum of Art, 1975. Extensive treatment of the subject with emphasis on the photographers Watkins, O'Sullivan, Muybridge, Russell, and Jackson.

Newhall, Beaumont. *The Daguerreotype in America*, 3rd ed. New York: Dover Publications, 1976.

————. *The History of Photography from 1839 to the Present*, rev. ed. New York: Museum of Modern Art, and Boston: New York Graphic Society, 1982. The most widely used basic text on the history of photography. Everyone else is a revisionist.

————. *Latent Image: The Discovery of Photography*. Garden City, NY: Doubleday, 1967. An interesting account of early photographic research and discoveries.

————, ed. *Photography: Essays and Images*. New York: The Museum of Modern Art, 1980.

O'Neal, Hank. *A Vision Shared: A Classic Portrait of America and Its People, 1935–1943*. New York: St. Martin's Press, 1976.

Petruck, Peninah R., ed. *The Camera Viewed: Writings on Twentieth Century Photography*. Vol. 1: *Photography Before World War II*. Vol. 2: *Photography After World War II*. New York: E. P. Dutton, 1979. A worthwhile anthology of hard-to-find writing.

Pollack, Peter. *The Picture History of Photography*. New York: Harry N. Abrams, 1969. Useful for its many illustrations.

Rudisill, Richard. *Mirror Image: The Influence of the Daguerreotype on American Society*. Albuquerque: University of New Mexico Press, 1971. Fascinating social history of the cultural, commercial, and social effects of the daguerreotype on mid-19th century America.

Scharf, Aaron. *Art and Photography*. Baltimore: Penguin Books, 1974. The interrelationship of photography and painting.

Sontag, Susan. *On Photography*. New York: Farrar, Straus and Giroux, 1977. The relation of photography to art, reality, and other matters.

Szarkowski, John. *Looking at Photographs*. New York: The Museum of Modern Art, 1973. Szarkowski discusses 100 pictures from the museum's collection. An insightful, very readable, and highly recommended book.

————. *Mirrors and Windows: American Photography Since 1960*. New York: The Museum of Modern Art, 1978.

————. *The Photographer's Eye*. New York: The Museum of Modern Art, 1966. Five major concerns of photographers—the photograph itself, the detail, the frame, time, and vantage point—with excellent illustrations for each concept.

Taft, Robert. *Photography and the American Scene*. New York: Dover Publications, 1964; reprint of 1938 edition. A detailed account of photography's introduction and growth in the United States between 1839 and 1889.

Tucker, Anne. *The Woman's Eye*. New York: Knopf, 1973. Biographies and statements of ten American women photographers and a portfolio of photographs by each. The book explores "the role played by sexual identity both in the creation and the evaluation of photographic art."

Witkin, Lee, and Barbara (Upton) London. *The Photograph Collector's Guide*. Boston: New York Graphic Society, 1979. Information of general photographic interest as well as for collectors, such as: biographical entries with illustrations for over 200 photographers; lists of over 8000 other photographers, museums, galleries, and so on.

Individual Photographers

The photographers listed below have pictures in this book.

Berenice Abbott
————. *Berenice Abbott: Photographs*. New York: Horizon Press, 1970.
————. *Changing New York*. Text by Elizabeth McCausland. New York: E. P. Dutton, 1939. Reprinted as *New York in the Thirties*. New York: Dover Publications, 1973.

Ansel Adams
————. *Ansel Adams: Images 1923–1974*. Foreword by Wallace Stegner. Boston: New York Graphic Society, 1974
————. *Yosemite and the Range of Light*. Intro. by Paul Brooks. Boston: New York Graphic Society, 1979.

Diane Arbus
————. *Diane Arbus*. ed. by Doon Arbus and Marvin Israel. Millerton, NY: Aperture, 1972.
————. *Diane Arbus Magazine Work*. Text by Thomas W. Southall. Millerton, NY: Aperture, 1984.
Bosworth, Patricia. *Diane Arbus: A Biography*. New York: Knopf, 1984.

Eve Arnold
————. *In China*. New York: Knopf, 1980.
————. *Unretouched Women*. New York: Knopf, 1976.

Eugène Atget
Abbott, Berenice. *The World of Atget*. New York: Horizon Press, 1964.
The Work of Atget. Ed. by John Szarkowski and Maria Morris Hambourg. New York: Museum of Modern Art, and Boston: New York Graphic Society. Vol. 1: *Old France*, 1981. Vol. 2: *The Art of Old Paris*, 1982. Vol. 3: *The Ancien Regime*, 1983. Vol. 4: *Modern Times*, 1984.

Morley Baer
Olmsted, Roger, and T. H. Watkins. *Here Today: San Francisco's Architectural Heritage*. San Francisco: Chronicle Books, 1968.

Cecil Beaton

———. *The Best of Beaton*. Intro. by Truman Capote. New York: Macmillan, 1968.

———. *Beaton*. Ed. James Danziger. New York: Viking, 1980.

Harry Benson

———. *Harry Benson on Photojournalism*. Text by Gigi and Harry Benson. New York: Harmony Books, 1982.

Ruth Bernhard

———. *The Big Heart*. Text by Melvin Van. New York: Fearon Publishers, 1957.

Margaret Bourke-White

———. *The Photographs of Margaret Bourke-White*. Ed. by Sean Callahan. Boston: New York Graphic Society, 1972.

———. *Portrait of Myself*. New York: Simon & Schuster, 1963.

Silverman, Jonathan. *For the World to See: The Life of Margaret Bourke-White*. New York: Viking, 1983.

Julia Margaret Cameron

Gernsheim, Helmut. *Julia Margaret Cameron: Her Life and Photographic Work*. Millerton, NY: Aperture, 1975.

A Victorian Album: Julia Margaret Cameron and Her Circle. Ed. by Graham Ovenden. New York: Da Capo, 1975.

Paul Caponigro

———. *Paul Caponigro*. Millerton, NY: Aperture, 1972.

———. *Landscape*. New York: McGraw-Hill, 1975.

———. *The Wise Silence*. Ed. by Marianne Fulton. Boston: New York Graphic Society, 1983.

Henri Cartier-Bresson

———. *Henri Cartier-Bresson*. Millerton, NY: Aperture, 1976.

———. *Henri Cartier-Bresson: Photographer*. Essay by Yves Bonnefoy. Boston: New York Graphic Society, 1979.

———. *The Decisive Moment*. New York: Simon & Schuster, 1952.

Marie Cosindas

———. *Marie Cosindas: Color Photographs*. Essay by Tom Wolfe. Boston: New York Graphic Society, 1978.

Robert Cumming

———. *Cumming Photographs*. Text by James Alinder. Carmel, CA: The Friends of Photography, 1979.

Imogen Cunningham

———. *Imogen! . . . Photographs 1910–1973*. Intro. by Margery Mann. Seattle: University of Washington Press, 1974.

Dater, Judy. *Imogen Cunningham: A Portrait*. Boston: New York Graphic Society, 1979.

L. J. M. Daguerre

———. *A Historical and Descriptive Account of the Various Processes of the Daguerreotype and the Diorama*, 1839. Reprint with introduction by Beaumont Newhall. New York: Winter House, 1971.

Gernsheim, Helmut and Alison. *L. J. M. Daguerre:*

The History of the Diorama and the Daguerreotype. London: Secker & Warburg, 1956. Bibliography. U.S. ed., New York: Dover, 1968.

Louise Dahl-Wolfe

———. *A Photographer's Scrapbook*. Preface by Frances McFadden. New York: St. Martin's/Marek, 1984.

Judy Dater

———. and Jack Welpott. *Women and Other Visions*. Dobbs Ferry, NY: Morgan & Morgan, 1975.

Bruce Davidson

———. *Bruce Davidson. Photographs*. Intro. by Henry Geldzahler. New York: Agrinde Publications, 1978.

———. *East 100th Street*. Cambridge, MA: Harvard University Press, 1970.

Lisl Dennis

———. *Travel Photography: Developing a Personal Style*. Somerville, MA: Curtin & London, 1983.

———. *How to Take Better Travel Photos*. Tucson, AZ: HP Books, 1979.

Robert Doisneau

———. *Three Seconds From Eternity*. Paris: Contrejour, and Boston: New York Graphic Society, 1979.

Maxime Du Camp

Flaubert in Egypt: A Sensibility on Tour—A Narrative Drawn from Gustave Flaubert's Travel Notes and Letters. Trans. and ed. by Francis Steegmuller. Boston: Little, Brown, 1972. Includes photographs and extracts from Du Camp's descriptions of the trip.

P. H. Emerson

Newhall, Nancy. *P. H. Emerson: The Fight for Photography as a Fine Art*. Millerton, NY: Aperture, 1975.

Turner, Peter, and Richard Wood. *P. H. Emerson: Photographer of Norfolk*. Boston: Godine, 1975.

Elliott Erwitt

———. *Photographs and Anti-Photographs*. Texts by Sam Holmes and John Szarkowski. Boston: New York Graphic Society, 1972.

———. *Recent Developments*. Intro. by Wilfred Sheed. New York: Simon & Schuster, 1978.

Walker Evans

———. *American Photographs*. Intro. by Lincoln Kirstein. New York: Museum of Modern Art, 1938. Reprint, New York: East River Press, 1975.

———. *First and Last*. New York: Harper & Row, 1978.

———. *Walker Evans*. New York: Museum of Modern Art, 1971.

———. *Walker Evans. Photographs for the Farm Security Administration 1935–1938*. Intro. by Jerald C. Maddox. New York: Da Capo Press, 1975. An illustrated catalog of photographic prints available from the Farm Security Administration Collection in the Library of Congress.

Agee, James, and Walker Evans. *Let Us Now Praise Famous Men*. Boston: Houghton-Mifflin, 1969.

Andreas Feininger

———. *Andreas Feininger*. Intro. by Ralph Hattersley. Dobbs Ferry, NY: Morgan & Morgan, 1973.

———. *Industrial America: 1940–1960*. New York: Dover, 1982.

Roger Fenton

———. *Roger Fenton: Photographer of the Crimean War. His Photographs and His Letters from the Crimea*. New York: Arno Press, 1973; reprint of 1954 edition.

Hannavy, John. *Roger Fenton of Crimble Hall*. Boston: Godine, 1976.

Carl Fleischhauer

Marshall, Howard, and Richard E. Ahlborn. *Buckaroos in Paradise: Cowboy Life in Northern Nevada*. Lincoln: University of Nebraska Press, 1981. Photographs by Fleischhauer and others.

Robert Frank.

———. *Les Américains*. Ed. by Alain Bosquet. Paris: Delpire, 1958. U.S. ed., *The Americans*. Intro. by Jack Kerouac. New York: Grove, 1959. Rev. eds., Millerton, NY: Aperture, 1969, 1978.

———. *The Lines of My Hand*. New York: Lustrum, 1972. Enlarged Japanese edition, Tokyo: Yugensha, 1972.

Jan Groover

———. *Jan Groover*. Intro. by Jane Livingston. Washington, DC: Corcoran Gallery of Art, 1976.

———. *Photographs*. Intro. by Alan Trachtenberg. Purchase, NY: Neuberger Museum, 1983.

Ernst Haas

———. *The Creation*. New York: Viking, 1971. Rev. ed. 1983.

Charles Harbutt

———. *Travelog*. Cambridge, MA: MIT Press, 1974.

David O. Hill and Robert Adamson

Bruce, David. *Sun Pictures: The Hill / Adamson Calotypes*. Boston: New York Graphic Society, 1974.

An Early Victorian Album: The Hill / Adamson Collection. Ed. and intro. by Colin Ford. Commentary by Roy Strong. London: Cape, 1974. U.S. ed., New York: Knopf, 1976.

Lewis W. Hine

Gutman, Judith M. *Lewis W. Hine and the American Social Conscience*. New York: Walker & Co., 1967.

Rosenblum, Walter, Naomi Rosenblum, and Alan Trachtenberg. *America & Lewis Hine: Photographs 1904–1940*. Millerton, NY: Aperture, 1976.

Kenneth Josephson

———. *Kenneth Josephson*. Chicago: Museum of Contemporary Art, 1983.

Art Kane

———. *The Persuasive Image*. Dobbs Ferry, NY: Morgan & Morgan, 1975.

Yousuf Karsh

———. *Faces of Our Time*. Toronto: University of Toronto Press, 1976.

———. *Karsh: A Fifty-Year Retrospective*. Boston: New York Graphic Society, 1983.

Gertrude Käsebier
    Homer, William Inness. *A Pictorial Heritage: The Photographs of Gertrude Käsebier.* Wilmington: Delaware Art Museum, 1979.
David Hume Kennerly
    ———. *Shooter.* New York: Newsweek Books, 1980.
André Kertész
    ———. *André Kertész: Sixty Years of Photography 1912–1972.* New York: Grossman Publishers, 1972.
    ———. *A Lifetime of Perception.* New York: Abrams, 1982.
Joseph Koudelka
    ———. *Gypsies.* Millerton, NY: Aperture, 1975.
Ellen Land-Weber
    ———. *The Passionate Collector.* New York: Simon & Schuster, 1980.
Dorothea Lange
    ———. *Photographs of a Lifetime.* Essay by Robert Coles. Millerton, NY: Aperture, 1982.
    Meltzer, Milton. *Dorothea Lange: A Photographer's Life.* New York: Farrar, Straus & Giroux, 1978.
Russell Lee
    Hurley, F. Jack. *Russell Lee: Photographer.* Dobbs Ferry, NY: Morgan & Morgan, 1978.
Herbert List
    ———. *Photographs 1930–1970.* Intro. by Gunter Metken. Munich: Schirmer / Mosel, 1976.
Danny Lyon
    ———. *Conversations with the Dead.* New York: Holt, Rinehart & Winston, 1971.
    ———. *Pictures From the New World.* Millerton, NY: Aperture, 1981.
Man Ray
    Penrose, Roland. *Man Ray.* Boston: New York Graphic Society, 1975
    Schwarz, Arturo. *Man Ray: The Rigour of Imagination.* New York: Rizzoli, 1977.
Mary Ellen Mark
    ———. *Falkland Road: Prostitutes of Bombay.* New York: Knopf, 1981.
    ———. *Ward 81.* New York: Simon & Schuster, 1979.
Susan Meiselas
    ———. *Nicaragua.* New York: Pantheon Books, 1981.
    El Salvador: Work of Thirty Photographers. Text by Carolyn Forché. Ed. by Harry Mattison, Susan Meiselas, and Fae Rubenstein. New York: Writers and Readers Publishing Cooperative, 1983.
Joel Meyerowitz
    ———. *Cape Light.* Boston: New York Graphic Society, 1978.
    ———. *St. Louis and the Arch.* Boston: New York Graphic Society, 1980.
Gjon Mili
    ———. *Photographs & Recollections.* Boston: New York Graphic Society, 1980.
László Moholy-Nagy
    Photographs of Moholy-Nagy. Ed. by Leland D.

Rice and David W. Steadman. Claremont, CA: Galleries of the Claremont Colleges, 1975.
    ———. *Moholy-Nagy: Photographs and Photograms.* Ed. by Andreas Haus. New York: Pantheon, 1980.
Wright Morris
    ———. *The Inhabitants.* New York: Scribner, 1946. Reprint, New York: Da Capo, 1973.
    ———. *The Home Place.* New York: Scribner, 1948. Reprint, Lincoln: University of Nebraska Press, 1968.
David Muench
    ———. *Washington Shores.* Portland, OR: Graphic Arts Center, 1981.
    ———. *Sierra Nevada.* Portland, OR: Graphic Arts Center, 1979.
Nickolas Muray
    ———. *Muray's Celebrity Portraits of the Twenties and Thirties.* Intro. by Marianne Fulton Margolis. New York: Dover Publications, 1978.
Eadweard Muybridge
    ———. *Muybridge's Complete Human and Animal Locomotion.* Intro. by Anita Ventura Mozley. 3 vols. New York: Dover Publications, 1979.
    Haas, Robert Bartlett. *Muybridge: Man in Motion.* Berkeley: University of California Press, 1976.
Arnold Newman
    ———. *Artists: Portraits From Four Decades.* Intro. by Henry Geldzahler. Boston: New York Graphic Society, 1980.
    ———. *One Mind's Eye.* Boston: Godine, 1974.
Ruth Orkin
    ———. *A World Through My Window.* Ed. by Arno Karlin. New York: Harper & Row, 1978.
    ———. *A Photo Journal.* New York: Viking, 1981.
Timothy H. O'Sullivan
    ———. *American Frontiers: The Photographs of Timothy H. O'Sullivan, 1867–1874.* Ed. by Joel Snyder. Millerton, NY: Aperture, 1981.
    Gardner, Alexander. *Gardner's Photographic Sketch Book of the War.* 2 vols. Washington, DC: Philip & Solomons, 1866. 45 albumen prints by O'Sullivan. Reprint, 1 vol. New York: Dover, 1959.
Paul Outerbridge
    ———. *Photographs.* Ed. by Graham Howe. New York: Rizzoli, 1980.
    ———. *Paul Outerbridge: A Singular Aesthetic, Photographs and Drawings 1921–1941.* Ed. by Elaine Dines. Santa Barbara, CA: Arabesque Books, 1983.
Bart Parker
    ———. *A Close Brush with Reality.* Rochester, NY: Visual Studies Workshop Press, 1981.
Olivia Parker
    ———. *Signs of Life.* Boston: Godine, 1983.
    ———. *Under the Looking Glass.* Boston: New York Graphic Society, 1983.
Gordon Parks
    ———. *A Poet and His Camera.* New York: Viking, 1968.
    ———. *Moments Without Proper Names.* New York: Viking, 1975.

Jeffrey Rotman
    Rotman, Jeffrey L., and Barry W. Allen. *Beneath Cold Seas: Exploring Cold Temperate Waters of North America.* New York: Van Nostrand-Reinhold, 1983.
Jack Sal
    ———. *Jack Sal: Mark/Making.* Greenfield Center, NY: Combinations Press, 1981.
Erich Salomon
    ———. *Erich Salomon.* Millerton, NY: Aperture, 1978.
August Sander
    ———. *Men Without Masks: Faces of Germany 1910–1938.* Boston: New York Graphic Society, 1973.
    ———. *August Sander: Photographs of an Epoch, 1904–1959.* Text by Robert Kramer and Beaumont Newhall. Millerton, NY: Aperture, 1980.
Norman Seeff
    ———. *Hot Shots.* New York: Flash Books, 1974.
Cindy Sherman
    ———. *Cindy Sherman.* Text by Peter Schjeldahl and I. Michael Danoff. New York: Pantheon, 1984.
Aaron Siskind
    ———. *Places.* New York: Light Gallery and Farrar, Straus & Giroux, 1976.
    ———. *Harlem Document, Photographs 1932–1946.* Providence, RI: Matrix, 1981.
    Chiarenza, Carl. *Aaron Siskind, Pleasures and Terrors.* Boston: New York Graphic Society, 1982.
Michael A. Smith
    ———. *Landscapes 1975–1979.* Revere, PA: Lodima Press, 1979.
W. Eugene Smith
    ———. *W. Eugene Smith: His Photographs and Notes.* Millerton, NY: Aperture, 1969.
    ———. *W. Eugene Smith: Master of the Photographic Essay.* Ed. and with commentary by William S. Johnson. Millerton, NY: Aperture, 1981.
    ———. *Minamata.* With Aileen M. Smith. New York: Holt, Rinehart & Winston, 1975.
Ralph Steiner
    ———. *Ralph Steiner: A Point of View.* Intro. by Willard VanDyke. Middletown, CT: Wesleyan University Press, 1978.
Alfred Stieglitz
    ———. *Alfred Stieglitz.* Intro. by Dorothy Norman. Millerton, NY: Aperture, 1976.
    ———. *Alfred Stieglitz: Photographs and Writings.* New York: Callaway Editions, 1983.
    America and Alfred Stieglitz. A Collective Portrait. Ed. by Waldo Frank, et al. Rev. ed. Millerton, NY: Aperture, 1979.
    Lowe, Sue Davidson. *Stieglitz: A Memoir / Biography.* New York: Farrar, Straus & Giroux, 1983.
Dennis Stock
    ———. *California Trip.* New York: Grossman, 1970.
    ———. *A Haiku Journey,* Tokyo: Kodansha, and New York: Harper & Row, 1975.

Paul Strand

Paul Strand: Sixty Years of Photographs. Profile by Calvin Tomkins. Millerton, NY: Aperture, 1976.

———. *Time in New England.* Ed. by Nancy Newhall. Millerton, NY: Aperture, 1977.

Josef Sudek

Bullaty, Sonja. *Sudek.* Intro by Anna Fárová. New York: Potter, 1978.

Joseph Szabo

———. *Almost Grown.* New York: Harmony, 1978.

William Henry Fox Talbot

Jammes, André. *William H. Fox Talbot: Inventor of the Negative-Positive Process.* New York: Macmillan, 1974.

Buckland, Gail. *Fox Talbot and the Invention of Photography.* Boston: Godine, 1980.

George A. Tice

———. *George A. Tice Photographs 1953–1973.* New Brunswick, NJ: Rutgers University Press, 1975.

———. *Urban Romantic.* Boston: Godine, 1982.

Philip Trager

———. *Photographs of Architecture.* Middletown, CT: Wesleyan University Press, 1977.

———. *New York.* Intro. by Louis Auchincloss. Middletown, CT: Wesleyan University Press, 1980.

Jerry N. Uelsmann

———. *Jerry N. Uelsmann: Silver Meditations.* Intro. by Peter C. Bunnell. Dobbs Ferry, NY: Morgan & Morgan, 1975.

———. *Jerry N. Uelsmann. Twenty Five Years: A Retrospective.* Text by James L. Enyeart. Boston: New York Graphic Society, 1982.

Weegee (Arthur Fellig)

Weegee. Ed. by Louis Stettner. New York: Knopf, 1977.

Weegee (Arthur Fellig). Intro. by Allene Talmey. Millerton, NY: Aperture, 1977.

William Wegman

———. *Man's Best Friend,* New York: Abrams, 1982.

———. *Wegman's World.* Minneapolis, MN: Walker Art Center, 1983.

Edward Weston

———. *The Daybooks of Edward Weston.* 2 vols., Millerton, NY: Aperture, 1973.

Maddow, Ben. *Edward Weston: Fifty Years.* Millerton, NY: Aperture, 1973. Bibliography. Another ed., Boston: New York Graphic Society, 1978.

Minor White

———. *Mirrors Messages Manifestations.* Millerton, NY: Aperture, 1969.

Minor White: Rites & Passages. Text by James Baker Hall. Millerton, NY: Aperture, 1978.

Garry Winogrand

———. *The Animals.* New York: Museum of Modern Art, 1969.

———. *Public Relations.* Texts by Tod Papageorge and John Szarkowski. New York: Museum of Modern Art, 1977.

Marion Post Wolcott

———. *Marion Post Wolcott: FSA Photographs.* Carmel, CA: The Friends of Photography, 1983.

Periodicals

A useful reference book that is in many libraries began as *An Index to Articles on Photography, 1977,* by William S. Johnson, Visual Studies Workshop Press. It appeared in that form again in 1978 and then appeared as the *International Photography Index: 1979,* by Johnson with Susan E. Cohen (Boston: G. K. Hall). Following behind the year being indexed by about two years, this publication includes approximately 7000 entries culled from over 100 foreign and domestic periodicals. As of this writing, the indexes for 1980 and 1981 have been published and 1982 is in progress.

American Photographer, 1515 Broadway, New York, NY 10036. Photography in all its forms; fame and fortune given an edge over fine art, with an emphasis on contemporary American work.

Aperture, Elm Street, Millerton, NY 12546. A superbly printed quarterly dealing with photography as an art form; founded by Minor White.

Artforum, 205 Mulberry Street, New York, NY 10012. This magazine, *Art in America,* and *Artnews* have occasional articles about photography as an art form in addition to reviews of photographic shows.

Art in America, 850 Third Avenue, New York, NY 10022.

Artnews, 5 West 37th Street, New York, NY 10018.

Modern Photography, 825 Seventh Avenue, New York, NY 10019. Along with *Petersen's* and *Popular Photography, Modern* is predominantly a magazine for hobbyists, mixing information about equipment and materials with portfolios and how-to articles.

Petersen's Photographic, 8490 Sunset Boulevard, Los Angeles, CA 90069.

Photo Communique, P.O. Box 129, Station M, Toronto, Ontario, Canada M6S 4T2. Canadian, but not exclusively so.

Photomethods, One Park Avenue, New York, NY 10016. For commerical and industrial photographers.

Popular Photography, One Park Avenue, New York, NY 10016. The editors also publish the Photography Annual, portfolios by well-known and emerging talent.

Print Collector's Newsletter, 16 East 82nd Street, New York, NY 10028. Regular articles on photography.

The Rangefinder, P.O. Box 1703, Santa Monica, CA 90406. Primarily for the professional studio portrait and wedding photographer.

Many institutions and non-profit groups involved with photography publish periodicals for their membership. Many cater to a specialized or regional interest, and they often serve as a springboard to national visibility for younger writers and photographers.

Afterimage, 31 Prince Street, Rochester, NY 14607. A tabloid-format monthly from the Visual Studies Workshop. Includes scholarly articles on photography, film, and video; listings of shows, events, publications, and opportunities nationwide.

Archive, The Center for Creative Photography, University of Arizona, 843 East University Boulevard, Tucson, AZ 85719. Scholarly and occasional.

CMP Bulletin, California Museum of Photography, University of California, Riverside, CA 92521. A bimonthly report on exhibits, activities, collections, and research of the CMP.

Exposure, Society for Photographic Education, PO Box 1651, FDR Post Office, New York, NY 10150. A periodical from an organization concerned with the teaching of photography, especially as a fine art.

History of Photography, University of Texas Press, PO Box 7819, Austin, TX 78712. Academic and technical, but unique.

Image, George Eastman House, 900 East Avenue, Rochester, NY 14607. Illustrated articles covering the curatorial interests of the museum, 19th and 20th century photography, and the histories of cinema and cameras.

Image, The Houston Center for Photography, 1441 West Alabama, Houston, TX 77006. Reviews of books and regional exhibitions; Texas photographers.

News Photographer, National Press Photographers Association, P.O. Box 1146, Durham, NC 27702. For working and student photojournalists.

Obscura, Los Angeles Center for Photographic Studies, 814 South Spring Street, Los Angeles, CA 90014. Critical writing about photography, mostly contemporary.

The Professional Photographer, The Professional Photographers of America, Inc., 1090 Executive Way, Des Plaines, IL 60018. Emphasis on portraits, weddings, and commercial photography.

Quarterly, San Francisco Camerawork, 70 12th Street, San Francisco, CA 94103.

Untitled, Friends of Photography, PO Box 500, Carmel, CA 93921. A four-times-yearly publication, it is more often a beautifully printed monograph than a magazine, and is always of exceptional quality.

Views, Photographic Resource Center, 1019 Commonwealth Avenue, Boston, MA 02215. A tabloid-format journal of New England photography.

Index

Page numbers in italics refer to illustrations of the subject or by the photographer mentioned.